Occult Holidays
or
God's Holy Days—Which?

by Fred R. Coulter

York Publishing Company
Post Office Box 1038
Hollister, California 95024-1

All New Testament Scriptures
used in this book are quoted from:
*The New Testament In Its
Original Order—A Faithful
Version With Commentary*
ISBN 978-0-9675479-3-0.
Old Testament Scriptures
quoted are from the
Authorized King James Version
unless otherwise noted.

About the Cover

The cover was designed by *Curley Creative*. The picture of the human skull, provided by punchstock.com, symbolically depicts the way of man that leads to death. The emblem of the Ten Commandments symbolizes God's way to life—"If you desire to enter into life, keep the commandments" (Matt. 19:17).

ISBN 978-0-9675479-7-0
Copyright 2006 ©
York Publishing Company
Post Office Box 1038
Hollister, California 95024-1038

Table of Contents

Forward

Confused and disillusioned, many today are wondering, "Is there a God? Where is He? What, if anything is God doing?" Mankind sees scant evidence in religion of God's direct involvement in the course of humanity. Shackled by tradition and religious myths, even professing "Christianity" gropes in a vacuum of ignorance regarding God's true plan for mankind.

Why? Because man has (for the most part, unknowingly) rejected the key to that plan—the knowledge of the seventh-day Sabbath and holy days of God. Instead, traditional holidays—including Sunday—have been adopted and accepted as "Christian."

Declaring the "end from the beginning," the true God of the Bible is actively involved in the affairs of man, ordering events according to His master plan as outlined by His Sabbath and feast days. Obviously, Satan the devil hates God's plan—for it also pictures his ultimate removal as the "god of this present age."

In what is perhaps one of the greatest conspiracies in the history of mankind, Satan has devised a cleverly disguised counterfeit "Christianity" to blind men from the knowledge of God's true plan. Analogous to King Jeroboam of ancient Israel—who substituted false "feast days" in place of God's true holy days—Satan has deceptively ensnared an unsuspecting world into believing that pagan occult holidays are acceptable forms of worship toward God.

In *Occult Holidays or God's Holy Days—Which?*, Fred R. Coulter brings to light this satanic conspiracy, uncovering in detail the occult roots of today's so-called "Christian" holidays—Halloween, Christmas, Easter, etc.—proving that such holidays are, in reality, a form of Satan worship.

Mr. Coulter proves how God's seven annual holy days form a kind of framework upon which are hung the various aspects of God's plan as they are fulfilled over time. This publication fully illustrates how God's seventh-day Sabbath and holy days picture His plan of salvation for all of mankind, concentrating on the establishment of the Kingdom of God and the eternal rule of Jesus Christ.

For a materialistic generation surrounded by religious indifference, intolerance and confusion, this book provides vital information. Emphasis is placed on the fact that the God of truth cannot be worshiped with pagan myths and forms of worship, as God can only be worshiped "in spirit and in truth."

In a world of relativism where the line between right and wrong, good and evil are increasingly blurred, Occult Holidays or God's Holy Days—Which? pulls no punches. Fred Coulter has captured, in a single book, the crux of the matter: Will we worship the true God, as He instructs—with the understanding of His true plan for mankind—or will we continue to look to myths, fables and false forms of worship that are of no avail?

The reader, indeed, will be compelled to choose—which?

Philip Neal
May 2006

About the Author

Fred R. Coulter attended the University of San Francisco and graduated from San Mateo State College before graduating from Ambassador University (Ambassador College), Pasadena, California, with a BA in Theology in 1964. He was ordained a minister of Jesus Christ in 1965 and pastored churches of God in the Pacific Northwest, the Mountain States, the greater Los Angeles area and Monterey, including the central coast area of California. Mr. Coulter completed advanced biblical and ministerial studies in 1972-75 under the Ambassador University Master's program. While completing these studies, he was encouraged by his professor of *Koiné* Greek to consider translating the books of the New Testament.

For the next twenty years, Mr. Coulter diligently studied, continuing to expand his knowledge of *Koiné* Greek. While undertaking a verse-by-verse study of the books of the New Testament, he was moved to translate the New Testament into clear, easy-to-read English for contemporary readers—resulting in *The New Testament In Its Original Order—A Faithful Version With Commentary*. He has consistently used this translation of the New Testament in his other publications.

Mr. Coulter has dedicated his life and talents to proclaiming Jesus Christ as personal Savior for all. Since 1983 Mr. Coulter has been the president of the Christian Biblical Church of God, headquartered in Hollister, California. He has an active ministry which reaches all parts of the United States and Canada, with additional offices in Australia, New Zealand, the United Kingdom, South Africa, Nigeria, and Kenya.

Each year nearly 400,000 people from around the world actively utilize the church's websites—where they find timely, inspiring weekly sermons and in-depth, verse-by verse biblical study materials covering virtually all of Scripture.

With his ministry now spanning over 40 years, Fred R. Coulter has again been inspired to take up the sword of God's Word and has published this most recent book: *Occult Holidays or God's Holy Days—Which?* The work documents the pagan and occult origins of the holidays accepted and celebrated today by Orthodox Christendom. The book then demonstrates in great detail God's true biblical feasts and holy days that He has commanded His people to keep—through which God actually reveals His plan and ultimate purpose for mankind, the pinnacle of His creation.

Acknowledgments

We first acknowledge God the Father and Jesus Christ, and thank them for preserving the Holy Bible—in spite of mankind's tumultuous history—so that today the truth is available for everyone. It is the very Word of God that gives us the true understanding of the purpose of human existence. Jesus said, "Your Word is the truth" (John 17:17), and "you shall know the truth, and the truth shall set you free" (John 8:32).

As with my other publications, many people have helped and shared in the production of this book. Their diligent work and support has made it possible. First, I give my heartfelt gratitude and appreciation to my loving, dear wife, Dolores, for her personal encouragement and assistance. Special thanks go to Kay Dye for contributing in the research of Halloween, Philip Neal and Duncan MacLeod for their diligent editing of the text and appendices, and Rod Repp and Rowan St. Clair Howell for proofreading. John and Hiedi Vogele are to be commended for the final formatting and proofreading of the entire text.

Fred R. Coulter
May 2006

Other Works by the Author

The New Testament In Its Original Order—A Faithful Version With Commentary is a new translation and is the only English version that has the books of the New Testament arranged in their original order. It retains the grace and grandeur of the King James Version while clarifying many of its problematic passages. Included are commentaries that answer such questions as: What is the New Testament? Who wrote it? When was it written? When was it canonized? Who canonized it? Other commentaries thoroughly explain the history and preservation of the Bible. Various appendices cover numerous controversial New Testament teachings in detail. This 928-page book is a vital tool for all Christians.

A Harmony of the Gospels In Modern English brings to life the message and purpose of the true Jesus, portraying His life and ministry in their true historical setting. This easy-to-understand, step-by-step account of the life of Jesus Christ is an indispensable study aid for every serious Bible student.

The Christian Passover details the scriptural and historical truths of the Passover in both the Old and New Testaments, leading the reader step-by-step through every aspect of one of the most vital and fundamental teachings revealed in the Bible. With over 500 pages, the book fully explains the meaning of the Christian Passover—a remembrance of the sacrifice of Jesus Christ, the Passover Lamb of God—in a most compelling and inspiring manner. The full meaning of the body and blood of Jesus Christ is revealed, showing the magnitude of God's love for every person.

The Day Jesus the Christ Died—the Biblical Truth About His Passion, Crucifixion and Resurrection is THE ONLY BOOK to present "the rest of the story"—left out by Mel Gibson in his epic movie The Passion of the Christ. Without the true historical and biblical facts, one cannot fully understand the meaning of Jesus Christ's horrific, humiliating and gruesome death by beating, scourging and crucifixion. The author presents the full biblical account in a most compelling way. As you will see, the truth is more astounding and profound than all of the ideas, superstitions, traditions and misbeliefs of men!

The Seven General Epistles is designed for an in-depth verse-by-verse study of the epistles of James; I and II Peter; I, II and III John and Jude. As part of the living Word of God, these epistles are as meaningful today for personal Christian growth as when they were written.

Lord, What Should I Do? is a book for Christians who are confused and bewildered by the escalating spiritual and doctrinal chaos in Christian churches today, which is undermining the true faith of the Bible. Any religious organization that teaches truths from the Word of God is a target for the forces of evil behind this chaos. This book clarifies the problem and offers the solution.

On-Line Studies for the serious Bible student—with additional written material and in-depth Bible studies in audio format—can be obtained at **www.cbcg.org** and **www.biblicaltruthministries.org**.

Preface

A carefully crafted worldview being disseminated in western society today is one which is not founded on the moral absolutes of yesteryear—a time when most people agreed on what was right and what was wrong, what was good and what was evil, who was wicked and who was righteous, and which things were true and which things were false. Instead, this new mind-set tenaciously maintains that individuals must "consider" all the different religious and lifestyle alternatives of a culturally diverse world, accepting all beliefs and customs as equal and valid (with the exception of the Christian viewpoint, which is rejected with hostility and disdain). In the name of "tolerance," judging moral behavior is simply not permitted.

The inevitable outcome of this approach is a world where it is believed there is no absolute truth, or if there is, it cannot be known. The individual becomes his own god, creating his own "reality"—and "truth" is whatever one wants or imagines it to be. This pervasive "postmodern thinking," as it is called, has gone mainstream in just one generation.

In his book *The Death of Truth*, Jim Leffel writes: "Postmodernists believe that truth is created, not discovered.... In a recent series of more than twenty interviews conducted at random at a large university, people were asked if there was such a thing as absolute truth—truth that is true across all times and cultures for all people. All but one respondent [a Bible-believing Christian] answered along these lines:
'Truth is whatever you believe.'
'There is no absolute truth.'
'If there *were* such a thing as absolute truth, how could we know what it is?'
'People who believe in absolute truth are dangerous.'"

Leffel continues: "Truth, declares a growing collective consciousness, is *relative*: what is true, right or beautiful for one person isn't necessarily true, right or beautiful for another. **Relativism says that truth isn't fixed by outside reality** [especially by a Creator God in heaven], but is decided by a group or individual for themselves. Truth isn't discovered, but manufactured. Truth is ever-changing not only in insignificant matters of taste or fashion, but in crucial matters of spirituality, morality, and reality" (pp. 20, 31, bold emphasis and bracketed comments added).

It is not difficult to follow this mindset to its logical conclusion. If twenty people have twenty different concepts about what is right and what is wrong, where does law and order fit in? Eventually, total lawlessness—even anarchy—is certain to follow. In trashing the truth of God, one falls prey to his own corrupt nature and his life becomes empty, void of purpose and understanding. As King David noted: "Behold, thou hast made my days *as* an handbreadth; and mine age *is* as nothing before thee: **verily every man at his best state *is* altogether vanity**.... Surely every man walketh in a vain show: surely they are disquieted in vain: he heapeth up *riches*, and knoweth not who shall gather them" (Psa. 39:5-6).

The apostle Paul prophesied of a time when lawlessness would reign in men's hearts. "Know this also, that in *the* last days perilous times shall come; for men will be **lovers of self**, **lovers of money**, braggarts, proud, blasphemers, disobedient to parents, unthankful, unholy, without natural affection, implacable, slanderers, without self-control, savage, despisers of those who are good, betrayers, reckless, egotistical, **lovers of pleasure rather than lovers of God**; having an outward appearance of godliness, but denying the power of *true* godliness. But *as for you*, turn away from *all* these…. *They are* always learning but *are* never able to come to *the* knowledge of *the* truth" (II Tim. 3:1-5, 7).

Although knowledge in the sciences has increased exponentially in this postmodern age, secular society has become spiritually crippled and incapable of attaining the truth of God in Christ Jesus because it has repudiated the Word of God.

The apostle Paul wrote that creation is a witness to all mankind of the truth of God and that in renouncing His visible truth as displayed throughout His creation, man becomes vulnerable to countless deceptions and chicanery: "For the invisible things of Him are perceived from *the* creation of *the* world, being understood by the things that were made—both His eternal power and Godhead—so that they are without excuse; because when they knew God, they glorified *Him* not as God, neither were thankful; but they became vain in their own reasonings, and their foolish hearts were darkened. While professing themselves to be *the* wise ones, they became fools and changed the glory of the incorruptible God into *the* likeness of an image of corruptible man, and of birds, and four-footed creatures, and creeping things.

"For this cause, God also abandoned them to uncleanness through the lusts of their hearts, to disgrace their own bodies between themselves, **who exchanged the truth of God for the lie; and they worshiped and served the created thing more than the one Who is Creator**, Who is blessed into the ages. Amen" (Rom. 1:20-25).

Satan the devil, who is "the prince of the power of the air" (Eph. 2:2) and anti-Christ, is behind the many deceptions that elevate the created above the Creator. One vehicle he utilizes to accomplish this in society today is, paradoxically, public education.

A former teacher, Beverly K. Eakman, is the current executive director of the National Education Consortium and the author of *Cloning of the American Mind: Eradicating Morality Through Education* (Huntington House). In in insightful her article "Bushwhacking Johnny," published in the September 2002 issue of *Chronicles Magazine*, Eakman expounded how the educational system is destroying truth, morals and independent thought in today's young students by using what is called "cognitive dissonance" to psychologically disorient them. She writes: "When cognitive dissonance is employed against an unsuspecting person—or worse, against a captive audience such as schoolchildren—the short-term objective is to prompt insecure individuals to find company, leading to a group (mob) mentality. **This**

makes it easier to reverse values held by the majority. 'Truth' can even be turned against itself—for example, 'freedom of speech' is now used to legitimize pornography [and other degrading immoral lifestyles]. The very people freedom of speech was designed to protect are left not only vulnerable but suspicious of the principle itself.

"What 'new values' are educators trying to instill? Here is a seven-point list, given to educators in North Carolina at an in-service workshop:

> **There is no right or wrong, only conditioned responses**.
> The collective good is more important than the individual.
> Consensus is more important than principle.
> Flexibility is more important than accomplishment.
> **Nothing is permanent except change.**
> **All ethics are situational; there are no moral absolutes.**
> There are no perpetrators, only victims.

"Notice that all of the items on this list involve no particular issue; rather, they reflect ethical 'outcomes' that a child is supposed to 'internalize.' "

Eakman continues: "Cognitive dissonance 'is a stressful mental or emotional reaction caused by trying to reconcile two opposing, inconsistent, or conflicting beliefs held simultaneously.'… So cognitive dissonance is not quite brainwashing, and it's not quite subliminal advertising, either. It's more like setting somebody up for a psychological fall. It plays with the mind by pitting various perceived 'authorities' against one another [parents, teachers, friends, political leaders, religious leaders and especially God and obedience to Him], exacerbating tensions [in the minds of the students]. After a while, intellectual deliberations shut down, and emotions take over. Only the strongest-willed individuals can hold out—[and they are labeled as] 'the troublemakers.'

"Thus was my generation (the Baby Boomers) educated to 'need' our peers more than we needed our principles, making us easy marks for such tactics as cognitive dissonance. Our children are now sitting ducks, with civilized norms forever under attack … all choices are equally legitimized.… Today, cognitive dissonance is an institutionalized method used to force-feed whatever is politically expedient" (www.BeverlyE.com, bold emphasis and bracketed comments added).

The use of cognitive dissonance is not limited to education. It is used in religion by clergy, in government by politicians and bureaucrats, in music, in entertainment and in all other forms of media. Consequently, many societies around the world are seemingly caught in a downward spiral of immorality that is rapidly approaching the degradation and hyper-immorality of Sodom and Gomorrah. Few voices of sanity are raised to warn against the onslaught of wickedness and immorality—and such voices are generally rejected, ridiculed or silenced.

Analyzing the marketing methods purveyors of evil have used in the past fifty years to achieve their goals, David Kupelian writes: "As Americans, we've come to tolerate, embrace, and even champion many things that would have horrified our parent's generation. Things like abortion-on-demand virtually up to the moment of birth, judges banning the Ten Commandments from public places, a national explosion of middle-school sex, the slow starvation of the disabled, thousands of homosexuals openly flouting the law and getting 'married,' and online porn creating late-night sex addicts in millions of middle-class homes.

"At the same time, our courts have scrubbed America's classrooms surgically clean of every vestige of religion on which this nation was founded—Christianity."

"The plain truth is, within the space of our lifetimes, much of what Americans once almost universally abhorred has been **packaged, perfumed, gift-wrapped, and sold to us as though it had great value**. By skillfully playing on our deeply felt national values of fairness, generosity, and tolerance, these marketers have persuaded us to embrace as enlightened and noble that which all previous generations since America's founding rejected as grossly self-destructive—in a word, evil" (*The Marketing of Evil*, pp. 11-12, bold emphasis added).

As a result, today's world is upside down! Because people have rejected God's truth, God has given them over to their own delusions. Truth, especially the truth of God's Word, has been branded as error and lies, and error and lies have been packaged as truth. A well-known quote by Dresden James illustrates this paradox:

> *"When a well-packaged web of lies*
> *has been sold gradually to the masses over*
> *generations, the truth will seem*
> *utterly preposterous and its*
> *speaker a raving lunatic."*

But you may ask, "What do occult holidays have to do with this? Aren't they wonderful times of year for children to have fun and for adults to party? How can the observance of these days possibly have anything to do with the death of truth? Aren't they, after all, 'Christian' celebrations?"

In *Occult Holidays or God's Holy Days—Which?*, you will understand the intense promotion and acceptance of the occult. Witchcraft, the feminine divine, New Age spirituality and Satanism have all been "jumpstarted" by the observance of Halloween and other "acceptable" occult holidays. **For centuries religious leaders have "sugar-coated, packaged, perfumed, gift wrapped and sold" these holidays to the masses "as though they had great value."**

We will begin by determining just how the "Christian" world has been duped. Then we will uncover the true origins of Halloween—which actually is the beginning and ending of the occult year—and progress through all the occult holidays. It will become transparent that they are not Christian! Yet, **the vast majority of church-going people have blindly accepted them** as such.

Upon examining the holy days and feasts of God, we will understand that God's holy days have deep spiritual meaning for true Christians, as well as all mankind, in His plan of salvation—past, present and future.

Prophecies of the Bible reveal that in the end time occult practices and open Satan worship will sweep the entire world. It's already happening. This generation is being prepared mentally, emotionally and spiritually to accept a universal deception which will usher in the final New World Order, the Antichrist and the False Prophet. **It will be Satan's finest hour!** Those who do not heed God's repeated warnings to repent—but reject the laws and commandments of God as well as the teachings of Jesus Christ and the New Testament—will be deluded. The masses will be deceived into accepting and worshiping the coming Antichrist—declared by the False Prophet to be the supreme manifestation of "God" in the flesh, the false savior of the world (II Thess. 2:1-12; Rev. 13:4-6).

PART ONE

Secrets of Halloween
and
Other Occult Holidays

CHAPTER ONE

How the "Christian" World Has Been Deceived

In spite of being forewarned in the Word of God, today the vast majority of professing "Christians" are deceived! Why? Because they do not read and study their Bibles for themselves, but believe the religious teachings of their leaders. As a result, most have failed to heed the repeated warnings of Jesus Christ and His apostles. Jesus specifically warned His disciples that false prophets would come in sheep's clothing, presenting themselves as messengers of God—and yet deceive many. While they would proclaim the name of Jesus and acknowledge Him as Savior, they would teach evil things in His name: "But beware of false prophets who come to you in sheep's clothing, for within *they* are ravening wolves. **You shall know them by their fruits**. They do not gather grapes from thorns, or figs from thistles, do they? In the same way, every good tree produces good fruit, but a corrupt tree produces evil fruit. A good tree cannot produce evil fruit, nor can a corrupt tree produce good fruit. Every tree *that is* not producing good fruit is cut down and is cast into the fire. Therefore, **you shall assuredly know them by their fruits**." (Matt. 7:15-20).

Knowing someone by their fruit involves examining their teachings and behavior. If such teachers do not conform to the teachings of Jesus Christ, then they are not of God—though they preach in His name and even perform miracles (Matt. 24:24). Jesus said they are workers of lawlessness! Inspired by Satan the devil, they substitute their own religious teachings and traditions for the commandments and laws of God. This is especially obvious in the holiday traditions of Orthodox Christendom and Protestantism*, many of which are rooted in abominable pagan religious practices.

How did the very abominations that God says He hates come to be observed by those who call themselves "Christians"?

A False Christianity Arises

Apostasy within the very Church of God began before the original apostles of Jesus Christ had even died. Shortly before his death, the apostle Peter gave this prophetic warning: "But there were also false prophets among the people, as indeed **there will be false teachers among you, who will stealthily introduce destructive heresies,** personally denying *the* Lord who bought them, and bringing swift destruction upon themselves. And many people will follow *as authoritative* their destructive ways; *and* be-

---

* *In this publication the term* Orthodox Christendom *includes Roman Catholicism, Eastern and Russian Orthodox and Protestant religions.*

cause of them, **the way of the truth will be blasphemed**. Also, through insatiable greed they will with enticing messages exploit you for gain; for whom the judgment of old is in *full* force, and their destruction is *ever* watching" (II Pet. 2:1-3).

In his epistle, Jude, a brother of the Lord Jesus Christ, emphatically warned the brethren to stand for the truth that was originally delivered by Jesus Christ and the apostles. He urged them to resist ungodly men who were infiltrating the churches and changing the grace of God into a lie: "Beloved, when personally exerting all *my* diligence to write to you concerning the common salvation, I was compelled to write to you, exhorting *you* to fervently fight for the faith, which once for all *time* has been delivered to the saints. For certain men have stealthily crept in, those who long ago have been written about, condemning *them* to this judgment. *They are ungodly men, who are perverting the grace of our God, turning it into licentiousness, and are personally denying the only Lord God and our Lord Jesus Christ*" (Jude 3-4).

The apostasy that began during the lifetimes of the apostles rapidly developed after the last original apostle, John, died in about 99-100 AD. Within twenty years of his death a vastly different, counterfeit "Christian" church began to emerge. Historian Jesse Lyman Hurlburt summarized this critical period: "At the end of the first century, the doctrines set forth by the Apostle Paul in the Epistle to the Romans were accepted throughout the church as the standards of the faith. The teachings of St. Peter and St. John in their epistles show a complete accord with the views of St. Paul. Heretical opinions were arising and sects were forming, the germs of which had been noted and warned against by the apostles, but their full development came later" (*The Story of the Christian Church*, p. 44).

It was not long before this apostasy gained popularity and power. As Hurlburt notes: "We name the last generation of the first century, from 68 to 100 A. D., 'The Age of Shadows,' partly because the gloom of persecution was over the church; but more especially because of all periods in the history, it is the one about which we know the least. We have no longer the clear light of the Book of Acts to guide us; and no author of that age has filled the blank of history. We would like to read of the later work by such helpers of St. Paul as Timothy, Apollos and Titus, but all these and St. Paul's other friends drop out of the record at his death. **For fifty years after St. Paul's life a curtain hangs over the church, through which we strive vainly to look; and when at last it arises, about 120 A. D. with the writings of the earliest church fathers, we find a church in many aspects very different from that in the days of St. Peter and St. Paul**" (Ibid., p. 42, bold emphasis added).

In succeeding centuries the religious leaders of this apostate Christianity further developed their counterfeit teachings, traditions and dogmas, branding many of the true teachings of Jesus and His apostles as "heresy." They continually adapted pagan practices—via various holidays—into Christendom. Over time these practices became so entrenched that today when "Christians" encounter the truth of the Word of God through public preaching or personal study, they find it almost unbelievable.

The Religious Traditions of Men

The easiest way to incorporate a teaching into a religious system is to surround it with tradition. In the case of Judaism, Scripture cites the "traditions of the elders." In the case of Christendom, traditions originated with the early "church fathers." In both cases, men brought in false doctrines by establishing traditions. Once a tradition has been established, it becomes "dogma"—considered to have equal or even greater authority over the religious faithful than the very Word of God.

The Traditions of Judaism. During His earthly ministry, Jesus continually confronted and rebuked the Jewish religious leaders for esteeming their traditions above the God-breathed Scriptures. While they hypocritically gave lip service to God, their traditions actually rejected and replaced the Word of God. We find an account of one such confrontation in the Gospel of Mark: "Then the Pharisees and some of the scribes from Jerusalem came together to Him. And when they saw some of His disciples eating with defiled hands (that is, unwashed *hands*), they found fault. **For the Pharisees and all the Jews, holding fast to the tradition of the elders**, do not eat unless they wash their hands thoroughly. Even *when coming* from the market, they do not eat unless they *first* wash themselves. And there are many other things that they have received to observe, *such as the* washing of cups and pots and brass utensils and tables. For this reason, the Pharisees and the scribes questioned Him, *saying*, '**Why don't Your disciples walk according to the tradition of the elders**, but eat bread with unwashed hands?'

"And He answered *and* said to them, 'Well did Isaiah prophesy concerning you hypocrites, as it is written, **"This people honors Me with their lips, but their hearts are far away from Me." But in vain do they worship Me, teaching *for* doctrine the commandments of men. For leaving the commandment of God, you hold fast the tradition of men**, *such as* the washing of pots and cups; and you practice many other things like *this*.' Then He said to them, '**Full well do you reject the commandment of God, so that you may observe your *own* tradition ... nullifying the authority of the Word of God by your tradition which you have passed down; and you practice many *traditions* such as this'** " (Mark 7:1-9, 13).

Some 1440 years before the ministry of Jesus Christ, God commanded the children of Israel not to add to or take away from the Word of God; neither were they to adopt the religious rituals of the Canaanites, who were idolaters and sun worshipers. Furthermore, they were not to worship the true God in the same manner that the heathen worshiped their idol gods: "When the LORD thy God shall cut off the nations from before thee, whither thou goest to possess them, and thou succeedest them, and dwellest in their land; **take heed to thyself that thou be not snared by following them, after that they be destroyed from before thee; and that thou inquire not** after their gods, saying, 'How did these nations serve their gods? even so will I do likewise.' Thou shalt not do so unto the LORD thy God: for every abomination to the LORD, which he hateth, have they done unto their gods; for even their sons and their daughters they have burnt in the fire to their gods. **What thing soever I command you, observe to do it: thou shalt not add thereto, nor diminish from it**" (Deut. 12:29-32). Nearly all the added traditions of Judaism violated this command of God. (The oral traditions of Judaism were later codified in the Mishna in the second century AD and in the Talmud in the fourth century AD. For interested readers, thousands of these oral laws have been compiled by Rabbi Solomon Ganzfried in the *Code of Jewish Law*, Hebrew Publishing Company, New York, 1993, ISBN 0-88482-779-8; Phone 1-518-392-3322).

The Traditions of Orthodox Christendom. While Orthodox Christendom maintains a pretense of upholding the Scriptures, it in fact holds the traditions of men on par with, or esteems them greater than the Scriptures. These traditions originated in the teachings of the so-called "early church fathers," who were some of the leading apostate teachers from the second to fourth centuries AD. For example, upon close examination, it becomes apparent that nearly all of the teachings of Roman Catholicism are based upon human traditions, arbitrary edicts of the popes and misinterpretations of Scripture, rather than on sound scriptural interpretation alone. Hence, just as in Judaism, their traditions have replaced the Word of God.

In the catechism book, *My Catholic Faith*, Louis LaRavoire Morrow writes: "Divine Revelation comes down to us by two means: through Holy Scripture, written down under divine inspiration, and through Tradition, handed down orally from Apostolic times. We read the Bible with great respect, for it is the Word of God. We treat Tradition with as great reverence, for God speaks through Tradition as well. **It is wrong to believe the Bible alone without Tradition**" (p. 22).

This is absolutely false! The Bible, and the Bible alone, is to be believed— it is the only standard upon which all teachings are to be based. The apostate traditions of men are to be rejected, not sanitized and given new "Christian" meanings so that "the faithful" may freely observe them.

Morrow further states that Roman Catholicism could preach the gospel without even having the Bible. "*It would have been possible* **for the Church to bring the truths of Jesus Christ to all mankind without the Bible**.... Even today it is possible for many people to learn about Jesus Christ without reading the Scriptures" (Ibid., p. 28, non-italicized bold emphasis added). This teaching is also patently contrary to the teaching of the Old and New Testaments.

When the apostle Paul wrote to instruct Timothy about what he was to teach, he made no appeal to the oral traditions of men. Instead, he clearly pointed to the Word of God as the only basis for sound teaching. "**Diligently** *study* **to present yourself approved unto God, a workman who** does not *need to be* ashamed, **rightly dividing the Word of the truth**; but avoid profane and vain babblings [the traditions and doctrines of men] because they will *only* give rise to more ungodliness, and their words will eat away at the body like gangrene; of whom are Hymeneus and Philetus, **who have gone astray from the truth**, claiming that the resurrection has already taken place, and are destroying the faith of some. Nevertheless, the foundation of God stands firm…" (II Tim. 2:15-19).

Paul further encouraged Timothy concerning the written Word of God: "But *as for* you, continue in the things that you did learn and were assured of, knowing from whom you have learned *them*; and that from a child **you have known the holy writings** [the Old Testament], which are able to make you wise unto salvation through faith, which *is* in Christ Jesus. **All Scripture** [New Testament, as well as Old Testament] *is* **God-breathed** and *is* profitable for doctrine, for conviction, for correction, for instruction in righteousness; so that the man of God may be complete, fully equipped for every good work" (II Tim 3:14-17).

Again, Paul did not make a single appeal to any so-called oral traditions of men for his authority, but only to the God-breathed Scriptures. (For an in-depth commentary on the history of the writing and preservation of the Bible, especially the New Testament, see *The New Testament In Its Original Order—A Faithful Version With Commentary* by Fred R. Coulter, 2004; ISBN 0-9675479-3-8; York Publishing Company, P.O. Box 1038, Hollister, California 95024-1038; also available through *amazon.com*.).

The apostle Peter—who Roman Catholicism falsely claims was the first pope—also condemned the vain traditions of men and upheld the authority of the Word of God. "**Knowing that you were not redeemed by corruptible things, by silver or gold, from your futile way of living, inherited** *by tradition* **from** *your* **forefathers**; but by *the* precious blood of Christ, as of a lamb without blemish and without spot; Who truly was foreknown before *the* foundation of *the* world, but was manifested in *these* last times for your sakes; *even for you* who through Him do believe in God, Who raised Him from *the* dead and gave Him glory, so that your faith and hope might be in God. Having purified your lives by obedience to the Truth unto unfeigned brotherly love through *the* Spirit, love one another fervently with a pure heart. *For* you have been begotten again, not from corruptible seed, but from incorruptible *seed*, **by** *the* **living Word of God,** *which* **remains forever**" (I Pet. 1:18-23).

The apostle Paul charged those who would preach to preach only the Word of God, Old and New Testaments. "I charge you, therefore, in the sight of God, even the Lord Jesus Christ, Who is ready to judge *the* living and *the* dead at His appearing and His kingdom: **Preach the Word! Be urgent in season and out of season; convict, rebuke, encourage, with all patience and doctrine**. For there shall come a time when they will not tolerate sound doctrine; but according to their own lusts they shall accumulate to themselves *a great number of* teachers, having ears itching *to hear what satisfies their cravings*; but **they shall turn away their own ears from the truth; and they shall be turned aside unto myths** [the traditions of men]" (II Tim. 4:1-4).

The apostle Peter wrote that the Word of God alone is the truth, not cleverly concocted myths. "Therefore, I will not neglect to make you always mindful of these things, although you *already* know them and have been established in **the present truth**…. But I will make every effort *that,* after my departure, you may always have a *written* remembrance of these things *in order* to practice *them* for yourselves, **for we did not follow cleverly concocted myths** *as our authority,* **when we made known to you the power and coming of our Lord Jesus Christ, but we were eyewitnesses of His magnificent glory**; because He received glory and honor from God *the* Father when *the* voice came to Him from the Majestic Glory, 'This is My Son, the Beloved, in Whom I am well pleased.' And this *is the* voice from heaven that we heard when we were with Him on the holy mountain. We also possess the confirmed prophetic Word [God-breathed New Testament] to which you do well to pay attention, as to a light shining in a dark place, until the day dawns and *the* morning star arises in your hearts; **knowing this first, that no prophecy of Scripture originated as anyone's own** *private* **interpretation; because prophecy was not brought at any time by human will, but the holy men of God spoke as they were moved by** *the* **Holy Spirit**" (II Pet. 1:12, 15-21).

Peter also wrote that there would be false teachers (inspired by Satan the devil), who would introduce destructive heresies (II Pet. 2:1-2).

Satan and his Ministers Appear to be Righteous

The master deceiver cleverly masquerades as an angel of light. He even quotes Scripture—but not for the sake of the truth. Instead, as he did when he tempted Jesus Christ for forty days and forty nights, Satan misapplies the truth of Scripture (Matt. 4:1-11; Luke 4:1-13). His ministers use the same tactic today.

The apostle Paul warned the Corinthians concerning these false apostles. He wrote, "But I fear, lest by any means, as the serpent deceived Eve by his craftiness, so your minds might be corrupted from *the* simplicity that *is* in Christ. For indeed, if someone comes **preaching another Jesus**, whom we did not preach, or you receive **a different spirit**, which you did not receive, or **a different gospel**, which you did not accept, you put up with it as *something* good…. For such *are* false apostles—deceitful workers who are transforming themselves into apostles of Christ. And *it is* no marvel, for **Satan himself transforms himself into an angel of light**. Therefore, *it is* no great thing if his servants also transform themselves as ministers of righteousness—whose end shall be according to their works" (II Cor. 11:3-4, 13-15).

The brethren of Corinth were allowing these false apostles to have authority over their lives, even to the point of spiritual abuse. Because of the seriousness of the situation, Paul attempted to bring them to their senses by exposing their foolishness for listening to such teachers. "Since many [false apostles] boast according to *the* flesh, I also will boast. **For since you are** *so* **intelligent** [thinking they knew more than Paul did], **you gladly bear** with fools. **For you bear** *it* **if anyone brings you into bondage, if anyone devours** *you***, if anyone takes** *from you***, if anyone exalts himself, if anyone beats you on the face**. I speak as though we were under reproach for being weak; but in whatever *way* anyone else is bold (I speak in foolishness), I also am bold. Are they Hebrews? So am I. Are they Israelites? So am I. Are they *the* seed of Abraham? So am I. **Are they servants of Christ? (I am speaking as if I were out of my mind.)**" (verses 18-23).

Likewise, the apostle Peter exhorted the brethren to beware of the teachings of men who use these devious tactics: "And bear in mind that the long-suffering of our Lord *is* salvation, exactly as our beloved brother Paul, according to the wisdom given to him, has also written to you; as *he has* also in all *his* epistles, speaking in them concerning these things; in which are some things *that are* difficult to understand, which **the ignorant and unstable are twisting** *and distorting***, as** *they* **also** *twist and distort* **the rest of the Scriptures, to their own destruction**. Therefore, beloved, since you know this in advance, be on guard against *such practices,* lest you be led astray with the error of the lawless ones, *and* you fall from your own steadfastness" (II Pet. 3:15-17). And again, Paul wrote, "For we are not like the many, who for *their own* profit are corrupting the Word of God; but we speak with sincerity, as from God, *and* before God, *and* in Christ" (II Cor. 2:17).

In his letter to the Thessalonians, Paul commanded the brethren to prove all things and to avoid every form of wickedness. "**Prove all things. Hold fast** *to that which* **is good. Abstain from every form of wickedness**" (I Thes. 5:21-22). Therefore, all religious teachings must be examined and judged in the light of God's Word, the God-breathed Scriptures, both Old and New Testaments. If any teaching does not conform to the teachings of the Bible—"if they speak not according to this word" (Isa. 8:20)—it is a false teaching promulgated by false prophets and is to be rejected.

In chapter two we will expose the pagan origins of Halloween—and examine ancient evidence proving that the holiday's origins predate its observance. Although promulgated as Christian, "Hallowed Eve" (or "Holy Evening") has nothing to do with holiness and the true Jesus Christ—but has everything to do with the worship of Satan the devil, the false god of this world.

CHAPTER TWO

_____

The Occult Origins of Halloween, Heathen Gods and Goddesses

Every year hundreds of millions of people throughout the world celebrate Halloween. During this celebration, children put on costumes or disguise themselves, walk through neighborhoods, knock on doors, and speak the words "trick or treat," expecting to receive candy or money. Many churches are involved, sponsoring Halloween parties for children, complete with costumes, games and apple bobbing contests. Adults attend glitzy Halloween costume parties, dances and balls, most of them oblivious to the fact that this night celebrates Wicca's most important "high Sabbat" in devotion to pagan gods and goddesses.

Centuries after the apostles' deaths, Orthodox Christendom appropriated Halloween as one of its official holidays, and Halloween's observance has been accepted as "Christian" ever since. However, it is anything but Christian! In fact, the custom originated in the ancient pagan world and was celebrated centuries before the New Testament Church was founded. In tracing the roots of this pagan holiday, it is necessary to go back to an early period in mankind's history, to the time just after sin entered the world through disobedience to God and His laws and commandments.

Pre-Christian History

After Adam and Eve were expelled from the Garden of Eden for their sins, their descendants continued to live in disobedience and wickedness. There were only a few who loved and obeyed God. After fifteen hundred years, all mankind had given themselves over to evil and wickedness, causing the Lord God to execute His judgment against them and destroy that world with a universal flood. "And God saw that the wickedness of man _was_ great in the earth, and _that_ every imagination of the thoughts of his heart _was_ only evil continually. And it repented the LORD that he had made man on the earth, and it grieved him at his heart. And the LORD said, I will destroy man whom I have created from the face of the earth; both man, and beast, and the creeping thing, and the fowls of the air; for it repenteth me that I have made them…. The earth also was corrupt before God, and the earth was filled with violence. And God looked upon the earth, and, behold, it was corrupt; for all flesh had corrupted his way upon the earth. And God said unto Noah, The end of all flesh is come before me; for the earth is filled with violence through them; and, behold, I will destroy them with the earth" (Gen. 6:5-7, 11-13). (See Appendix A, _Halloween and the Flood of_

Noah—Is There a Link? p. 206.) Because Noah was a just man and walked with God, he found "grace in the eyes of the Lord." In His mercy God rescued Noah, his wife, his three sons and their wives. In addition, God selected certain animals, and together they were all saved in the ark from the destruction of that world by the flood (Gen. 6:8-8:22).

After the flood, however, mankind soon returned to their wicked ways in rebellion against God and began following Nimrod. "And Cush begat Nimrod: **he began to be a mighty one in the earth**. He was a mighty hunter before [in place of] the LORD: wherefore it is said, 'Even as Nimrod the mighty hunter before [in place of] the LORD.' And the beginning of his kingdom was Babel, and Erech, and Accad, and Calneh, in the land of Shinar" (Gen. 10:8-10).

At the tower of Babel, Nimrod and his wife, Semiramis, established a religious system in rebellion against God—wherein they and their followers also tried to establish a dictatorial government, "a tower to reach unto heaven." They believed Satan's lie that if they worshiped him they would become gods in the flesh. See *The Two Babylons* by Alexander Hislop for a complete and detailed historical documentation: available at www.cbcg.org or www.biblicaltruthministries.org.

The book of Genesis contains this account: "And the whole earth was of one language, and of one speech. And it came to pass, as they journeyed from the east, that they found a plain in the land of Shinar; and they dwelt there. And they said one to another, 'Go to, let us make brick, and burn them thoroughly.' And they had brick for stone, and slime had they for mortar. And they said, 'Go to, let us build us a city and a tower, whose top *may reach* unto heaven; and let us make us a name, lest we be scattered abroad upon the face of the whole earth.' And the LORD came down to see the city and the tower, which the children of men builded. And the LORD said, '**Behold, the people *is* one, and they have all one language; and this they begin to do: and now nothing will be restrained from them, which they have imagined to do.** Go to, let us go down, and there confound their language, that they may not understand one another's speech.' So the LORD scattered them abroad from thence upon the face of all the earth: and they left off to build the city. Therefore is the name of it called Babel; because the LORD did there confound the language of all the earth: and from thence did the LORD scatter them abroad upon the face of all the earth" (Gen. 11:1-9).

Wherever the people were scattered, they took their false religion with them. Since their one language was changed into many languages, thus we find in antiquity various names for the same false gods and goddesses (or demons).

In his epistle to the Romans, the apostle Paul wrote that because men did not want to retain the knowledge of God, He abandoned them to their own depraved imaginations: "**And in exact proportion as they did not consent to have God in *their* knowledge, God abandoned them to a reprobate mind...**" (Rom. 1:28-32).

The worship of the sun (symbolized by the sacred serpent), along with nature worship, has its roots in this rejection of God and His Word. In rebellion, mankind watched the changing of the seasons and observed the life and death of crops, perceiving such natural processes as mystic. They developed fertility cults with gods and goddesses who died and were reborn. Thus the worship of the earth's "spirit" as a mother and the incarnation of the earth's fertility forces within dying gods and goddesses developed into one of the most widespread forms of pagan religion recorded in antiquity.

Whether it was Inanna of the Sumerians, Ishtar of the Babylonians, or Fortuna of the Romans, every civilization had a sect of religion based on the embodiment of the earth's spirit as a caring mother-goddess. The Egyptians worshipped Hathor in this manner, as did the Chinese with Shingmoo. The Germans worshipped Hertha as the great Mother Earth, and the apostate Jews idolized "the queen of heaven." In Greece, Gaia is Mother Earth, the creator of all things. Beneath her were many other earth goddesses including Demeter, Artemis, Aphrodite, and Hecate.

Hecate, the Titan earth mother of the wizards and witches, was considered to be the underworld sorceress of all that is demonic.

Goddess Hecate. As the dark goddess of witchcraft, Hecate was worshiped with mystical rites and magical incantations. Her name was most likely derived from the ancient Egyptian word Heka ("sorcery" or "magical"), which may explain her association with the Egyptian frog goddess of the same name. This may also explain the affiliation of frogs with witchcraft.

Hecate's followers sincerely believed in and feared her magic and presence, and magical ritual was used to appease her. This appeasement of the dark goddess was primarily due to her role as the sorceress of the afterlife, but pagans also thought she had the ability to afflict the mind with madness.

Physical locations that had a history of violence were believed to be magnets for malevolent spirits, a concept similar to that of "haunted houses." If one wanted to get along with the local resident ghosts, he needed to sacrifice to the ruler of the darkness, Hecate. A night owl was thought to announce the acceptance of these sacrifices, and those who gathered on the eve of the full moon perceived its hoot as a good omen. Hecate's devotees left food offerings for the goddess ("Hecate's Supper") and sometimes sacrificed puppies and female black lambs.

Deformed and vicious owl-like affiliates of Hecate called "strigae" were thought to fly through the night feeding on the bodies of unattended babies. During the day the strigae appeared as simple old women, and such folklore may account for the myths of flying witches. The same strigae hid amidst the leaves of trees during the annual festival of Hecate, held on August 13, when Hecate's followers offered up the highest praise to the goddess, communed with the tree spirits (earth spirits, including Hecate, were thought to inhabit trees—the basis for the modern radical ecology movement) and summoned the souls of the dead from the mouths of nearby caves. It was here that Hecate was known as Hecate-Chthonia ("Hecate of the earth"), a depiction in which she most clearly embodied the popular earth-mother-spirit—or Mother Nature.

Hecate was known by other names throughout the pagan world. Some people regarded her as Hecate-Propylaia, "the one before the gate," a role in which she guarded the entrances of homes and temples from nefarious outside evils. Others knew her as Hecate-Propolos, "the one who leads" as an underworld guide. Finally, she was known as Hecate-Phosphoros, "the light bearer," her most sacred title and one that recalls another powerful underworld spirit, Satan, who appears as a messenger of light. However, it was her role as the feminist earth-goddess-spirit Hecate-Chthonia that popularized her divinity (Anderson, D., *Happy Halloween?* 2004).

Modern pagans perceive the earth similarly, often referring to the earth as Gaia—a living, caring entity. They believe that people are one of Mother Earth's species rather than her dominators. She provides the living biosphere: the regions on, above, and below her surface, where created things, both physical and spiritual, live (Anderson, *What Witches Do After Halloween,* 2004).

Wiccans (modern pagans) and witches acknowledge all of the so-called deities (demons) that ancient peoples worshipped. However, the primary deities are "the Goddess and the God," the Great (Earth) Mother and her horned consort, the "Horned God," the ancient god of fertility.

Horned God. The Horned God is actually a modern term invented in the 20th century to link together numerous male nature gods out of such widely dispersed and historically unconnected mythologies as the Celtic Cernunnos, the Welsh Caerwiden, the English Herne the Hunter, the Hindu Pashupati, the Greek Pan and the satyrs, and even a Paleolithic cave painting known as "the Sorcerer" in the Cave of the Three Brothers in France.

The Greek god Pan is perhaps the most familiar form of the Horned God/Wild Man archetype. The ancient scholars of Alexandria believed that Pan personified the Natural Cosmos, and the word Pantheism is derived from this idea in which all Nature is God and God is All Nature. Arcadian Greece first recorded Pan's worship.

The Horned One, or Cernunnos, is a Celtic god of fertility, life, animals, wealth, and the underworld. His worship spread throughout Gaul and into Britain as well. Paleolithic cave paintings found in France that depict a stag standing upright or a man dressed in stag costume seem to indicate that Cernunnos' origins date to those times. Known to the Druids as Hu Gadarn, he was the god of the underworld and astral planes and the consort of the great goddess.

The Horned God has cloven hoofs or the hindquarters of a goat with a human torso and a human but goat-horned head. The god's horns are seen as phallic symbols, representing male potency, strength and protection. As a symbol of sexuality, the Horned God is complementary to female fertility deities known collectively as the Great Mother. In this context, he is sometimes referred to as the Great God or the Great Father. He impregnates the

Goddess and dies during the autumn and winter months and is reborn gloriously in spring, while the goddess always lives on as Mother Earth, giving life to the Horned God as he moves through the eternal cycle of life, death, and rebirth. He alternates with the goddess of the moon in ruling over life and death, continuing the cycle of death, rebirth, and reincarnation (Wikipedia, *Horned God,* 2005; Smith, Dr. A., *Cernunnos,* 1997, 1999).

This pagan belief in a cycle of life, death and rebirth as portrayed by the seasons of the year can be found in every ancient culture.

Druid Origins and Customs of Halloween

The origins of Halloween specifically can be traced to the ancient Celts (who lived in what is now known as Ireland, Scotland, Wales and Northern France) and their Druid priests. The end of October commemorated their festival of the waning year, when the sun began its downward course and the fields yielded ripened grain. "Samhain" or "Summer's End," as this feast to the dying sun was called, was celebrated with human sacrifice, divination or soothsaying and prayers. Druids believed that during this season spirits walked, and evil held power over the souls of men.

On October 31, their New Year's Eve, great bonfires were kindled, which were thought to simulate the sun and to procure blessings for the entire succeeding year. The fires remained burning as a means to frighten away evil spirits. The Druids held these early Halloween celebrations in honor of Samhain, also known as Lord of the Dead, whose festival fell on November 1. These bonfires, or "bone fires," were also used in animal and human sacrifice—thus the name. The tradition of lighting a bonfire has continued to modern times.

The Druids believed that people needed to be cleansed after they died. Samhain supposedly condemned the souls of the departed to inhabit the bodies of animals. Kurt Koch writes in *Occult ABC,* "During the night of October 31, the enchanted souls were freed by the Druid god, Samhain, and taken together into the Druid heaven. This festival was always accompanied by animal and sometimes human sacrifices and linked with all kinds of magic" (p. 87). The Druids held back no cruelty in attempting to please the Lord of the Dead!

During the festival of Samhain, people believed that there was a very thin veil between the living and the dead, and they feared that the dead would come back in search of bodies to possess. Fearing possession, people did many things to trick the spirits such as dressing up to look like them. Druid priests wore masks, so they would not be recognized and attacked by evil spirits. Others wore frightening costumes to scare the evil spirits away. Celts also hollowed out a turnip, on which they carved a grotesque face to fool demons. They carried lanterns to light their way in the dark and to ward off evil spirits (*Pagan Traditions of the Holidays*, p. 79-80).

Druid Jack-O-Lantern and Trick-or-Treat. The Druids originated the practice of hollowing out turnips or potatoes (Jack-O-Lanterns) and filling them with human fat. Whenever a raiding party came to a home to demand of the husband that someone inside be surrendered as a human sacrifice, they would light a Jack-O-Lantern filled with human fat; if the husband relented and provided one of his loved ones as a sacrifice, the Druid party would leave the burning Jack-O-Lantern on the porch. This lantern would tell the other raiding parties and the demonic host that this party had surrendered a human for sacrifice and that the remaining people inside were to be left alone. This guarantee that no one else in the house would be harmed was the "treat."

If the husband refused to surrender one of his loved ones, a "trick" would be placed upon the house. The members of the raiding party would draw a large hexagram using human blood on the front door. (They got the blood for the hexagram from a dead body which they dragged around with them.) The demonic host would be attracted to this hexagram and would invade the house, causing one or more of the inhabitants to either go insane or die from fright (*America's Occult Holidays*, p. 20)

Various names for the Jack-O-Lantern through the years have included "Lantern Men," "Hob-O-Langer," "Will-O-The-Wisp," "Fox Fairy," etc. "Jack" is a nickname for "John," which is a common slang word meaning, "man." Thus, "Jack-O-Lantern" literally means, "man with a lantern."

Many legends have grown up around the lore of the Jack-O-Lantern. According to some, Jack is a wandering soul trapped between heaven and hell. Another tale—about a drunk named Jack who made a deal with the devil—claims to be the true origin of the Jack-O-Lantern myth. In *Halloween,* Helen Borten writes:

> *An Irish legend tells how this [lantern] custom began. A man named Jack was kept out of Heaven because he was stingy. The gates of Hell were closed to him, too, because he had played jokes on the Devil. Poor Jack, carrying a lantern to light his way, was supposed to walk the earth forever.*

Whatever the true roots of the Jack-O-Lantern, it has become a predominant symbol of Halloween.

Games to divine the future have always been popular Halloween rituals. "Bobbing for apples" was a game played during the ancient Roman Pomona's festival (Pomona was the goddess of fruit), which occurred at about the same time after the autumn equinox. This game was later adopted by the Celts, who used it to divine the future. A young man who was able to secure an apple between his teeth was assured of his girl's love for the coming year. The Snap Apple game was one in which each person, in his turn, would spring up in an attempt to bite an apple that was being twirled on the end of a stick. The first to succeed would be the first to marry.

Questions concerning marriage, luck, health, and the time of one's death were popular subjects of divination. In Scotland, young people pulled shoots out of the ground to ascertain which of them would marry during the coming year and in what order the marriages should occur.

Owls, bats, cats and toads were an essential part of Halloween divination. Witches considered these creatures to be demon-possessed and controlled. Traditionally they were known as the "witch's familiars." A divining "familiar" was the species of animal whose shape Satan would assume in order to aid the witch in divining the future. A witch would closely watch the animal's movements (whether slow or fast)—and she would note the direction in which the animal moved and the kinds of sounds it made in order to foretell length of life and/or impending illness (*Pagan Traditions of Holidays*, p. 75-76).

Today in parts of Ireland, October 31 is still known as "Oidhch Shamhna," or "Vigil of Saman."

In the next chapter, we will learn how Halloween became an official holiday of Orthodox Christendom.

CHAPTER THREE

Halloween and Orthodox Christendom

The general practice of the Christianized Roman Empire was to try to convert pagans as quickly as possible. However, the pagans were reluctant to give up their false gods and ancient practices, so pagan religious practices were appropriated in order to encourage the pagans' conversion. This was accomplished by renaming pagan holidays and changing their symbolism to reflect "Christian" themes. In his catechism book, *My Catholic Faith,* Louis LaRavoire Morrow proudly boasts of the Roman Catholic Church's practice of renaming pagan festivals in order to encourage conversions to the church. "In the history of the Church we find that she often christened pagan festivals, making use of dates and ceremonies, and endowing them with an entirely new and Christian significance" (p. 416). In her book *Witches*, Erica Jong writes, "Christian holidays were deliberately set at times that had been sacred since the earliest Pagan days. The Christians knew the power Paganism had over the people and usually renamed rather than reinvented holidays" (p. 124).

The pagan festival of the dead continued to be observed until the sixth century, when it was slowly integrated into Christian practice. Pope Gregory the Great (540-604 AD) advised the Archbishop of Canterbury to retain the Druid sacrifices and celebrate them in honor of Christian saints. The Roman Church first introduced All Saints' Day on May 13, 609 AD, to commemorate all those saints and martyrs who had no special day of recognition. In the 8th century, the day was moved from May 13 to November 1 to counteract the pagan celebrations held on that same day. By the ninth century the Roman Church was holding a Eucharist of reconciliation for those dead who had not been named among the saints. The evening before, October 31, was called "All Hallowed Eve" (holy evening).

In the tenth century, "All Souls' Day" was added to the Roman Catholic calendar on November 2 for the souls still suffering in purgatory. A popular practice became visiting cemeteries and setting out "soul cakes" (currant buns), wine, tobacco and gifts for the dead. People went from house to house begging for these soul cakes, and in return, these house callers would offer up prayers for the souls of the giver's dead relatives. This was referred to as "a souling."

During the Reformation, Protestant authorities saw fit to remove "All Souls" from the church calendar. John King reveals, "The feast was restored only as late as 1928, when it was presumably felt that superstition or the pagan influence no longer offered any significant danger to Christian orthodoxy" (King, *The Celtic Druids' Year: Seasonal Cycles of the Ancient Celts,* p. 28).

Morrow writes of the significance of the feast of "All Saints Day," November 1, for the Roman Catholic Church: "On this day *the Church honors the Angels and Saints* in heaven. *It is a holy day of obligation.* This day is a great family feast. It has its origin in the year 610, when Boniface IV dedicated the Pantheon of Rome to the Blessed Virgin and all the martyrs. *It is in special commemoration of the millions of Saints in heaven who have not been officially canonized by the Church,* and thus have no special commemoration during the year" (*My Catholic Faith*, p. 417). Since Scripture condemns the worship of angels, men and any other "deity" besides God Himself, Morrow's reference to honoring "Angels," "Saints," and the "Blessed Virgin" can only be referring to pagan deities or demons, disembodied souls, and the mother goddess.

Likewise, November 2 is the feast of "All Souls Day." Morrow explains its meaning for Catholics: "This day commemorates *all the souls in purgatory.* It is a day for *pious remembrance of the dead,* and for offering of Masses and prayers for them. On this day as on Christmas, priests are allowed to say three Masses, for the souls of the departed, that they may be free from Purgatory" (Ibid., p. 417). The concept of "souls in purgatory" closely resembles the wandering disembodied souls of the Druid religion who have not gained entrance into heaven.

The Roman Catholic Church's historical practice of appropriating pagan celebrations and giving them new "Christian" names and meanings is quite universal—with far too many instances to be covered in depth in this book. However, Sir James George Frazer gives this succinct summary: "**Taken altogether, the coincidences of the Christian with the heathen festivals are too close and too numerous to be accidental**. They mark the compromise which the Church in the hour of its triumph was compelled to make with its vanquished yet still dangerous rivals. The inflexible Protestantism of the primitive missionaries, with their fiery denunciation of heathendom, had been exchanged for the supple policy, the easy tolerance, the comprehensive charity of shrewd ecclesiastics, who clearly perceived that if Christianity was to conquer the world it could do so only by relaxing the too rigid principles of its Founder, by widening a little the narrow gate which leads to salvation" (*The Golden Bough*, p. 419, bold emphasis added).

Modern Celebration

"All Hallowed Eve" or Halloween was nearly absent in America during the first few hundred years of settlement. Adhering to the Word of God, the English Puritans in America (a strict Protestant sect) rejected Halloween as a Catholic and pagan holiday. Over two hundred years later, the Irish potato famine of the 1840s brought thousands of Irish immigrants to America, who in turn brought the Halloween custom with them. At that time Halloween was regarded as a night of fear—and wise men, respectful of hobgoblins and wandering demons, stayed indoors. Only in modern times has Halloween developed into a festive time for children.

Direct parallels can be made between pagan traditions and modern customs of Halloween. Trick or treating rehearses the ancient custom of people visiting neighborhood homes on Halloween night to represent the dead in search of food. Those who pass out candy represent the homes visited by the dead and may also represent worried individuals seeking to appease Hecate and other nighttime terrors. Many children and adults disguise themselves today with masks and costumes on Halloween. Such masks of devils and hobgoblins symbolize evil spirits seeking mischief, as well as represent an attempt to scare evil spirits away.

Yet, there are even more sinister re-enactments on Halloween that have been largely ignored by society.

Wicca and Satanist High Sabbat. For modern pagans, Wiccans, witches and Satanists, Halloween is the holiest day of the year—a High Sabbat—and a serious celebration. Celebrated above all other occult holidays, Halloween is a festival of the dead and represents both the end and the beginning of the occult year. It also marks the beginning of the death and destruction associated with winter. "At this time the power of the underworld is unleashed, and spirits are supposedly freed to roam about the earth; it is considered the best time to contact spirits" (*Halloween and Satanism,* p. 146).

As in times past, modern pagans celebrate Samhain Sabbat (Halloween) because they believe that at this time of the year the veil between the living and the dead is at its thinnest, allowing communication with the spirit world.

Historically, real witches were known to revel on Halloween night. According to *Man, Myth & Magic,* the witches of Aberdeen danced "round an old grey stone at the foot of the hill at Craigleuch, the Devil himself playing music before them." Modern Wiccans practice a similar sky-clad (nude) Halloween tradition, calling on earth spirits and goddesses to visit their knife drawn circles of power. It is preferable to hold this sky-clad circle of power in an evergreen grove, especially when Halloween falls on the night of a full moon. Halloween is strongly associated with goddess worship. "It is a time when the summer goddess (the Great Mother) relinquishes her power to the winter god (the Horned God)" (*Witches,* p. 122).

For Satanists, who celebrate the holiday as one of two *highest* holy days, Halloween is the sinister, direct celebration of Satan and death. Sacrifices are performed by a select few at the highest levels of witchcraft covens, satanic cults and various occult secret societies. "**At Halloween the sacrifices of some of these satanic cults are unspeakably vicious and brutal**. This includes a series of six weeks of rituals including the slaughter of a small animal like a bird or cat, progressing through each week with a larger animal such as a goat, and **then the murder of a small infant or child until the final night where they ritually murder not only another child but also an adult female**" (*Like Lambs To The Slaughter,* pp. 190, 192).

Every year there are hundreds, perhaps thousands, of missing children and young adults who are never found, nor are their bodies ever recovered. Are these victims of secret occultists' human sacrifices? Only God knows!

How ironic and tragic that on a night when paganism and occultism are at their zenith and unspeakably vile and violent acts are being played out among Wiccans and Satanists, many Christians—rather than involving themselves in prayer and repentance—are having their own Halloween celebrations!

Halloween's Popularity. In the past few decades Halloween's popularity has grown by leaps and bounds. Second only to Christmas, Halloween is the biggest shopping holiday for many retailers, generating more than $6 billion in sales. More candy is sold for Halloween than is sold for Valentine's Day, and there are more Halloween parties than New Year's Eve parties! Two-thirds of all adults celebrate Halloween, and consumers send each other 28 million Halloween cards (*The Halloween Industry,* 2001-2002*)*.

An example of Halloween's growing popularity can be seen in San Francisco. Halloween in San Francisco is what Mardi Gras, another occult celebration, is to New Orleans—one of the biggest events of the year. No other city in America has anything to equal it. Promoted as a peaceful and happy event, it is the biggest impromptu bash of its kind, bringing out a quarter of a million revelers to the Castro and Market Street neighborhood.

The following excerpt was written by an eager traveler from the United Kingdom who celebrated Halloween in San Francisco. "Firstly, unlike in the U.K., Halloween in America is a big deal. Whilst we half-heartedly celebrate it, over here it's one of the biggest holidays of the year. So it is by luck that I found myself in San Francisco, which happens to host the biggest Halloween celebration in the world with 300,000 people taking to the Castro area of San Francisco [which is otherwise the epicenter of gay culture in San Francisco]. The party however soon turned to violence, and multiple arrests were made as seven people were stabbed, and police in riot gear had to step in. A friend I was with was attacked by several black men. I could only watch as they tore into him" (*Brian Webb's Travel Journal*).

Halloween Is Darkness

Visions of Jack-O-Lanterns with burning candles inside to make the jeering faces look even more eerie; thoughts of skeletons and ghosts, goblins and devils; the use of black, a favorite color of Halloween; rooms made to be dark and scary—all point to **the theme of Halloween, which is clearly darkness**. I John 1:5 states that "God is light and there is no darkness in Him." Jesus Christ tells us in John 8:12, "I am the light of the world; the one who follows Me shall never walk in darkness, but shall have the light of life." Through the prophet Isaiah, God solemnly warns, "Woe unto them that call evil good, and good evil; that put darkness for light, and light for darkness; that put bitter for sweet, and sweet for bitter!" (Isa. 5:20).

Halloween is the very antithesis of true Christianity. Its images are images of death, demons, ghosts, goblins, spiritism and Satanism. All this is absolutely contrary to God's Word. Halloween is about the dead, whereas the true God is the God of the living! Further, Halloween glorifies the spirit realm—a realm composed of fallen angels or demons and Satan, its ruler, who are opposed to God and to the truth.

The Spiritual Realm

The Scriptures teach that demonic spiritual forces are bound in the physical earth. In Revelation 9:14, John writes of "the four angels which are bound in the great river Euphrates." Likewise, Job 26:5 says, "Dead *things* are formed from under the waters." A literal Hebrew translation would read, "The Rafa [fallen angels] are made to writhe from beneath the waters."

Additional biblical references indicate that some places on the earth are a kind of holding tank, or prison, where God has bound certain fallen entities (II Pet. 2:4; Jude 6). As revealed in Scripture, such fallen spirits seek to communicate with men and to participate in their affairs. The Hebrew people were warned that earth spirits pretending to be gods might seek communion with men. In I Sam. 28:13 we read that the witch of Endor summoned such a fallen spirit, which ascended from "out of the earth." These and other Scriptures reveal that the dynamic (or energy) behind the earth-goddess-spirits of Halloween is indeed real—and is the same power behind the legions of fallen spirits bound within the earth.

Sadly, as in antiquity, those who practice modern paganism are deceived into worshipping "devils" (Rev. 9:20). Dogma embraced as the wisdom of goddesses is defined in the Scriptures as "doctrines of devils." The apostle Paul said, "The things which the Gentiles sacrifice, they sacrifice to demons" (I Cor. 10:20). In Acts 7:41-42 we read that those who worship idols are joined to the "army of heaven" (Greek, *stratos*, a "fallen angel army"). Psalm 96:5 concludes that "all the gods of the nations are idols" (Hebrew, *elilim*, nothing, vanity; the LXX translates *elilim* as *daimonia*, or demons). Thus, the pagan images which represented the ancient gods and goddesses were "elilim"—empty, nothing, vanity. But behind such empty idols were the living dynamics of idolatry itself and the very objects of heathen adoration—demons and Satan the devil himself.

Because the Bible clearly defines earth-centered goddess worship as actually paying homage to Satan and his demons—and since demons are eternal personalities who desire the worship of humans—it is clear that Wiccan deities are, in reality, nothing more than neo-pagan titles given to demon spirits (*Happy Halloween?*).

Satan the Devil Is the God of This World

The New Testament reveals that Satan the devil is the god of this world, as the apostle Paul wrote: "For we [the apostles and true Christians] have personally renounced the hidden things of dishonest gain, not walking in *cunning* craftiness, nor handling the Word of God deceitfully; but by manifestation of the truth, we are commending ourselves to every man's conscience before God. But if our gospel is hidden, it is hidden to those who are perishing; in whom **the god of this world has blinded the minds of those who do not believe**, lest the light of the gospel of the glory of Christ, Who is *the* image of God, should shine unto them" (II Cor. 4:2-4).

Satan is also called the prince of the power of the air. This is why he can deceive people into following him and rejecting the true God and His Son Jesus Christ. Paul reminded the Ephesians that before their conversion they were dead in their sins: "Now you were dead in trespasses and sins, in which you walked in times past according to the course of this world, **according to the prince of the power of the air, the spirit that is now working within the children of disobedience**; among whom also we all once had our conduct in the lusts of our flesh, doing the things willed by the flesh and by the mind, and were by nature *the* children of wrath, even as the rest *of the world*" (Eph. 2:1-3).

Satan's spiritual power extends into high places in government and religion (Eph. 6:11-18). He uses these institutions to further deceive the whole world. Indeed, the apostle John described him as "the great dragon … **the ancient serpent who is called the Devil and Satan, who is deceiving the whole world**" (Rev. 12:9).

Many who profess to be Christians have been deceived into celebrating Halloween. In Revelation two, Jesus Christ personally rebukes the church of Thyatira, saying, "I have a few things against you, because you allow the woman Jezebel, who calls herself a prophetess, to teach and to seduce My servants into committing fornication [spiritual fellowship with satanic religions] and eating things sacrificed to idols [the Catholic Eucharist is sacrificed to idols]. And I gave her time to repent of her fornication, but she did not repent. Behold, I will cast her into a bed, and those who commit adultery with her into great tribulation, unless they repent of their works. **And I will kill her children with death**; and all the churches shall know that I am He Who searches *the* reins and hearts; and I will give to each of you according to your works. But to you I say, and to *the* rest who *are* in Thyatira, **as many as do not have this doctrine, and who have not known the depths of Satan**, as they speak; I will not cast upon you any other burden" (Rev. 2:20-24).

The "depths of Satan" are found not only in Halloween, but also in all the other occult holidays of this world. In chapter four we will take a more in-depth look at how Satan is deceiving the world through occult saturation.

CHAPTER FOUR

Secrets of the Occult
Saturate the World Today

The Occult: What is it? The word *occult* comes from the Latin *occultus,* which means "concealed." In its ordinary usage, it means "beyond the bounds of ordinary knowledge—the mysterious, the concealed, or that which is hidden from view." Witchcraft, magic, etc., are occult substitutes for Bible miracles. Whereas God does miracles for His people, believers in the occult seek miracles by appealing to spirit powers (demons).

Students of the occult frequently divide occult phenomena into three areas: (1) forms of divination, (2) types of mystical experience, and (3) magical manipulation.

Divination is an attempt to obtain, by supernatural means, information which cannot be obtained by the natural processes of study and investigation. Divination seeks especially to foretell the future. Just as magic is the occult substitute for divine miracles, divination is the occult substitute for God-inspired prophecy. God drove Israel into captivity because they practiced sins that included divination (II Kings 17:17-18) or soothsaying.

Augury (another form of divination) involves interpreting omens— and is based on the belief that the activities of gods could be predicted. This is done by observing events in nature (the weather, behavior of animals, the movement of stars, etc.), or by observing the results of ritual ceremonies involving chance (casting lots, tossing arrows, etc.). King Manasseh of Israel practiced such and did evil before God (II Kings 21:6; II Chron. 33:6). The most common form of divination (augury) today is astrology. Other examples of divination include reading palms (palmistry), ouija boards, tarot cards, crystal balls, and interpretation of dreams.

Any attempt to transcend the bounds of the physical world with out-of-body experiences such as astral flight or levitation fits into category two—types of mystical experience. Séances, necromancy, and psychic healing also fit into this category.

Necromancy is the alleged power to communicate with the spirits of dead people ("ghosts"). The Scriptures call this "having a familiar spirit." Today, people who do this are called spiritists, spiritualists, or mediums. There are millions of people in South America who claim this power, and hundreds of thousands in the US, many of whom are members of the hundreds of spiritualist or spiritist churches (*The Occult: Witchcraft, Magic, Divination and Psychics*).

Magical manipulation—using hidden forces of the spiritual realm to manipulate people and circumstances—is the third category. Practitioners include sorcerers, witches, and witch doctors (*The Occult Connection*).

Today, the tentacles of occult philosophy reach into every area of society. Police departments request psychics to help solve crimes; universities offer courses in paranormal and occult science; well-known science fiction writers mask occult doctrines in their works through pseudo-scientific language; and, a leader of the women's movement urges her followers to return to the ancient religions in which female deities were worshiped (witchcraft). Even the American Medical Society endorses the search for "new" powers to aid the healing process.

Is this saturation of occult philosophy a mere coincidence—or is there an agenda being implemented by these varied, seemingly unconnected disciplines?

Occult Saturation: Preparation for a New World Order

Within the past few decades many voices have been crying for a *New World Order.* These include, among others, past and present presidents of the United States, the Pope, the president of Russia and the prime minister of England. What is being declared as "new" is really not new at all, but is a renewed attempt by mankind to unite in order to build a kingdom or government without God's intervention or rulership. It is in fact a continuation of the ancient Tower of Babel and is the driving philosophical/religious force behind the United Nations and the planned New World Order. Scholars believe that the Babylonian Tower was a type of pyramid. This pyramid was never completed because God intervened and confused the languages of man, dispersing humanity over all the earth.

The unfinished pyramid on the back of the U.S. one-dollar bill depicts the renewal of this one-world vision. The all-seeing eye above the pyramid is thought by some to represent "big brother" or the ruling Elite, but it is also thought to represent Lucifer or the occult force behind the New World Order. One writer notes: "The New World Order as envisioned by the Elite is hardly a recent undertaking. Theirs is a philosophy rooted in ancient occult traditions. Success is near, and the infiltration of society by New Age occultism is the reason for this success. The New World Order has never been solely about world government; rather, from the beginning its proponents have been privy to secret doctrines and **it is a spiritual plan more than anything**" (*New World Order or Occult Secret Destiny? The New Age Movement and Service to The Plan*).

Robert Hieronimus is a proponent of the New Age and the Secret Brotherhood's plan for a New World Order. In his book, *America's Secret Destiny*, he traced the spiritual vision of America's founding fathers and the plan's eventual fruition in the New World Order and the New Age Movement (both of which are synonymous).

Willy Peterson, though writing from the opposite camp, confirms the assertions of Hieronimus. "In order to reach their aims of world unity and thus engage the whole world in service to the Plan, 'enlightened' Freemasons and New Agers have been pushing for collectivist motifs that promote monistic pantheism and unity. This is why the chief instigators to the globalist League of Nations and the United Nations have been Theosophists, trying to work out the plan. This is why the verbiage and aims at the UN is for world peace and brotherhood. It is a spiritual undertaking in a secular world."

These so-called "enlightened people" are considered to be the torchbearers of a spiritual plan that can be traced to the time of Nimrod and the Tower of Babel, up through to the Illuminati and onwards. David Allen Lewis writes in *Dark Angels of Light,* "Whether the Illuminati has one special organization that is its original descendant ... its philosophical torchbearers are represented by literally hundreds of organizations and individuals in many diverse realms."

A Blueprint for Destiny

It is no coincidence that America has become the center of New Age and New World Order conspiracies. Heironomus states that "America's Great Seal may be seen as a blueprint for the elevation of consciousness. It says, in part, that we must transform ourselves before we can change the world, and it is during the process of self-transformation that we can catch a glimpse of what part we are to play in national and global transformation."

Texe Marrs, author of *Dark Secrets of the New Age,* writes: "The New World Order, or rather the philosophy its deliverers hold to be true, is one and the same as the New Age ideal of man's divinity and self-transformation. In order to partake ... one must awaken to the original sin of Lucifer, as proposed to Eve in the Garden of Eden, that 'we can be as Gods' [now in this physical life]." (See Gen. 3:5.) It is not surprising, then, that Christians are often cited as the main obstacle hindering its success.

True Christians proclaim only one Savior—Jesus Christ—and only one salvation through Him. On the other hand, the New Age belief allows for many 'saviors' and enlightened teachers, masters and gurus, and hence many ways to salvation. Therefore, the only belief system not compatible with the New Age and coming New World Order is true Christianity.

"The New Age is a universal open-arms religion that excludes from its ranks only those who believe in Jesus Christ and a Personal God. Buddhists, Shintoists, Satanists, Secular Humanists, witches, witch doctors and shamans—and all who reject Christianity are invited to become trusted members of the New Age family. Worshippers of separate faiths and denominations are to be unified in a common purpose: THE GLORIFICATION OF MAN" (Ibid.).

Secular Humanism. The glorification of man is both the philosophy and goal of Secular Humanism. The Humanist Manifesto I was written in 1933. A second addition, Humanist Manifesto II, was completed in 1973 and signed by such notables as the author Isaac Asimov; professors Brand Blanshard, Anthony Flew, and A.J. Ayer; psychologist B.F. Skinner; situational ethicist Joseph Fletcher; and biologist Jacques Monod. The following are selections that show the general direction of the statement.

"'Promises of immortal salvation and fear of eternal damnation are both illusory and harmful.' Why? Because 'they distract humans from present concerns, from self-actualization, and from rectifying social injustices.' Moreover, science has found 'no credible evidence that life survives the death of the body.'

"'We affirm that moral values derive their source from human experience. Ethics is autonomous and situational, needing no theological or ideological sanction.'

"'In the area of sexuality, we believe that intolerant attitudes, often cultivated by orthodox religions and puritanical cultures, unduly repress sexual conduct.' The authors affirm 'the right to birth control, abortion, and divorce.' They also permit any form of 'sexual behavior between consenting adults,' for 'short of harming others or compelling them to do likewise, individuals should be permitted to express their sexual proclivities and pursue their lifestyles as they desire' " (McCallum, D., *Optimistic Secular Humanism*, 2004).

Secular Humanism has dominated western thinking and is finding its ultimate expression in plans for a New World Order. And one way to get all people—including professing Christians—mentally prepared for this New World Order is to desensitize them by saturating them with teachings and practices of humanism, sexual promiscuity, eastern mysticism, witchcraft, satanism, paganism and occultism as well as ethnic diversity and politically correct "tolerance" propaganda. Astrology is one such example.

Astrology

In 2003 a U.S. public opinion poll was taken regarding beliefs in astrology. Of those participating, 31%, or nearly 1 in 3 people, believed in the accuracy of astrology—and among those aged 25 to 29 that number rose to 46%, nearly 1 in 2. Belief by people over age 64 was only 17%, or about 1 in 6. These statistics clearly show how influential this saturation campaign has been at all levels of society in changing beliefs in just one generation.

In the United States and Canada, 1,800 newspapers print daily horoscopes. Twelve thousand Americans claim to be full-time astrologers, and another 200,000 work at it part-time. Author Linda Goodman's two books on astrology have sold an incredible 60 million copies. The phenomenon of astrology is growing.

God's View of Astrology. Throughout history, man has searched the heavens for answers to life's questions. And throughout history, God has condemned such practices.

The prophet Isaiah proclaimed, "Let now the astrologers, the stargazers, the monthly prognosticators, stand up, and save thee from *these things* that shall come upon thee. Behold, they shall be as stubble; the fire shall burn them; they shall not deliver themselves from the power of the flame; *there shall* not *be* a coal to warm at, *nor* fire to sit before it. Thus shall they be unto thee with whom thou hast laboured, *even* thy merchants, from thy youth; they shall wander every one to his quarter; none shall save thee" (Isaiah 47:13-15).

As Isaiah explains, astrologers do not have the power to save anyone from troubles or death. Reading the stars and planets will not tell man what he needs to know. God Himself reveals what man needs to know, as the biblical account of Daniel and his companions shows. "And in all matters of wisdom *and* understanding that the king inquired of them, he found them [Daniel and his friends] ten times better than all the magicians *and* astrologers that *were* in all his realm.... Daniel answered in the presence of the king, and said, 'The secret which the king has demanded cannot the wise *men*, the astrologers, the magicians, the soothsayers, show unto the king; **but there is a God in heaven that revealeth secrets, and maketh known to the king Nebuchadnezzar what shall be in the latter days'** " (Daniel 1:20 and 2:27-28).

Therefore, people who use astrology are using witchcraft. It makes no difference if it is checking their astrological birth sign in the daily newspaper, making and using astrological charts, or consulting with astrologers. True Christians live by the Word of God and walk in faith, believing God the Father and Jesus Christ, and do not seek to know the future through astrology.

The Occult and Violence in Films

The desensitization towards and seduction into postmodern pagan spirituality in our modern culture can also be illustrated by the popularity of occult themes in entertainment. Occult themes provide popular material for TV shows and movies. Escalating in the 1960s with the hit *Rosemary's Baby* (1968), Hollywood began to churn out increasing numbers of films with dark occult themes. *Rosemary's Baby* featured a young woman who mothered a child by the devil. As the decade of the seventies progressed, violence, sadism, brutality, slasher films, victims of possession, and graphic blood-and-gore tales became more frequent. *Deliverance* (1972) included graphic mutilation and sodomy by crazed hillbillies upon an unsuspecting group of wilderness adventurers. The influential and acclaimed independent-sleeper horror classic *Halloween* (1978), with its creepy soundtrack, featured a knife-wielding killer of teenage babysitters. This popular serial killer slasher film inspired numerous sequels—seven more by the year 2002.

Evil spirits possessed the body of a twelve-year-old girl in the box-office success *The Exorcist* (1973). Its horrific visuals terrified audiences. The blockbuster, about the attempted exorcism of a demonic entity by two priests, inspired sequels of its own, e.g., *Exorcist II: The Heretic* (1977), *The Exorcist III* (1990) and *Exorcist: The Beginning* (2004).

Other devil-possession movies in the late 70s and early 80s included *The Amityville Horror* (1979), about a devilish haunted house, and *Poltergeist*, a story about menacing spirits that kidnap a young child by sucking her into a TV set and taking her into a parallel dimension. *Poltergeist* encouraged a sequel in 1986, and another in 1988. *The Omen* (1976), about a young adopted son named Damien—Satan's son—also inspired two sequels: *Damien: Omen II* (1978) and *The Final Conflict* (1981). There was also a made-for-cable TV sequel titled *Omen IV: The Awakening* in 1991. Other devil films included *The Devil's Advocate* (1997) and *End of Days* (1999) with the lead character as the seductive Devil Lord.

Horror films in the mid-1990s surprised the industry with their phenomenal success. *The Craft* (1996), about schoolgirls dabbling in witchcraft and black magic, and the horror/thriller *Scream* (1996), are two examples. The end of the century's expressionistic docu-horror, *The Blair Witch Project* (1999), was filmed using a hand-held camera which enhanced its suggestive, understated horror (Dirks, T., *Horror Films*, 1996-2005).

The Occult and Violence in Electronic Games

Children have long played elaborate imaginative games with dolls, toy soldiers, forts, tanks, boats and planes—all without causing harm. But times have changed. Violence and horror themes have taken center stage in electronic video games—along with fantasy in role-playing games like *Dungeons & Dragons, Vampire, Werewolf* and *GURPS*. The same goes for card games like *Magic the Gathering, Battle Tek* and *Star Wars,* as well as computer simulation and virtual reality games.

The largest provider of violent and occult games is Wizards of the Coast, producers of *Magic the Gathering* and publisher of *Dungeons and Dragons. Magic the Gathering,* an occult card trading game, was released in late 1993 and sold out its first 10 million cards in six weeks (instead of the projected six months). More than 500 million cards have been sold, and there are more than five million game enthusiasts in 52 countries, surpassing both *Monopoly* and *Trivial Pursuit.*

Most of such games take place in a setting where the distinctions between good and evil are blurred. This promotes the lie that there is "white" magic, which can be good, and "black" magic, which is bad. A player doesn't merely observe the occult aspects of the game—he is immersed in that environment and must participate in the occult to survive. Some games are filled with violence, destruction, murder, human sacrifice, spells, demons and psychic powers. Nearly all of the games present a view that is hostile to a Christian worldview, incorporating themes which either mock or misinterpret biblical truths.

"Virtual reality" computer games, where participants perceive that they are actually involved in the action, are particularly sinister because players directly participate in witchcraft and the occult and are immersed in activities with familiar spirits.

Doom, by Id Software, is considered by many to be the greatest game of all time. The first episode, "Knee Deep in the Dead," features pentagrams, a Wicca or witchcraft symbol. Toward the end of the episode the hero of the game exits by stepping onto a platform with the symbol of a goat behind a pentagram. An inverted cross (a symbol of Satanism) can be found near the beginning of the second episode, "The Shores of Hell." The third episode, called "Inferno," features more pentagrams. Teleporters, which move the player to different areas, also utilize pentagrams.

When exiting the shareware version of the game, there is a screen with more information about what is in the full registered version. In part, it states: "Sure, don't order *DOOM*. Sit back with your milk and cookies and let the universe go to Hell. Don't face the onslaught of demons and spectres that await you on The Shores of Hell. Avoid the terrifying confrontations with cacodemons and lost souls that infest Inferno. Or, act like a man! Slap a few shells into your shotgun and let's kick some demonic butt. Order the entire *DOOM* trilogy now! After all, you'll probably end up in Hell eventually. Shouldn't you know your way around before you make the extended visit?"

In *Afterlife,* by Lucasarts, players develop a Heaven and Hell that are far different from the Heaven and Hell of the Bible. The plotline is that the player is a local deity who must take care of Heaven and Hell. What each soul **believes** determines where they will **go**. For example, if one believes in a religion that involves reincarnation, they will return to earth with another life at a later time.

Quake, another game by Id Software, is much like *Doom* but more technologically advanced. While uploading *Quake* or *Doom*, there is a loading indicator on the top or bottom right of the screen. In *Doom*, the indicator is a small picture of a disk, but in *Quake*, it is a pentagram. One of the powerups in *Quake* is called "the pentagram of protection." It makes one's character invincible for a brief period of time. While the powerup is in effect, the character's armor rating turns to "666," and the character gradually begins to look more sinister.

In the controversial *Duke Nukem 3d*, created by 3D Realms, the third level in the first episode is called "Death Row." In an area near the beginning of the level (a prison facility), there is a chaplain and a cross on the wall. If Duke Nukem, the game's morally decayed hero, touches a gray portrait in front of the cross, it will invert.

In *Warcraft 2*, by Blizzard Entertainment, one of the buildings, the altar of storms, has a pentagram on it. In *Diablo*, another game made by Blizzard, pentagrams can be found rather easily in the menus of the game (Andrew, *Computer Games Used as a Tool to Praise Satan*).

The games mentioned above are just a small sampling of what is being created and marketed to desensitize people to occult symbols and practices, witchcraft, and Satanism. Countless numbers of children and adults are mesmerized by and enslaved to these games, including many professing Christians and their children.

Desensitization of Children by the Media

Children are being continuously bombarded with occult symbols, witchcraft, and eastern religion by the electronic media. Many television commercials reflect reincarnation, yoga, and subliminal New Age beliefs. The world famous Disney Productions is one the world's foremost promoters of the occult and Satanism in its cartoons, videos, movies and theme parks.

Most cartoon shows abound in occult themes, which are actually designed to indoctrinate young children, preparing them to reject true Christianity. Some contain overt messages, such as Jim Henson's *Dark Crystal, Thunder Cats, She-Ra, He-Man,* and *Master of the Universe.*

"Others, like Ted Turner's *Captain Planet and the Planeteers,* are more subtle as they promote the New Age version of ecology.... Popular movies such as *Field of Dreams, E.T., Close Encounters of the Third Kind,* the *Star Wars* trilogy, *Raiders of the Lost Ark,* and *Temple of Doom,* although often beautifully entertaining, are laced with the New Age messages of benevolent space creatures, positive psychic powers and a blending of evil and good characters and themes.

"The sheer volume and the escalating intensity of these programs in a culture of diminishing Biblical values [clouds] children's minds so that they can no longer discern between the real and unreal or even between right and wrong" (Branch, C., *The Media or the Medium?,* 2000).

In addition, public and school libraries, as well as bookstores, are full of witchcraft books for children—and whole sections of these libraries are devoted to New Age books.

Occult Influences in Schools

The public school system has become an important vehicle for promoting the anti-God, anti-Christ, humanist and occult agenda of the New World Order. The assault on children's minds under the guise of education is reflected in this brief sampling of actual events that have occurred in various public schools across America:

"*The Witches,* by Roald Dahl, was read aloud to second graders ...during regular school hours.... The book starts out with the caveat: This is NOT a Fairy Tale. This is about REAL witches! The book goes on to say that real witches dress in ordinary clothes; look like ordinary women; hate children; and get their pleasure from doing away with one child [i.e., human sacrifice] a weekend, 52 a year. The parents learned about this horrendous instruction only when their second graders had nightmares.

"Seventh graders ... have for years been assigned to read the guide to the London Dungeon, a British museum where tourists can see frightening displays of wax figures demonstrating hideous torture practices that were used in bygone eras. The guide itself states that the exhibition is not recommended to unaccompanied or young children. The class assignment instructed the children to write a paragraph describing their own form of torture. One child announced that he was going home to try this kind of torture on his little brother.

"In another school, eleven-year-olds were given a book called *The Headless Cupid,* which is about a girl practicing to be a witch. The book graphically describes the First Amendment-protected religion of witchcraft, occult practices, spirit guides, séances and initiation rites.

"A class of sixth graders was shown the R-rated movie *Dawn of the Dead* as a reward after they had finished a test. Parents were not informed in advance, and when they finally reviewed the film, were shocked to find that it contained cannibalism, brutally violent scenes and was steeped in satanic and occult-related themes.

"In still another American school, the film *The Sword and the Sorcerer* was shown to sixth graders. Parents complained because it shows a witch calling up the devil from the pit of hell while the walls appeared to be coming alive with humans who are bleeding and screaming in agony. The witch worships the devil by licking and kissing him, calling him 'my god and my master' " (*The NCSCIA FOCUS Pre-Halloween, 2001 Edition*).

What about the popularity of the Harry Potter books and films? Should they be considered serious occult influences upon children (and adults) who read them, or are they just a source of creative, harmless entertainment? Some leading evangelical leaders have given them their stamp of approval. Yet, many other Christian pastors and leaders are shouting an alarm—and for good reason. The level of occult information contained in the Harry Potter series reveals that the author has a highly sophisticated knowledge of the occult, which she is passing on to her readers.

The following is a personal testimony from a former witch that has been edited:

Harry Potter: What Does God Have to Say?—by David Meyer

"I am writing this urgent message because I was once a witch. I lived by the stars as an astrologer and numerologist casting horoscopes and spells. I lived in the mysterious and shadowy realm of the occult. By means of spells and magic, I was able to invoke the powers of the 'controlling unknown' and fly upon the night winds transcending the astral plane. **Halloween was my favorite time of the year, and I was intrigued and absorbed in the realm of Wiccan witchcraft**. All of this was happening in the decade of the 1960s when witchcraft was just starting to come out of the broom closet.

"It was during that decade of the 1960s, in the year 1966, that a woman named J.K. Rowling was born. This is the woman who has captivated the world in this year of 2000 with four books known as the 'Harry Potter Series.' [Note: As of this publication, Rowling has written two more and is finishing a third to bring the total to seven.] These books are orientational and instructional manuals of witchcraft woven into the format of entertainment. These four books by J. K. Rowling teach witchcraft! I know this because I was once very much a part of that world.

"Witchcraft was very different in the 1960s. There were a lot fewer witches, and the craft was far more secretive. At the end of that spiritually troubled decade, I was miraculously saved by the power of Jesus Christ and His saving blood. I was also delivered from every evil spirit that lived in me and was set free. However, as I began to attend fundamental Christian churches, I realized that even there witchcraft had left its mark. Pagan holidays and Sabbats were celebrated as 'Christian holidays.'

"As time went on, I watched the so-called 'Christian' churches compromising and unifying. I also watched with amazement as teachings from eastern religions and 'New Age' doctrine began to captivate congregations. It was a satanic set-up ... bringing forth a one-world religion with a cleverly concealed element of occultism interwoven in its teachings.

"In order to succeed in bringing witchcraft to the world and thus complete satanic control, an entire generation would have to be induced and taught to think like witches, talk like witches, dress like witches, and act like witches. The occult songs of the 1960s launched the Luciferian project of capturing the minds of an entire generation....

"As a former witch, I can speak with authority when I say that I have examined the works of Rowling and that the Harry Potter books are training manuals for the occult. Untold millions of young people are being taught to think, speak, dress and act like witches by filling their heads with the contents of these books. Children are so obsessed with the Harry Potter books that they have left television and video games to read these witchcraft manuals.

"The first book of the series, entitled *Harry Potter and the Sorcerer's Stone*, finds the orphan, Harry Potter, embarking into a new realm when he is taken to 'Hogwart's School of Witchcraft and Wizardry.' At this occult school, Harry Potter learns how to obtain and use witchcraft equipment. Harry also learns a new vocabulary, including words such as 'Azkaban,' 'Circe,' 'Draco,' 'Erised,' 'Hermes,' and 'Slytherin'; all of which are names of real devils or demons. These are not characters of fiction!

"How serious is this? By reading these materials, many millions of young people are learning how to work with demon spirits. They are getting to know them by name. Vast numbers of children professing to be Christians are also filling their hearts and minds, while willingly ignorant parents look the other way."

"The titles of the books should be warning enough to make us realize how satanic and anti-Christ these books truly are. The aforementioned title of the first book, *Harry Potter and the Sorcerer's Stone* (1998), was a real give-away. The second book was called *Harry Potter and the Chamber of Secrets* (1999), while the third book was entitled *Harry Potter and the Prisoner of Azkaban* (1999)." The fourth book in the series is *Harry Potter and the Goblet of Fire* (2000), fifth is *Harry Potter and the Order of the Phoenix* (2003) and the sixth is *Harry Potter and the Half-blood Prince* (2005), with the seventh expected to be released soon. To show the impact and influence of these books on people, especially the younger generation, the total number of books sold worldwide is over 270 million and they have been translated into 62 languages.

"As a real witch, I learned about the two sides of 'the force'.... When real witches have Sabbats and esbats and meet as a coven, they greet each other by saying 'Blessed be,' and when they part, they say 'The Force be with you.' Both sides of this 'Force' are Satan. It is not a good side of the force that overcomes the bad side of the force, but rather it's the blood of Jesus Christ that destroys both supposed sides of the satanic 'Force.'

"High level witches believe that there are seven satanic princes and that the seventh, which is assigned to Christians, has no name. In coven meetings, he is called 'the nameless one.' In the Harry Potter books, there is a character called 'Voldemort.' The pronunciation guide says of this being: 'He who must not be named.'

"On July 8 [2000] at midnight, bookstores everywhere were stormed by millions of children to obtain the latest and fourth book of the series known as *Harry Potter and the Goblet of Fire.* These books were taken into homes everywhere with a real evil spirit following each copy to curse those homes.... Now we have learned that the public school system is planning to use the magic of Harry Potter in the classrooms, making the public schools centers of witchcraft training.

"What does God have to say about such books as the Harry Potter series? In the Bible, in the book of Acts, we read the following in the 19th chapter, verses 18-20: "And many that believed came, and confessed, and showed their deeds. Many of them also which used curious arts brought their books together and burned them before all men: and they counted the price of them, and found it fifty thousand pieces of silver. So mightily grew the Word of God and prevailed."

"As parents, we will answer to God if we allow our children to read witchcraft books. The Word of God will prevail mightily in your life only if such things of Satan are destroyed." (Meyer, D., *Harry Potter: What Does God Have to Say?*)

The Occult and the Feminine Divine

Under the guise of New Age spirituality, feminine occult practices and Satanism are increasing in scope and activity. For example, at the 13th annual Women of Wisdom Conference held in Seattle, February 16-21, 2005, the theme was "Living Boldly With Heart, Intention & Commitment." It was billed as, "A week of lectures, performances and experiential workshops, with presenters from diverse ethnic and spiritual backgrounds exploring the Divine Feminine."

The WOW New Age workshops bring in elements from diverse perspectives, such as Hindu, Wiccan, Celtic and others, incorporating occult practices such as tarot reading, meditation, chanting, ecstatic drumming, and "ecstatic tantric dancing." They dwell on issues such as sexuality, eroticism, feminine consciousness, and personal altars as well as healing with chakras, medicine wheels, crystals, and colors.

Examples of the various features of New Age workshops follow.

Sharron Rose, a 56-year-old DVD producer/distributor in Shoreline, Wash., taught a full-day workshop on *Tantric Dance of Durga.* Rose, also a teacher and choreographer who has studied dance and spirituality in India, focused on the mythical teachings of Durga, a Hindu goddess of power and beauty. In her teachings, Rose said, she wants to remind women of how females in various spiritual traditions have always been "the spirit and foundation of everything."

Danielle Rama Hoffman, LMP, a self-proclaimed energy healer, transformational trainer and leader of spiritual tours to Egypt, hosted *Awaken the Sekhmet Within: Solar Feminine Power*. Her summary said: "Fortify your feminine nature with the solar power of Sekhmet: the Egyptian lioness goddess of courage, compassion and healing."

Suzanna McCarthy, LlCSW, Spiritual Director, Wisdom's Gate, offered *Traversing the Dark Night of the Soul—Companioned by Hecate and Isis-Wisdom-Sophia*. The pamphlet for her workshop read: "The Dark Night of the Soul is a solitary experience that follows the path of 'no path.' The 'self' is stripped away; slowly, the true SELF emerges. Realizing that matters are out of our control, we enter into the mystery. This journey requires courage and consciousness as the outcome is unwritten. **Powerful allies Hecate and Isis-Wisdom-Sophia provide ancient wisdom and spiritual gifts** as they companion us during our journey."

Joanne Halverson, LMHC, and Margaret Riordan, PhD, IFCM, (with 20 years of experience in goddess spirituality and shamanism), presented *Ancient Power, Ancient Healing: the Sacred Snake, the Eternal Goddess and the Feminine Face of the Divine*. Their ad read: "Explore the ancient power of the Divine Feminine, delving into archaic stories, myths and images centered around the Sacred Snake and her association with the Mother Goddess. **The Sacred Snake was a symbol of female power and holiness in many pre-patriarchal cultures**. Her energy represents wisdom, strength, healing, transformation and a capacity for ecstatic experience of the Divine in one's life. Reclaim this mysterious and awesome power, bringing this transformative gift into your daily life." (Adapted from *www.womenofwisdom.org*, bold emphasis added.)

The above excerpts reveal the underlying philosophies and the satanic spiritual powers behind feminist movements worldwide.

Divine Goddess Worship in Modern Israel. While normative Judaism proudly boasts that it worships the one true God of the Old Testament (while rejecting Jesus Christ and the New Testament), some modern Jews are reviving goddess worship and occult practices in the land of Israel—just as it was in ancient Judah. The Jerusalem Post gives the following report on a group of goddess worshipers who worship Mother Earth: "Thirteen men and women are seated around the artifacts. A bag of instruments is passed around, and a shrine with Neolithic goddess figurines, babushkas, photographs of goddess statues, and a ceramic plate painted with a spiral design is quietly constructed. The earth below is the archeological site of a civilization over 8,000 years old. A few hundred meters away, one of the oldest known wells, now covered, marks the spot where people of the Yarmukian society once came to fill buckets of fresh water for pottery, drinking and bathing.

"We are in Kibbutz Sha'ar Hagolan, south of Lake Kenneret, but the modern blessing ceremony some Israeli women have invented might have origins much older than was previously imagined. They have chosen this place to conduct their ritual because of the goddess figurines recently found in this area. Iris Yotvat, one of the leaders of the goddess spirituality movement in Israel and a former movie star, leads the group in songs and prayers. As a chalice filled with water passes from hand to hand, each person places a few drops on their skin and thanks Mother Earth for her blessings.

"Some of the women remind everyone that we were not here first, and we will not be here last. A thin bundle of smoking sage, tightly bound with white string, is passed around for meditation and cleansing. After each person says his or her blessings and thoughts, Yotvat begins to sing to the beat of a slow drum. Tambourines, flutes, shakers and darbukas join in the songs of praise to the Great Mother, the creator of life.

"For many of the men and women seated here, the power of the circle represents a sacred space. It provides a medium for group meditation and unity. It relates to the moon and the ancient symbol of eternity, where time has no end and no beginning. The goddess worshipers believe that a divine goddess was praised thousands of years ago when agricultural societies lived in relative peace, and that the loss of that feminine spirit is part of what ails our modern culture.

"Despite their marginality, their convictions are supported by a growing body of archeological evidence and by many biblical scholars. **Many of those who believe in a divine feminine recently united in the Negev desert for a Shakti festival to learn more about ancient goddess figurines and how they connect to their lives today**" (The Jerusalem Post, April 28, 2005).

These modern-day Jews are worshiping the queen of heaven, as the ancient Jews did before God sent them into exile for these and other occult, pagan religious practices. They have forgotten that those who are involved in goddess worship of any kind, whether Jew or Gentile, are in direct defiance of Almighty God! In fact, they are committing gross, abominable sins in transgressing the first and second commandments. God's fierce judgment against these practices is revealed in Jeremiah 44, and once again will be executed against such sins.

Feminine Divine—Virgin Mary and Pagan Goddess Worship. Roman Catholicism makes "the Virgin Mary" the central focus of its worship and blasphemously calls her "the Queen of Heaven," "co-Mediatrix" and "co-Redemptrix" with Jesus Christ—Who, in fact, is the **only** Redeemer and Mediator (see Hislop, pp. 264-267). Notwithstanding, the Bible exposes an entirely different panorama of the "queen of heaven."

Mary Ann Collins, a former Catholic nun, has written extensively on her web site on numerous topics related to Roman Catholicism. The following section is excerpted from her article, "Mary Worship?"

"Goddess worship is not ancient history. It is going on today. It is practiced in Wicca and a variety of modern pagan religions. (Wicca is a religion based on witchcraft. It involves goddess worship, rituals and spells.)

"The credibility of goddess worship has been increased through its acceptance by university professors and its incorporation into textbooks. Wiccan doctrines are being promoted in publicly funded, accredited colleges and universities. Nursing school textbooks are overtly promoting goddess worship, including textbooks written by the National League for Nursing (an accrediting agency for nursing schools).

"In the following table, I will compare Catholicism's version of Mary with the goddess who is worshiped by Wiccans and modern pagans. My reason for doing this is that Wiccans and modern pagans live in modern America. If I compared Catholic doctrine about Mary with the goddess worship of ancient civilizations, it would seem remote and far removed from the real world. It would seem like a legend instead of real life.

"[O]vert goddess worship has infiltrated a number of main-line Protestant denominations. There have been some conferences in which Catholics and representatives of various Protestant groups worshiped the goddess Sophia and openly said that Jesus Christ is irrelevant.

"All Christian groups need to guard against goddess worship. According to the Bible, God's people are not supposed to worship any other deities. The Old Testament prophets often rebuked the people of Israel for worshiping 'foreign gods.' The people who worshiped the goddess Sophia at those conferences were doing the same kind of thing that the ancient Israelites did. They claimed to be God's people, but they were worshiping a 'foreign god.'

"The table compares the Mary of Roman Catholic theology and religious practice with the Biblical portrayal of Mary and with the goddess which is worshipped by Wiccans and modern pagans. My information about Wicca comes from the book, 'Wicca: Satan's Little White Lie,' by Bill Schnoebelen (who was the high priest of a Wiccan coven before he became a Christian), the 'World Book,' and the on-line version of 'The Encyclopedia Britannica.'

"One popular prayer in Mary's honor is the 'Hail Holy Queen,' which is known in Latin as the 'Salve Regina.' It is traditionally included as part of praying the rosary.

'Hail, holy Queen, Mother of Mercy! Our life, our sweetness and our hope! To thee do we cry, poor banished children of Eve. To thee do we send up our sighs, mourning and weeping, in this valley of tears. Turn, then, most gracious Advocate, thine eyes of mercy toward us; and after this our exile show unto us the blessed fruit of thy womb, Jesus. O clement, O loving, O sweet Virgin Mary.' "

Marian Apparitions. Collins continues: "On May 13, 1981, a man shot Pope John Paul II. As the ambulance carried him to the hospital, the Pope kept praying, 'Mary, my mother! Mary, my mother!' One year later, the Pope made a pilgrimage to Fatima to thank Our Lady of Fatima for saving his life and to consecrate the entire human race to her. The video 'Catholicism: Crisis of Faith' shows the Pope kissing the feet of a statue of Mary.

Biblical Mary	*Catholic Mary*	*The Goddess*
Humble and obedient. Calls herself "the handmaid of the Lord."	The Pope officially gave Mary the title "Queen of Heaven" and established a feast day honoring Mary, Queen of Heaven.	Wiccans call their goddess the "Queen of Heaven."
Knew she needed a savior: "And my spirit hath rejoiced in God my saviour" (Luke 1:47)	"Immaculate Conception" (Mary was conceived sinless, without original sin) and "All-Holy" (Mary lived a sinless life).	Goddesses don't need salvation. They make the rules.
Wife and mother who had other children (Mk. 6:3-4).	"Perpetual Virginity" (Jesus' brothers and sisters are considered to be cousins).	Goddesses don't have human children.
No biblical evidence that Mary didn't die like a normal person.	"Glorious Assumption" (Mary was bodily taken up into Heaven).	Goddesses don't die.
Jesus told John to take Mary into his home and take care of her as if she was his own mother.	Catholics are the adopted children of Mary. "Woman behold your son" (John 19:26) is taken to apply literally to every Catholic.	Witches are the adopted, "hidden children" of the Queen of Heaven.
Normal woman.	Sometimes pictured standing on a crescent moon, wearing a crown or with a circle of stars around her head.	Moon goddess.
Normal woman.	Supernatural (apparitions accompanied by miracles and healings).	Supernatural.
Points people to Jesus. Mary said, "Whatsoever he saith unto you, do it." (John 2:5)	Can make Jesus do things. A full page newspaper ad showing Mary and Jesus says, "He hasn't denied her anything in 2,000 years. What would you have her ask Him?" This is not official Catholic doctrine, but it is a widespread attitude which is encouraged by pious literature.	Points to herself. Wants to be worshipped.
Knew that she needed a savior. (Luke 1:47)	Apparitions of "Mary" have promised that if people wear certain objects (such as a Scapular or Miraculous Medal) or say certain prayers then they are guaranteed to go to Heaven. The Catholic Church has not officially approved of these practices, but it has also not discouraged them.	Invoked to make supernatural things happen through witchcraft (the use of special objects and special verbal formulas). Goddesses don't need a savior.

"Millions of pilgrims go to shrines which honor apparitions of Mary. Every year fifteen to twenty million pilgrims go to Guadalupe in Mexico, five and a half million go to Lourdes in France, five million go to Czestochowa (Jasna Gora) in Poland, and four and a half million go to Fatima in Portugal....

"Are these pilgrims worshipping Mary? You can observe them and see for yourself, thanks to a video entitled 'Messages from Heaven.'

"If you watch the video, you will see the Pope bow in front of a painting of Mary and cover the area with incense. You will see a million pilgrims walking in a procession, following a statue of Our Lady of Fatima and singing songs in her honor. You will see several million people in a procession following a painting of Our Lady of Guadalupe. You will see people weeping and raising their arms towards Mary. You will see the largest assembly of bishops and cardinals since the Second Vatican Council, gathered together to join Pope John Paul II in solemnly consecrating the entire world to the Immaculate Heart of Mary. [You can watch this video online; the information is available on Collins' website.]

"Goddess worship has infiltrated mainline Christian denominations. In November 1993, a Re-Imagining Conference was held in Minneapolis, Minnesota. Most of the 2,000 participants were women. This ecumenical church conference was sponsored by and attended by members of over a dozen denominations, including Presbyterians, Episcopalians, Catholics, Lutherans and Methodists. They prayed to Sophia, the goddess of Wisdom, calling her their Creator. They did rituals for this goddess, including a communion service where bread and wine were replaced by milk and honey. They openly rejected the doctrines of the incarnation and the atonement. This conference was repeated in 1996, 1998 and 2000.

"There are Wiccan web sites with web pages devoted to individual goddesses. The Virgin Mary is included among the goddesses of the following web sites: The Spiral Goddess Grove, The White Moon, and Goddess 2000. They consider Mary to be the 'Divine Feminine' and say that for centuries, many people have 'blended' their ancient goddesses with Mary." (See *www.catholicconcerns.com/MaryWorship.html*.)

In II Thessalonians two, Paul writes about the Mystery of Iniquity that was already at work in the first-century Church. The mixing in of pagan and occult beliefs and practices has no place in the true Church of God, which acknowledges Jesus Christ as its Head (Eph. 1:22-23) and worships God the Father in spirit and in truth (John 4:23-24).

Deepak Chopra and Occult Eastern Spirituality

Eastern spirituality has attracted many followers in the past four decades. In the Western Hemisphere, especially in America, Deepak Chopra is the most prominent and widely known teacher, author and advocate of Eastern spirituality. His teachings are a combination of Buddhism and Hinduism. Chopra does not believe that God is a Spirit Being, nor does he believe in a personal God as the Bible teaches. Rather, he believes in a pantheistic God that is a force of pure energy. Since everything is based on energy, and God is energy, God is in everything. Since God is in everything, God also exists in everyone. Therefore, Chopra teaches that in order to know God, one needs to find the deepest inner self. Consequently, when a person connects with that pure spiritual energy of the self, *then* one knows God.

Chopra teaches that one knows God through seven stages of spiritual development. The end result is "nirvana," a state of enlightenment that supposedly puts one on the same level as God. To achieve this, a person has to empty his mind through yoga and meditation until he hears nothing. What Chopra calls God and knowing God through yoga and meditation is, in reality, being familiar with and submitting to demon spirits, principalities and powers—for Satan is "the god of this world" (II Cor. 4:4).

Eastern spirituality as taught by Chopra is cloaked in the same lie that Satan told Eve in the Garden of Eden. Satan told her that if she and Adam ate of the fruit of the tree of the knowledge of good and evil, they would "become as God." Chopra has developed this satanic philosophy into a highly sophisticated seven-step process in his book, *How to Know God— The Soul's Journey into the Mystery of Mysteries* (all quotes are from the Large Print Edition).

Of nirvana, Chopra writes: "However long it takes, according to Buddhism, my mind will eventually desire the opposite of what I have. The karmic pendulum swings until it reaches the extreme of poverty, and then it will pull me back toward wealth again. Since only God is free from cause and effect, to want nirvana means that you want to attain God-realization [i.e., you realize that you yourself are God]. In the earlier stages of growth this ambition would be impossible, and most religions condemn it as blasphemy. **Nirvana isn't moral. Good and evil don't count anymore, once they are seen as the two faces of the same duality**" (*How to Know God*, p. 258).

This duality—good and evil co-existing in God—is nearly the same belief as that of Witchcraft, which believes that good and evil are embodied in the "Force." Yet, the Scriptures teach that God is light, and there is no darkness in Him at all!

Chopra continues: "For the sake of keeping society together, religions hold it as a duty to respect goodness and abhor evil. Hence a paradox: the person who wants to be liberated [where nothing is good or evil] is acting against God. Many devout Christians find themselves baffled by Eastern spirituality because they cannot resolve this paradox. How can God want us to be good and yet want us to go beyond good?" (Ibid., p. 258.) Chopra misunderstands because he does not know the true God of the Bible. Jesus Christ said that the only one Who is good is GOD (Matt. 19:17). To go "beyond good" is to go beyond God—be greater than God Himself— which is an absolute impossibility.

Yet, there is another meaning that Chopra is implying. In going "beyond good," one may choose a life of sin or lawlessness without guilt. Hence, one is "liberated." To substantiate this claim, he shows that according to Hinduism there is a right-hand and a left-hand path to God: "The answer takes place in consciousness. Saints in every culture turn out to be exemplars of goodness, shining with virtue. But the *Bhagavad-Gita* [Hindu religious writings] informs us that there are no outward signs of enlightenment, which means that **saints do not have to obey any conventional standards of behavior**. In India there exists the 'left-hand path' to God. On this path a devotee shuns conventional virtue and goodness. Sexual abstinence is often replaced with sexual indulgence (usually in a highly ritualized way). One might give up a loving home to live in a graveyard; some tantric devotees go so far as to sleep with corpses and eat the most repulsive decayed food. In other words, the left-hand path is not so extreme, but it is always different from orthodox religious observance.

"The left-hand path may seem like the dark side of spirituality, totally deluded in its barbarity and insanity—certainly Christian missionaries to India had no problem holding that interpretation. They shuddered to look upon Kali [an Indian goddess] with her necklace of skulls and blood dripping from her fangs. What kind of mother was this? But the left-hand way is thousands of years old, its origins are in the sacred texts that exhibit as much wisdom as any in the world. They state that God cannot be confined in any way. His infinite grace encompasses death and decay; he is in the corpse as well as the newborn baby. For some (very few) people, to see this truth isn't enough; they want to experience it. And God will not deny them. In the West our abhorrence of the left-hand path doesn't need to be challenged. Cultures each go their own way" (Ibid., pp. 259-260).

The Effects of the Left-Hand Path on Youth Culture Today: David Kupelian, in his book *The Marketing of Evil*, explains the adoption of the "left-hand path" by the modern youth culture today. Those who promote this kind of aberrant behavior do not refer to it as the left-hand path of Hinduism. Rather, they promote it as "freedom of expression" that has deep "spiritual" qualities: "[S]omething … is intent on degrading this generation so totally that little hope would be left for the next generation of Americans" (p. 70).

"Hollywoods depictions [of Sodom and Gomorrah] don't even *begin* to capture the shocking reality of what is going on in America's culture today—they're not even close.

"First of all, there's sex. Very simply, there seem to be neither boundaries nor taboos any more when it comes to sex. Anything goes—from heterosexual to homosexual to bi-, trans-, poly-, and you-don't-want-to-know sexual experiences. Sex has become a ubiquitous, cheap, meaningless quest for ever-greater thrills …"

"Moreover, with the evolution of online pornography, every type of sexual experience has literally been shoved under the noses of millions of Americans against their will, who find their e-mail in-boxes filled with hardcore sexual images. As a result, many pastors are struggling with how to deal with large numbers of churchgoers reportedly caught up with Internet Pornography.

"What about body piercing? It has progressed from traditional earrings for females, to earrings for males (eager to display their 'feminine side' which the '60 cultural revolution sold them), to multiple piercings for both males and females in literally every part of the body—the tongue, nose, eyebrow, lip, cheek, navel, breasts, genitals—again, things you don't really want to know.

"It's the same progression to extremes with tattooing. But why stop with 'conventional' piercing and tattooing? Ritual scarification and 3D-art implants are big. So are genital beading, stretching and cutting, transdermal implants, scrotal implants, tooth art and facial sculpture.

"How about tongue splitting? How about branding? How about amputations? That's right—amputations. Some people find these activities a real 'turn-on.'

"There are no bounds—no lower limits. Whatever you can imagine, even for a second in the darkest recesses of your mind, know that someone somewhere is actually doing it, praising it, and drawing others into it via the Internet.

"**Strangest of all is the fact that any behavior, any belief—no matter how obviously insane—is rationalized so it sounds reasonable, even spiritual. Satanism itself, and especially its variant, the worship of Lucifer** (literally, 'Angel of Light') **can be made to sound almost enlightened—of course, only in a perverse way**. But if you were sufficiently confused, [Satan is the author of confusion] rebellious and full of rage—if you had been set up by cruelty or hypocrisy (or both) to rebel against everything 'good'—the forbidden starts to be mysteriously attractive.

"Let's pick just one of these bizarre behaviors. How about hanging by your skin from hooks? It's called 'suspension.' In literally any other context, this would be considered a **gruesome torture**. But to many people who frequent 'suspension parties,' it's a **spiritual experience**. Consider carefully what 'Body Modification Ezine' (www.bmezine.com)—the Web's premiere site for body modification—says about 'suspension':

" 'What is suspension?

'The act of suspension is hanging the human body from (or partially from) hooks pierced through the flesh in various places around the body.

'Why would someone want to do a suspension?

'There are many different reasons to suspend, from pure adrenaline or endorphin rush, to conquering one's fears, to **trying to reach a new level of spiritual** consciousness and everything in between. In general, people suspend to attain some sort of "experience."

'Some people are seeking the opportunity to discover a deeper sense of themselves and to challenge pre-determined belief systems which may not be true. Some are **seeking a rite of passage or a spiritual encounter** to let go of the fear of not being whole or complete inside their body.

'Others are looking for control over their body, or seek to prove to themselves that they are more than their bodies, or are not their bodies at all. Others simply seek to explore the unknown.

'Many people believe that learning how one lives inside one's body and seeing how that body adapts to stress—and passes through it—**allows one to surrender to life and explore new realms of possibility**.

"Gosh—'control over their body, 'discover a deeper sense of themselves, 'conquering ones fears,' '**trying to reach a new level spiritual consciousness**.' What could be wrong with that?

"Or, how about tongue splitting—literally making yourself look like a human lizard—how could that be a positive, spiritual experience?

" 'The tongue,' explains the BME website, 'is one of the most immense nervous structures in your body. We have incredibly fine control over it and we receive massive feedback from it. When you dramatically alter its structure and free yourself of the physical boundaries your biology imposes, **in some people it triggers a larger freeing on a spiritual level'** " (Ibid. 71-73).

The left-hand path is an occultic, demonic, bizarre corruption of the mind and body that breeds a culture of rebellion and death. While the right-hand path of Eastern spirituality leads to worship of self as "God."

*Spiritual Evolution—Idolatry of Self***:** Chopra defines the spiritual evolution of coming to know God as a seven-step union of the mind, soul and God—which is nothingness: "Believe it or not, we find ourselves very close to the soul now. We have whittled away the scientific objections to God by placing him outside the reach of measurement. This means that a person's subjective experience of God can't be challenged—at the quantum level, objectivity and subjectivity merge into each other. The point of the merger is the soul [demon possession]; therefore knowing God comes down to this: like a photon nearing a black hole, your mind hits a wall as it tries to think about the soul. The soul is comfortable with the uncertainty; it accepts that you can be two places at once (time and eternity); it observes cosmic intelligence at work and is not bothered that the creative force is outside the universe....

"The mind is creeping closer and closer to the soul, which sits on the edge of God's world, at the event horizon. The gap of separation is wide when there is no perception of spirit; it grows smaller as the mind figures out what is happening. Eventually the two will get so close that mind and soul have no choice but to merge [demon possession]. When that happens, the resemblance to a black hole is striking. To the mind, it will be as if falling into God's world lasts forever, an eternity in bliss consciousness. From God's side, the merging takes place in a split second; indeed, if we stand completely in God's world, where time has no meaning, the whole process never even occurred. The mind was part of the soul all along, only without knowing it" (Ibid., pp. 487-489, bold emphasis and bracketed comments added).

Chopra describes his seven-step processes: "If you regard the soul as a kind of force field steadily pulling the mind toward it, every one of the seven stages can be described as closing the separation:

Stage One: *I am in such separation that I sense deep fear inside.*
Stage Two: *I don't feel so separate; I am gaining a sense of power.*

Stage Three: *Something larger than me is drawing near;*
                 I feel much more peaceful.
Stage Four: *I am beginning to intuit what that larger thing is—it*
                 must be God.
Stage Five: *My actions and thoughts are drawing on God's force field,*
                 as if we are both involved in everything.
Stage Six: *God and I are almost together now. I feel no separation;*
                 my mind is God's mind*.*
Stage Seven: ***I see no difference between myself and God"***
                 (Ibid., p. 490, bold emphasis added).

Chopra's seven-step thought process creates in a person a kind of "self idolatry." One will never come to know the true God through such means—for He reveals Himself to the humble. The prophet Ezekiel warned the leaders of ancient Israel, who had set up idols in their hearts: "And the word of the LORD came unto me, saying, '**Son of man, these men have set up their idols in their heart**, and put the stumbling block of their iniquity before their face: should I be inquired of at all by them? Therefore speak unto them, and say unto them, Thus saith the Lord GOD: Every man of the house of Israel that setteth up his idols in his heart, and putteth the stumbling block of his iniquity before his face, and cometh to the prophet; I the LORD will answer him that cometh according to the multitude of his idols; that I may take the house of Israel in their own heart, because they are all estranged from me through their idols.

"Therefore say unto the house of Israel, Thus saith the Lord GOD; **Repent, and turn *yourselves* from your idols; and turn away your faces from all your abominations**. For every one of the house of Israel, or of the stranger that sojourneth in Israel, which separateth himself from me, and setteth up his idols in his heart, and putteth the stumbling block of his iniquity before his face, and cometh to a prophet to inquire of him concerning me; I the LORD will answer him by myself: and I will set my face against that man, and will make him a sign and a proverb, and I will cut him off from the midst of my people; and ye shall know that I *am* the LORD' " (Ezekiel 14:2-8).

Besides idolatry of the self, Chopra's teachings illustrate a renaissance of ancient yoga philosophies as he states, "In ancient India this closing of the gap was described as *yoga* or union (the same Sanskrit root gave us the verb 'to yoke') [that is, in bondage to the elemental spirits of the world—Satan, his principalities, powers and demons]. Because the Indian sages had thousands of years to analyze it, the entire process of joining the soul was turned into a science. Yoga precedes Hinduism, which is a particular religion, and at its inception, the practices of Yoga [that are also taught by "Yoda," the master teacher of the mysteries in the *Star Wars* movies] were intended to be universal. The ancient sages had at their disposal the power to witness their own spiritual evolution, which boiled down to watching the mind approach the soul.

"What they discovered can be stated in a few cardinal points:
Evolution takes place inside. It isn't a matter of pilgrimages, observances, and obeying religious rules. No codes of conduct can alter the fact that every mind is on a soul journey.
Evolution is automatic. In the larger view, the soul is always pulling at us. Its force field is inescapable.
A person is required to pay attention. Since the journey to the soul happens only in awareness, if you block out awareness you impede your progress; if you pay attention, you build up momentum.
The final goal is inevitable. No one can resist the soul forever. Saints and sinners are on the same road.
"You can accurately graph a person's spiritual growth on this scale alone. The ego moves from an isolated, helpless state to a realization that it might have power; then it looks where the power comes from, at first deciding that it must be external, in the form of money and status, but in time realizing that the power source is internal. More time passes and the difference between inner and outer power dissolves. All reality is perceived as having one source; **in the end, you are that source**...."

Chopra continues, describing how "faith" is involved: "FAITH ...

Stage One: *Faith is a matter of survival. If I don't pray to God, he can destroy me.*

Stage Two: *I'm beginning to have faith in myself. I pray to God to help me get what I want.*

Stage Three: *Faith brings me peace. I pray that life should be free from turmoil and distress.*

Stage Four: *I have faith that inner knowledge will uphold me. I pray for more insight into God's ways.*

Stage Five: *Faith tells me that God will support my every desire. I pray that I am worthy of his faith in me* [God puts faith in no man, nor is any man worthy].

Stage Six: *Faith can move mountains. I pray to be God's instrument of transformation.*

Stage Seven: *Faith melts away into universal being. When I pray, **I find that I am praying to myself*** [because I become a god, 'I am']"

(Ibid., pp. 490-495, bold emphasis and bracketed comments added).

Like all other religious systems that man has fabricated, Chopra's belief hangs precariously upon the ability of the individual to achieve salvation by vain philosophy and empty works. This is clearly a deception.

In his epistle to the Colossians, the apostle Paul warned the brethren not to be deceived by such ideas: "Beware lest anyone takes you captive through **philosophy and vain deceit**, according to the **traditions of men**, according to the elements [elemental spirits] of the world, and not according to Christ. For in Him dwells all the fullness of the Godhead bodily; and you are complete in Him, Who is the Head of all principality and power" (Col. 2:8-10).

Voodoo and the Occult

While the Western Hemisphere has absorbed Eastern spirituality, Voodoo (also known as Vodun), is practiced by over 60 million people worldwide, predominantly in the Southern Hemisphere and many Island countries.

The Encyclopedia Britannica 2003 contains this entry on voodoo: "**VOODOO:** Also spelled Voudou, French Vaudou, national religious folk cult of Haiti. **Voodoo is a mixture of Roman Catholic ritual elements, which date from the period of French colonization**, and African theological and magical elements, which were brought to Haiti by slaves formerly belonging to the Yoruba, Fon, Kongo, and other peoples of Africa. The term voodoo is derived from the word vodun, which denotes a god, or spirit, in the language of the Fon people of Benin (formerly Dahomey, which also included parts of today's Togo, and Nigeria).

"Although voodooists profess belief in a rather distant supreme God, the effective divinities are a large number of spirits called the **loa**, which can be variously identified as local or African gods, deified ancestors, or Catholic saints. The loa are believed to demand ritual service, which thereby attaches them to individuals or families. In voodoo ritual services, a number of devotees congregate at a temple, usually a humble meeting place, where a priest or priestess leads them in ceremonies involving song, drumming, dance, prayer, food preparation, and the ritual sacrifice of animals [including drinking the blood of the animal]. The voodoo priest, or houngan, and the priestess, or mambo, also act as counselors, healers, and expert protectors against sorcery or witchcraft.

"The loa are thought by voodoo devotees to act as helpers, protectors, and guides to people. **The loa communicate with an individual during the cult services by possessing him during a trance state** in which the devotee may eat and drink, perform stylized dances, give supernaturally inspired advice to people, perform medical cures, or display special physical feats; these acts exhibit the incarnate presence of the loa within the entranced devotee. Many urban Haitians believe in two sharply contrasting sets of loas, a set of wise and benevolent ones called Rada loas, and a harsher, more malevolent group of spirits called Petro loas. Petro spirits are called up by more agitated or violent rituals than Rada spirits are evoked by.

"A peculiar, and much sensationalized, aspect of voodoo is the zombie. A zombie is regarded by voodooists as being either a dead person's disembodied soul that is used for magical purposes, or an actual corpse that has been raised from the grave by magical means and is then used to perform agricultural labour in the fields as a sort of will-less automaton. In actual practice, certain voodoo priests do appear to create 'zombies' by administering a particular poison to the skin of a victim, who then enters a state of profound physical paralysis for a number of hours.

"For decades the Roman Catholic church in Haiti denounced voodoo and even advocated the persecution of its devotees, but because voodoo has remained the chief religion of at least 80 percent of the people in Haiti, **the Catholic church by the late 20th century seemed resigned to coexisting with the cult**" (CD-ROM Version, bold emphasis and bracketed comments added).

The modern Roman Church's inability to triumph over occult religious belief and practice in Haiti—and her eventual willingness to coexist with it—recalls her early history in which she absorbed many of the occult beliefs and practices of Roman paganism.

The Only Way to Know the True God is through Jesus Christ

God cannot be known through Eastern mystic philosophy. He cannot be known through any religious system. The only way to know God the Father is through Jesus Christ. "Jesus said to him, 'I am the way, and the truth, and the life; no one comes to the Father except through Me' " (John 14:6). Jesus is the only one who can reveal the Father to a person. "At that time Jesus answered and said, 'I praise You, O Father, Lord of heaven and earth, that You have hidden these things from the wise and intelligent, and have revealed them to babes. Yes, Father, for it was well pleasing in Your sight *to do* this. **All things were delivered to Me by My Father; and no one knows the Son except the Father; neither does anyone know the Father except the Son, and the one to whom the Son personally chooses to reveal *Him*' " (Matt. 11:25-27).

And again Jesus said, "No one can come to Me unless the Father, Who sent Me, draws him; and I will raise him up at the last day…. For this reason, I have said to you, no one can come to Me unless it has been given to him from My Father" (John 6:44, 65).

God also revealed through the prophet Isaiah that if a person truly seeks Him, he or she will find Him, because Jesus will reveal Him. "**Seek ye the LORD while he may be found**, call ye upon him while he is near: **Let the wicked forsake his way, and the unrighteous man his thoughts** [of self-worship and self-idolatry]: and let him return unto the LORD, and he will have mercy upon him; and to our God, for he will abundantly pardon" (Isa. 55:6-7).

Jesus Himself promised, "Ask, and it shall be given to you. Seek, and you shall find. Knock, and it shall be opened to you. For everyone who asks receives, and the one who seeks finds, and to the one who knocks it shall be opened" (Matt. 7:7-8).

Obedience—Key to Knowing God. Anciently, when King David handed over the twelve-tribe Kingdom of Israel to his son Solomon, he gave this charge: "Now therefore in the sight of all Israel the congregation of the LORD, and in the audience of our God, **keep and seek for all the commandments of the LORD your God**: that ye may possess this good land, and leave *it* for an inheritance for your children after you for ever. And thou, Solomon my son, **know thou the God of thy father**, and serve him with a perfect heart and with a willing mind: for the LORD searcheth all hearts, and understandeth all the imaginations of the thoughts: **if thou seek him, he will be found of thee**; but if thou forsake him, he will cast thee off for ever" (I Chron. 28:8-9).

The New Testament shows that in order to truly know God one must first repent of all sin—and sin is the transgression of God's law (I John 3:4). Afterwards, a person must be baptized for the forgiveness of those sins: "Repent and be baptized each one of you in the name of Jesus Christ for *the* remission of sins, and you yourselves shall receive the gift of the Holy Spirit" (Acts 2:38).

The Holy Spirit enables a person to obey God. And a person who knows God will be obedient to His standards. This is the opposite of what Chopra advocates when he claims that "**saints do not have to obey any conventional standards of behavior**." The apostle John wrote that Christians who know God will be keeping His commandments: "And by this *standard* **we know that we know Him**: if we keep His command-ments. **The one who says, 'I know Him,' and does not keep His com-mandments, is a liar, and the truth is not in him**. On the other hand, *if* **anyone is keeping His Word, truly in this one the love of God is being perfected**. By this *means* we know that we are in Him. Anyone who claims to dwell in Him is obligating himself also to walk even as He Himself walked" (I John 2:3-6).

In the next chapter we will discuss the origins of other religious holidays observed in Christendom.

CHAPTER FIVE

The Origins of Other
Occult Holidays
Observed in Christendom

Orthodox Christendom has adopted a number of other holidays that have their origins in pagan and occult religious observances. However, the majority of professing Christians today who observe these holidays are simply unaware of their origins. Little do they know that beneath the Christianized veneer of these holidays lie ritualized "mysteries" that continue within secret societies, occult groups and witchcraft covens—with sinister, esoteric occult celebrations that even include human sacrifice to the god of death, Satan the devil! These human sacrifice rituals have a long and bloody history.

Human Sacrifice in Ancient and Modern Occult Worship

In ancient civilizations, the practice of human sacrifice was an open part of occult worship. In his epochal work, *The Golden Bough—A Study in Magic and Religion*, Sir James George Frazer exposes the occult practices and holidays that have been accepted in every age and nation in the world as part of the idolatrous worship of the sun, moon, planets and stars. (The reader is encouraged to read Frazer's single-volume Abridged Edition, The Macmillan Company, 1972.). Frazer details how human sacrifice was an integral part of such religious ceremonies. The following pages reference some of the countries where this occurred: Mexico, 91, 680; South Sea Islands, 110-111; India, 130, 324; Sumatra, 134-135; Japan, Annam, Senegambia, Scandinavia and Scotland, 169; Sweden, 325; Carthage 327; Greece, 337-338, 670; Western Asia Minor, 340; Phoenicia and Moab, 341; Phrygia, 411; Philippine Islands, 412; Egypt, 439, 441; Thrace and New Guinea, 440; Eastern Caucasus, 662; Europe, 706; also Scotland, 715; by the Celts, 757; and by the Druids in Europe, 761-762. These references are given to show that the practice of human sacrifice was nearly universal.

Frazer writes: "Sometimes these human gods [i.e., men proclaimed to be a god or demigod—undoubtedly demon possessed] are restricted to purely supernatural or spiritual functions. Sometimes they exercise supreme political power in addition. In the latter case they are kings as well as gods, and the government is a theocracy. Thus in [the] Marques or Washington Islands there was a class of men who were deified in their lifetime. They were supposed to wield a supernatural power [demonic powers from Satan and his principal demons] over the elements: they could give abundant harvests or smite the ground with barrenness; and they could inflict disease or death. **Human sacrifices** were offered to them to avert their wrath. There were not many of them [god-men], at the most one or two on each island. They lived in mystic seclusion. Their powers were sometimes, but not always, hereditary. A missionary has described one of these human gods from personal observation. The god was a very old man who lived in a large house within an enclosure. In the house was a kind of altar, and on the beams of the house and on the trees round it were hung human skeletons, head down. No one entered the enclosure except the persons dedicated to the service of the god; only on days when human victims were sacrificed might ordinary people penetrate into the precinct. This human god received more sacrifices than all the other gods; often he would sit on a sort of scaffold in front of his house and call for two or three human victims at a time. They were always brought, for the terror he inspired was extreme. He was invoked all over the island, and offerings were sent to him from every side. Again on the South Sea Islands in general we are told that each island had a man who represented or personified the divinity. Such men were called gods, and their substance was confounded with that of the deity. The man-god was sometimes the king himself; [more often] he was a priest or subordinate chief" (Ibid., pp. 110-111, bracketed comments and bold emphasis added).

Human sacrifice was an accepted part of the worship of gods in ancient civilized Greece (e.g., the sun god, Zeus) and also in Crete. Frazer describes human sacrifice to the sun-idol Minotaur on the island of Crete: "Stripped of his mystical features [it] was nothing but a bronze image of the sun represented as a man with a bull's head. In order to renew the solar fires, human victims may have been sacrificed to the idol by being roasted in its hollow body or placed on its sloping hands and allowed to roll into a pit of fire. It was in the latter fashion that the Carthaginians sacrificed their offspring to Moloch [Molech]. The children were laid on the hands of the calf-headed image of bronze, from which they slid into the fiery oven, while the people danced to the music of flutes and timbrels to drown out the shrieks of the burning victims" (Ibid., pp. 326-327).

The most bloodthirsty were the Aztecs and Mayans in Central America. In their occult devotion and worship of the sun god, the high priest (high atop a steep pyramid) would cut open the chest of a human victim and quickly cut out his or her heart and thrust it still beating into the air in sacrifice to the sun. Frazer writes: "The ancient Mexicans conceived the sun as the source of all vital force; hence they named him Ipalnemohuani, 'He by whom men live.' But if he bestowed life on the world, he needed also to receive life from it [i.e., the beating heart of the human sacrifice]. And as the heart is the seat and symbol of life, bleeding hearts of men and animals were presented to the sun to maintain him in vigour and enable him to run his course across the sky. Thus the Mexican sacrifices to the sun were magical rather than religious, being designed, not so much to please and propitiate him, as physically to renew his energies of heat, light and motion.

The constant demand for human victims to feed the solar fire was met by waging war every year on the neighboring tribes and bringing back troops of captives to be sacrificed on the altar. Thus the ceaseless wars of the Mexicans and their cruel system of human sacrifices, the most monstrous on record, sprang in great measure from a mistaken theory of the solar system" (Ibid., p. 91, bracketed comments added).

The Mexicans also conducted special human sacrifices to represent the growth of maize from planting to harvest. "For when a god is represented by a living person, it is natural that the human representative should be chosen on the ground of his supposed resemblance to the divine original. Hence the ancient Mexicans, conceiving the maize as a personal being who went through the whole course of life between seed-time and harvest, sacrificed newborn babes when the maize was sown, older children when it had sprouted, and so on till it was fully ripe, when they sacrificed old men. A name for Osiris [to whom human sacrifices were offered in Egypt] was the 'crop' or 'harvest'; and the ancients sometimes explained him as a personification of the corn [or grain]" (Ibid., p. 441, bracketed comments added).

The Aztecs were consumed and obsessed with human sacrifice, perhaps more than any other ancient culture. Frazer writes: "By no people does the custom of sacrificing the human representative of a god appear to have been observed so commonly and with so much solemnity as by the Aztecs of ancient Mexico. With the ritual of these remarkable sacrifices we are well acquainted, for it has been fully described by the Spaniards who conquered Mexico in the sixteenth century, and whose curiosity was naturally excited by the discovery in this distant region of a barbarous and cruel religion which presented many curious points of analogy to the doctrine and ritual of their own church. 'They took a captive,' says the Jesuit Acosta, 'such as they thought good; and afore they did sacrifice him unto their idols, they gave him the name of the idol, to whom he should be sacrificed, and apparelled him with the same ornaments like their idol, saying, that he did represent the same idol. And during the time that this representation lasted, which was for a year in some feasts, in others six months, and in others less, they reverenced and worshipped him in the same manner as the proper idol; and in the meantime he did eat, drink and was merry. When he went through the streets, the people came forth to worship him, and every one brought him an alms, with children and sick folks, that he might cure them, and bless them, suffering him to do all things at his pleasure, only he was accompanied with ten or twelve men lest he should fly. And he (to the end he might be reverenced as he passed) sometimes sounded upon a small flute, that the people might prepare to worship him. The feast being come, and he grown fat, they killed him, opened him, and ate him, making a solemn sacrifice of him.'

"This general description of the custom may now be illustrated by particular examples. Thus at the festival called Toxcatl, the greatest festival of the Mexican year, a young man was annually sacrificed in the character of Tezcatlipoca, 'the god of gods,' after having been maintained and worshipped as the great deity in person for a whole year. According to the old Franciscan monk Sahagun, our best authority on the Aztec religion, **the sacrifice of the human god fell at Easter** or a few days later, so that, if he is right, it would correspond in date as well as in character to the Christian festival of the death and resurrection of the Redeemer" (Ibid., p. 680).

Abortion—the Sacrifice of the Unborn. Just as it was in ancient civilizations, in today's modern society human sacrifice (to Satan the devil) is still being committed with full government sanction. **It is legalized murder, and it is called abortion**. Under the feminist ideology that women have a "right to choose," millions of unborn babies are killed in the womb—sacrificed to the god of this so-called "right to choose." **Thus, the modern abortion clinic becomes the temple, the abortion table becomes the altar, and the doctor becomes the high priest attending to the bloody sacrifice. Scientists, as well, become gods, experimenting with the body parts of the sacrificial offerings.**

In addition to the open sacrificial slaughter of the unborn, secret adult human sacrifice is being conducted on specified occult holidays. Mac Dominick has written about this at his web site, www.cuttingedge.org/news/n1796.cfm. Some of the following material has been adapted or quoted from this site with his permission.

How America Has Copied Occult Holidays

Too many Christians are enthusiastically celebrating pagan holidays, thinking they are Christian. Once you understand how thoroughly pagan America and the rest of the Western world have become, you will see why God's judgment cannot be far behind.

God reveals His coming judgment against all the systems of the world—religious, political and economic—in the Book of Revelation: "And he [the mighty angel] cried out mightily with a loud voice, saying, 'Babylon the Great is fallen, is fallen, and has become a habitation of demons, and a prison of every unclean spirit, and a prison of every unclean and hated bird; because all nations have drunk of the wine of the fury of her fornication, and the kings of the earth have committed fornication with her, and the merchants of the earth have become rich through the power of her luxury.' And I heard another voice from heaven, saying, '**Come out of her, My people, so that you do not take part in her sins, and that you do not receive of her plagues, for her sins have reached as far as heaven, and God has remembered her iniquities**' " (Rev. 18:2-5).

The Corruption of Christianity. During the reign of Constantine, Christianity began to be thoroughly corrupted by pagan practices. With state and religious authority, Constantine permitted the apostate practice of combining Christian doctrine, art, and objects with those of paganism (a process called "syncretization"). While Constantine sanctioned the practice, the Roman Catholic Church perfected it!

In Satanism, the obelisk is the symbol of the male phallus, while the circle represents the female vulva. (Remember, paganism is defined as worshiping the creature rather than the Creator—Romans 1:25—and one of the easiest aspects of creation to worship has been sex.) Whenever Satanists wanted to represent the sex act, they merely placed the phallus of the obelisk into the vulva of the circle.

Catholic popes have falsely believed that they could "Christianize" a Satanic symbol of worship by praying over it and/or anointing it with "holy oil," thus making the object suitable for Christian use. For example, as one can see in any picture of St. Peter's Basilica, there is an obelisk standing in the middle of the huge circular assembly area. Look closely at this obelisk and you will note that it is standing in the middle of an eight-fold path of Satanic Enlightenment. One of the greatest ironies of all time is that the Roman Catholic Church has had (since the seventh century) this permanent symbol of Satanic sex worship standing in front of St. Peter's Basilica, where the Pope faces it daily—even though the Vatican is the world's greatest proponent of celibacy!

For the past 1,400 years, the Roman Catholic Church has led Western Civilization down the horrid road of syncretization, where Satanic worship has been mixed with Christian worship. Once we understand their pagan foundations, we can then find it easier to refuse to participate in those holidays that have their origins in the world of Satanism and the occult.

Occult Holidays and Sabbats

The Satanist believes that numbers contain inherent power—thus, they literally order their lives by occult numerology. Such numerology also is a key component in astrology, another system of divining that Satanists observe very closely. The occult solar calendar is divided into four segments of thirteen weeks each. These periods are as follows, with significant dates noted:

Winter Solstice: 13 weeks—Minor Sabbat
- December 21-22—Winter Solstice/Yule; one of the Illuminati's **human sacrifice** nights.
- February 1 and 2—Candlemas and Imbolg, (Groundhog's Day); one of the Illuminati's **human sacrifice** nights.
- February 14—Valentine's Day

Spring Equinox: 13 weeks—Minor Sabbat, but does require **human sacrifice**.
- March 21-22—Goddess Ostara; Easter is the first Sunday after the first new moon after Ostara; March 21 is one of the Illuminati's **human sacrifice** nights.
- April 1—All Fool's Day, precisely 13 weeks from New Year's Day!
- April 19-May 1—Blood sacrifice to the beast; fire sacrifice is required on April 19.
- April 30-May 1—Beltaine Festival, also called Walpurgis Night; this is the highest day on the Druidic witch's calendar. May 1 is the Illuminati's second most sacred holiday; **human sacrifice** is required.

Summer Solstice: 13 weeks—When the sun reaches its northern most point in its journey across the sky.
- June 21-22—Summer Solstice
- June 21—Litha, one of the Illuminati's **human sacrifice** nights.
- July 4—America's Independence Day, 13 days after the Day of Litha.
- July 19—13 days before Lughnasa.
- July 31-August 1—Lughnasa, Great Sabbat Festival; August 1 is one of the Illuminati's **human sacrifice** nights

Autumnal Equinox: 13 weeks—Minor Sabbath, but does require **human sacrifice.**
- September 21—Mabon, one of the Illuminati's **human sacrifice** nights.
- September 21-22—Autumnal Equinox
- October 31—Samhain, also known as Halloween, or All Hallows Eve. This date is the Illuminati's highest day of **human sacrifice**.

The annual calendar for the entire Western world is ordered by these Satanic festival times and days!

Specific Dates Within the Occult Solar Calendar

December 21-22, Yule

When the sun begins its northward trek in the sky, and days began to grow longer again, pagans celebrated the Winter Solstice by burning the Yule log. Since the sun had reversed itself and was now rising in the sky, pagans believed this was a sign that the human sacrifices carried out in Samhain (Halloween) had been accepted by the gods. Yet, as professing Christians, we continue to sing, "Deck the halls with boughs of holly ... troll the ancient Yuletide carol ... See the blazing Yule before us. Fa la la la la la la la la" (*Pagan Traditions of the Holidays*, David Ingraham, p. 71).

The Roman Catholic Church later changed the Winter Solstice celebration to December 25, calling it "Christmas."

Christmas. The festival of Christmas was celebrated by pagan societies many centuries before the birth of Christ. Historian Alexander Hislop wrote extensively about this festival in his book, *The Two Babylons*. Regarding its origin, he states, "Indeed, it is admitted by the most learned and candid writers of all parties that the day of our Lord's birth cannot be determined [However, today it can be determined with great accuracy that Jesus was born near October 2, 5 BC—see *A Harmony of the Gospels in Modern English: the Life of Jesus Christ*, Coulter; York Publishing Co.; Hollister, California; ISBN 978-0-9675479-1-1], and that *within the Christian Church* **no such festival as Christmas was ever heard of** *till the third* **century**, and that not till the *fourth* century was far advanced did it gain much observance. How then, did the Romish Church fix on December 25th as Christmas-day? Why thus: Long before the fourth century, and long before the Christian era itself, a festival was celebrated among the heathen, at the precise time of the year, in honour of the birth of the son of the Babylonian queen of heaven; and it may fairly be presumed that, in order to conciliate the heathen, and to swell the number of nominal adherents of Christianity, the same festival was adopted by the Romish Church, giving it only the name of Christ.

"**That Christmas was originally a Pagan festival, is beyond all doubt**. The time of the year, and the ceremonies with which it is still celebrated, prove its origin. In Egypt, the son of Isis, the Egyptian title for the queen of heaven, was born at this very time, '**about the time of the winter solstice**.'

"The Christmas tree, now so common among us, was equally common in Pagan Rome and Egypt. In Egypt that tree was a palm-tree; in Rome it was the fir; the palm-tree denoting the Pagan Messiah, as Baal-Tamar, the fir referring to him as Baal-Berith. The mother of Adonis, the Sun-God and great mediatorial divinity, was mystically said to have been changed into a tree, and when in that state to have brought forth her divine son. If the mother was the tree, the son must have been recognised as the 'Man the branch' " (Hislop, *The Two Babylons*, pp. 92-93, bold emphasis and bracketed comments added).

The Word of God reveals that the custom of the "Christmas tree" is vanity. "For the customs of the people are vain: for one cutteth a tree out of the forest, the work of the hands of the workman, with the ax. They deck it with silver and with gold; they fasten it with nails and with hammers, that it move not" (Jer. 10:3-4). While God calls such customs an abomination, people have been misled into believing that such practices honor God. Yet, every year at Christmas time, religious leaders and historians readily admit that Christmas was originally a holiday in celebration of the pagan sun god. Hislop writes: "Therefore, the 25th of December, the day that was observed at Rome as the day when the victorious god reappeared on earth, was held at the Natalis invieti solis, 'the birth-day of the unconquered Sun' " (Hislop, *The Two Babylons*, pp. 97-98).

The birthday of the "unconquered Sun" is further described by Samuele Bacchiocchi in his book, *From Sabbath to Sunday*. "The adoption of the 25th of December for the celebration of Christmas is perhaps the most explicit example of sun-worship's influence on the Christian liturgical calendar. It is a known fact that the pagan feast of the *dies natalis Solis Invicti*—the birthday of the Invincible Sun—was held on that date…. It was a solemn rite among the pagans to celebrate the festival of the rising of the sun on this very day, December 25th.

"That the Church of Rome introduced and championed this new date [December 25] is accepted by most scholars. For instance Mario Righetti, a renowned Catholic liturgist writes: '… the Church of Rome, to facilitate the acceptance of the faith by the pagan masses, found it convenient to institute the 25th of December as the feast of the temporal birth of Christ, to divert them from the pagan feast, celebrated on the same day in honor of the "Invincible Sun," Mithras, the conqueror of darkness.'

"It is sufficient to notice that the adoption of the date of December 25th for the celebration of Christ's birth provides an additional example not only of the influence of the Sun-cult, but also of the primacy exerted by Rome in promoting liturgical innovations.... J. A. Jungmann summarizes it well when he writes that 'Christianity absorbed and made its own what could be salvaged from pagan antiquity, not destroying it but converting it, Christianizing what could be turned to good' " (Bacchiocchi, *From Sabbath to Sunday*, pp. 256-257, and footnote 72; 260-261).

In *The Golden Bough*, Frazer further instructs us about the preeminence of Christmas in the pagan world: "An instructive relic of the long struggle [between true Christianity and occult Christianity (Mithraism)] is preserved in our festival of Christmas, which **the Church seems to have borrowed directly from its heathen rival**. In the Julian calendar the twenty-fifth of December was reckoned the winter solstice, and it was regarded as the nativity of the Sun, because the day begins to lengthen and the power of the sun to increase from that turning point of the year.... The Egyptians even represented the new-born sun by the image of an infant, which on his birthday, the winter solstice, they brought forth and exhibited to his worshippers [called a "nativity scene" today]. No doubt the Virgin who thus conceived and bore a son on the twenty-fifth of December was the great Oriental goddess whom the Semites called the Heavenly Virgin or simply the Heavenly Goddess; in the Semitic lands she was a form of Astarte [the queen of heaven]. Now Mithra [the infant savior] was regularly identified by his worshippers with the sun, the Unconquered Sun, as they called him; hence his nativity also fell on the twenty-fifth of December" (Frazer, *The Golden Bough*, p. 416, bold emphasis and bracketed comments added).

Almost identical to the ancient Egyptian practice, "Christians" have for centuries (in their churches, cathedrals and city squares) exhibited a nativity scene, replete with a crib, the little infant "Jesus," and Mary and Joseph. *"The Church* celebrates the Nativity on *December 25.... Many* churches and homes *set up a crib at Christmas*. This custom, although of very ancient origin [in ancient pagan Egypt], *was popularized by St. Francis of Assisi. In the year 1223*, he visited Pope Honorius III and sought approval of his plans to make a scenic representation of the Nativity. Having obtained the Pope's consent, Francis left Rome and arrived at Greccio on Christmas Eve. *There in the church he constructed a crib*, grouping the images of the Blessed Virgin and St. Joseph, of the shepherds, the ox, and the ass. At the Midnight Mass St. Francis acted as a deacon. *After singing the words of the Gospel, 'And they laid Him in a manger,'* he knelt down to meditate on the great gift of the Incarnation. And people around saw in his arms a Child, surrounded by a most brilliant light. *Since then the devotion to the crib has spread far and wide"* (Morrow, *My Catholic Faith*, p. 71).

Worshiping a baby in a manger has continued in modern times to be a prominent theme of the Christian Christmas. The birth of the Savior is re-enacted each year at the same time that pagan cultures anciently re-enacted the "birth" of the sun. In spite of its clearly pagan origin, Orthodox Christendom has made Christmas a major holiday for its faithful, perpetuating the lies associated with its celebration (such as Jesus having been born in December at the time of the Winter Solstice).

Consider the pagan roots of these popular Christmas symbols:

(1) **Christmas Tree**—The sacred tree of the winter-god; the Druids believed the spirit of their gods resided in the tree. Most ancient pagans knew the tree represented Nimrod—reincarnated into Tammuz! Pagans also looked upon the tree as a phallic symbol.

(2) **Star**—A five-pointed star, the pentalpha is a powerful symbol of Satan, second only to the hexagram. The star is the sacred symbol of Nimrod, and has nothing to do with Christianity.

(3) **Candles** represent the sun god's newly born fire. Pagans the world over love and use candles in their rituals and ceremonies. Certain colors are also thought to represent specific powers. The extensive use of candles is usually a very good indication that a service is pagan, regardless of the outward trappings.

(4) **Mistletoe** is the sacred plant of the Druids, symbolizing pagan blessings of fertility—thus, kissing under the mistletoe is the first step in the reproductive cycle.

(5) **Wreaths** are associated with fertility and the "circle of life." Being circular, they also represent the female sexual organ.

(6) **Santa Claus**—The mythical attributes and powers ascribed to Santa are eerily close to those possessed by Jesus Christ.

(7) **Reindeer** are horned animals representing the "horned-god" or the "stag-god" of pagan religion. Santa traditionally has a team of eight reindeer; in Satanic geomantic, eight is the number of "new beginnings" or the cycle of reincarnation.

(8) **Elves** are imp-like creatures who are Santa's little helpers (or Satan's demons).

(9) **Green and Red** are the traditional colors of the season, as they are the traditional pagan colors of winter.

(10) **December 25** was also known to the Romans as "Saturnalia," a time of deliberate debauchery. Drinking through repeated toasting—known as 'wassail'—was a feature of this celebration. The mistletoe symbolized fornication, and the entire event was finished with a Great Feast, the Christmas Dinner.

February 1 and 2: Candlemas and Imbolg—or Groundhog's Day

The popular "Punxsutawney Phil" groundhog comes out of his burrow to divine the next few weeks of weather. If he sees his shadow, there will be six more weeks of bad weather until Spring finally arrives; if he does *not* see his shadow, the next seven weeks before Spring will be good weather. What most people do not realize is that the pagan view of Groundhog's Day (Imbolg) represents the Earth Mother. Consider the uncanny parallels between the groundhog and the Earth Mother: as the Earth Goddess sleeps inside the earth during the Winter season, so does the groundhog; both the goddess and the groundhog awaken in the Spring; both the goddess and the groundhog represent the cycle of "rebirth" and "renewal"; and, both the goddess and the groundhog complete the "cycle of reincarnation."

February 14: Valentine's Day

Valentine's Day is a pagan festival that encourages physical lust. It is celebrated precisely thirteen days after Imbolg, thus it carries the number "thirteen"—Satan's number of extreme rebellion. While most people view this day as the day to honor your wife or your lover, this celebration is steeped in paganism. Consider the camouflaged occult gods of Valentine's Day: 1) Cupid, the son of Venus, is really Tammuz, son of Semiramis; 2) Jupiter, the head deity and sun god, is Nimrod, Semiramis' husband; and 3) Venus, the daughter of Jupiter, is really Semiramis herself—the "queen of heaven."

Nigel Pennick, author of *The Pagan Book of Days*, describes February, the month in which Valentine's Day falls. "The name of this month comes from the Roman goddess Februa and St. Febronia (from *Febris*, the fever of love). She is the patroness of the passion of love…. Her orgiastic rites are celebrated on 14 February—still observed as St. Valentine's Day—when, in Roman times, young men would draw billets naming their female partners…. This is a time of clear vision into other worlds, expressed by festivals of purification. On the 1st of February is the celebration of the cross-quarter day, or fire festival (Imbolg), a purificatory festival. It is followed on the 2nd by its Christian counterpart, Candlemas, the purification of the Virgin Mary" (p. 37).

Valentine's Day is a day of "orgiastic rites" in which pagans encouraged the flow of lustful passion.

Ostara, Ishtar or "Eostre"

Easter is a shifting date using the common practice of astrology. It is celebrated on the first Sunday after the first new moon after Ostara. This date has nothing to do with the resurrection of our Lord Jesus Christ! Rather, this day in the pagan tradition celebrates the return of Semiramis into her reincarnated form as the Spring Goddess. Pagans observe an "Easter Friday," which has historically been timed to be the third full moon from the start of the year. Since the merging of pagan Easter with Jesus' resurrection, however, Good Friday has been permanently fixed on the Friday prior to Easter.

The Babylonian goddess, Ishtar, the one for whom Easter is named (Ingraham, *Pagan Traditions of the Holidays*, p. 9), is another pseudonym for Semiramis, the wife of Nimrod, and the real founder of the Babylonian cult. After Nimrod died, she created the legend that he was a Divine Son born to her while a virgin. She is considered to be the co-founder of all occult religions.

Easter, or *the day of Ishtar*, is celebrated widely among various cultures and religions. According to a Babylonian legend, a huge egg fell from heaven, landing in the Euphrates River. The goddess Ishtar broke out of this egg. Later, the feature of "egg nesting" was introduced—a nest where the egg could incubate until hatched. A "wicker" or reed basket was used to nest the Ishtar egg (hence the Easter-egg basket).

The Easter egg hunt is based on the notion that if anyone found Ishtar's egg while she was being "reborn," she would bestow a blessing upon that lucky person. Because this was a joyous Spring festival, eggs were colored with bright Spring (pastel) colors.

The Easter Bunny. Among the Celts, custom dictated that "the goddess' totem, the Moon-hare, would lay eggs for good children to eat.... Eostre's hare was the shape that Celts imagined on the surface of the full moon..." (Ibid., p. 10).

Since Ishtar, or Eostre, was a goddess of fertility—and because rabbits procreate quickly—the rabbit became associated with the sexual act, and the egg became symbolic of "birth" and "renewal." Together, the Easter bunny and Easter egg symbolize the sexual union that produced Tammuz, the son and false messiah of Semiramis, the queen of heaven.

It is a very serious spiritual matter, indeed, when so-called "Christian" churches participate in the pagan Easter tradition—complete with an Easter egg hunt for "resurrection eggs"—by which they are clearly guilty of combining Christianity with paganism. Such a combination is a lethal cocktail the Lord Jesus will always reject! "***Wherefore come out from among them, and be ye separate, saith the Lord, and touch not the unclean thing***." (See II Cor. 6:17, KJV.)

Easter offerings are derived from a tradition in which priests and priestesses brought offerings to the pagan temples for Easter. A popular Easter offering was freshly made or purchased clothes. The priests wore their best clothes, while the vestal virgins wore newly made white dresses. They also wore headgear, like bonnets, and many adorned themselves in garlands of Spring flowers. They placed freshly cut Spring flowers on the altar of the idol they worshipped. In addition, they carried wicker baskets filled with foods and candies to offer to the pagan gods and goddesses.

Easter sunrise services originated with the Babylonian priesthood to symbolically hasten the reincarnation of Ishtar.

Easter Traditions and Queen of Heaven Worship. The Easter hot cross buns and traditional dyed eggs have their earliest origins in similar ancient Chaldean pagan religious traditions. Hislop informs us about these early traditions: "The popular [Easter] observances that still attend the period of celebration amply confirm the testimony of history as to its Babylonian character. The hot cross buns of Good Friday, and the dyed eggs of Pasch or Easter Sunday, figured in the Chaldean rites just as they do now. The 'buns,' known too by that identical name, were used in the worship of the queen of heaven, the goddess of Easter, as early as the days of Cecrops, the founder of Athens—that is, 1500 years before the Christian era.... The origin of the Pasch eggs is just as clear. The ancient Druids bore an egg, as the sacred emblem of their order. In the Dionysiaca, or the mysteries of Bacchus, as celebrated in Athens, one part of the nocturnal ceremony consisted in the consecration of an egg. The Hindoo fables celebrate their mundane egg as of a golden colour. The people of Japan make their sacred egg to have been brazen. In China, at this hour, dyed or painted eggs are used on sacred festivals, even as in this country [England]. In ancient times eggs were used in religious rites of the Egyptians and the Greeks, and were hung up for mystic purposes in their temples" (Hislop, *The Two Babylons*, pp. 108-110).

Through the prophet Jeremiah, God warned of impending judgment for the practices associated with worshiping the queen of heaven. "Seest thou not what they do in the cities of Judah and in the streets of Jerusalem? The children gather wood, and the fathers kindle the fire, and the women knead *their* dough, to **make cakes to the queen of heaven, and to pour out drink offerings unto other gods**, that they may provoke me to anger. Do they provoke me to anger? saith the LORD: *do they* not *provoke* themselves to the confusion of their own faces? Therefore thus saith the Lord GOD; **Behold, mine anger and my fury shall be poured out upon this place**, upon man, and upon beast, and upon the trees of the field, and upon the fruit of the ground; and it shall burn, and shall not be quenched" (Jer. 7:17-20).

Lent is a commemoration of Tammuz' death. The legend of his death claims that he was killed by a wild boar when he was 40 years old. Therefore, Lent is celebrated one day for each year of Tammuz' life (Doc Marquis, *America's Occult Holidays*). Participants are to express their sorrow over Tammuz' untimely death by weeping, fasting, and self-chastisement. Lent was observed exactly 40 days prior to the celebration of Ishtar/Esotre and other goddesses by the Babylonians and, at times, by the ancient Israelites. Lent is observed today by Mexicans, Koordistanians, Roman Catholics and by liberal Protestant churches. We can see God's anger over the celebration of Lent in Ezekiel 8:13-18—and God's judgment for such abominations is described in Ezekiel 9. (We suggest you read these passages carefully, for God has stated that He will similarly punish any nation who does not "hear and obey" His commands—Jeremiah 12:17.)

April 19, Blood Sacrifice to the Beast

April 19 is the first day of the 13-day Satanic ritual relating to fire—the fire god, Baal, or Molech/Nimrod (the sun god). Fire sacrifice is required on April 19, with an emphasis on children. To pagans, this is one of the most important human sacrifice days.

A number of historic events have been staged on April 19 in order to meet this blood sacrifice. For example: the Battle of Lexington & Concord in 1775, which made the Masonic-led Revolutionary War inevitable (war is a most propitious way to sacrifice, for it kills both children and adults); the storming of the compound of David Koresh at Waco, Texas in 1993, which fulfilled the basic requirements for a human sacrifice (trauma, fire, and young sacrificial victims); and the 1995 Oklahoma City bombing (once again, many young children were killed).

April 30-May 1, Beltaine Festival

Since the Beltaine celebration officially begins the night before Beltaine, a tradition has developed among occultists to celebrate Beltaine as a two-day ceremony. Great bonfires are lit on the Eve of Beltaine, April 30, in order to welcome the Earth Goddess. Participants hoped to gain favor with this goddess so that she might bless their families with procreative fertility. The Royal House of Windsor lights a Beltaine "Balefire" every year (Marquis, *America's Occult Holidays*, p. 30).

The "Maypole" observance originated from the celebration of Beltaine. Since fertility is being asked of the Earth Goddess, the Maypole becomes a phallic symbol around which a circular dance is performed. The dance circle is symbolic of the female sex organ. Four, six-foot ribbons with alternating red and white colors are connected to the pole. Men would dance counterclockwise, while ladies danced clockwise. The union of the intertwining red and white ribbons symbolized the act of copulation.

Such are the origins of the occult holidays practiced by Orthodox Christendom.

Obviously, the majority of those who observe such holidays are not involved in the secret, esoteric, demonic occult practices (such as human sacrifices). Most professing Christians, however, continue to celebrate these days because they are simply ignorant of their satanic origins. Furthermore, religious leaders have assured their "faithful" that the "church" has sanitized, Christianized and sanctioned such holidays. Consequently, people believe that they are at liberty to embrace such practices, since they are no longer celebrating them to honor Satan, but to honor Jesus Christ.

In the next chapter we will learn that God the Father and Jesus Christ **do not accept** worship toward them through the means of pagan practices and occult holidays. In fact, quite the opposite is true—because God commands us **not to learn the way of the heathen**.

PART TWO

Survey of Occult Holidays
and
Practices in the Bible

CHAPTER SIX

"Learn Not the Way of the Heathen"

In the previous chapter, we learned that those who observe occult holidays claim to be worshiping the true God. They rationalize that He now accepts such worship. Yet, the Scriptures do not support these assertions. God says, "**I *am* the LORD, I change not**" (Mal. 3:6). And again, the New Testament declares: "Jesus Christ *is* the same yesterday, and today, and forever" (Heb. 13:8). Paul, the apostle to the Gentiles, affirms that Christians cannot worship the true God with pagan, occult rituals and holidays. "But that which the Gentiles sacrifice, they sacrifice to demons, and not to God; and I do not wish you to have fellowship with demons. **You cannot drink *the* cup of *the* Lord, and *the* cup of demons. You cannot partake of *the* table of *the* Lord, and *the* table of demons**. Now do we provoke the Lord to jealousy? Are we stronger than He?" (I Cor. 10:20-22.)

As we will see, the same pagan holidays that were celebrated by the apostate children of Israel and Judah thousands of years before Christ are the same days apostate Orthodox Christendom hallows today. Yet, God has commanded His people to *not* learn the way of the heathen: "Hear ye the word which the LORD speaketh unto you, O house of Israel: Thus saith the LORD, '**Learn not the way of the heathen** [occult practices and the worship of false gods] and be not dismayed at **the signs of heaven** [as in astrology and witchcraft]; for the heathen are dismayed at them' " (Jer. 10:1-2).

Idol Worship at the Temple

In a vision, God told the prophet Ezekiel, " 'Son of man, lift up thine eyes now the way toward the north.' So I lifted up mine eyes the way toward the north, and behold northward at the gate of **the altar this image of jealousy in the entry** [an image of Baal, the sun god]" (Ezk. 8:5). In addition to erecting an image of Baal at the north gate, the priests and leaders of ancient Judah secretly worshiped idols and committed other abominations in temple meeting rooms. "He said furthermore unto me, 'Son of man, seest thou what they do? *even* **the great abominations that the house of Israel committeth here**, that I should go far off from my sanctuary? but turn thee yet again, *and* **thou shalt see greater abominations**.' And he brought me to the door of the [temple] court; and when I looked, behold a hole in the wall. Then said he unto me, 'Son of man, dig now in the wall:' and when I had digged in the wall, behold a door. And he said unto me, 'Go in, and behold the **wicked abominations** that they do here.' So I went in and saw; and behold every form of creeping things, and abominable beasts, and **all the idols of the house of Israel**, portrayed upon the wall round about. And there stood before them seventy men of the ancients of the house of Israel [the Senate of Israel], and in the midst of them stood Jaazaniah the son of Shaphan [a priest], with every man his censer in his hand; and a thick cloud of incense went up. Then said he unto me, 'Son of man, hast thou seen what the ancients of the house of Israel do in the dark, every man in the chambers of his imagery? for they say, "The LORD seeth us not; the LORD hath forsaken the earth" ' " (verses 6-12).

"He said also unto me, 'Turn thee yet again, *and* thou shalt see greater abominations that they do.' Then he brought me to the door of the gate of the LORD'S house which *was* toward the north; and, behold, **there sat women weeping for Tammuz**" (verses 13-14).

The Worship of Tammuz. The son of Nimrod, Tammuz was the ancient false messiah who allegedly died and was resurrected each year. On the worship of and weeping for Tammuz, Frazer writes: "Nowhere, apparently, have these [magical] rites been more widely and solemnly celebrated than in the lands which border the Eastern Mediterranean. Under the names of Osiris, Tammuz, Adonis, and Attis, the peoples of Egypt and Western Asia represented the yearly decay and revival of life, especially of vegetable life, which they personified as a god who annually died and rose again from the dead. In name and detail the rites varied from place to place: in substance they were the same. The supposed death and resurrection of this oriental deity, a god of many names but essentially [of] one nature, is now examined. We begin with Tammuz or Adonis.

"The worship of Adonis was practiced by the Semitic peoples of Babylon and Syria, and the Greeks borrowed it from them as early as the seventh century before Christ. The true name of the deity was Tammuz.... In the religious literature of Babylonia, Tammuz appears as the youthful spouse or lover of Ishtar, the great mother goddess, the embodiment of the reproductive energies of [Mother] nature.... [E]very year Tammuz was believed to die, passing away from the cheerful earth to the gloomy subterranean world, and every year his divine mistress journeyed in quest for him ... that the two might return together to the upper world, and that with their return all nature might revive.

"Laments for the departed Tammuz are contained in several Babylonian hymns.... His death appears to have been annually mourned, to the shrill music of flutes, by men and women about midsummer in the month named after him, the month Tammuz" (Frazer, *The Golden Bough*, pp. 378-79, bracketed comments added).

Orthodox Christendom practices a similar ceremony in the spring of the year at Easter time. This ceremony begins on "Good Friday" evening with mourning for the crucified Jesus (as was done for Tammuz) and is continued through Saturday night. In some predominantly Roman Catholic countries, women beat themselves with whips and weep in an attempt to enter into the physical sufferings of Jesus. At the stroke of midnight, beginning Easter Sunday, the mourning is turned to joy with shouts, "He is risen! He is risen!" These familiar Good Friday and Easter rituals are clearly derived from pagan Babylonian practices.

  The Worship of the Sun at the Temple of the Lord. In all the ceremonies and sacrifices that God commanded to be performed at the temple, the priests and Levites always faced toward the west, not the east. However, when the apostate Israelites and Jews worshiped the sun god Baal, they worshiped toward the east with their backs to the temple of God. Ezekiel recorded God's own description: "Then said he unto me, 'Hast thou seen *this*, O son of man? turn thee yet again, *and* thou shalt see greater abominations than these.' And he brought me into the inner court of the LORD'S house, and, behold, at the door of the temple of the LORD, between the porch and the altar, *were* about five and twenty **men, with their backs toward the temple of the LORD, and their faces toward the east; and they worshipped the sun toward the east**. Then he said unto me, 'Hast thou seen *this*, O son of man? Is it a light thing to the house of Judah that they commit the abominations which they commit here? for they have filled the land with violence, and have returned to provoke me to anger: and, lo, they put **the branch** [a symbol of Tammuz, the son of the sun god, Nimrod] to their nose' " (Ezk. 8:15-17).

God's Warnings Against Serving Other Gods or Practicing Any Form of the Occult

  Thousands of years ago, before He brought them into the Promised Land, God warned the Israelites *not* to follow the customs of the nations around them. "Ye shall not do after all *the things* that we do here this day, every man whatsoever *is* right in his own eyes.... Take heed to thyself that thou be not snared by following them, after that they be destroyed from before thee; and that thou inquire not after their gods, saying, 'How did these nations serve their gods? even so will I do likewise [the customs of the heathen].' **Thou shalt not do so unto the LORD thy God: for every abomination to the LORD, which he hateth, have they done unto their gods; for even their sons and their daughters they have burnt in the fire to their gods. What thing soever I command you, observe to do it: thou shalt not add thereto, nor diminish from it**" (Deut. 12:8, 30-32).

  God made no exceptions when He also commanded Moses to write, "If there arise among you a prophet, or a dreamer of dreams, and giveth thee a sign or a wonder, and the sign or the wonder come to pass, whereof he spake unto thee, saying, 'Let us go after other gods, which thou hast not known, and let us serve them;' t**hou shalt not hearken unto the words of that prophet, or that dreamer of dreams**: for the LORD your God proveth you, to know whether ye love the LORD your God with all your heart and with all your soul. Ye shall walk after the LORD your God, and fear him, and keep his commandments, and obey his voice, and ye shall serve him, and cleave unto him. And that prophet, or that dreamer of dreams, shall be put to death; because he hath spoken to turn *you* away from the LORD your God, which brought you out of the land of Egypt, and redeemed you out of the house of bondage, to thrust thee out of the way which the LORD thy God commanded thee to walk in. So shalt thou put the evil away from the midst of thee.

"If thy brother, the son of thy mother, or thy son, or thy daughter, or the wife of thy bosom, or thy friend, which *is* as thine own soul, **entice thee secretly, saying, 'Let us go and serve other gods,' which thou hast not known, thou, nor thy fathers;** *namely,* **of the gods of the people which** *are* **round about you, nigh unto thee, or far off from thee, from the** *one* **end of the earth even unto the** *other* **end of the earth**; thou shalt not consent unto him, nor hearken unto him" (Deut. 13:1-8).

In Leviticus, God specifically warned against becoming involved with the magic arts, and those known to be involved were to be put to death. "Regard not them that have familiar spirits, neither seek after wizards, to be defiled by them: I *am* the LORD your God.... And the soul [any person] that turneth after such as have familiar spirits, and after wizards, to go a whoring after them, I will even set my face against that soul, and will cut him off from among his people.... A man also or woman that hath a familiar spirit, or that is a wizard, shall surely be put to death: they shall stone them with stones: their blood *shall be* upon them" (Lev. 19:31; 20:6, 27).

Both the Old and New Testament Scriptures uphold God's ban on occult practices, which are named in the book of Deuteronomy. "When thou art come into the land which the LORD thy God giveth thee, **thou shalt not learn to do after the abominations of those nations. There shall not be found among you** *any one* **that maketh his son or his daughter to pass through the fire,** *or* **that useth divination,** *or* **an observer of times, or an enchanter, or a witch, or a charmer, or a consulter with familiar spirits, or a wizard, or a necromancer**. For all that do these things *are* an abomination unto the LORD: and because of these abominations the LORD thy God doth drive them out from before thee. Thou shalt be perfect with the LORD thy God. For these nations, which thou shalt possess, hearkened unto observers of times, and unto diviners: but as for thee, the LORD thy God hath not suffered [allowed] thee so *to do*" (Deut. 18:9-14).

The Scriptures do not make a distinction between using witchcraft or sorcery to achieve a "good" purpose or an evil purpose. Despite the intention, all such practices are inherently evil because they **make an appeal to a forbidden source of power—Satan and the demons**. The Church has the obligation to disfellowship the person or persons committing such sins (Matt. 18:15-17; I Cor. 5:4-13). Individuals themselves are obligated to separate from a congregation where the majority have accepted false doctrines—or where the worship of other gods or images, or other occult practices, are involved. As Paul wrote to Timothy, "If anyone teaches any different doctrine, and does not adhere to sound words, *even those* of our Lord Jesus Christ.... **From such withdraw** *yourself*" (I Tim. 6:3-5).

God Hates the Abominable Occult Holidays

God is a jealous God and will not give His glory to any other so-called god, nor to images: "I *am* the LORD: that *is* my name: and my glory will I not give to another, neither my praise to graven images" (Isa. 42:8). Therefore, it is *impossible* to worship God by the means of occult holidays and/or rituals. Yet, Israel and Judah repeatedly went into apostasy wherein they denied the true God and worshiped false gods.

As Jeremiah testified, they exchanged God's seventh day Sabbath and annual holy days for the practices of the other nations. But God proclaims that He hates those practices: "I hate, I despise your feast days, and I will not smell in your solemn assemblies. Though ye offer me burnt offerings and your meat offerings, I will not accept *them*: neither will I regard the peace offerings of your fat beasts. Take thou away from me the noise of thy songs; for I will not hear the melody of thy viols.... Have ye offered unto me sacrifices and offerings in the wilderness forty years, O house of Israel? But ye have borne the tabernacle of your Moloch and Chiun your images, the star of your god, which ye made to yourselves" (Amos 5:21-26).

Again, Isaiah witnessed against the children of Israel because the priests, Levites and people practiced abominable rituals and sacrifices at the temple of God. Notice Isa. 1:10-12: "Hear the word of the LORD, ye rulers of Sodom; give ear unto the law of our God, ye people of Gomorrah. 'To what purpose *is* the multitude of your sacrifices unto me?' saith the LORD: 'I am full of the burnt offerings of rams, and the fat of fed beasts; and I delight not in the blood of bullocks, or of lambs, or of he goats. When ye come to appear before me, who hath required this at your hand, to tread my courts?' "

"Bring no more vain oblations; incense is an abomination unto me; the new moons and sabbaths [of Baal], the calling of assemblies, I cannot away with; *it is* iniquity, even the solemn meeting. Your new moons and your appointed feasts my soul hateth: they are a trouble unto me; I am weary to bear *them*. And when ye spread forth your hands, I will hide mine eyes from you: yea, when ye make many prayers, I will not hear: your hands are full of blood" (verses 13-15).

Ancient Israel and Judah became so corrupt that they had the gall and hardheartedness to actually worship other gods at the temple of the true God in Jerusalem!

The prophet Jeremiah continually warned Israel that God's judgment was coming because of these abominable idolatries. He constantly called them to repentance, to turn from their idolatry and obey the words of God in the Law and the words of God that Jeremiah was commanded to speak. "The word that came to Jeremiah from the LORD, saying, 'Stand in the gate of the LORD'S house, and proclaim there this word, and say, "Hear the word of the LORD, all *ye of* Judah, that enter in at these gates to worship the LORD. Thus saith the LORD of hosts, the God of Israel, Amend your ways and your doings, and I will cause you to dwell in this place" ' " (Jer. 7:1-3).

"**Trust ye not in lying words, saying, 'The temple of the LORD, The temple of the LORD, The temple of the LORD, *are* these.'** For if ye thoroughly amend your ways and your doings; if ye thoroughly execute judgment between a man and his neighbour; *if* ye oppress not the stranger, the fatherless, and the widow, and shed not innocent blood in this place, neither walk after other gods to your hurt: Then will I cause you to dwell in this place, in the land that I gave to your fathers, for ever and ever.

"**Behold, ye trust in lying words, that cannot profit. Will ye steal, murder, and commit adultery, and swear falsely, and burn incense unto Baal, and walk after other gods whom ye know not; and come and stand before me in this house, which is called by my name, and say, 'We are delivered to do all these abominations?' Is this house, which is called by my name, become a den of robbers in your eyes? Behold, even I have seen *it*, saith the LORD**" (verses 4-11). In effect, by embracing these abominable heathen practices at the temple in the name of the Lord, the Jews made God to serve with their sins: "Thou hast made me to serve with your sins, thou hast wearied me with thine iniquities" (Isa. 43:24).

Modern Christendom is doing the same today. In the name of Jesus Christ, ministers, priests and popes command the faithful to worship on occult holidays. They teach people to sin against God while claiming that God has sanctioned these abominable iniquities and lies. Yet, these are the same pagan occult days of worship that ancient Israel and Judah observed when they apostatized—falling away from the living God.

Finally, after much patience, God sent the armies of Nebuchadnezzar, king of Babylon, to execute His judgment against Jerusalem and the Jews for serving false gods—including the queen of heaven. In 585 BC, Jerusalem was burned and its temple destroyed.

The New Testament Supports the Old Testament in its Condemnation of Witchcraft and the Occult

The New Testament teachings of Jesus Christ and the apostles confirm all the Old Testament commands and prohibitions against witchcraft and occult practices, which are an appeal to the power of Satan.

Just before Jesus Christ began His public ministry, He was tempted by Satan the devil for forty days and forty nights. Satan tried to induce Jesus to actually tempt God, and to use His God-given powers as if He were a magician. Satan even audaciously asked Jesus to worship him as God. Matthew wrote, "And when He had fasted *for* forty days and forty nights, afterwards He was famished. And when the tempter came to Him, he said, 'If You are the Son of God, command that these stones become bread.' But He answered *and* said, 'It is written, "Man shall not live by bread alone, but by every word that proceeds out of *the* mouth of God."' Then the devil took Him to the holy city and set Him upon the edge of the temple, and said to Him, 'If You are the Son of God, cast Yourself down; for it is written, "He shall give His angels charge concerning You, and they shall bear You up in *their* hands, lest You strike Your foot against a stone." ' Jesus said to him, 'Again, it is written, "You shall not tempt *the* Lord your God." ' After that, the devil took Him to an exceedingly high mountain, and showed Him all the kingdoms of the world and their glory, and said to Him, 'All these things will I give You, if You will fall down and worship me.' Then Jesus said to him, 'Begone, Satan! For it is written, "You shall worship the Lord your God, and Him alone shall you serve" ' " (Matt. 4:2-10).

All through His ministry, Jesus healed the sick and cast out demons from those who were possessed. "And Jesus went throughout all Galilee, teaching in their synagogues, and preaching the gospel of the kingdom, and healing every disease and every bodily ailment among the people. Then His fame went out into all Syria; and they brought to Him all who were sick, oppressed by various diseases and torments, and possessed by demons, and lunatics, and paralytics; and He healed them" (Matt. 4:23-24).

The demons knew that Jesus was, in fact, the Son of God—they even talked to Him. "And they were astonished at His doctrine; for He was teaching them as *one* having authority, and not as the scribes. Now in their synagogue there was a man with an unclean spirit; and it cried out, saying, 'Ah! What have we to do with You, Jesus, *the* Nazarene? Have You come to destroy us? I know Who You are—the Holy *One* of God!' But Jesus rebuked it, saying, 'Be silent, and come out of him.' And after throwing him into convulsions and crying out with a loud voice, the spirit came out of him" (Mark 1:22-26).

In one biblical account, a man who was possessed with multiple numbers of demons confronted Jesus. No human power had been able to control the man, but Jesus cast them all out. Luke wrote this account: "Then they sailed down to the country of the Gadarenes, which is across from Galilee. And when He went out on the land, *there* met Him a certain man from the city who had *been possessed by* demons for a long time; and he was not wearing *any* clothes, and did not dwell in a house, but in the tombs. Now when he saw Jesus, he cried out and fell down in front of Him, and said with a loud voice, 'What do You have to do with me, Jesus, Son of God the Most High? I beseech You, do not torment me.'

"For He had commanded the unclean spirit to come out of the man. For many times it had seized him, and *each time* he was restrained, being bound with chains and fetters; but *after* breaking the bonds, he was driven by the demon into the desert. And Jesus asked it, saying, 'What is your name?' And it said, 'Legion,' because many demons had entered into him. Then it begged Him that He would not command them to go away into the abyss [a prison for demons]. Now there was a herd of many swine feeding there on the mountain, and they begged Him that He would allow them to enter into the *swine*; and He gave them permission. And the demons went out of the man *and* entered into the swine, and the *whole* herd rushed *headlong* down the steep *slope* into the lake and were drowned. Now when those who were feeding *the swine* saw what had taken place, they fled; and they went *and* reported *it* to the city and to the country. And those *who heard* went out to see what had taken place; and they came to Jesus, and found the man from whom the demons had gone out, clothed and of a sound mind, seated at Jesus' feet. And they were afraid" (Luke 8: 26-35).

Jesus also gave power and authority to His apostles and disciples to cast out demons because they would encounter them when preaching the gospel (Luke 10:10-20; Mark 16:17-18).

The Apostles Confront a Powerful Occult Leader in Samaria. The early New Testament Church was confronted with an occult adversary who was a powerful religious leader in Samaria. His name was Simon Magus (i.e., *magician*), a false prophet who bewitched his followers with sorcery. "But *there was* a certain man named Simon, who had from earlier times been **practicing sorcery** [witchcraft] in the city and astounding the nation of Samaria, proclaiming himself to be some great one. To him they had all given heed, from the least to the greatest, saying, '**This man is the great power of God.' Now they were giving heed to him because *he* had for a long time bewitched them with sorceries**. But when they believed Philip, who was preaching the gospel—the things concerning the kingdom of God and the name of Jesus Christ—they were baptized, both men and women" (Acts 8:9-12).

When the apostles in Jerusalem heard of the situation they sent Peter and John down to Samaria. Simon Magus approached Peter and John and offered them money to buy the Holy Spirit. "Now when Simon saw that the Holy Spirit was given by the laying on of the hands of the apostles, he offered them money, saying, 'Give this authority to me also, so that on whomever I lay hands, he may receive *the* Holy Spirit.' But Peter said to him, '**May your money be destroyed with you because you thought that the gift of God might be purchased with money. You have neither part nor lot in this matter, for your heart is not right before God**. Repent, therefore, of this your wickedness, and beseech God, if perhaps the thought of your heart may be forgiven you; for I perceive *that* you are in *the* gall of bitterness and *the* bondage of unrighteousness' " (verses 18-23).

History shows that Simon Magus never repented. Rather, he devised a counterfeit Gnostic religion—which has become the world's greatest "Christian" religion with its headquarters in Rome. (See the entry on Simon Magus in *The Encyclopedia of Religion and Ethics*.)

The Apostle Paul and His Encounters with Occult Opposition. On Paul's first evangelistic trip, he was confronted with a false prophet named Elymas Bar-Jesus: "And when they had gone through the island as far as Paphos, they found a certain sorcerer [a wizard], a false prophet, a Jew whose name *was* Bar-jesus. He was with the proconsul Sergius Paulus, an intelligent man, who called Barnabas and Saul to *him*, desiring to hear the Word of God. But **Elymas the sorcerer** (for so was his name interpreted) **withstood them**, seeking to turn away the proconsul from the faith. But Saul, who *was* also *called* Paul, being filled with *the* Holy Spirit, fixed his eyes on him, *and* said, '**O full of all guile and all craftiness, *you* son of**

the devil *and* **enemy of all righteousness, will you not cease to pervert the straight ways of** *the* **Lord**? And now behold, *the* hand of the Lord *is* upon you, and you shall be blind, not seeing the sun for a season.' And immediately a mist and darkness fell upon him, and he went about seeking someone to lead *him* by the hand" (Acts 13:6-11).

On another occasion, when Paul and those with him were evangelizing in the Grecian city of Philippi, they were confronted with a woman possessed with a divining spirit. "Now it came to pass that as we were going to prayer, a certain damsel who had a spirit of Python met us; *and* she brought her masters much gain by divining. She followed Paul and us *and* cried out, saying, 'These men are servants of the Most High God, and are preaching to us *the* way of salvation.' Now she did this for many days. Then Paul, being grieved, turned to the spirit and said, 'I command you in the name of Jesus Christ to come out of her.' And it came out the same hour" (Acts 16:16-18).

After Paul came to Athens, he witnessed to the philosophers and religious thinkers gathered at Mars' hill, the center of pagan Greek religious and philosophical thought. The Greeks did not worship the true God and had never heard of Jesus Christ. They worshiped all the known gods and goddesses of their region, and they even had an altar dedicated to an *unknown god.*

"Then Paul stood in *the* center of Mars' hill *and* said, 'Men, Athenians, I perceive *that* in all things you are very reverent to deities [demons]; for *as* I was passing through and observing the objects of your veneration, I also found an altar on which was inscribed, "To an unknown God." So then, He Whom you worship in ignorance *is* the one *that* I proclaim to you. He *is* the God Who made the world and all things that *are* in it. Being *the* Lord of heaven and earth, He does not dwell in temples made by hands; nor is He served by the hands of men, as *though* He needs anything, *for* He gives to all life and breath and all things. And He made of one blood all the nations of men to dwell upon all the face of the earth, having determined beforehand *their* appointed times and the boundaries of their dwelling; in order that they might seek the Lord, if perhaps they might feel after Him and might find Him; though truly, He is not far from each one of us, for in Him we live and move and have our being; as some of the poets among you also have said, "For we are His offspring." Therefore, since we are the offspring of God, we should not think that the Godhead *is* like that which *is made* of gold, or silver, or stone—a graven thing of art *devised by the* imagination of man; for *although* God has indeed overlooked the times of this ignorance, **He now commands all men everywhere to repent**' " (Acts 17:22-30).

Paul evangelized and taught in Ephesus for over three years. In the city of Ephesus there was a great temple dedicated to the pagan goddess Diana. Devotees from all over the world came to worship there. When Paul preached in Ephesus, God performed great miracles by his hands and, as a result, thousands were converted from the pagan goddess religion. The new converts destroyed their demonic idols and burned their occult books in a public repudiation of Diana worship. They abandoned the goddess Diana and her great temple for the true God and Jesus Christ, the Son of God, the true Savior of the world. The mass conversion of former worshipers of Diana was so vast that it had an enormous impact on the local economy, causing a depression in the idol and book making industries associated with the temple. A riot of newly unemployed craftsmen followed, and Paul had to escape to avoid being killed (Acts 19).

In all of the Gentile areas where Paul preached the gospel of the salvation of God through Jesus Christ's crucifixion and resurrection, he encountered pagan religions and idolatry. As in Ephesus, the believers in Galatia had previously worshipped false gods and idols as well as practiced witchcraft. Some time after their conversion, a number of them began to apostatize from the teachings of Jesus Christ that Paul had taught them and began reverting to pagan practices. Paul instructs them in his epistle: "**[W]hen you did not know God, you were in bondage to those who are not gods by nature**.... [Now] after having known God—rather, after having been known by God—**how** *is it that* **you are turning again to the weak and impotent elements, to which you again desire to be in bondage? You are** *of* **your own selves observing [pagan] days, and months, and times and years**. I am afraid for you, lest somehow I have labored among you in vain" (Gal. 4:8-11).

Although these verses are commonly interpreted to mean that the Galatians were observing God's Sabbath and holy days (hatefully denounced as "Jewish" days), such an interpretation is incorrect. From what Paul wrote, it is clear that the Galatians were backsliding into their former paganism, observing occult religious days, months, times and years. In order to revert back to these observances, they were, in fact, forsaking the worship of the true God. (See Appendix B, *The Weekly Sabbath and Annual Feasts and Holy Days,* p. 208.)

In the same epistle, Paul writes that those who practice such things shall not inherit the kingdom of God. "Now the works of the flesh are manifest, which are *these*: adultery, fornication, uncleanness, **licentiousness, idolatry**, **witchcraft** [hence, all pagan occult observances and practices], hatred, strifes, jealousies, indignations, contentions, divisions, sects, envyings, murders, drunkenness, revelings, and such things as these; concerning which I am telling you beforehand, even as I have also said in the past, that **those who do such things shall not inherit *the* kingdom of God**" (Gal. 5:19-21).

When Paul wrote to the Colossians, he urged them to stand fast in Jesus Christ and not be led away by **vain philosophy and the worship of angels**. "Therefore, as you have received Christ Jesus the Lord, be walking in Him; being rooted and built up in Him, and being confirmed in the faith, exactly as you were taught, abounding in it with thanksgiving. **Beware lest anyone takes you captive through philosophy and vain deceit, according to the traditions of men, according to the elements** [elemental spirits or demons] **of the world, and not according to Christ**. For in Him dwells all the fullness of the Godhead bodily; and you are complete in Him, Who is the Head of all principality and power.... **Do not allow anyone to defraud you of the prize** *by* **doing** *his* **will in self-abasement and** *the* **worship of angels, intruding into things that he has not seen, vainly puffed up by his own carnal mind**" (Col. 2:6-10, 18).

Since the time of the apostles to today, Satan and his demons have continued their relentless attacks to subvert the gospel of Jesus Christ and the true Church of God through vain philosophies and the traditions of men. When Jesus instructed John to write the book of Revelation, He gave him stern and specific warnings for the seven churches of God that existed in Asia in the early centuries.

Jesus Christ's Warnings to the Churches. Jesus' warnings in letters to the seven churches of Revelation 2-3 are also prophetic admonitions for the Church today. These ominous warnings carry the authority of Jesus Christ, meaning that every true Christian **must** heed them. (To get the full impact of Christ's personal messages to His Church, please read the letters in their entirety.)

A summary of Jesus' warnings follows:

Ephesus: "Therefore, remember from where you have fallen, and repent, and do the first works; for if *you do* not, I will come to you quickly; and I will remove your lampstand out of its place unless you repent" (Rev. 2:5).

Smyrna: "I know your works and tribulation and poverty (but you are rich), and **the blasphemy of those who declare themselves to be Jews and are not, but** *are* **a synagogue of Satan**. Do not fear any of the things that you are about to suffer. Behold, the devil is about to cast *some* of you into prison, that you may be tried; and you shall have tribulation ten days. Be faithful unto death, and I will give you a crown of life" (Rev. 2:9-10).

Pergamos: "I know your works and where you dwell, where the throne of Satan *is*; but you are holding fast My name, and did not deny My faith, even in the days in which Antipas *was* My faithful witness, who was killed among you, where Satan dwells. But I have a few things against you because you have there *those* who hold the teaching of Balaam, who taught Balak to cast a stumbling block before the children of Israel, **to eat things sacrificed to idols and to commit fornication. Moreover, you also have** *those* **who hold the doctrine of the Nicolaitanes, which thing I hate**. Repent! For if *you* do not *repent*, I will come to you quickly, and will make war against them with the sword of My mouth" (Rev. 2:13-16).

Thyatira: "I have a few things against you, because you allow **the woman Jezebel**, [a teacher of the Canaanite religion] who calls herself a prophetess, **to teach and to seduce My servants into committing fornication and eating things sacrificed to idols**. And I gave her time to repent of her fornication, but she did not repent. Behold, I will cast her into a bed, and those who commit adultery with her into great tribulation, unless they repent of their works. And I will kill her children with death; and all the churches shall know that I am He Who searches *the* reins and hearts; and I will give to each of you according to your works. **But to you I say, and to** *the* rest who *are* in Thyatira, as many as do not have this doctrine, and who have not known the depths of Satan, as they speak; I will not cast upon you any other burden" (Rev. 2:20-24).

Sardis: "Be watchful, and strengthen the things that remain, which are about to die. **For I have not found your works complete before God.** Therefore, remember what you have received and heard, and hold on *to this*, and repent. Now then, if you will not watch, I will come upon you as a thief, and you shall by no means know what hour I will come upon you" (Rev. 3:2-3).

Philadelphia: Of the seven churches, Philadelphia and Smyrna are the only two churches that remained faithful to Jesus Christ and were not seduced by satanic false doctrines. Smyrna resisted the synagogue of Satan and was commended by Jesus for being faithful in martyrdom. Philadelphia resisted the synagogue of Satan and was faithful in love, patience, endurance and doctrine. By loving God the Father and Jesus Christ, they faithfully preserved the truth of God and resisted all the satanic doctrinal assaults against them. Jesus commended them because they were faithful—and wherever the prophetic, end-time Philadelphian church of God is today, they are still faithful.

"I know your works. Behold, I have set before you an open door, and no one has the power to shut it because you have a little strength, and **have kept My word, and have not denied My name.** Behold, I will make those of the synagogue of Satan, who proclaim themselves to be Jews and are not, but do lie—behold, I will cause them to come and worship before your feet, and to know that I have loved you. **Because you have kept the word of My patience, I also will keep you from the time of temptation which *is* about to come upon the whole world to try those who dwell on the earth**" (Rev. 3:8-10).

Laodicea: "I know your works, that you are neither cold nor hot; I would *that* you be *either* cold or hot. So then, because you are lukewarm, and *are* neither cold nor hot, I will spew you out of My mouth. For you say, 'I am rich, and have become wealthy, and have need of nothing'; and you do not understand that you are wretched, and miserable, and poor, and blind, and naked. I counsel you to buy from Me gold purified by fire so that you may be rich; and white garments so that you may be clothed, and the shame of your nakedness may not be revealed; and to anoint your eyes with eye salve, so that you may see. As many as I love, I rebuke and chasten. Therefore, be zealous and repent" (Rev. 3:15-19).

These are direct warnings from Jesus Christ, the Head of the true Church of God! All who profess His name must **heed these warnings** and repent of following Satan and his demons and their teachings—which have been cleverly sugar-coated, packaged, perfumed, gift wrapped and sold as though they had great value to apostate Christendom and its followers.

In the next chapter we will examine the origin of the most commonly accepted day of "Christian" worship—Sunday, the so-called, "Lord's Day."

CHAPTER SEVEN

Sunday—an Occult Day of Worship or a Christian Day of Worship—*Which?*

We have now examined how leaders of Orthodox Christendom and other Christian-professing churches have officially sanctioned and established occult holidays as observances for their followers.

Furthermore, for over sixteen hundred years Orthodox Christendom has sanctified Sunday as its Sabbath. This is in addition to the "Christian" annual holidays. Today, millions of the devout and faithful assemble each Sunday either to celebrate Mass and partake of the Eucharist, or to listen to a sermon and, at times, partake of communion. Convinced they are doing the will of God, they sincerely believe that going to church on Sunday is the Christian thing to do. Their priests and ministers have assured them, and they have blindly concurred, that Sunday keeping is a commandment of God. (See Appendix C, *The Biblical Truth About Sunday Keeping,* page 210.)

What about Sunday keeping? Did God ever command the faithful to keep Sunday, or is it a *tradition* of men? What is the true origin of Sunday worship? When, how, and by whose authority was Sunday instituted as the weekly day of worship? To answer these questions, we will examine the ancient origin of Sunday observance as well as survey the practice of occult sun worship by the children of Israel and Judah as recorded in the Scriptures.

The Ancient Origin of Sunday

Shortly after the flood, Nimrod began to establish his despotic kingdom. He and his wife Semiramis introduced the apostate religious system known as the Babylonian Mysteries, from which all ancient and modern-day pagan religions originated. (See *The Two Babylons* by Alexander Hislop, available online at www.biblicaltruthministries.org and www.cbcg.org.)

Nimrod was a legendary warrior and a champion of the people in their rebellion against God. Yet, it was Satan who inspired the building of Nimrod's kingdom and the tower of Babel, as well as his occult religion—all in defiance of God. He received man's worship under the guise of the sun or fire god and the sacred serpent. Hislop comments on this early apostasy and the red dragon of Revelation 12:3: "[T]he word rendered 'Red' properly means 'Fiery'; so that the 'Red Dragon' signifies the 'Fiery Serpent' or 'Serpent of Fire.' Exactly so does it appear to have been the first form of idolatry that under the patronage of Nimrod appeared in the ancient world. The 'Serpent of Fire' in the plains of Shinar seems to have been the grand object of worship. There is the strongest evidence that apostasy among the sons of Noah began in fire-worship, and that in connection with the symbol of the serpent" (Hislop, *Two Babylons*, pp. 226).

The apostasy begun by Nimrod found its zenith in the lavish temples and huge pyramids dedicated to the sun god, where men offered animal and human sacrifices. Hislop writes about the origin of sun worship as follows: "The beginning, then, of sun-worship, and of the worship of the host of heaven [astrology], was a sin against the light [against the true God Himself]—a presumptuous, heaven-daring sin. As the sun in the heavens was the great object of worship, so *fire* was worshipped as its earthly representative.

"Along with the sun, as the great fire-god, and in due time, identified with him, was the serpent worshipped. 'In mythology of the primitive world,' says Owen, 'the serpent is universally the symbol of the sun.' In Egypt, one of the [most common] symbols of the sun, or sun god, is a disk with a serpent around it. The original reason was that identification seems just to have been that, as the sun was the great enlightener of the physical world, so **the serpent was held to have been the great enlightener of the spiritual, by giving mankind the *'knowledge of good and evil.'*...** At all events, we have evidence, both Scriptural and profane, for the fact, that the worship of the serpent began side by side with the worship of fire and the sun" (Ibid., pp. 226-227, bold emphasis and bracketed comments added).

The worship of the sun has a long and daring history, dating from prehistoric times to the close of the fifth century of the Christian era. Together with all of its mystical rituals and sacrifices, it spread from "Mother Babylon" to Egypt, Greece, Rome, Europe, India, China, all of Southeast Asia, Africa, and Central and South America—the entire world. All of these civilizations had highly developed forms of sun worship. The belief in and practice of astrology was predominant in sun worship. Therefore, the worship of the six then-known planets was incorporated into the worship of the sun.

The Romans named the seven days of the week in honor of the seven known planets, which were also their pagan deities (Mercury, Venus, Mars, Jupiter, Saturn, the sun and the moon). Later, the pagan Germans renamed some of the days in honor of the Germanic gods, whose names and qualities corresponded to those of the Roman gods. Therefore, the day of the Sun became Sunday; the day of the Moon became Monday; the day of Mars (the Roman god of war) became Tuesday (after Tiw, pronounced *too*, the German god of war—"Tiw's Day"); the day of Mercury became Wednesday (Woden's Day, the Germanic version of Mercury); the day of Jupiter became Thursday (Thor's Day, the Germanic version of Jupiter); the day of Venus became Friday (after the Germanic female god Frigg or Freyja— pronounced *fry-ya*); and the day of Saturn became Saturday.

These descriptive names of the days of the week demonstrate that Sunday worship was pagan long before it allegedly became a Christian institution. The day of the Sun, *dies Solis*, or Sunday, was pre-eminent over all other days of the week. Although other so-called gods had days named after them, only *dies Solis* was proclaimed to be holy.

Bacchiocchi writes: "There is no question that the existence of the planetary week with its 'Sun-day'—*dies Solis*—is crucial for determining any influence of Sun-worship on the Christian adoption of Sunday observance, inasmuch as the Sun before the existence of a weekly 'Sun-day' was venerated every morning" (*From Sabbath to Sunday*, p. 237).

"The *dies Solis* was evidently the most sacred [day] of the week for the faithful of Mithra and like the [professing] Christians, they had to keep Sunday holy and not [the seventh-day] Sabbath…. The gods have arranged the days of the week, whose names the Romans have dedicated to certain stars. The first day [of the week] they called the day of the sun because it is the ruler of all the stars" (Ibid., p. 250, footnote 53, bracketed comments added).

As it was then, so it is today: the day of the Sun, *dies Solis*, Sunday, was always the most prominent day of worship and stood at the head of all the days of the week. Sunday has always been the predominant pagan occult day of worship to the sun god.

But *when* did Sunday, which was venerated by pagan sun worshippers, become the holiest day of the week for Christians?

It was the Roman emperor Constantine who first issued an edict concerning Sunday in A.D. 321: "Let all the judges and town people, and the occupation of all trades, rest on **the venerable day of the sun**; but let those who are situated in the country, freely and at full liberty, attend to the business of agriculture because it often happens that no other day is so fit for sowing corn and planting vines, lest the critical moment being let slip, men should lose the commodities granted them by heaven" (*Corpus Juries Civilis Cod.* Liv. 3, Tit. 12:30).

This pagan Sunday law was henceforth enforced as a Christian festival. The church historian Eusebius, in his Commentary on the Psalms, indicates that from the time of Constantine's Sunday edict, the sanctity of the Sabbath was transferred to the first day of the week. "And all things whatsoever that it was duty to do on the Sabbath, these we have transferred to the Lord's Day, as more appropriately belong to it, because it has a precedence and is first in rank, and more honourable than the Jewish Sabbath" (Cox's *Sabbath Literature,* Volume 1, p. 361).

Thus, since this fourth-century edict, much of Orthodox Christendom has accepted Sunday as the "Lord's Day," or the so-called "Christian Sabbath." To this day the Roman Catholic Church pontifically claims that it had the authority to change God's Fourth Commandment and transfer the solemnity of the seventh-day weekly Sabbath to Sunday, the first day of the week. This flagrant, bold boast of authority is diametrically opposed to the Word of God. God has never relinquished His authority to any man at any time to change His Sabbath commandment! After Jesus' resurrection and just before He ascended to heaven, He told His disciples, "**All authority in heaven and on earth has been given to Me**. Therefore, go *and* make disciples in all nations, baptizing them into the name of the Father, and of the

Son, and of the Holy Spirit; **teaching them to observe all things that I have commanded you**. And lo, I am with you always, *even* until the completion of the age" (Matt. 28:18-20).

There is no question that the Roman Catholic Church fully comprehends that **the Scriptures absolutely require the observance of the biblical Sabbath**, the seventh day of the week, called Saturday today. Cardinal James Gibbons fully admits that Sunday keeping is a Catholic institution based solely on the traditions of the "early church fathers," the edicts of Emperor Constantine (321 AD) and the ecclesiastical authority of the Catholic Church in the Councils of Laodicea (336, 364 AD). Gibbons also admits that the establishment of Sunday worship is not based on the authority of the Scriptures: "**You may read the Bible from Genesis to Revelation, and you will not find a single line authorizing sanctification of Sunday. The Scriptures enforce the religious observance of Saturday, a day which we never sanctify.**" (Gibbons, *Faith of Our Fathers*, 1892, p. 111). Rome's challenge to Protestants is that if they truly believed the rallying cry of the Reformation—"*solo scriptura*"—they would reject the Catholic tradition of Sunday keeping and would be ardently keeping the seventh-day Sabbath as God commands. (See Appendix D, *Rome's Challenge to the Protestants*, page 212.)

As we peel back the layers of historical and scriptural evidence of sun worship/Sunday keeping, it is undeniable that this false teaching is a **great sin** against God and violates the Fourth Commandment. Yet, Orthodox Christendom continues to channel mankind into the mire of its humanly-devised tradition of Sunday worship—a day originally devised by Nimrod and Semiramis to worship Satan the devil. Sunday keeping is part of the "Mystery of Iniquity," Satan's grand counterfeit that *looks* Christian and proclaims to *be* Christian, but is, in fact, *false* (II Thes 2:3-12; Rev. 13:11-14).

A Survey of Occult Sun Worship in the Bible

For most of their history, Israelites and Jews have worshiped the false gods of the nations around them. They dealt in witchcraft and divination, consulted familiar spirits, and used occult practices. While serving false gods instead of the true God, Israel worshiped the sun god on his day, Sunday. The Bible reveals that Israel, at one time or another, observed all the pagan holidays—which later came to be known as Halloween, Christmas, Lent, Easter, and so on. Moreover, they, without shame, committed these abominations in the **name** of the LORD their God!

Typically, except for brief periods of time in their history, Israel and Judah did not faithfully keep God's Sabbaths and holy days as He had commanded. A complete biblical record of this fact is found in all the books of the Old Testament—specifically from Exodus to II Chronicles.

In spite of their sins, God faithfully continued to deal with Israel and Judah because of His promises to Abraham, Isaac and Jacob, and for His own reputation's sake among the nations. God's covenant with Israel had guaranteed blessings if they obeyed Him and curses if they disobeyed Him. A summation of these blessings and curses is found in Deuteronomy 28 and Leviticus 26. (For a complete understanding of these blessings and cursings, the reader is encouraged to read these chapters in their entirety.)

Ancient Israel and Sun Worship in Egypt

Approximately nine hundred years after God scattered mankind from the tower of Babel into the entire world, the children of Israel were enslaved in Egypt. During this time, they were mostly serving the gods of Egypt. Of all the gods of Egypt, the chief god was the sun god, whose symbols were the sun disk, the sacred cobra, and the sacred bull with a disk of the sun between its horns. Pharaoh, the king and absolute ruler of Egypt, was worshiped as the incarnation of the sun god. On his crown in the center of his forehead was a protruding hooded cobra, demonstrating that he derived his power and authority—both civil and religious—from Satan the devil.

The book of Exodus gives the account of how God miraculously delivered the twelve tribes of Israel from their harsh slavery with great signs and awesome plagues. To show His supreme power over all the demon gods of Egypt, God judged Pharaoh and the Egyptians by using against them the very things they worshiped. God used serpents, turned water into blood, and sent plagues of frogs, lice, fleas, flies, and murrain against their animals. Yet, Pharaoh stubbornly refused to let the children of Israel go. Therefore, God intensified the plagues and afflicted the Egyptians with boils.

Still defiant, Pharaoh resolutely would not let the Israelites go. In answer to Pharaoh's implacable defiance, God demonstrated His awesome power and authority as the one true God by using the elements and powers of the earth to further afflict the Egyptians. He sent destructive hail, thunder and lightning, swarms of locusts, and finally three days of thick, tangible darkness. The Egyptians could not venture out of their houses because of the darkness. Yet, in Goshen, the children of Israel had light. Still, Pharaoh refused to relent. Therefore, God brought one last mighty plague upon the Egyptians—the supernatural death of all their firstborn, both man and beast.

In order to spare the firstborn of the children of Israel, God instructed Moses and Aaron to command all the Israelite heads of households to prepare a special domestic sacrifice called the Passover. It is called the Passover because on that night God "passed over" the houses of the children of Israel, sparing their firstborn—while at midnight He killed all the firstborn of the Egyptians, man and beast.

Why did God do this?

God did this not only to release the children of Israel from their Egyptian slavery, but also to execute His judgment against the gods of Egypt. It was a massive display of God's sovereign, almighty power and authority. Through this act God demonstrated that He alone is the true God. All of the impotent gods of Egypt were proven false—and hence, all of the

Satan-inspired, man-made gods throughout all time are nothing! Notice what the Lord God said: "For I will pass through the land of Egypt this night, and will smite all the firstborn in the land of Egypt, both man and beast; and **against all the gods of Egypt I will execute judgment**: I *am* the LORD" (Ex. 12:12). After God's devastating judgment against the Egyptians and their false gods with the killing of their firstborn, Pharaoh finally let the Israelites go free.

God Gives Israel the Ten Commandments and His Laws at Mount Sinai

With the protection and guidance of God, Moses and Aaron led the Israelites out of Egypt and through the Red Sea on dry ground. After Israel made it safely across the sea, Pharaoh and his pursuing armies attempted to follow. As soon as the Egyptians were in the middle of the dry sea bottom, God commanded the waters to return. All were trapped and destroyed.

On their way to Mount Sinai, God performed additional miracles—providing fresh water to drink, quail to eat, and manna (bread from heaven) to eat. After arriving at Mount Sinai, God displayed His awesome power and glory from the top of the mount while Israel assembled itself at the base. "And Moses brought forth the people out of the camp to meet with God; and they stood at the nether part of the mount. And mount Sinai was altogether on a smoke, because the LORD descended upon it in fire: and the smoke thereof ascended as the smoke of a furnace, and the whole mount quaked greatly. And when the voice of the trumpet sounded long, and waxed louder and louder, Moses spake, and God answered him by a voice" (Ex. 19:17-19).

God told Moses to warn the people concerning the base of the mountain, not to come past it, to touch it, or to allow an animal to come near it. After manifesting His incredible power, God personally spoke the Ten Commandments to the children of Israel. We will focus on the first four commandments, which pertain to our personal relationship with God.

The First Commandment: "And God spake all these words, saying, I *am* the LORD thy God, which have brought thee out of the land of Egypt, out of the house of bondage. **Thou shalt have no other gods before me.**"

The Second Commandment: "**Thou shalt not make unto thee any graven image, or any likeness** *of any thing* that *is* in heaven above, or that *is* in the earth beneath, or that *is* in the water under the earth: thou shalt not bow down thyself to them, nor serve them: for I the LORD thy God *am* a jealous God, visiting the iniquity of the fathers upon the children unto the third and fourth *generation* of them that hate me; and showing mercy unto thousands of them that love me, and keep my commandments."

The Third Commandment: "**Thou shalt not take the name of the LORD thy God in vain**; for the LORD will not hold him guiltless that taketh his name in vain."

The Fourth Commandment: "**Remember the sabbath day, to keep it holy**. Six days shalt thou labour, and do all thy work: but the seventh day *is* the sabbath of the LORD thy God: *in it* thou shalt not do any work, thou, nor thy son, nor thy daughter, thy manservant, nor thy maidservant, nor thy cattle, nor thy stranger that *is* within thy gates: for *in* six days the LORD made heaven and earth, the sea, and all that in them *is*, and rested the seventh day: wherefore **the LORD blessed the sabbath day, and hallowed it**" (Ex. 20:1-11). (See Appendix E, *Biblical Truth About Sabbath Keeping*, page 235.)

These commandments are the very words of God Himself. They are not complicated or difficult to comprehend; rather, they are clear, and easy to understand and keep. Contrary to what most professing Christians believe, Jesus did not come to abrogate or abolish the Law or the Prophets with the advent of the New Covenant. Jesus Christ, as God manifested in the flesh—who was the Lord God of the Old Testament and who spoke the Ten Commandments to Israel—emphatically said: "Do not think that I have come to abolish the Law or the Prophets; I did not come to abolish, but to fulfill. For truly I say to you, **until the heaven and the earth shall pass away, one jot or one tittle shall in no way pass from the Law until everything has been fulfilled**" (Matt. 5:17-18).

What Jesus declared, as recorded by Matthew, is verified throughout all Scripture from Genesis to Revelation. Isaiah recorded similar words of God: "Lift up your eyes to the heavens, and look upon the earth beneath: for the heavens shall vanish away like smoke, and the earth shall wax old like a garment, and they that dwell therein shall die in like manner: but my salvation shall be for ever, and **my righteousness shall not be abolished**" (Isa. 51:6). Again, David said, "The works of his hands *are* verity and judgment; **all his commandments *are* sure. They stand fast for ever and ever, *and are* done in truth and uprightness**" (Psa. 111:7-8).

When the leaders of Orthodox Christendom make false claims about God's Word, they are taking His name in vain and following in the sinful footsteps of ancient Israel's religious leaders. The prophet Ezekiel wrote this indictment of such leaders: "And the word of the LORD came unto me, saying,... '*There is* a **conspiracy of her prophets** [whenever there is a conspiracy, those involved know better] in the midst thereof, like a roaring lion ravening the prey; they have devoured souls; they have taken the treasure and precious things; they have made her many widows in the midst thereof. **Her priests have violated my law**, and have **profaned mine holy things**: they have put no difference between the holy and profane, neither have they showed *difference* between the unclean and the clean, **and have hid their eyes from my sabbaths**, and I am profaned among them.... And her prophets have daubed them with untempered *mortar*, **seeing vanity, and divining lies unto them, saying, 'Thus saith the Lord GOD', when the LORD hath not spoken**' " (Ezek. 22:23-28).

As we will see, almost immediately after God spoke the Ten Commandments to Israel at Mount Sinai, certain leaders began speaking lies in God's name—thus taking His name in vain.

Israel and Sun Worship in the Wilderness

When Moses received the Ten Commandments and other laws from God, he wrote them down in the Book of the Law. Afterwards, Moses read all of God's words to the people, and the covenant was ratified (Ex. 21-24). They promised in their covenant pledge with God to be obedient to all the words that He had spoken.

"And Moses came and told the people all the words of the LORD, and all the judgments: and all the people answered with one voice, and said, 'All the words which the LORD hath said will we do.' And Moses wrote all the words of the LORD, and rose up early in the morning, and builded an altar under the hill, and twelve pillars, according to the twelve tribes of Israel. And he sent young men of the children of Israel, which offered burnt offerings, and sacrificed peace offerings of oxen unto the LORD. And Moses took half of the blood, and put *it* in basins; and half of the blood he sprinkled on the altar. **And he took the book of the covenant, and read in the audience of the people: and they said, 'All that the LORD hath said will we do, and be obedient.' And Moses took the blood, and sprinkled it on the people, and said, 'Behold the blood of the covenant, which the LORD hath made with you concerning all these words'** " (Ex. 24:3-8).

Afterwards, Moses went up Mount Sinai to commune with God for forty days and forty nights. There he received the Ten Commandments, written by the finger of God on tables of stone. In addition, he received all of God's instructions for the tabernacle and the altars as well as the ritual laws that the priests and Levites were to perform.

The last words that God spoke to Moses concerned His holy Sabbaths—both His annual Sabbaths and the weekly seventh-day Sabbath: "And the LORD spake unto Moses, saying, 'Speak thou also unto the children of Israel, saying, "**Verily my sabbaths ye shall keep: for it *is* a sign between me and you throughout your generations; that *ye* may know that I *am* the LORD that doth sanctify you**" ' " (Ex. 31:12-13).

God continued: "Ye shall keep the sabbath therefore; for it *is* holy unto you: every one that defileth it shall surely be put to death: for whosoever doeth *any* work therein, that soul shall be cut off from among his people. Six days may work be done; but in the seventh *is* the sabbath of rest, holy to the LORD: whosoever doeth *any* work in the sabbath day, he shall surely be put to death. **Wherefore the children of Israel shall keep the sabbath, to observe the sabbath throughout their generations,** *for* **a perpetual covenant**. It *is* a sign between me and the children of Israel for ever: for *in* six days the LORD made heaven and earth, and on the seventh day he rested, and was refreshed" (verses 14-17).

"And he gave unto Moses, when he had made an end of communing with him upon mount Sinai, **two tables of testimony, tables of stone, written with the finger of God**" (verse 18).

What occurred next was, perhaps, one of the greatest ironies in the history of the Israelite nation. The last words that God spoke to Moses concerned Israel's keeping His Sabbaths—weekly and annual—as a perpetual covenant. However, while God was instructing Moses during the forty days and forty nights, his brother Aaron was causing the people of Israel to greatly sin—virtually in the presence of God at the foot of Mount Sinai as they waited for Moses to return.

Israel Worships the Golden Calf. Aaron was the first priest of Israel to speak lies, to sanction pagan sun worship and to lead the people into committing idolatry, all in the name of the Creator, the Lord God—even though all Israel had previously heard God speak the Ten Commandments.

"And when the people saw that Moses delayed to come down out of the mount, **the people gathered themselves together unto Aaron, and said unto him, 'Up, make us gods**, which shall go before us; for *as for* this Moses, the man that brought us up out of the land of Egypt, we wot [know] not what is become of him.'

"And Aaron said unto them, 'Break off the golden earrings, which *are* in the ears of your wives, of your sons, and of your daughters, and bring *them* unto me.' And all the people brake off the golden earrings which *were* in their ears, and brought *them* unto Aaron. And he received *them* at their hand, and **fashioned it with a graving tool, after he had made it a molten calf**: and they said, **'These** *be* **thy gods, O Israel, which brought thee up out of the land of Egypt.'** And when Aaron saw *it*, he **built an altar before it**; and **Aaron made proclamation, and said, 'To morrow** *is* **a feast to the LORD.'** And they rose up early on the morrow, and offered burnt offerings, and brought peace offerings; and the people sat down to eat and to drink, and rose up to play [a sex orgy]. And the LORD said unto Moses, 'Go, get thee down; for thy people, which thou broughtest out of the land of Egypt, have corrupted *themselves*: **They have turned aside quickly out of the way which I commanded them: they have made them a molten calf, and have worshipped it, and have sacrificed thereunto, and said, "These** *be* **thy gods**, O Israel, which have brought thee up out of the land of Egypt" ' " (Ex. 32:1-8).

The molten calf that Aaron fashioned with his own hands undoubtedly was a replica of the golden Egyptian sacred bull with the sun disk between its horns. After making the calf, Aaron told the people that they could use the idol—the very symbol of the sun god and of Satan—to worship God Himself. This action was a transgression of the First and Second Commandments. He then proclaimed, "To morrow *is* a feast to the LORD," taking the name of the Lord God in vain and thus transgressing the Third Commandment.

Therefore, in defiance of God, Aaron led the people back into a familiar celebration of the false gods of Egypt and proclaimed this idolatrous abomination as a sanctified "feast unto the Lord" (thereby breaking the Fourth Commandment). Similarly, very early in its history, Orthodox Christendom used this same deceitful slight of hand in taking to itself pagan holidays and sanctioning them as "feasts unto the Lord"—and in taking idolatrous religious rituals and incorporating them into its worship services.

And this has all been done "in the name of the Lord," just as Aaron had claimed.

Israel's Great Sin of Sun Worship. God first reacted by determining to destroy the children of Israel for their presumptuous, rebellious sin of worshiping the golden calf. Moses, however, interceded for the people, and God had mercy. Moses then came down from the mount, carrying the tables of stone with the Ten Commandments written by the finger of God. As he approached the camp he heard the people singing: "And it came to pass, as soon as he came nigh unto the camp, that he saw the calf, and the dancing: and Moses' anger waxed hot, and he cast the tables out of his hands, and brake them beneath the mount. And he took the calf which they had made, and burnt *it* in the fire, and ground *it* to powder, and strowed *it* upon the water, and made the children of Israel drink *of it*.

"And Moses said unto Aaron, **'What did this people unto thee, that thou hast brought so great a sin upon them?'** And Aaron said, 'Let not the anger of my lord wax hot: thou knowest the people, that they *are set* on mischief. For **they said unto me, "Make us gods,** which shall go before us: for *as for* this Moses, the man that brought us up out of the land of Egypt, we wot [know] not what is become of him." And I said unto them, "Whosoever hath any gold, let them break *it* off." So they gave *it* me: then I cast it into the fire, and there came out this calf.'

"And when Moses saw that the people *were* naked; (for Aaron had made them naked unto *their* shame among their enemies:) then Moses stood in the gate of the camp, and said, **'Who *is* on the LORD'S side?** *let him come* unto me.' And all the sons of Levi gathered themselves together unto him. And he said unto them, 'Thus saith the LORD God of Israel, "Put every man his sword by his side, *and* go in and out from gate to gate throughout the camp, and slay every man his brother, and every man his companion, and every man his neighbour." ' And the children of Levi did according to the word of Moses: and there fell of the people that day about three thousand men.... And it came to pass on the morrow, that **Moses said unto the people, 'Ye have sinned a great sin**: and now I will go up unto the LORD; peradventure I shall make an atonement for your sin' " (Ex. 32:19-30).

The children of Israel sinned greatly in this rebellion, and God left **no doubt that those who did so were worthy of death**. However, because of Moses' intercession, Aaron and most of the people were spared. Yet, three thousand died by the sword of the sons of Levi—for as the Scriptures teach, "The wages of sin is death" (Rom. 6:23).

This incident as recorded in the book of Exodus shows that God will judge disobedience. What happened at Mount Sinai was a prophetic prelude to a long history of Israelite rebellion and disobedience toward God during which they served the false gods of the nations around them, while engaging in occult practices and keeping occult holidays.

The book of Numbers records Israel's repeated apostasy. In chapter 25, just before they entered the "Promised Land," we find this account: "And Israel abode in Shittim, and **the people began to commit whoredom** with the daughters of Moab. And they called the people unto the sacrifices of their gods: and the people did eat, and bowed down to their gods. And Israel joined himself unto Baalpeor: and the anger of the LORD was kindled against Israel. And the LORD said unto Moses, 'Take all the heads of the people, and hang them up before the LORD against the sun, that the fierce anger of the LORD may be turned away from Israel.' And Moses said unto the judges of Israel, 'Slay ye every one his men that were joined unto Baalpeor.'... And those that died in the plague were twenty and four thousand" (Num. 25:1-5, 9).

Israel and Occult Worship in the Promised Land

After forty years of vacillating rebellion and wandering in the wilderness of Sinai, God finally brought the children of Israel to the Promised Land as He had promised Abraham, Isaac, and Jacob. Moses and Aaron died without entering the Land. God appointed Joshua to succeed Moses, and Aaron's son, Eleazar, to succeed Aaron. God was with them, and they conquered the land of the Canaanites in seven years, after which God gave them rest from their enemies and divided the land among the twelve tribes.

As long as Joshua and the elders—who had come through the forty years of wandering in the wilderness—lived, the children of Israel followed God: "And the people served the LORD all the days of Joshua, and all the days of the elders that outlived Joshua, who had seen all the great works of the LORD, that he did for Israel. And Joshua, the son of Nun, the servant of the LORD, died, *being* an hundred and ten years old.... And also all that generation were gathered unto their fathers: and **there arose another generation after them, which knew not the LORD**, nor yet the works which he had done for Israel" (Judges 2:7-10).

When these godly leaders died, the children of Israel again turned their backs on God and went after the occult gods of the heathen nations around them. "And the children of Israel did evil in the sight of the LORD, and served Baalim [Hebrew plural for *Baal*, meaning various versions of the sun god]: and they forsook the LORD God of their fathers, which brought them out of the land of Egypt, and followed other gods, of the gods of the people that *were* round about them, and bowed themselves unto them, and provoked the LORD to anger.

"**And they forsook the LORD, and served Baal** [the sun god] **and Ashtaroth** [the queen of heaven; often spelled *Ashtoreth*]. And the anger of the LORD was hot against Israel, and he delivered them into the hands of spoilers that spoiled them, and he sold them into the hands of their enemies round about, so that they could not any longer stand before their enemies" (Judges 2:11-14).

In captivity the children of Israel would typically repent, and God would raise up a righteous judge who would deliver them out of their enemies' hands. The children of Israel would then follow God as long as the godly judge lived. However, as soon as the judge died, they would again reject the true God and begin serving the false gods of the nations—Baal, the sun god, and Ashtoreth, the queen of heaven. Such is the entire story of the book of Judges, covering a period of over 400 years. The last verse of the book of Judges summarizes this entire period: "In those days *there was* no king in Israel: every man did *that which was* right in his own eyes" (Judges 21:25).

Samuel, the Last Judge of Israel. Samuel was the last ruling judge to lead the children of Israel. He was also a priest and a prophet. He taught the children of Israel the true way of God and caused many of the people to serve the Lord instead of the gods of the land—Baalim and Ashtoreth. God restored the Ark of the Covenant that the Philistines had captured because of the sins of the children of Israel and the former priesthood of Eli and his sons. It remained in the house of Abinadab until the time of King David: "And it came to pass, while the ark abode in Kirjathjearim, that the time was long; for it was twenty years: and all the house of Israel lamented after the LORD.

"And Samuel spake unto all the house of Israel, saying, '**If ye do return unto the LORD with all your hearts,** *then* **put away the strange gods and Ashtaroth from among you, and prepare your hearts unto the LORD, and serve him only: and he will deliver you out of the hand of the Philistines.**' Then the children of **Israel did put away Baalim and Ashtaroth**, and served the LORD only" (I Sam. 7:2-4).

This revival of the true worship of the Lord was short lived. When Samuel was old and because of the corruption of his sons (who he had appointed as judges), the leaders of the children of Israel demanded that he appoint a king over the nation. They wanted a king to rule them, rather than the judges that God had appointed.

Samuel warned them that if they had a king like the other nations, there would be consequences. "But the thing displeased Samuel, when they said, 'Give us a king to judge us.' And Samuel prayed unto the LORD. And the LORD said unto Samuel, 'Hearken unto the voice of the people in all that they say unto thee: for they have not rejected thee, but **they have rejected me, that I should not reign over them**. According to all the works which they have done since the day that I brought them up out of Egypt **even unto this day**, wherewith **they have forsaken me, and served other gods**, so do they also unto thee. Now therefore hearken unto their voice: howbeit yet protest solemnly unto them, and show them the manner of the king that shall reign over them' " (I Sam. 8:6-9).

Although Israel rejected His rulership, God promised that he would still bless them if they followed Him instead of false gods. Thus when Saul was installed as Israel's first king, Samuel proclaimed, "Now therefore behold the king whom ye have chosen, *and* whom ye have desired! and, behold, the LORD hath set a king over you. If ye will fear the LORD, and serve him, and obey his voice, and not rebel against the commandment of the LORD, then shall both ye and also the king that reigneth over you continue following the LORD your God: but if ye will not obey the voice of the LORD, but rebel against the commandment of the LORD, then shall the hand of the LORD be against you, as *it was* against your fathers" (I Sam. 12:13-15).

David Succeeds Saul as King of Israel. Saul failed to follow God's instructions and rebelled against Him. Therefore, he was rejected from being king (I Sam. 15). God then sent Samuel to anoint David, the youngest son of Jesse, as the new king of Israel (I Sam. 16). Although David was not blameless, God said that he was a man after His own heart. David was the most righteous of all the kings of Israel and reigned for forty years. He wrote hundreds of Psalms and Proverbs that have been preserved in the Scriptures.

Solomon Succeeds David. Before David died, God gave him the plans for the temple of God that David's son Solomon would build (I Chron. 28-29). As king, young Solomon started out well. His desire for wisdom pleased God so much that God blessed him not only with great wisdom but also with great wealth—making him the wisest and richest man on earth (perhaps in the history of the world). Solomon finished the temple and consecrated it to God. Through the blessings of God, His kingdom prospered. All the kings of the earth sought Solomon's wisdom—and, in tribute, brought gifts of gold and other valuables to Solomon year by year (I Kings 1-10).

Intermarriage Causes Solomon to Forsake the True God. Solomon had the greatest blessings, wealth and power of all the kings of Israel. He wrote hundreds of Proverbs and the book of Ecclesiastes, which are part of the Old Testament, preserved for us to read and study today. But Solomon forsook God because of his many wives who worshiped false gods.

"But king Solomon **loved many strange women**, together with the daughter of Pharaoh, women of the Moabites, Ammonites, Edomites, Zidonians, *and* Hittites; of the nations *concerning* which the LORD said unto the children of Israel, 'Ye shall not go in to them, neither shall they come in unto you: *for* surely they will turn away your heart after their gods:' Solomon clave unto these in love.

"And he had seven hundred wives, princesses, and three hundred concubines: and **his wives turned away his heart**. For it came to pass, when Solomon was old, *that* his wives turned away his heart **after other gods**: and his heart was not perfect with the LORD his God, as *was* the heart of David his father. **For Solomon went after Ashtoreth** [the queen of heaven] the goddess of the Zidonians, and **after Milcom the abomination of the Ammonites. And Solomon did evil in the sight of the LORD**, and went not fully after the LORD, *as did* David his father. Then did Solomon build an high place for **Chemosh**, the abomination of Moab, in the hill that *is* before Jerusalem, and for **Molech** [where children were sacrificed in its flaming arms and belly], the abomination of the children of Ammon. And likewise did he for all his strange wives, which **burnt incense and sacrificed unto their gods**" (I Kings 11:1-8).

This historical account should serve as a profound, continuous lesson and warning to all who read it. Solomon had the privilege of building the temple of God in Jerusalem. He and all the twelve tribes of Israel had received the blessings of God in great abundance. However, toward the end of his life, he became corrupted through the worship of false gods. Moreover, the people of Israel followed him into apostasy.

What a tragedy! The one who built the temple of God also became the master builder of temples and incense altars for the false gods of his seven hundred wives. Solomon constructed them on a hill west of the temple, later called the Hill of Abomination. "And the LORD was angry with Solomon, because his heart was turned from the LORD God of Israel, which had appeared unto him twice, and had commanded him concerning this thing, that he should not go after other gods: but he kept not that which the LORD commanded. Wherefore the LORD said unto Solomon, 'Forasmuch as this is done of thee, and thou hast not kept my covenant and my statutes, which I have commanded thee, **I will surely rend [take] the kingdom from thee**, and will give it to thy servant. Notwithstanding in thy days I will not do it for David thy father's sake: *but* I will rend it out of the hand of thy son. Howbeit I will not rend away all the kingdom; *but* will give one tribe to thy son for David my servant's sake, and for Jerusalem's sake which I have chosen' " (I Kings 11:9-13).

God Gives the Kingship of the Ten Tribes of Israel to Jeroboam. Jeroboam was Solomon's servant, a general in Solomon's army and a ruler over the house of Joseph. After Solomon died, God sent the prophet Ahijah to tell Jeroboam that He had chosen him to be king over the ten tribes of Israel. Solomon's son, Rehoboam, would rule over Judah in Jerusalem (I Kings 11:28-32).

Ahijah told Jeroboam that God was dividing the kingdom because of the sins of Solomon and the children of Israel. "**Because that they have forsaken me, and have worshipped Ashtoreth the goddess of the Zidonians, Chemosh the god of the Moabites, and Milcom the god of the children of Ammon, and have not walked in my ways**, to do *that which is* right in mine eyes, and *to keep* my statutes and my judgments, as *did* David his father" (verse 33).

God promised Jeroboam that if he would do that which was right in His sight, He would establish his kingdom just as He had for David, "And it shall be, if thou wilt hearken unto all that I command thee, and wilt walk in my ways, and do *that is* right in my sight, to keep my statutes and my commandments, as David my servant did; that I will be with thee, and build thee a sure house, as I built for David, and will give Israel unto thee" (verse 38).

Thus Jeroboam knew that God had divided the kingdom because Solomon grievously sinned by forsaking Him and exchanging the worship of the one true God for the worship of false gods. However, Jeroboam did not listen to the words of God by Ahijah. Neither did he walk in God's ways, but transgressed worse than Solomon did.

Jeroboam feared that if the people went to Jerusalem to keep the feasts of God, they would align themselves with Rehoboam. In order to prevent this, he appointed a feast day of his own choosing and made two golden calves for the people to worship.

"Whereupon the king took counsel, and **made two calves** *of* **gold**, and said unto them, 'It is too much for you to go up to Jerusalem: **behold thy gods, O Israel, which brought thee up out of the land of Egypt** [the same sin as Aaron].' And he set the one in Bethel, and the other put he in Dan. **And this thing became a sin: for the people went** *to worship* **before the one,** *even* **unto Dan**" (I Kings 12:28-30).

"And he made an house of high places, and made priests of the lowest of the people, which were not of the sons of Levi. And Jeroboam **ordained a feast in the eighth month**, on **the fifteenth day of the month**, like unto the feast that *is* in Judah, and he offered upon the altar. So did he in Bethel, sacrificing unto the calves that he had made: and he placed in Bethel the priests of the high places which he had made. So he offered upon the altar which he had made in Bethel the fifteenth day of the eighth month, *even* in the month **which he had devised of his own heart; and ordained a feast unto the children of Israel**: and he offered upon the altar, and burnt incense" (verses 31-33).

Jeroboam also forced the Levites to leave the ten tribes, so he could establish his own priesthood for the golden calf worship: "For the Levites left their suburbs and their possession, and came to Judah and Jerusalem: for Jeroboam and his sons had cast them off from executing the priest's office unto the LORD: and **he ordained him priests for the high places, and for the devils, and for the calves which he had made**" (II Chron. 11:14-15).

God sent another prophet to warn Jeroboam, but he refused to listen and repent. "After this thing Jeroboam returned not from his evil way, but made again of the lowest of the people priests of the high places: whosoever would, he consecrated him, and he became *one* of the priests of the high places. **And this thing became sin** unto the house of Jeroboam, even to cut *it* off, and to destroy *it* from off the face of the earth" (I Kings 13:33-34).

As a consequence of Jeroboam's sins, the ten tribes of Israel completely forsook the Lord God. God sent many prophets to warn them to repent and return to the true God. However, none of the kings and only very few of the people ever repented. It is recorded that during the time of Elijah the prophet, there were just seven thousand who had not "bowed the knee to Baal" (I Kings 19:18).

After Elijah, God sent the prophet Elisha. In spite of Elisha's powerful ministry and miracles—and some reprieve from the wars with the Syrians—Israel would not repent from worshiping false gods, but plunged deeper and deeper into sun worship, witchcraft and occult practices.

The Ten Tribes of Israel Go into Captivity Because of Their Sins. For approximately 300 years after Jeroboam's reign, the ten tribes of Israel continued to serve false gods and idols. They used witchcraft and other occult practices (Micah 5:12-14). They worshiped Baal, the sun god, and Ashtoreth, the "queen of heaven."

In spite of the fact that the priests, Levites, and people of Israel had the book of the Law of God—the five books of Moses—to instruct them, they repeatedly failed to obey the Word of God and to keep His commandments and statutes. Finally, God used Shalmaneser, king of Assyria, to punish Israel. The Assyrians besieged Samaria for three years, 721-718 BC, and afterwards took the Israelites into captivity.

The story is recorded in the book of II Kings:

"In the ninth year of Hoshea [king of Israel] the king of Assyria took Samaria, and carried Israel away into Assyria, and placed them in Halah and in Habor *by* the river of Gozan, and in the cities of the Medes. For *so* it was, that **the children of Israel had sinned against the L**ORD **their God**, which had brought them up out of the land of Egypt, from under the hand of Pharaoh king of Egypt, and **had feared other gods, and walked in the statutes of the heathen**, whom the LORD cast out from before the children of Israel, and of the kings of Israel, which they had made. And the children of Israel **did secretly** *those* **things that** *were* **not right** against the LORD their God, and they built them high places in all their cities, from the tower of the watchmen to the fenced city. And they set them up **images and groves in every high hill**, and under every green tree: And there they **burnt incense in all the high places**, as *did* the heathen whom the LORD carried away before them; and **wrought wicked things to provoke the L**ORD **to anger**: for they **served idols**, whereof the LORD had said unto them, 'Ye shall not do this thing.'

"Yet the LORD testified against Israel, and against Judah, by all the prophets, *and by* all the seers, saying, '**Turn ye from your evil ways, and keep my commandments** *and* **my statutes**, according to all the law which I commanded your fathers, and which I sent to you by my servants the prophets.' Notwithstanding **they would not hear, but hardened their necks**, like to the neck of their fathers, that did not believe in the LORD their God. And **they rejected his statutes, and his covenant that he made with their fathers**, and his testimonies which he testified against them; and **they followed vanity, and became vain, and went after the heathen** that *were* round about them, *concerning* whom the LORD had charged them, that they should not do like them. And **they left all the commandments of the L**ORD **their God, and made them molten images,** *even* **two calves, and made a grove, and worshipped all the host of heaven, and served Baal. And they caused their sons and their daughters to pass through the fire, and used divination and enchantments, and sold themselves to do evil in the sight of the L**ORD**, to provoke him to anger**. Therefore the LORD was very angry with Israel, and removed them out of his sight: there was none left but the tribe of Judah only.

"And the LORD rejected all the seed of Israel, and afflicted them, and delivered them into the hand of spoilers, until he had cast them out of his sight. For he rent Israel from the house of David; and they made Jeroboam the son of Nebat king: and **Jeroboam drave Israel from following the L**ORD**, and made them sin a great sin**. For the children of Israel walked in all the sins of Jeroboam which he did; they departed not from them; until the LORD removed Israel out of his sight, as he had said by all his servants the prophets. So was Israel carried away out of their own land to Assyria **unto this day** [apparently an editorial comment added by Ezra the priest around 500 BC]. And the king of Assyria brought *men* from Babylon, and from Cuthah, and from Ava, and from Hamath, and from Sepharvaim, and placed *them* in the cities of Samaria instead of the children of Israel: and they possessed Samaria, and dwelt in the cities thereof" (II Kings 17:6-18, 20-24).

While the ten northern tribes of Israel and their kings never repented and returned to God, the southern kingdom of Judah, which retained the area of Judea and the city of Jerusalem, experienced periods of repentance and revival. The books of II Kings and II Chronicles record the history of the kings of Judah. Judah, however, failed to return wholeheartedly to God even after the ten tribes of Israel were taken into Assyria. "Also Judah kept not the commandments of the LORD their God, but walked in the [apostate] statutes of Israel which they [had] made [in rebellion]" (II Kings 17:19).

The Kingdom of Judah Also Rebels Against God. Some of the kings of Judah led the Jews to repentance. Others were wicked and followed in the way of Jeroboam, leading the people to sin greatly against God. Of all the kings of Judah, Manasseh, who reigned for fifty-five years, was undoubtedly the most wicked.

Manasseh defied God and rebelled against Him, overturning all the righteous reforms that his father Hezekiah had instituted during his reign. The kingdom of Judah was transformed into a sun-worshiping occult society under his leadership.

"Manasseh *was* twelve years old when he began to reign, and he reigned fifty and five years in Jerusalem: **but did *that which was* evil in the sight of the LORD, like unto the abominations of the heathen**, whom the LORD had cast out before the children of Israel. For he built again the high places which Hezekiah his father had broken down, and he reared up altars for Baalim [sun god worship], and made groves [for witchcraft], and worshipped all the host of heaven [the worship of Satan and demons], and served them.

"Also he **built altars** in the house of the LORD, whereof the LORD had said, 'In Jerusalem shall my name be for ever.' And he **built altars for all the host of heaven** in the two courts of the house of the LORD" (II Chron. 33:1-5). Manasseh deliberately desecrated the temple of God, converting it into a pagan monument devoted to sun worship—replete with occult rituals and Satan worship.

"And he caused his children to pass through the fire in the valley of the son of Hinnom: also **he observed times, and used enchantments, and used witchcraft, and dealt with a familiar spirit, and with wizards: he wrought much evil in the sight of the LORD, to provoke him to anger. And he set a carved image, the idol which he had made, in the house of God**, of which God had said to David and to Solomon his son, 'In this house, and in Jerusalem, which I have chosen before all the tribes of Israel, will I put my name for ever: neither will I any more remove the foot of Israel from out of the land which I have appointed for your fathers; so that they will take heed to do all that I have commanded them, according to the whole law and the statutes and the ordinances by the hand of Moses.' **So Manasseh made Judah and the inhabitants of Jerusalem to err, *and* to do worse than the heathen**, whom the LORD had destroyed before the children of Israel. And the LORD spake to Manasseh, and to his people: but they would not hearken" (verses 6-10).

"Moreover Manasseh shed innocent blood very much, till he had filled Jerusalem from one end to another; beside his sin wherewith he made Judah to sin, in doing *that which was* evil in the sight of the LORD" (II Kings 21:16).

Therefore, God sent Manasseh into captivity before the rest of the Jews: "Wherefore the LORD brought upon them the captains of the host of the king of Assyria, which took Manasseh among the thorns, and bound him with fetters, and carried him to Babylon" (II Chron. 33:11).

In prison, Manasseh repented of his sins. He humbled himself, and God restored him to his throne. "And when he was in affliction, **he besought the LORD his God, and humbled himself greatly before the God of his fathers**, and prayed unto him: and he was entreated of him, and heard his supplication, and brought him again to Jerusalem into his kingdom. Then Manasseh knew that the LORD he *was* God" (II Chron. 33:12-13).

This account of Manasseh's repentance shows that God will forgive and restore people who wholeheartedly turn to Him and repent of their sins and transgressions. When Manasseh was returned to his throne in Jerusalem, he destroyed the idols that he had built and restored the true worship of God at the temple. "And he took away the strange gods, and the idol out of the house of the LORD, and all the altars that he had built in the mount of the house of the LORD, and in Jerusalem, and cast *them* out of the city. **And he repaired the altar of the LORD, and sacrificed thereon peace offerings and thank offerings, and commanded Judah to serve the LORD God of Israel**. Nevertheless the people did sacrifice still in the high places, *yet* unto the LORD their God only. Now the rest of the acts of Manasseh, and his prayer unto his God, and the words of the seers that spake to him in the name of the LORD God of Israel, behold, they *are written* in the book of the kings of Israel" (verses 15-18).

From Judah's Captivity in Babylon until the Time of Jesus Christ. Over a twenty-year period, from 605 BC to 585 BC, King Nebuchadnezzar's armies attacked Judah and finally removed the Jews to Babylon. After seventy years of captivity, a few thousand Jews returned to Judea under the leadership of Ezra and Nehemiah. Then, for a period of about 120 years—during the time of Ezra and the priests of the Great Synagogue (which ended in 305 BC)—the Jews properly kept the Sabbath and holy days.

The Jews were greatly influenced by the Greek civilization imposed on them by Alexander the Great and his successors. During this time, they again apostatized from God and thoroughly adopted the customs and language of the Greeks. By the 170s BC, the Jews had totally polluted the temple of God and were again worshiping pagan gods. God sent the armies of

Antiochus Epiphanes to punish them. In 168 BC, Antiochus desecrated God's temple in Jerusalem by setting up an image of the sun god and slaughtering a swine on the altar of burnt offerings.

There were various revivals during the Maccabean era (from 167 BC to 63 BC). Rome conquered Palestine at the end of that era. The Hellenistic Sadducees retained control of the temple during this period—but only in competition with the Pharisees, another major religious sect of the Jews. From this time on through the ministry of Jesus Christ and the apostles, God's seventh-day Sabbath and annual holy days were continually observed. New Testament Gentile Christians also observed these weekly and yearly holy days.

In the next chapter we will take a closer look at the seventh-day Sabbath—the day God created holy and commanded His people to observe.

PART THREE

God's Feasts
And
Holy Days

Who and What Is a True Christian?

The world has various ideas about who and what a "Christian" is or isn't. Some think a Christian is anyone born into a Christian-professing family and christened by a priest or minister. Others say a Christian is one who has "given his heart to the Lord" and is "born again"—or perhaps one who simply **claims** to be a Christian.

Is it possible, however, for someone to live and die **assuming** that he or she is a Christian—only to find out in the Judgment that God **never recognized their brand** of "Christianity"? Christ, in fact, warned of that very possibility in Matt. 7:21-23.

What truly makes a person a Christian? How does GOD describe a Christian in His inspired word—the Bible?

Serious followers of Christ will diligently study their Bibles to understand the true definition of a Christian—and to make sure that they are, indeed, true Christians (II Tim. 3:15-17). They will have their minds and hearts set to love God the Father and Jesus Christ with all their hearts and all their minds and all their strength (Mark 12:28-30). They will be committed to **live by every word of God** (Matt. 4:4; Luke 4:4; Deut 8:3), proving all things from the Scriptures (I Thess. 5:21; Acts 17:10-12).

No Longer Under the Penalty of Sin

Crucial to understanding the **Bible definition** of a Christian is the fact that all human beings have been sinners, including ourselves (Rom. 3:23). The penalty for sin is permanent death (Rom. 6:23). A Christian is one who has come to realize that he or she had been under that death penalty and in need of a Savior. A Christian understands that Jesus Christ **paid that penalty** by dying on the cross when He was completely innocent of any sin (II Cor. 5:21; I John 2:2; 4:10; Rev. 1:5; 5:9).

A Christian learns just **what, specifically, is sin**—and what brought the death penalty upon them in the first place. Again, the world has its own ideas about what sin is or isn't, but the Bible defines sin for us as the **transgression of the law** of God (I John 3:4).

A true Christian, then, is one who has had the blood of Jesus Christ's sacrificial death applied to him or to her—but only after having acknowledged and **repented** of their sins (toward God the Father) and accepted Christ as their personal Savior (Acts 3:19; 2:38; Ezek. 18:21-23). Repentance literally means a change of mind and attitude, as well as a complete **change of conduct.** In repentance, one literally **turns from** the way of sin (breaking God's law) that leads to death (Prov. 14:12; 16:25; Matt. 7:13) and begins walking God's way—the true, Christian **way of life** (John 14:4-6; Acts 16:17; 18:25-26; I John 2:3-6).

Living in God's Grace

In order to become a Christian one has to be baptized, by full water immersion, into the name of the Father, the Son and the Holy Spirit. After the laying on of hands (Heb. 6:2), the new convert receives the gift of the Holy Spirit from Christ and the Father, by which a person is begotten as a new creation in Jesus Christ (Mark 1:8; Acts 2:38; 8:14-17; II Cor. 1:22; I John 3:9, 22-24).

By simply believing in Jesus Christ and in His name, repenting of sin, and asking God the Father's forgiveness, one comes under God's saving **grace** (Rom. 3:23-26; 6:23) This grace (which is so precious!) is a **free gift** from God—totally undeserved by anyone. No amount of effort by anyone could ever come close to earning this gift of God's favor. Being a "good person" will not earn you salvation—for God does not "owe" salvation to anyone! "For by grace you have been saved through faith, and this *especially* is not of your own selves; *it is* the gift of God" (Eph. 2:8-9).

Once baptized—and having received the gift of God's Holy Spirit—what should the newly converted Christian then do? Can a true Christian continue living as before? Does being "under grace" mean that one can go back and continue practicing what he or she supposedly repented of? Absolutely not! The apostle Paul makes it clear that one is not to continue to **live in sin**—continually transgressing the laws and commandments of God. Notice Romans 6:1-3: "What then shall we say? **Shall we continue in sin, so that grace may abound**? MAY IT NEVER BE! We who died to sin, how shall we live any longer therein? Or are you ignorant that we, as many as were baptized into Christ Jesus, were baptized into His death?"

A New Life in Christ

Notice how Paul goes on in Romans six to describe the **new life** of a true Christian. "Therefore, we were buried with Him through the baptism into the death; so that, just as Christ was raised from *the* dead by the glory of the Father, in the same way, we also should **walk in newness of life**. For if we have been conjoined together in the likeness of His death, so also shall we be *in the likeness* of *His* resurrection. Knowing this, that our old man was co-crucified with *Him* in order that the body of sin might be destroyed, so that we might no longer be enslaved to sin; because the one who has died *to sin* has been justified from sin. Now if we died together with Christ, we believe that we shall also live with Him, knowing that Christ, having been raised from *the* dead, dies no more; death no longer has any dominion over Him. For when He died, He died unto sin once for all; but in that He lives, He lives unto God. In the same way also, you should indeed reckon yourselves to be **dead to sin, but alive to God** through Christ Jesus our Lord. Therefore, do not let sin rule in your mortal body by obeying it in the lusts thereof. Likewise, do not yield your members as instruments of unrighteousness to sin; rather, yield yourselves to God as those who are alive from *the* dead, and your members *as* instruments of right-eousness to God" (Rom. 6:4-13, emphasis added).

In both the parable of the pounds (Luke 19:11-27) and the parable of the talents (Matt. 25:14-30) Christ makes it clear that once having received a gift from God, one is not expected to sit on it or bury it—but to **build on it**, to increase it. Christians are to grow spiritually to become ever more like Jesus and the Father (II Pet. 1:3-11; 3:18; Eph. 4:11-13; 5:1). With this goal in mind, the true Christian studies his or her Bible regularly (II Tim. 2:15) to learn to **follow the example** set by Christ when He walked the earth in the flesh (John 13:15; 14:6; I Pet. 2:21; I John 2:6). In this way, God leads one through the power of His Holy Spirit and creates in each Christian His godly character (Eph. 2:10) and the mind of Christ (Phil. 2:5).

Christ's Example Shows the Way

What was the example Jesus Christ set for His followers? For starters, He perfectly kept His Father's commandments (John 15:10). His life's example, however, was not merely a legalistic, letter-of-the-law obedience—it was obedience from the heart, be-cause He loved the Father with his **whole being**. A true Christian is to love God the Father and Jesus Christ with all his heart, all his mind, all his soul, and all his strength—which is the greatest com-mandment of all (Matt. 22:37-40). In this passage Jesus declares that LOVE, whether toward God or neighbor, is the basis for all of God's spiritual law. Each precept of the law merely tells us **how to love**. Also, there is a **spirit and intent** behind every law or com-mand of God—and that intent is best summed up in one word, LOVE. If God tells us to do (or not to do) something, His motiva-tion is always love (I John 4:8).

In the Sermon on the Mount (Matt. 5, 6, 7), Christ outlined how the spirit and intent of the law translates into personal conduct. Belief in the principles He has taught, however, is not enough—for they are of value only IF one **applies and lives by them** (Matt.

7:24-27).   A true Christian—who loves God and knows that His laws are based on love—will in faith obey from the heart whatever He asks of him or her (John 14:15; I John 5:3).   And a Christian's obedience will not be based on fear (of losing salvation, etc.), or because it "earns" them anything—but will be motivated by their love toward God, and because they understand that heartfelt obedience empowers them to become more and more like God the Father and Jesus Christ.

Many, unfortunately, mistakenly think that love and obedience to God's commandments are somehow opposites—in conflict with one another.   Nothing could be further from the truth!   Often, those who claim to be Christian will say they "love the Lord" or "know the Lord"—yet they fail to obey Him.   The apostle John has an answer for such people.   "And by this *standard* we know that we know Him: if we keep [obey] His commandments.   The one who says, 'I know Him,' and does not keep [obey] His commandments, is a liar, and the truth is not in him.   On the other hand, *if* anyone is keeping [obeying] His Word, truly in this one the love of God is being perfected.   By this *means* we know that we are in Him.   Anyone who claims to dwell in Him is obligating himself also to walk even as He Himself walked" (I John 2:3-6).

A Spirit-led Life

Many churchgoers assume they are already pretty good people.   The apostle Paul, on the other hand—after relating how he also did that which was not right—said of himself, "O wretched man that I am!" (Rom. 7:14-24).   Why did a holy apostle and man of God call himself "wretched"?   Because he understood that his own human nature was not godly—and he was honest and humble enough to admit it.   He likewise admitted that—even after conversion—his old carnal nature still led him to sin for which he had to repent and ask forgiveness.

Notice his explanation of human nature in Romans 8:7-14: "Because the carnal mind [the mind of the unconverted] *is* enmity against God, for it is not subject to the law of God; neither indeed can it *be*.   Now then, those who are in *the* flesh cannot please God.   However, you are not in *the* flesh, but in *the* Spirit, if *the* Spirit of God is indeed dwelling within you.   But if anyone does not have *the* Spirit of Christ, he does not belong to Him.   Now if Christ *be* within you, the body *is* indeed dead because of sin; however, the Spirit *is* life because of righteousness.   Now if the Spirit of Him Who raised Jesus from *the* dead is dwelling within you, He Who raised Christ from *the* dead will also quicken your mortal bodies because of His Spirit that dwells within you.   So then, brethren, we are not debtors to the flesh, to live according to *the* flesh; because if you are living according to *the* flesh, you shall die; but if by *the* Spirit you are putting to death the deeds of the body, you shall live. For as many as **are led by *the* Spirit of God**, these are *the* sons of God" (emphasis added).

A true Christian is one who is **led by the Spirit of God**. In order to grow in that Spirit, which is needed to obey God and grow more like Him, a true Christian draws on the Holy Spirit through regular prayer and Bible study and occasional fasting. Christ taught His disciples to pray (Matt 6:5-15; Luke 18:1-14) and set an example by beginning each day with prayer (Mark 1:35). The Bible is the "God-breathed" words of God (II Tim. 3:16; I Pet. 1:11-12), and is also a powerful source of God's Spirit. Concerning the very words which He spoke, Christ said "they are spirit and they are life" (John 6:63). He also taught the right approach to fasting (Matt. 6:16-18).

One might ask, "How does **faith** fit into all of this?" In the 11th chapter of Hebrews (often called the "faith chapter"), we find example after example of those who **"by faith"** performed something that God had commanded. In each case, those faithful demonstrated their faith by obedience to God. Clearly, **faith and obedience go hand in hand** (Heb. 11:7-38; Rev. 14:12). To think they are somehow at odds with one another is a gross error. A true Christian's faith will **show in what he or she does** (James 2:17-18, 26). It was Abraham's **obedience** to God, by faith, that made him "the father of the faithful" (James 2:21-24). When Christ returns, He will bring His reward with Him and render to each person "according as his **work** shall be" (Rev. 22:12).

Finally, a true Christian will fellowship with others of like mind when possible—again following the example of Jesus Christ (Mark 1:21; Heb. 10:25). By fellowshiping with one another, Christians also fellowship with God (I John 1:3)—thus strengthening their relationship with God and growing in His Way. A true Christian **demonstrates his or her love** for one another by serving and giving materially to those in need (Matt. 25:31-46; I John 3:17, 18)—as well as by praying for and encouraging one another (James 5:16). All of these are expressions of the true love of God.

This, then, is the **Bible description of a true Christian**— one who, through God's grace, has turned from a life of sin and death to a life of love, obedience and the good works of faith as led and empowered by God's Holy Spirit.

CHAPTER EIGHT

Which Day of Worship
Did God Make Holy?

Throughout their history the children of Israel and Judah continually rejected the commandments of God. In particular, they refused to keep God's Sabbath and holy days. At the temple of God in Jerusalem, they literally turned their backs on God to worship the sun and various occult gods. Generation after generation, they repeatedly and grievously transgressed against God. Yet, in His love and mercy for His people and for the sake of His promises to Abraham, God sent numerous faithful prophets over hundreds of years with warnings and calls to repentance. In spite of the repeated warnings, both Israel and Judah refused to repent. Finally, as punishment for their sins, God sent them into captivity at the hands of their enemies.

Ignoring the record of the Old Testament, apostate Orthodox Christendom has in defiance of God **perpetuated the sins of ancient Israel and Judah**. While its leadership professes to represent the God of the Bible and to claim His authority, its popes, priests, ministers and evangelists actually oppose God by **rejecting** much of His Word. In fact, the Roman Catholic Church today accepts and observes the *traditions* of the "church fathers" and various papal proclamations—claiming that they are as binding and authoritative as the Word of God. In practice, however, such traditions and papal proclamations actually *supersede* the authority of the Word of God. Protestants also accept as authoritative the traditions of the "church fathers," and falsely teach that Jesus abolished the Law of God. As a result, they practice the very things God commands them to avoid—even while professing to serve Him! (See Appendix F, *Rome's War Against Against the Christian Passover, God's Sabbath and Holy Days*, p. 238)

The apostle Peter prophesied that this would happen. "But there were also false prophets among the people [of ancient Israel and Judah], as indeed there will be **false teachers among you, who will stealthily introduce destructive heresies, personally denying *the* Lord who bought them**, and bringing swift destruction upon themselves. And many people will follow *as authoritative* their destructive ways; *and* because of them, **the way of the truth will be blasphemed**. Also, through insatiable greed they will with enticing messages exploit you for gain; for whom the judgment of old is in *full* force, and their destruction is *ever* watching" (II Pet. 2:1-3).

The Scriptures: The Word of Truth from the God of Truth

God is the God of truth, and it is impossible for Him to lie. The apostle Paul wrote, "Paul, *a* servant of God and *an* apostle of Jesus Christ, according to *the* faith of God's elect and *the* knowledge of *the* truth that *is* according to godliness; in *the* hope of eternal life, which **God Who cannot lie** promised before the ages of time" (Titus 1:1-2). Also: "In this *way* God, desiring more abundantly to show the heirs of the promise the unchangeable nature of His own purpose, confirmed *it* by an oath; so that by two immutable things, in which *it was* **impossible** *for* **God to lie…**" (Heb. 6:17-18).

In addition, the God of truth keeps truth *forever*. As the psalmist wrote, the one Who "made heaven, and earth, the sea, and all that [are] therein" also **"keepeth truth for ever"** (Psa. 146:6). The heavens and the earth are witnesses of His truth: "Give ear, **O ye heavens**, and I will speak; and hear, **O earth**, the words of my mouth. My doctrine shall drop as the rain, my speech shall distil as the dew, as the small rain upon the tender herb, and as the showers upon the grass: because I will publish the name of the LORD: ascribe ye greatness unto our God. *He is* the Rock [i.e., Jesus Christ, I Cor. 10:4], **his work** *is* **perfect: for all his ways** *are* **judgment: a God of truth and without iniquity, just and right** *is* **he**" (Deut. 32:1-4).

Jesus Christ, the true Savior of the world, verified the truth of God, saying, **"Your Word is the truth"** (John 17:17). Of Himself, He said, "**I am the way, and the truth, and the life**; no one comes to the Father except through Me" (John 14:6); and, "The heaven and the earth shall pass away, but **My words shall never pass away**" (Mark 13:31).

Much of the truth of God has been revealed to men through the laws and commandments that God has given. Psalm 119 says: "Thy righteousness *is* an everlasting righteousness, and **thy law** *is* **the truth**" (verse 142); "Thou *art* near, O LORD; and **all thy commandments** *are* **truth**" (verse 151); "Therefore **I esteem all** *thy* **precepts** *concerning* **all** *things to be* **right;** *and* **I hate every false way**" (verse 128). The reader is encouraged to read and study all of Psalm 119, as the chapter is a prophecy of Jesus' own attitude toward God's Word. Because Jesus Himself esteemed God's Word as truth, we can be sure that His Word *is* the absolute truth—God-breathed from the God of truth (II Tim. 3:15-16).

With this in mind, we ought to eagerly examine the Scriptures in search of the truth. First century believers in Berea were commended for their diligence in searching the Scriptures, as the writer of the book of Acts notes: "Now these [of Berea] were more noble than those in Thessalonica, *for* they received the Word with all **readiness of mind** *and* **examined the Scriptures daily** *to see* if these things were so" (Acts 17:11).

We also ought to study so that we might learn to *rightly divide* the Word of truth. The apostle Paul encouraged Timothy: "**Diligently** *study* to show yourself approved unto God, a workman who does not *need to be* ashamed, **rightly dividing the Word of the truth**" (II Tim. 2:15). Paul wrote to the believers in Thessalonica, "**Prove all things**. Hold fast *to that which* is good" (I Thes. 5:21).

David wrote, "Teach me thy way, O LORD; **I will walk in thy truth** [as a way of life]" (Psa. 86:11). And Jesus said, "Man shall not live by bread alone, but by every word of God that proceeds out of the mouth of

God" (Matt. 4:4; Luke 4:4). This teachable attitude and approach—coupled with the *Fourteen Rules of Bible Study* (See Appendix G, Page 242)—will bring us understanding of the truth of the Word of God.

A Survey of the Seventh-Day Sabbath in the Old Testament

The following account from the book of Genesis reveals that the weekly seventh-day Sabbath is a special creation of God set aside by Him from the beginning. "Thus the heavens and the earth were finished, and all the host of them. And on [or, "by the beginning of"] the seventh day God ended his work which he had made; and he rested on the seventh day from all his work which he had made. **And God blessed the seventh day, and sanctified it: because that in it he had rested from all his work which God created and made**" (Gen. 2:1-3).

Sanctifying the Sabbath means that God **set it apart** or **made it holy**. Since God is holy, only He has the power and authority to make or declare something holy. God made the Sabbath day holy by personally taking five specific actions: 1) God created it; 2) God blessed it; 3) God sanctified it; 4) God put His presence in it; and, 5) God rested on it. **Therefore, no man has the power or authority to change, annul or abrogate what God has personally made holy**.

The weekly cycle of seven days has been the same from creation. On the Roman calendar today, the seventh-day Sabbath is called Saturday. This day is the weekly Sabbath of God that He personally set aside and made holy from the beginning of creation.

The Ancient Righteous Patriarchs Kept the Sabbath. The laws of God have been in effect from the beginning (Rom. 5:12-14). If there was no law for the 2,500 years from Adam to Moses, there would have been no sin—because where there is no law, sin is not imputed (Rom. 4:15). Sin is the transgression of the law (I John 3:4)—therefore if there is sin, there is law. The fact that God passed judgment on mankind and destroyed them with a universal flood because of gross wickedness and sin (Gen. 6:5-13), proves that the laws and commandments of God have always been in effect.

The patriarchs Abel, Enoch, and Noah walked with God (Gen. 5:22; 6:9). They were righteous in that they believed God and kept His laws and commandments (Heb. 11:4-5, 7; 12:24). Since all the commandments of God are righteousness, this means the patriarchs kept the seventh-day Sabbath as well as all the other commandments.

After the flood, Abraham, the father of the faithful, received God's promises because he believed and obeyed Him (Gen. 12:1-4; 22:1-18). Abraham's faith was counted as righteousness (Gen. 15:6). Abraham also had righteous works. The apostle James, the brother of the Lord Jesus, writes of Abraham's faith and works: "But are you willing to understand, O foolish man, that faith without works is dead? Was not Abraham our father justified by works when he offered up Isaac, his own son, upon the altar?

Do you not see that faith was working together with his works, and by works *his* faith was perfected? And the scripture was fulfilled which says, 'Now Abraham believed God, and it was reckoned to him for righteousness;' and he was called a friend of God. You see, then, that a man is justified by works, and not by faith only" (Jas. 2:20-24).

When the promises given to Abraham were passed on to his son Isaac, God specifically told Isaac that he was receiving the promises because of Abraham's obedience. The Lord appeared to Isaac and said, "Sojourn in this land, and I will be with thee, and will bless thee; for unto thee, and unto thy seed, I will give all these countries, and I will perform the oath which I sware unto Abraham thy father; and I will make thy seed to multiply as the stars of heaven, and will give unto thy seed all these countries; and in thy seed shall all the nations of the earth be blessed; **because that Abraham obeyed my voice, and kept my charge, my commandments, my statutes, and my laws**" (Gen. 26:3-5).

Since God does not change (Mal. 3:6), and Jesus Christ is "the same, yesterday, today and forever" (Heb. 13:8), we can conclude that the laws, commandments and statutes that Abraham kept were the same as those given later to Israel at Mount Sinai.

Weeks before the Israelites arrived at Mount Sinai, God miraculously provided manna for them to eat. On the sixth day of the week, God sent a *double portion* of manna; He sent none on the seventh day. Thus the children of Israel would not need to gather food on the seventh day and could observe the Sabbath rest. Some, however, went out on the Sabbath to gather manna anyway—but didn't find any. Through Moses, God asked, "How long refuse ye to keep my commandments and my laws?" (Ex. 16:28).

At Mount Sinai God expounded upon the Fourth commandment, saying, "**Remember the sabbath day, to keep it holy**. Six days shalt thou labour, and do all thy work: **but the seventh day *is* the sabbath of the LORD thy God**: *in it* thou shalt not do any work, thou, nor thy son, nor thy daughter, thy manservant, nor thy maidservant, nor thy cattle, nor thy stranger that *is* within thy gates: for *in* six days the LORD made heaven and earth, the sea, and all that in them *is*, and rested the seventh day: wherefore the LORD blessed the sabbath day, and hallowed it" (Ex. 20:8-11).

Moses recounted the Ten Commandments in Deuteronomy five, stressing that God's Sabbath was not only to be *remembered*, it was to be *kept*: "**Keep the sabbath** day to sanctify it, as the LORD thy God hath commanded thee. Six days thou shalt labour, and do all thy work: **but the seventh day *is* the sabbath of the LORD thy God**: *in it* thou shalt not do any work, thou, nor thy son, nor thy daughter, nor thy manservant, nor thy maidservant, nor thine ox, nor thine ass, nor any of thy cattle, nor thy stranger that *is* within thy gates; that thy manservant and thy maidservant may rest as well as thou. And remember that thou wast a servant in the land of Egypt, and *that* the LORD thy God brought thee out thence through a mighty hand and by a stretched out arm: **therefore the LORD thy God commanded thee**

to keep the sabbath day" (Deut. 5:12-15).

In Leviticus, God declares that the Sabbath is a holy convocation: "Six days shall work be done: but the seventh day *is* the sabbath of rest, an holy convocation; ye shall do no work *therein*: it is the sabbath of the LORD in all your dwellings" (Lev. 23:3).

Sabbath-Keeping Is A Perpetual
Sign Between God and His People

There are a number of key Scriptures concerning Sabbath-keeping as a special sign between God and His people. For example:

"And the LORD spake unto Moses, saying, 'Speak thou also unto the children of Israel [The true Church of God is called the "Israel of God" in Gal. 6:16.], saying, "Verily **my sabbaths** ye shall keep: for it [the keeping of God's Sabbaths] *is* a **sign between me and you** throughout your generations; that *ye* **may know that I** *am* **the LORD that doth sanctify you**. Ye shall keep the sabbath therefore; for it *is* holy unto you: every one that defiles it shall surely be put to death [The wages of sin is death, Rom. 6:23, and sin is the transgression of the law, I John 3:4.]: For whosoever doeth *any* work therein, that soul shall be cut off from among his people" ' " (Ex. 31:12-14)

"Six days may work be done: but in the seventh *is* the sabbath of rest, holy to the LORD: whosoever doeth *any* work in the sabbath day, he shall surely be put to death. **Wherefore the children of Israel shall keep the sabbath, to observe the sabbath throughout their generations,** *for* **a perpetual covenant. It** *is* **a sign between me and the children of Israel forever:** for *in* six days the LORD made heaven and earth, and on the seventh day he rested and was refreshed" (verses 15-17).

God declared, "My sabbaths ye shall keep." (As we will see in the next chapter, this means not only the weekly seventh-day Sabbath, but also the annual holy days—all of which are Sabbaths.) The keeping of His Sabbaths is a sign between God and His people. Those who do not keep His Sabbaths are transgressing God's commandments, regardless of what they profess.

This **perpetual covenant**—meaning it cannot be changed or abolished—of Sabbath-keeping is **in addition** to the covenant that was ratified between God and the children of Israel as recorded in Exodus 24. As such, the Sabbath covenant of Exodus 31 supersedes or transcends all other covenants. There is little doubt that this perpetual covenant of Sabbath-keeping was included in every covenant of God from creation—because the Sabbath was *from the beginning*!

Sabbath Breaking Is Rebellion Against God

In Ezekiel twenty, God commanded the children of Israel to put away the idols of Egypt and keep His laws and Sabbaths. "And I gave them my statutes, and showed them my judgments, which *if* a man do, he shall live in them. Moreover also I gave them **my sabbaths**, to be a sign between me and them, that they might know that I *am* the LORD that sanctify them.

"**But the house of Israel rebelled against me in the wilderness**: they walked not in my statutes, and they despised my judgments, which *if* a man do, he shall even live in them; and **my sabbaths they greatly polluted**..." (Ezk. 20:11-13). Because of the sins of the children of Israel in the wilderness, God punished them with forty years of wandering—until all those over twenty years of age died (Num. 14:34).

At the end of the forty years, and just before they went into the Promised Land, God again pleaded with the children of Israel: "But I said unto their children in the wilderness, 'Walk ye not in the statutes of your fathers, neither observe their judgments, nor defile yourselves with their idols: I *am* the LORD your God; walk in my statutes, and keep my judgments, and do them; and **hallow my sabbaths; and they shall be a sign** between me and you, that ye may know that I *am* the LORD your God' " (Ezk. 20:18-20).

Verse 21: "Notwithstanding, the children **rebelled** against me: they walked not in my statutes, neither kept my judgments to do them, which *if* a man do, he shall even live in them: **they polluted my sabbaths**...." Israel rejected God's pleas to obey Him and keep His Sabbaths. They rebelled and refused to keep His commandments and laws. In their rebellion against God, they worshipped the gods of the nations around them.

Blessings of Sabbath-Keeping

The prophet Isaiah prophesied that in the end times, just before the return of Jesus Christ, salvation would directly involve Sabbath-keeping. "Thus says the LORD, 'Keep ye judgment and do justice: for my salvation *is* near to come [beginning with Jesus' ministry in 26 AD until His second coming], and my righteousness to be revealed. Blessed *is* the man *that* doeth this, and the son of man *that* layeth hold on it; that keepeth the sabbath from polluting it, and keepeth his hand from doing any evil.... [Blessed also are] the sons of the stranger, that join themselves to the LORD [the conversion of Gentiles through Jesus Christ], to serve Him, and to love the name of the LORD, to be his servants, [and] every one that keepeth the sabbath from polluting it, and **taketh hold of my covenant** [the perpetual Sabbath-keeping covenant of Exodus 31 and the New Covenant through Jesus Christ]' " (Isa. 56:1-2, 6).

God blesses those who seek to please Him by keeping His holy Sabbath. "If thou turn away thy foot from the sabbath, *from* doing thy pleasure on my holy day: and call the sabbath a delight, the holy of the LORD, honourable; and shalt honour him, not doing thine own ways, nor finding thine own pleasure, nor speaking *thine own* words: Then shalt thou delight thyself in the LORD; and I will cause thee to ride upon the high places of the earth, and feed thee with the heritage of Jacob thy father; for the mouth of the LORD hath spoken *it*" (Isa. 58:13-14).

Sabbath-keeping is not a curse as so many "Christians" have been wrongly taught. Rather, there are **many blessings** for keeping the seventh-day Sabbath. The fact is, curses are the *result of sin*—and sin is the transgression of God's law. Curses do not come from keeping the Sabbath—curses come from breaking the Sabbath. Anyone who rejects the Fourth Commandment and does not keep the seventh-day Sabbath **is sinning**.

The Old Testament reveals the following truths about the Sabbath:

• The Sabbath is a weekly memorial of God's creation of heaven and earth.
• The Sabbath is a great *gift* from God *to mankind.*
• The Sabbath is the only day of the week that God has specifically blessed and made holy.
• The Sabbath is a day of ceasing from all labor.
• The Sabbath is a holy convocation—a day of assembly and worship.
• God commands *all* mankind to keep the Sabbath.
• God gave the Sabbath as a sign of remembrance of His covenant with His people.
• Sabbath-keeping is a perpetual covenant.
• God owns the Sabbath. "**But the seventh day is the Sabbath of the Lord**."

This brief survey concerning Sabbath-keeping has covered only the more important Old Testament passages. The reader is encouraged to study the many other scriptures directly relating to the Sabbath.

A Survey of the Seventh-Day Sabbath in the New Testament

In the beginning God created all things, and the one Who did the actual creating was the one Who became Jesus Christ. The apostle John wrote of this fundamental truth: "In *the* beginning was the Word, and the Word was with God, and the Word was God. He was in *the* beginning with God. All things came into being through Him, and not even one *thing* that was created came into being without Him.... And the Word became flesh, and tabernacled among us (and we ourselves beheld His glory, *the* glory as of *the* only begotten with *the* Father), full of grace and truth" (John 1:1-3, 14). The book of Hebrews confirms this understanding. "God, Who spoke to the fathers at different times in the past and in many ways by the prophets, has spoken to us in these last days by *His* Son, Whom He has appointed heir of all things, **by Whom also He made the worlds**; Who, being *the* brightness of *His* glory and *the* exact image of His person, and upholding all things by the word of His own power, when He had by Himself purged our sins, sat down at *the* right hand of the Majesty on high" (Heb. 1:1-3).

Again, the apostle Paul wrote that Jesus Christ created all things: "Because by Him [Jesus Christ] were all things created, the things in heaven and the things on earth, the visible and the invisible, whether *they be* thrones, or lordships, or principalities, or powers: all things were created by Him and for Him. And He is before all, and by Him all things subsist. And He is the Head of the body, the church; Who is *the* beginning, *the* firstborn from among the dead, so that in all things He Himself might hold the pre-eminence" (Col. 1:16-18, also see Heb. 2:9-10).

This knowledge is of the utmost significance because it means that **Jesus Christ is the Creator of the seventh-day Sabbath. He is the Lord God Who blessed it, sanctified it, and commanded men to keep it as a perpetual covenant**. Moreover, as the Lord God of the Old Testament, He gave the Ten Commandments and all of the laws, commandments, statutes and judgments to ancient Israel at Mt. Sinai.

Jesus Christ did not Abolish the Law or the Prophets

When Jesus Christ began His ministry, He taught concerning the laws and commandments of God, and the prophets, saying, "**Do not think** [do not even let it enter your mind] **that I have come to abolish the Law or the Prophets; I did not come to abolish, but to fulfill**. For truly I say to you, **until the heaven and the earth shall pass away, one jot or one tittle shall in no way pass from the law until everything has been fulfilled**" (Matt. 5:17-18). Since heaven and earth still exist, **the laws and commandments of God are still in full force and effect**!

Jesus further taught regarding the commandments: "Therefore, whoever shall break one of these least commandments, and shall teach men so, shall be called least in the kingdom of heaven; **but whoever shall practice and teach *them*, this one shall be called great in the kingdom of heaven**" (verse 19). Christ Himself made it clear that we are blessed, not cursed, if we do and teach even the "least" of the commandments.

In another account, when a young rich man asked Jesus what he must do to inherit eternal life, Jesus gave this answer: "If you desire to enter into life, keep [Greek, *poiew*, meaning, "to practice," "to do"] the commandments" (Matt. 19:17). The man responded by saying that he had kept the commandments from his childhood. Jesus then told the young man that he should sell all that he owned and give to the poor, because commandment-keeping—while required to enter into life—is not enough by itself.

The apostles also taught commandment-keeping to New Testament Christians. In the 90s AD, the apostle John wrote that Christians were to keep the commandments of God. "And whatever we may ask we receive from Him **because we keep His commandments and practice those things that are pleasing in His sight.... And the one who keeps His commandments is dwelling in Him, and He in him**; and by this we know that He is dwelling in us: by the Spirit which He has given to us" (I John 3:22, 24).

When Peter and the other apostles were called before the Sanhedrin for preaching salvation through Jesus Christ, they gave this answer: "**We are obligated to obey God rather than men**.... And we are His witnesses of these things, as *is* also **the Holy Spirit, which God has given to those who obey Him**" (Acts 5:29, 32). We must obey God over men—and where the teachings of men contradict the Word of God, we must be willing to discard such teachings. If we are obedient to His Word, God will enable us to further discern truth from error.

God's laws, commandments, statutes and judgments are holy, righteous and good—and God has given them to us for our well-being, **so that He might bless us in everything**, because He loves us. (See Deut. 4:1, 39-40; 5:29-33; 6:1-6, 17-18, 24-25; 7:6-15; 10:12-15; 11:1-28.)

Contrary to the Word of God, Dr. Russell K. Tardo typifies the **lawless** Protestant viewpoint by claiming that all the laws and commandments of God have been abolished, rendered inoperative, or fulfilled. "In fact, the whole law of Moses has been rendered inoperative. The New Testament message is clear for all who have 'ears to hear.' **The whole of the law of Moses has been rendered inoperative by the death of the Lord Jesus. The law, in its entirety, no longer has any immediate and forensic authority or jurisdiction whatsoever over anyone**.... Christ is the complete end and fulfillment of all of the laws' 613 commandments, ending their jurisdiction over us completely" (Tardo, *Sunday Facts & Sabbath Fiction*, p. 26-27). To allege that Christ completely fulfilled the Law and brought it to an end is absolute nonsense—the idea creates an untenable "lawless grace"—contradicting Jesus Christ's own plain teachings.

All of God's Laws are Based on Love

Jesus Christ taught that the whole foundation for the laws and commandments of God is the **love of God**. A doctor of the law asked Jesus, "Master, which commandment *is the* great commandment in the law?" Jesus answered, "'**You shall love *the* Lord your God with all your heart, and with all your soul, and with all your mind.' This is *the* first and greatest commandment**; and *the* second *one is* like it: '**You shall love your neighbor as yourself**.' **On these two commandments hang all the Law and the Prophets.**" (Matt. 22:36-40; also see Deut. 6:4-5).

Love is *not* contrary to commandment-keeping, as many religious teachers ignorantly affirm. Rather, all the Law and the Prophets hang on the love of God. In other words, the love of God is the underlying basis for all the laws and commandments of God—the reason they exist in the first place. Law is not opposed to the love of God; instead, law and love complement each other.

Jesus **amplified the meaning** of these two great commandments. Christ, as God manifested in the flesh, was the Lord God of the Old Testament. Therefore, what Jesus said about the commandments of God refers not only to *His* commandments in the New Testament, but also to the commandments *He gave* as the God of the Old Testament. Jesus said, "If you love Me, keep the commandments—namely, My commandments.... **The one who has My commandments and is keeping them, that is the one who loves Me; and the one who loves Me shall be loved by My Father,**

and I will love him and will manifest Myself to him.... If anyone loves Me, he will keep My word; and My Father will love him, and We will come to him and make Our abode with him. **The one who does not love Me does not keep My words; and the word that you hear is not Mine, but the Father's, Who sent Me**" (John 14:15-24).

As this precise translation of the Greek shows, if anyone loves God the Father and Jesus Christ, that love will be made evident by obedience. This means that it is impossible to love God while rejecting or denouncing the laws and commandments of God, regardless of one's "profession of love" toward God. Keeping the commandments of God, which includes the seventh-day weekly Sabbath, is the standard by which we know that we love God. The apostle John wrote, "By this *standard* we know that we love the children of God: **when we love God and keep His commandments. For this is the love of God, that we keep His commandments; and His commandments are not burdensome**" (I John 5:2-3).

John even went so far as to say, "**The one who says, 'I know Him,' and does not keep His commandments, is a liar, and the truth is not in him**. On the other hand, *if* anyone is keeping His Word, truly in this one the love of God is being perfected. By this *means* we know that we are in Him. **Anyone who claims to dwell in Him is obligating himself also to walk even as He Himself walked**" (I John 2:4-6). It is through obedience that the love of God is being perfected in His followers.

How did Jesus walk before God the Father? He loved God and kept His commandments, always doing the things that pleased the Father. "Then Jesus said to them, 'When you have lifted up the Son of man, then you yourselves shall know that I AM, and *that* I do nothing of Myself. But as the Father taught Me, these things I speak. And He Who sent Me is with Me. The Father has not left Me alone because I always do the things that please Him' " (John 8:28-29). Thus, if we are Christ's, then we will love God, keep His commandments, and please Him in everything as Jesus did. "And in this *way* we know that **we are of the truth**, and shall assure our hearts before Him.... And whatever we may ask we receive from Him **because we keep His commandments and practice those things that are pleasing in His sight**" (I John 3:19, 22).

When we keep the Sabbath in a loving and godly way, and worship God "in spirit and truth," it is most pleasing to Him—and our spiritual fellowship is with the Father and the Son. "That which we have seen and have heard we are reporting to you in order that you also may have fellowship with us; for the fellowship—indeed, our fellowship—*is* with the Father and with His own Son, Jesus Christ" (I John 1:3).

Jesus' Teaching and Example
Concerning the Seventh-Day Sabbath

Jesus Christ Kept the Sabbath. Jesus Christ observed the weekly seventh-day Sabbath as a custom. "And He came to Nazareth, where He had been brought up; and **according to His custom, He went into the**

synagogue on the Sabbath day and stood up to read." (Luke 4:16). On that Sabbath, Jesus read from the scroll of Isaiah where it foretold of His ministry of love, mercy, forgiveness and redemption. "And there was given Him *the* book of the prophet Isaiah; and when He had unrolled the scroll, He found the place where it was written, '*The* Spirit of *the* Lord *is* upon Me; for this reason, He has anointed Me to preach the gospel to *the* poor; He has sent Me to heal those who are brokenhearted, to proclaim pardon to *the* captives and recovery of sight to *the* blind, to send forth in deliverance those who have been crushed, to proclaim *the* acceptable year of *the* Lord' " (verses 17-19).

After Jesus left Nazareth, He continued to teach the people throughout all Galilee—particularly on the Sabbath. He never at any time claimed that He had come to do away with the Sabbath commandment. "Then He went down to Capernaum, a city of Galilee, and **taught them on the Sabbath days**. And they were astonished at His teaching: for His word was with authority" (Luke 4:31-32).

The Sabbath, as we have previously discussed, was made to be a blessing for all mankind. Jesus used the Sabbath to preach the gospel, to teach and to personally administer God's love, mercy and blessings through healing and the casting out of demons. Jesus Christ used the Sabbath to release people from sin—**not to lead them into sin**! Hence, Jesus revealed that the Sabbath day is a day of love, mercy, forgiveness, redemption and salvation—a day of blessing!

Jesus Healed on the Sabbath Day

Mark recorded Jesus' healing of a man on the Sabbath day as follows: "And again He went into the synagogue, and a man who had a withered hand was there. And they were watching Him, *to see* if He would heal him **on the Sabbath**, in order that they might accuse Him [notice the picky, hateful, unmerciful attitude of the Jewish religious leaders]. Then He said to the man who had the withered hand, 'Stand up *here* in the center.' And He said to them, 'Is it lawful to do good on the Sabbaths, or to do evil? To save life, or to kill?' But they were silent. **And after looking around at them with anger, being grieved at the hardness of their hearts**, He said to the man, 'Stretch out your hand.' And he stretched *it* out, and his hand was restored *as* sound as the other. Then the Pharisees left *and* immediately took counsel with the Herodians *as to* how they might destroy Him" (Mark 3:1-6).

John also recorded how Jesus healed a man on the Sabbath: "Now a certain man was there who had been *suffering with* an infirmity for thirty-eight years. Jesus saw him lying *there*, and, knowing that he had been there a long time, said to him, 'Do you desire to be made whole?' And the infirm *man* answered Him, 'Sir, I do not have anyone to put me in the pool after the water has been agitated [by an angel]. But while I am going, another *one* steps down before me.' Jesus said to him, 'Arise, take up your bedroll and walk.' And immediately the man was made whole; and he took up his bedroll [probably not much bigger than a small sleeping bag] and walked. Now that day was a Sabbath.

"For this reason, the Jews said to the man who had been healed, 'It is *the* Sabbath *day*. It is not lawful for you to take up your bedroll.' He answered them, 'The one Who made me whole said to me, "Take up your bedroll and walk." ' Then they asked him, 'Who is the one Who said to you, "Take up your bedroll and walk"?' But the man who had been healed did not know Who it was, for Jesus had moved away, *and* a crowd was in the place.

"After these things, Jesus found him in the temple and said to him, 'Behold, you have been made whole. **Sin no more, so that something worse does not happen to you.**'

"And for this cause, the Jews persecuted Jesus and sought to kill Him, because He had done these things on a Sabbath. But Jesus answered them, '**My Father is working until now, and I work**.' So then, on account of this *saying*, the Jews sought all the more to kill Him, not only because He had loosed the Sabbath, but also *because* He had called God His own Father, making Himself equal with God. Therefore, Jesus answered and said to them, 'Truly, truly I say to you, the Son has no power to do anything of Himself, but only what He sees the Father do. For whatever He does, these things the Son also does in the same manner' " (John 5:5-19).

The Jews did not understand that **spiritual works** such as healing the sick, casting out demons, and helping the poor and destitute **on the Sabbath day glorify God**. These acts are a part of the good works of keeping the Sabbath day holy. Jesus did not work for gain. Rather, His was a spiritual work. Moreover, by healing the man and commanding him to pick up his bedroll, Jesus loosed a traditional law of Judaism that had made the Sabbath a burden. In this account, He most assuredly did not abrogate the Sabbath or any other laws of God, as some misguided theologians allege.

God never made the Sabbath day to be a burden for people—for as John wrote, "His commandments are not burdensome." However, the Jewish religious leaders legislated hundreds of letter-of-the-law "do's and don'ts" which burdened the people with rigorous, harsh restrictions. As a result of these man-made laws, the Sabbath became a yoke of bondage to the people. Jesus condemned the scribes and Pharisees for putting these heavy burdens on the people (Matt. 23:4, 14-15). These added traditional laws made it nearly impossible to truly keep the Sabbath as God intended it, as a day for rest, rejoicing, and worshiping God the Father and Jesus Christ in spirit and in truth.

Lord of the Sabbath. Another dispute arose because Christ and His disciples had plucked ears of grain to eat on the Sabbath day. Afterward, Jesus announced, "The Sabbath was made for man, *and* not man for the Sabbath. **Therefore, the Son of man is Lord even of the Sabbath**" (Mark 2:27-28).

Jesus Himself is Lord of the Sabbath because He created, blessed, and sanctified the day. It is the *true* "Lord's Day." **The Sabbath day is the** seventh day of the week, known as Saturday. The Lord's Day of the New Testament is the seventh-day weekly Sabbath—not Sunday, the first day of the week!

The Apostles Kept the Sabbath

Throughout the book of Acts, we find that the apostle Paul taught on the Sabbath. When Paul first began preaching in Greece proper, he observed the Sabbath day, as was his custom. Because there was no synagogue in the area, Paul and his entourage sought out a place of prayer where people were keeping the Sabbath. Luke writes: "And from there *we went* to Philippi, which is *the* primary city in *that* part of Macedonia, *and* a colony. And we stayed in this city *for* a number of days. Then **on the Sabbath**, we went outside the city by a river, where *it* was customary *for* prayer to be *made*; and after sitting down, we spoke to the women who were gathered *there*" (Acts 16:12-13).

When Paul came to Thessalonica, he taught on the Sabbath at a synagogue of the Jews: "And as was the custom with Paul, **he went in to them and for three Sabbaths reasoned with them from the Scriptures**, expounding and demonstrating that it was necessary for Christ to suffer and to rise from *the* dead, and *testifying*, 'This Jesus, Whom I am proclaiming to you, is the Christ.' Now some of them were convinced, and joined themselves to Paul and Silas, including **a great multitude of devout Greeks** [Gentile converts], and of the chief women not a few" (Acts 17:2-4).

Again, in Antioch, Paul taught on the Sabbath at the synagogue. "They came to Antioch of Pisidia: and they went into the synagogue on the Sabbath day *and* sat down" (Acts 13:14). After Paul preached Jesus Christ to them, many of the Jews were offended. However, some of the Jews—and most of the Gentiles—wanted to hear more about the gospel of Jesus Christ. "And when the Jews had gone out of the synagogue, the Gentiles entreated *him* that **these words might be spoken to them on the next Sabbath**. Now after the synagogue had been dismissed, many of the Jews and the proselytes [Gentile converts] who worshiped *there* followed Paul and Barnabas, who, speaking to them, **persuaded them to continue in the grace of God. And on the coming Sabbath** [not the next day, Sunday—but the next *Sabbath*], **almost the whole city was gathered together to hear the Word of God**" (Acts 13:42-44).

If it were indeed true—as taught by theologians and believed by millions of churchgoers—that after the resurrection of Christ the apostles changed the Sabbath from the seventh day of the week to the first day, Paul certainly would have instructed these worship-seekers to come back the very next day, Sunday—but he didn't!

When the apostle Paul was in Corinth, he taught **every Sabbath** for one and a half years. "And he reasoned in the synagogue every Sabbath, and persuaded *both* Jews and Greeks. Now when Silas and Timothy came down from Macedonia, Paul was stirred in his spirit and was earnestly testifying to the Jews *that* Jesus *was* the Christ. But when they set themselves in opposition and were blaspheming, *Paul* shook *his* garments *and* said to them, 'Your blood *be* upon your heads. I am pure *of it*. **From this time forward I will go to the Gentiles.**'

"And after departing from there, he came into *the* house of a certain one named Justus, who worshipped God, whose house adjoined the synagogue. But Crispus, the ruler of the synagogue, believed in the Lord with his whole house; and many Corinthians who heard, believed and were baptized. And the Lord said to Paul in a vision in *the* night, 'Do not be afraid; but speak, and do not be silent, for I am with you; and no one shall set upon you to mistreat you because I have many people in this city.' **And he remained** *there for* **a year and six months teaching the Word of God among them**" (Acts 18:4-11).

These scriptures prove that Paul did not institute Sunday-keeping as a replacement for the seventh-day weekly Sabbath among the Gentile communities.

Grace Does Not Eliminate Sabbath-Keeping. In no way does being under grace eliminate the need to obey the Fourth Commandment. Sabbath-keeping is not opposed to grace. In fact, Paul often taught Gentiles on the Sabbath day about the grace of God. In his epistle to the Romans, Paul taught that grace does not abolish law, rather it establishes law. "[There is] indeed one God Who will justify *the* circumcision by faith, and *the* uncircumcision through faith. Are we, then, abolishing law through faith? MAY IT NEVER BE! Rather, we are establishing law!" (Rom. 3:30-31).

Later in this same epistle to the Romans, Paul refutes the idea that since God's grace covers sin, the more one sins, the more grace is manifest. He makes it clear that a Christian cannot continue to live in sin, transgressing the commandments of God—including the Fourth Commandment. "What then shall we say? **Shall we continue in sin, so that grace may abound? MAY IT NEVER BE! We who died to sin, how shall we live any longer therein**? Or are you ignorant that we, as many as were baptized into Christ Jesus, were baptized into His death?

"Therefore, we were buried with Him through the baptism into the death; so that, just as Christ was raised from *the* dead by the glory of the Father, in the same way, we also should walk in newness of life. For if we have been conjoined together in the likeness of His death, so also shall we be *in the likeness* of *His* resurrection. **Knowing this, that our old man was co-crucified with** *Him* **in order that the body of sin might be destroyed, so that we might no longer be enslaved to sin**; because the one who has died *to sin* [through the operation of baptism] has been justified from sin" (Rom. 6:1-7).

There is not even the slightest hint in the New Testament Scriptures that the apostles of Jesus Christ—including Paul, who was the apostle to the Gentiles—taught that Sunday was the Gentile Sabbath. **Never at any time did they teach that Sunday would replace the seventh-day Sabbath.** All the way through the book of Acts, and in the writings of all the apostles, the Sabbath is upheld.

If You Transgress One of the Commandments, You are Guilty of Breaking them All

From the days of Constantine, Orthodox Christendom has rejected the Fourth Commandment and has replaced it with Sunday-keeping. Yet, as strange as it may seem, those who reject this commandment will insist that since they keep other commandments of God, they are still living within the will of God. But is this true?

In his epistle, James shows that Jesus' teachings concerning the spirit of the law in no way eliminate the need to obey the letter of the law. James explains that Jesus' command to "love your neighbor as yourself" requires **obedience to all of God's commandments**. James specifically refers to the Sixth and Seventh Commandments, and makes it clear that to break any of God's commandments is sin: "**If you are truly keeping** *the* **Royal Law according to the scripture**, 'You shall love your neighbor as yourself,' you are doing well. But if you have respect of persons, **you are practicing sin, being convicted by the law as transgressors; for** *if* **anyone keeps the whole law, but sins in one** *aspect*, **he becomes guilty of all**. For He Who said, 'You shall not commit adultery,' also said, 'You shall not commit murder.' Now if you do not commit adultery, but you commit murder, you have become a transgressor of *the* law. In this manner speak and in this manner behave: as those who are about to be judged by *the* law of freedom" (James 2:8-12).

It is clear that when James wrote of "the Royal Law," he was referring to the laws and commandments of God. Likewise, "the law of freedom" is another reference to the commandments of God—meaning that when people keep the laws and commandments of God, they are **free from sin**. On the other hand, when people do not keep the commandments, they are sinning and are automatically judged by "the Royal Law, the law of freedom."

To borrow from James, "if anyone keeps nine of the commandments, but sins only by breaking the Sabbath command, he is still guilty of being a lawbreaker, as if he had broken them all."

Many Scholars Understand New Testament Sabbath-Keeping

Many theologians have misconstrued Jesus' declaration that He is "Lord of the Sabbath" to mean that He was using His authority to abolish the Sabbath. This interpretation of Jesus' words is completely unfounded. Among those scholars who understand the true meaning of Sabbath-keeping scriptures are the writers of *The Anchor Bible Dictionary*. Note what they have written about these critical verses: "At times Jesus is interpreted to have abrogated or suspended the sabbath commandment on the basis of the controversies brought about by sabbath healings and other acts. Careful analysis of the respective passages does not seem to give credence to this interpretation. The action of plucking the ears of grain on the sabbath by the disciples is particularly important in this matter. Jesus makes a foundational pronouncement at that time in … [an authoritatively] structured statement of antithetic [contrasting] parallelism: 'The sabbath was made for man and not man for the sabbath' (Mark 2:27). The disciples' act of plucking the grain infringed against the rabbinic *halakhah* of minute casuistry [i.e., the Jews' use of false reasoning to create traditional laws to define trivial, frivolous matters] in which it was forbidden to reap, thresh, winnow, and grind on the sabbath (*Sabb.* 7.2). Here again rabbinic sabbath *halakhah* is rejected [by Jesus], as in other sabbath conflicts. **Jesus reforms the sabbath and restores its rightful place as designed in creation, where the sabbath is made for all mankind and not specifically for Israel, as claimed by normative Judaism** (*cf. Jub.* 2:19-20, see D.3). The subsequent logion, "The Son of Man is Lord even of the sabbath" (Mark 2:28; Matt. 12:8; Luke 6:5), indicates that man-made sabbath *halakhah* does not rule the sabbath, but that **the Son of Man as Lord determines the true meaning of the sabbath**. The sabbath activities of Jesus are neither hurtful provocations nor mere protests against rabbinic legal restrictions, but are part of Jesus' essential proclamation of the inbreaking of the kingdom of God in which man is taught the original meaning of the sabbath as the recurring weekly proleptic [anticipated] 'day of the Lord' in which God manifests his healing and saving rulership over man" (*The Anchor Bible Dictionary*, Vol. 5, pp. 854-55, bold emphasis and bracketed comments added).

There Remains Sabbath-Keeping for the People of God

As these scholars have written, the Gospel accounts do not support the widespread belief that Jesus abolished the Sabbath day. Rather, as the Lord of the Sabbath, He taught the true meaning of the Sabbath day and set the example for its proper observance. Christ's apostles continued to keep the Sabbath and to teach the early believers to keep it, as Paul's epistle to the Hebrews clearly demonstrates. The apostle Paul wrote this epistle in 61 AD, more than thirty years after the beginning of the New Testament Church. Even at that time, false ministers were beginning to teach that Sunday, the first day of the week, had replaced the Sabbath. To counter these false teachings, Paul gave the brethren a sober warning that to reject the Sabbath and accept Sunday was sin—just as the children of Israel sinned when they rebelled against God in the wilderness.

Paul drew the comparison between the rebellious Israelites—who were not allowed to enter the Promised Land because of their Sabbath-breaking and occult worship of the sun god—and professing Christians who harden their hearts in disobedience to God. He warned them that just as the Israelites were not allowed to enter the Promised Land because of their unbelief and Sabbath-breaking, they likewise would not enter into the Kingdom of God because of their unbelief and Sabbath-breaking. "For He spoke in a certain place about the seventh *day* in this manner: '**And God rested on the seventh day from all His works**'; and again concerning this: 'If they shall enter into My rest—' Consequently, since it remains *for* some to enter into it, and those who had previously heard the gospel did not enter in because of disobedience, again He marks out a certain day, 'Today,' saying in David after so long a time (exactly as it has been quoted above), 'Today, if you will hear His voice, harden not your hearts.' For if Joshua had given them rest, He would not have spoken *long* afterwards of another day. **There remains therefore, Sabbath-keeping** [Greek, σαββατισμος—*sabbatismos*] **for the people of God**" (Heb. 4:4-9).

Paul does not say, "There remains Sabbath-keeping for the Jews." He clearly declared, "There remains Sabbath-keeping for **the people of God**"—Gentiles as well as Jews (I Pet. 2:10 and Eph. 2:11-13).

Paul carries his instruction even further, showing that we must keep the Sabbath or risk losing salvation. "For the one who has entered into His rest [keeps the Sabbath], he also has ceased from his own works, as God *did* from His own *works* [when He created the Sabbath day by resting]. We should be diligent therefore to enter into that rest [Sabbath-keeping, as well as striving to enter into the Kingdom of God], lest anyone fall after the same example of disobedience. For the Word of God *is* living, and powerful, and sharper than any two-edged sword, piercing even to the dividing asunder of the soul and spirit, *and* of both *the* joints and *the* marrow, and *is* able to discern *the* thoughts and intents of *the* heart" (Heb. 4:10-12). (See Appendix H, *The True Meaning of Sabbatismos in Hebrews 4:9*, page 242, for a detailed analysis of the Greek word σαββατισμος—*sabbatismos*, Sabbath-keeping.)

What could be clearer? God's Holy Word reveals that if we want to be true Christians, we must love God the Father and Jesus Christ. We must be following the example of Jesus Christ, living by every word of God and keeping all of His commandments. Our very calling and hope of salvation requires that we observe the seventh-day weekly Sabbath as the day of rest, worship and fellowship. (See Inset, *Who and What Is a True Christian*, p.92.)

Summary

We have seen from God's Word the following truths about the **seventh-day holy Sabbath of God**:

- God created the seventh-day Sabbath as a day of rest for all of mankind from the beginning of the creation.
- Abraham kept the Sabbath.
- The Sabbath commandment was given to the Israelites before Mt. Sinai.
- The Sabbath commandment is the fourth of the Ten Commandments, and we are commanded to remember the seventh-day Sabbath to keep it holy.
- God owns the Sabbath.
- Jesus Christ was the Creator of the Sabbath.

• Jesus Christ is Lord of the Sabbath day, which means that the Lord's Day is the seventh day—not Sunday, the first day of the week.

• Jesus Christ observed the Sabbath, and taught and healed on the Sabbath.

• The apostles never changed the day of worship to the first day of the week.

• The apostle Paul taught the Gentiles to observe the Sabbath.

• The apostle Paul taught that grace and Sabbath-keeping go hand-in-hand.

• The Bible nowhere teaches that the Sabbath was changed to Sunday.

• Heb. 4:9 is a direct command for Christians today to keep the Sabbath.

• Sabbath-keeping is essential for salvation and is a sign that we love God and keep His commandments.

In the next chapter we will survey God's annual feasts and holy days in the Old Testament. Just as God commanded the twelve tribes of Israel to keep the weekly seventh-day Sabbath, God likewise commanded that they keep His annual feasts and holy days.

CHAPTER NINE

A Survey of God's Feasts
and Holy Days in the Old Testament

Since God has **never at any time** accepted any pagan occult holiday as a day of worship toward Him, what then are the *true* feasts and holy days of God? To answer this question, we will begin by examining the Old Testament scriptures. We will learn that throughout history God has used His annual feasts and holy days to **make Himself known** to the people of Abraham, Isaac and Jacob—the children of Israel—and to the world in special, powerful ways. In fact, the biblical feasts and holy days have great significance to God's people and the world because they **outline His plan** for mankind.

God Planned for His Feasts
and Holy Days from the Beginning

In the beginning God created the seven-day weekly cycle with the seventh day being His holy Sabbath. Likewise, from the beginning God created the yearly cycle for His annual feasts and holy days. In Genesis we read: "And God said, 'Let there be lights in the firmament of the heaven to divide the day from the night; and let them be for signs, and for seasons, and for days, and years' " (Gen. 1:14). The **signs** are the stars and heavenly bodies which continually testify that God is Creator of the heavens and the earth. The **seasons** are for the annual feasts of God that He commands to be observed at their appointed times. The **days** are not only for the weekly cycle and the **seventh day Sabbath**, but are also for the **annual holy days— yearly Sabbath days** that are in addition to the weekly Sabbath.

God also testifies that the Fourth Commandment—regarding the seventh-day Sabbath—is the foundational bedrock of all His annual feasts and holy days. "And the LORD spake unto Moses, saying, 'Speak unto the children of Israel, and say unto them, "*Concerning* **the feasts of the LORD, which ye shall proclaim** *to be* **holy convocations,** *even* **these are my feasts**. Six days shall work be done: but the seventh day *is* the sabbath of rest, an holy convocation; ye shall do no work *therein*: it *is* the sabbath of the LORD in all your dwellings" ' " (Lev. 23:1-3). God's instructions to Moses concerning the weekly Sabbath are vital, because they specifically point to the Sabbath command as the sanctifying command for the seasonal feasts of God as found in the next verse: "**These** *are* **the feasts of the LORD,** *even* **holy convocations, which ye shall proclaim in their seasons**" (verse 4).

There is no doubt that God has commanded His yearly feasts to be proclaimed in their seasons. These annual holy days are also sabbaths—holy convocations. Most people, however, have been misled into believing that the weekly Sabbath day as well as the annual feasts and holy days of God are only for the Jews. Countless theologians and churches declare that because God brought the temple rituals and animal sacrifices to a conclusion through the sacrifice of Jesus Christ, people are not required to keep the biblical Sabbath, holy days and feasts. All such claims are unfounded. These days **belong** to God, He created them, He owns them and He demands that we keep them—weekly and annually in their seasons.

What are the annual feasts and Sabbaths that God commands us to keep? When are they to be kept?

The Calculated Hebrew Calendar. God has not left men to their own self-serving inventions to determine when the annual feasts and holy days are to be kept. We need to realize that God calculates time differently than we do today with our Roman calendar. First, the Bible teaches that a day is reckoned from sunset to sunset (Lev. 23:32), rather than from midnight to midnight. Second, God has set the months and the year based on the earth's relationship to the sun and the moon. In order to know when God's annual Sabbaths are to be kept, He has given His people the sacred, calculated Hebrew calendar—as was undoubtedly used by the ancient Hebrews, including Abraham, Isaac and Jacob. Later, when God established His covenant with Israel, He provided the methods of calculation for the priests and Levites, so that they could establish the annual feasts of God in their seasons. According to the Hebrew Calendar, God has set the first month of the sacred year to begin in the Spring, which corresponds to March/April on the Roman calendar. The first month was originally named Abib, which means "green ears" of grain (Ex. 13:4). Later, after the Babylonian captivity, it was called Nisan.

(For detailed information about the sacred, calculated Hebrew calendar, please visit www.cbcg.org.)

The Scriptures demonstrate that God has **always used His feasts and holy days to fulfill His promises and to accomplish His will in significant, powerful and profound ways**—often involving **history-making events**. From the beginning of time, God's feasts and holy days have revealed His direct, major interventions in His dealings with Abraham, Isaac and Jacob, the twelve tribes of Israel and the world—past, present and future. They also foreshadowed and prophesied of the first coming of the Messiah, Jesus Christ, "the Lamb of God Who takes away the sin of the world." It is through the knowledge and keeping of God's feasts and holy days that He continues to impart understanding to His people concerning His plan of salvation and prophetic events yet to be fulfilled.

God's Feasts and Holy Days in the Old Testament Were Not Dependent on Rituals and Sacrifices

It is imperative to understand that God commanded His feasts to be kept **before** He gave any command to Moses concerning animal sacrifices and rituals at the tabernacle/temple. Consequently, the holy days and feasts of God do not stand or fall because of sacrifices and rituals performed on these days.

We now know that the seventh-day weekly Sabbath is to be kept without regard to animal sacrifices or priestly rituals. Since the holy days are annual Sabbaths, they too are to be kept without regard to such sacrifices. This understanding is punctuated by the historical fact that before and after the final destruction of the temple in 70 AD, faithful Jews of the Diaspora kept the Sabbath and holy days wherever they were—completely cut off from the temple rituals. This clearly proves that the observance of God's holy days was not, and is not now, dependent on sacrifices and rituals.

In the following verses, we find that there is **not a single reference to any sacrifice or ritual**: "Three times thou shalt keep a feast unto me in the year. Thou shalt keep the feast of unleavened bread: (thou shalt eat unleavened bread seven days, as I commanded thee, in the time appointed of the month Abib; for in it thou camest out from Egypt: and none shall appear before me empty:) And the feast of harvest, the firstfruits of thy labours, which thou hast sown in the field [the feast of firstfruits of the barley/wheat harvest—also called Pentecost]: and the feast of ingathering, *which is* in the end of the year, when thou hast gathered in thy labours out of the field [the Feast of Tabernacles]" (Ex. 23:14-16).

In Exodus 34, after Israel's rebellion at Sinai with the golden calf, God restated His commandments to Moses and the children of Israel. Here, God mixes His commands to keep the annual feasts with some of the Ten Commandments. By doing this, He shows that His commands to keep His feasts are just as important as the Ten Commandments. "For thou shalt worship no other god [the First Commandment]: for the LORD, whose name is Jealous, is a jealous God.... Thou shalt make thee no molten gods [the Second Commandment]. **The feast of unleavened bread shalt thou keep. Seven days thou shalt eat unleavened bread**, as I commanded thee, in the time of the month Abib: for in the month Abib thou camest out from Egypt. All that openeth the matrix *is* mine; and every firstling among thy cattle, *whether* ox or sheep, *that is male*. But the firstling of an ass thou shalt redeem with a lamb: and if thou redeem *him* not, then shalt thou break his neck. All the firstborn of thy sons thou shalt redeem. And none shall appear before me empty.

"**Six days thou shalt work, but on the seventh day thou shalt rest: in earing time and in harvest thou shalt rest** [the Fourth Commandment]. **And thou shalt observe the feast of weeks**, of the firstfruits of wheat harvest [Pentecost], and the feast of ingathering [Tabernacles] at the year's end.

"Thrice in the year shall all your men children appear before the Lord GOD, the God of Israel.... And the LORD said unto Moses, 'Write thou these words: for after the tenor of these words I have made a covenant with thee and with Israel.' And he was there with the LORD forty days and forty nights; he did neither eat bread, nor drink water. **And he wrote upon the tables the words of the covenant, the ten commandments**" (Ex. 34:14, 17-28).

Forty years later, Moses vigorously restated the commandments and covenant of God to the children of Israel just before they entered the Promised Land. Again, we see that God makes no mention of sacrifices in these verses: "Three times in a year shall all thy males appear before the LORD thy God in the place which he shall choose; in **the feast of unleavened bread**, and in **the feast of weeks** [Pentecost], and in the feast of tabernacles: and they shall not appear before the LORD empty: every man *shall give* as he is able, according to the blessing of the LORD thy God which he hath given thee" (Deut. 16:16-17).

A Listing of All the Feasts and Holy Days of God

In Leviticus 23, God lists all the feasts and holy days He commands His people to keep, beginning with the weekly seventh-day Sabbath. Before we turn there, it should be noted that Leviticus is basically a book of instructions for the priests and Levites, giving detailed instructions on how they were to carry out their duties at the tabernacle/temple. In chapters 1-7, God instructed the priests and Levites concerning all animal sacrifices, oblations and meal/cereal offerings to be offered at the tabernacle/temple. Also, in Numbers 28-29, God gave a complete listing of all the sacrifices the priests were to offer—covering daily, Sabbath, monthly, and holy day sacrifices. However, as we have seen, the feasts and holy days of God were not dependent on animal sacrifices or other rituals. (A complete study of the Hebrew sacrificial system is contained in the book *The Law of the Offerings*, by Andrew Jukes, ISBN 0-8254-2957-9. He details how every aspect of the sacrifices and physical rituals were, in reality, prophetic types of Jesus Christ's sacrifice and priesthood.)

Now we can examine the feasts and holy days of God in Leviticus 23, summarizing their significance and meaning as found in the Old Testament.

All are Holy Convocations: "And the LORD spake unto Moses, saying, 'Speak unto the children of Israel, and say unto them, "*Concerning* the **feasts of the LORD**, which ye shall proclaim *to be* **holy convocations**, *even* these *are* **my feasts**" ' " (verses 1-2). Again, the Lord makes it abundantly clear that all the holy days and feasts belong to God—*not* to the Jews.

The Weekly Sabbath: "Six days shall work be done: but the seventh day *is* the sabbath of rest, **an holy convocation**; ye shall do no work *therein*: it is the sabbath of the LORD in all your dwellings" (verse 3).

The Annual Feasts of the Lord: "These *are* the **feasts of the LORD, *even* holy convocations**, which ye shall proclaim in their seasons" (verse 4).

The Passover: "In the fourteenth *day* of the first month at even *is* **the LORD'S passover**" (verse 5).

The Feast of Unleavened Bread: "And on the fifteenth day of the same month *is* the **feast of unleavened bread unto the LORD**: seven days ye must eat unleavened bread. In the **first day ye shall have an holy convocation** [a holy day]: ye shall do no servile work therein. But ye shall offer an offering made by fire unto the LORD seven days: in **the seventh day *is* an holy convocation** [a holy day]: ye shall do no servile work *therein*" (verses 6-8).

The Wave Sheaf Offering Day: The Wave Sheaf offering day is a special day, but it is not a holy day. This day is always the first day of the week during the seven-day Feast of Unleavened Bread. On this day a special offering of the first of the firstfruits of the barley/wheat harvest was made by the high priest. It is the first day of the fifty-day count to the Feast of Firstfruits—also known as Pentecost (which means "count fifty"). The Wave Sheaf offering signaled the beginning of the barley/wheat harvest, and the Israelites were not to eat of the new grain until the Wave Sheaf was offered (verses 9-16).

The Feast of Firstfruits—Pentecost: The Feast of the Firstfruits, a holy day, is the fiftieth day from the Wave Sheaf—seven complete weeks, plus one day. (It is also called the Feast of Weeks in Deuteronomy 16:9-10, because of the counting of seven full weeks.) This is the only holy day of God that always falls on the first day of the week, Sunday. Israel was to count, "Even unto the morrow after the seventh sabbath [which would be a Sunday] shall ye number fifty days; and ye shall offer a new meat [meal or cereal] offering unto the LORD. Ye shall bring out of your habitations **two wave loaves of two tenth deals: they shall be of fine flour; they shall be baken with leaven;** *they are* **the firstfruits unto the LORD**" (verses 16-17).

On this holy day, each family was to present two freshly-baked loaves of leavened bread made with the new barley/wheat of the harvest to the priests and Levites, who waved them before the Lord. "And the priest shall wave them with the bread of the firstfruits *for* a wave offering before the LORD with the two lambs: they shall be holy to the LORD for the priest. And ye shall proclaim on the selfsame day [the fiftieth day—Pentecost], *that* it may be **an holy convocation unto you**: ye shall do no servile work *therein: it shall be* a statute for ever in all your dwellings throughout your generations" (verses 20-21).

The Feast of Trumpets: Trumpets is the first of four holy days that God commanded to be kept in the seventh month, known also as the month "Tishri." The seventh month of the Hebrew Calendar corresponds to September/October of the Roman year. "And the LORD spake unto Moses, saying, 'Speak unto the children of Israel, saying, "In the seventh month, in the first *day* of the month, shall ye have **a sabbath**, a memorial of blowing of trumpets, an holy convocation. Ye shall do no servile work *therein*: but ye shall offer an offering made by fire unto the LORD" ' " (verses 23-25).

The Day of Atonement: The day of Atonement is a special day of fasting to God: "And the LORD spake unto Moses, saying, 'Also on the tenth *day* of this seventh month *there shall be* a day of atonement: it shall be an holy convocation unto you; and ye shall afflict your souls [meaning a complete fast—no food or water for the day], and offer an offering made by fire unto the LORD. And ye shall do no work in that same day: for it *is* a day of atonement, to make an atonement for you before the LORD your God. For whatsoever soul *it be* that shall not be afflicted in that same day, he shall be cut off from among his people. And whatsoever soul *it be* that doeth any work in that same day, the same soul will I destroy from among his people. Ye shall do no manner of work: *it shall be* a statute for ever throughout your generations in all your dwellings. **It *shall be* unto you a sabbath of rest**, and ye shall afflict your souls: in the ninth *day* of the month at even, **from even unto even, shall ye celebrate your sabbath**" ' " (verses 26-32).

The Feast of Tabernacles and Last Great Day: "And the LORD spake unto Moses, saying, 'Speak unto the children of Israel, saying, "The fifteenth day of this seventh month *shall be* the feast of tabernacles *for* seven days unto the LORD. **On the first day *shall be* an holy convocation**: ye shall do no servile work *therein*. Seven days ye shall offer an offering made by fire unto the LORD: on **the eighth day** [the Last Great Day] **shall be an holy convocation** unto you; and ye shall offer an offering made by fire unto the LORD: it *is* a solemn assembly; *and* ye shall do no servile work *therein*.... Also in the fifteenth day of the seventh month, when ye have gathered in the fruit of the land, ye shall keep a feast unto the LORD seven days: on **the first day *shall be* a sabbath**, and on **the eighth day *shall be* a sabbath**" (verses 33-36, 39).

Again, God emphatically states that His holy days are Sabbaths: "**These *are* the feasts of the LORD**, which ye shall proclaim *to be* **holy convocations**, to offer an offering made by fire unto the LORD, a burnt offering, and a meat offering, a sacrifice, and drink offerings, every thing upon his day: beside **the sabbaths of the LORD** [all the holy days are Sabbaths], and beside your gifts, and beside all your vows, and beside all your freewill offerings, which ye give unto the LORD" (verses 37-38).

As we will see, God's feasts and holy days are intrinsically connected to each other—and reveal, step-by-step, **God's master plan for mankind**.

We will begin with the Passover and Feast of Unleavened Bread.

The Passover and Feast of Unleavened Bread in the Old Testament

God commanded the children of Israel to observe their first Passover while they were still in Egypt (Ex. 12). He instructed the heads of households to select a male lamb of the first year, without blemish (a type of Christ), on the 10th day of the first month. They were to then kill the lamb on the 14th, just after sunset (which also ended the 13th day of the month). As instructed, they smeared some of the blood on the doorposts and upper lintels of the doors of their houses. The blood was a sign for protection—so that God would spare the firstborn of the children of Israel from the death sentence that He was to execute against the Egyptians. Next, they were to roast the lamb with fire and eat it that night with unleavened bread and bitter herbs. The remainder of the lamb was to be burned by morning (verse 10). Finally, they were not to leave their houses until morning, at sunrise (verse 22).

At midnight on the 14th, the Lord passed through the land of Egypt and killed all the Egyptian firstborn of man and beast. "For I will pass through the land of Egypt this night, and will smite all the firstborn in the land of Egypt, both man and beast; and against all the gods of Egypt I will execute judgment: I *am* the LORD. And the blood shall be to you for a token upon the houses where ye *are*: and when I see the blood, I will pass over you, and the plague shall not be upon you to destroy *you*, when I smite the land of Egypt. And this day shall be unto you for a memorial; and ye shall keep it a feast to the LORD throughout your generations; ye shall keep it a feast by an ordinance for ever" (verses 12-14).

The 14th day of the first month is called the "Passover" because God *passed over* Israel's houses at midnight, sparing their firstborn. "And it shall come to pass, when your children shall say unto you, 'What mean ye by this service?' That ye shall say, 'It is the sacrifice of **the LORD'S passover**, **who passed over the houses of the children of Israel in Egypt**, when he smote the Egyptians, and delivered our houses.' And the people bowed the head and worshipped" (verses 26-27). God commanded them to keep the Passover as a memorial of His sparing their firstborn: "And this day shall be unto you for a memorial; and ye shall keep it a feast to the LORD throughout your generations; ye shall keep it a feast by an ordinance for ever" (verse 14).

The Feast of Unleavened Bread. At sunrise, beginning the day portion of the 14th, the children of Israel left their houses, gathered their livestock, and continued to spoil the Egyptians as they made their way to the city of Rameses—the assembly area from which they would begin the Exodus. "And the children of Israel did according to the word of Moses; and they borrowed [spoiled] of the Egyptians jewels of silver, and jewels of gold, and raiment: and the LORD gave the people favour in the sight of the Egyptians, so that they lent [gave] unto them *such things as they required*. And **they spoiled the Egyptians**" (Ex. 12:35-36). It must have taken most of the daylight portion of the 14th for the children of Israel to assemble at Rameses. The Exodus then began at sunset, which ended the 14th and began the 15th day of the month—the first day of the Feast of Unleavened Bread.

God directed the children of Israel to observe the Feast of Unleavened Bread for seven days, beginning on the 15th day of the first month: "Seven days shall ye eat unleavened bread; even the first day ye shall [have] put away leaven out of your houses: for whosoever eateth leavened bread from the first day until the seventh day, that soul shall be cut off from Israel. **And in the first day** *there shall be* **an holy convocation, and in the seventh day there shall be an holy convocation to you**; no manner of work shall be done in them, save *that* which every man must eat, that only may be done of you. And ye shall observe *the feast of* unleavened bread; **for in this selfsame day** [that night] **have I brought your armies out of the land of Egypt**: therefore shall ye observe this day in your generations by an ordinance for ever.... And the children of Israel journeyed from Rameses to Succoth, about six hundred thousand on foot *that were* men, beside children" (verses 15-17, 37).

"And they departed from Rameses in the first month, on the fifteenth day of the first month; on the morrow after the passover the children of Israel went out with an high hand in the sight of all the Egyptians" (Num. 33:3). Therefore, the children of Israel left Egypt by night: "Observe the month of Abib, and keep the passover unto the LORD thy God [on the 14th]: for in the month of Abib the LORD thy God brought thee forth out of Egypt by night [on the 15th]" (Deut. 16:1).

The Night to be Much Observed. The Exodus actually commenced as the sun was setting on the 14th and the 15th was beginning. (Remember, God reckons each day from sunset to sunset.) God brought the children of Israel out of Egypt by night—the night of the 15th—which is a special night to be "much observed to the Lord" as the Feast of Unleavened Bread begins. "And it came to pass at the end of the four hundred and thirty years, even the selfsame day it came to pass, that all the hosts of the LORD went out from the land of Egypt. **It** *is* **a night to be much observed unto the LORD for bringing them out from the land of Egypt: this** *is* **that night of the LORD to be observed of all the children of Israel in their generations**" (Ex. 12:41-42).

"The Night to be Much Observed" also commemorates another immortalized event that happened on the same night 430years earlier. By a special covenant oath, the Lord God confirmed His promises to Abraham that He would indeed bring the children of Israel out of captivity in Egypt on **this particular night**—the night of the 15th. (This special covenant that God made with Abraham took place over a two day period, the 14th and 15th—and is actually the origin of the Passover and Feast of Unleavened Bread for both the Old and New Testaments. In the book, *The Christian Passover*, by Fred R. Coulter, a detailed explanation of the significance of God's special covenant with Abraham is found on pp. 266-298).

The First Day of the Feast of Unleavened Bread. On the first day of the Feast of Unleavened Bread, Moses explained the purpose of the first holy day: "And Moses said unto the people, '**Remember this day, in which ye came out from Egypt**, out of the house of bondage; for by strength of hand the LORD brought you out from this *place*: there shall no leavened bread be eaten. This day came ye out in the month Abib. And it shall be when the LORD shall bring thee into the land of the Canaanites, and the Hittites, and the Amorites, and the Hivites, and the Jebusites, which he sware unto thy fathers to give thee, a land flowing with milk and honey, that thou shalt keep this service in this month. Seven days thou shalt eat unleavened bread, and in the seventh day *shall* be a feast to the LORD.

" 'Unleavened bread shall be eaten seven days; and there shall no leavened bread be seen with thee, neither shall there be leaven seen with thee in all thy quarters. And thou shalt show thy son in that day, saying, *"This is done* because of that *which* the LORD did unto me when I came forth out of Egypt." And it shall be for **a sign** [Gen. 1:14, Ex. 31:13; the keeping of the Feast of Unleavened Bread is a sign] unto thee upon thine hand, and for a memorial between thine eyes, **that the LORD'S law may be in thy mouth**: for with a strong hand hath the LORD brought thee out of Egypt. Thou shalt therefore keep this ordinance in his season from year to year' " (Ex. 13:3-10).

One final, important note: beginning the night of the Exodus, God provided a pillar of fire by night and a pillar of cloud cover by day (verses 21-22).

God has revealed that the purpose of the Feast of Unleavened Bread was: 1) to teach Israel that only God could deliver them from bondage in Egypt and bring them to the Promised Land; and 2) to be a sign "that the Lord's law may be in thy mouth."

The Seventh Day of the Feast of Unleavened Bread. The chronology of the Exodus shows that the children of Israel had arrived at the Red Sea by the sixth day of the Feast of Unleavened Bread. Meanwhile, Pharaoh had already gathered his army—all the chariots of Egypt, plus six hundred chosen chariots—and was in pursuit. The Egyptian army caught up with the Israelites as they camped along the shore of the Red Sea. At first the people were afraid and complained to Moses, but he told them: "Fear ye not, stand still, and see the salvation of the LORD, which he will show to you to day: for the Egyptians whom ye have seen to day, ye shall see them again no more for ever. **The LORD shall fight for you, and ye shall hold your peace**" (Ex. 14:13-14).

"And the LORD said unto Moses, 'Wherefore criest thou unto me? Speak unto the children of Israel, that they go forward: but lift thou up thy rod, and stretch out thine hand over the sea, and divide it: and the children of Israel shall go on dry *ground* through the midst of the sea. And I, behold, I will harden the hearts of the Egyptians, and they shall follow them: and I will get me honour upon Pharaoh, and upon all his host, upon his chariots, and upon his horsemen' " (verses 15-17).

That night God miraculously parted the waters of the Red Sea with a strong east wind. In the early dawn hours of the seventh day of the Feast of Unleavened Bread, the children of Israel walked across the dry floor of the sea and made it safely to the other side. When the Egyptians saw this, they pursued headlong into the Red Sea after the children of Israel—in a final, futile attempt to bring them back to Egypt and enslave them again. But God powerfully intervened and rescued the children of Israel from the Egyptians: "And the LORD said unto Moses, 'Stretch out thine hand over the sea, that the waters may come again upon the Egyptians, upon their chariots, and upon their horsemen.' And Moses stretched forth his hand over the sea, and the sea returned to his strength when the morning appeared; and the Egyptians fled against it; and **the LORD overthrew the Egyptians in the midst of the sea**. And the waters returned, and covered the chariots, and the horsemen, *and* all the host of Pharaoh that came into the sea after them; there remained not so much as one of them.

"But the children of Israel walked upon dry *land* in the midst of the sea; and the waters *were* a wall unto them on their right hand, and on their left. **Thus the LORD saved Israel** that day out of the hand of the Egyptians; and Israel saw the Egyptians dead upon the sea shore. And Israel saw that great work which the LORD did upon the Egyptians: and the people feared the LORD, and believed the LORD, and his servant Moses" (Ex. 14:26-31).

God used the Passover day and the Feast of Unleavened Bread to fulfill His promises to Abraham, Isaac and Jacob and the children of Israel. Not only do these days picture momentous events that God has performed for Israel, they also contain vital lessons for us today. In keeping these days, the children of Israel were to remember always that the blood of the Passover lamb **spared their firstborn**. As well, they were to keep the first day of the Feast of Unleavened Bread in remembrance of their **release from bondage** and their Exodus from Egypt. The significance of the seventh day of the feast is to be found in the account of Israel's crossing of the Red Sea: 1) We are not to be afraid or complain, because **God will fight our battles for us**; and 2) It takes the **power of God to rescue u**s from Satan the devil and his legions of demons, as symbolized by Pharaoh and his armies who were drowned in the Red Sea.

Throughout the Bible God shows that Egypt is a type of sin, as well as a type of this satanic, sinful society. Once the children of Israel had kept the Passover, they had to leave Egypt and their way of life as slaves and servants of sin. Thus, in keeping the Feast of Unleavened Bread today, we learn a great spiritual lesson: only God can release us from the bondage of sin, grant us salvation and lead us in His way.

Passover and Unleavened Bread Under Hezekiah. We find that when the children of Israel obeyed God and kept His Sabbath, feasts and holy days, He richly blessed them. However, in their many rebellions and sins against the Lord, the children of Israel and Judah also suffered curses under the corrective hand of God.

In the days of King Ahaz, God's people rejected Him and worshiped various false gods. Ahaz walked in the ways of the kings of Israel and Jeroboam, causing the people of Israel to sin greatly—in sacrificing to other gods, erecting molten images of Baal (the sun god), and burning children in the fire to Moloch. "And in the time of his distress did he trespass yet more against the LORD: this *is that* king Ahaz. For he sacrificed unto the gods of Damascus, which smote him: and he said, 'Because the gods of the kings of Syria help them, *therefore* will I sacrifice to them, that they may help me.'

But they were the ruin of him, and of all Israel.

"**And Ahaz gathered together the vessels of the house of God, and cut in pieces the vessels of the house of God, and shut up the doors of the house of the LORD, and he made him altars in every corner of Jerusalem. And in every several city of Judah he made high places to burn incense unto other gods, and provoked to anger the LORD God of his fathers**" (II Chron. 28:22-25).

Again, we see the illogical pattern of sin, rebellion and the worship of false gods by the kings and people of Israel and Judah. However, because God is merciful, whenever the children of Israel would repent of their sins and apostasy and of serving false gods, He would forgive them. Then, for a time, Israel would return to God and keep His commandments, the Passover and holy days.

Ahaz died in 723 BC, and his son Hezekiah became king. Hezekiah instituted a great reformation and led Israel back to serving and worshiping the true God. Ahaz had brazenly desecrated the temple to such an extent that—when Hezekiah began his revival—the priests and Levites could not cleanse it in time to keep the Passover in the first month. Consequently, Hezekiah made a decree throughout all the land that Israel would celebrate the Passover on the 14th day of the *second* month, just as God had provided for in Numbers chapter nine (II Chron. 30:1-6).

"And the children of Israel that were present at Jerusalem kept the [Passover and the] **feast of unleavened bread seven days** with great gladness: and the Levites and the priests praised the LORD day by day, singing with loud instruments unto the LORD. And Hezekiah spake comfortably unto all the Levites that taught the good knowledge of the LORD: and they did eat throughout the feast seven days, offering peace offerings, and making confession to the LORD God of their fathers. And the whole assembly took counsel to keep other seven days: and they kept *other* seven days with gladness…. So there was great joy in Jerusalem: for since the time of Solomon the son of David king of Israel *there was* not the like [festival observance] in Jerusalem. Then the priests the Levites arose and blessed the people: and their voice was heard, **and their prayer came *up* to his holy dwelling place, *even* unto heaven**" (II Chron. 30:21-23, 26-27).

King Hezekiah and the people then continued to carry out their reformation by destroying all idols, occult images and groves. "Now when all this was finished [the Passover and Feast of Unleavened Bread], all Israel that were present went out to the cities of Judah, and brake the images in pieces, and cut down the groves, and threw down the high places and the altars out of all Judah and Benjamin, in Ephraim also and Manasseh, until they had utterly destroyed them all. Then all the children of Israel returned, every man to his possession, into their own cities" (II Chron. 31:1).

After Hezekiah had reigned for 29 years, his twelve-year-old son Manasseh was anointed king. Throughout most of his 55-year reign, Manasseh led the children of Israel into apostasy—causing them to reject God and instead serve false gods, as well as to observe satanic occult holidays.

One of the most wicked kings of Judah, Manasseh completely desecrated the temple of God, rededicating it to Baal. After his death, his son Amon reigned for only two years—and he sinned far greater than his father. As a result, he was killed at the hands of his own servants (II Chron. 33:21-25).

Then, Amon's eight-year-old son, Josiah, became king.

Passover and Unleavened Bread Under Josiah. When Josiah was twenty-six, he began to restore Judah's relationship with God. While cleansing the temple from Manasseh and Amon's abominations, Hilkiah the priest found a copy of the Book of the Law. Shaphan the scribe brought the book to Josiah and read it to him. Upon hearing the warnings of God's judgment for sin and rebellion—and because he knew of the sins and wickedness of the people—Josiah personally repented and led the children of Judah into a special covenant of repentance and return to God. "Then the king sent and gathered together all the elders of Judah and Jerusalem. And the king went up into the house of the LORD, and all the men of Judah, and the inhabitants of Jerusalem, and the priests, and the Levites, and all the people, great and small: and he read in their ears all the words of the book of the covenant that was found in the house of the LORD.

"**And the king stood in his place, and made a covenant before the LORD, to walk after the LORD, and to keep his commandments, and his testimonies, and his statutes, with all his heart, and with all his soul, to perform the words of the covenant which are written in this book**. And he caused all that were present in Jerusalem and Benjamin to stand *to it*. And the inhabitants of Jerusalem did according to the covenant of God, the God of their fathers. And Josiah took away all the abominations out of all the countries that *pertained* to the children of Israel, and made all that were present in Israel to serve, *even* to serve the LORD their God. *And* all his days they departed not from following the LORD, the God of their fathers" (II Chron. 34:29-33).

"Moreover Josiah **kept a passover unto the LORD** in Jerusalem: and they killed the passover on **the fourteenth** *day* **of the first month**.... **And the children of Israel that were present kept the passover at that time, and the feast of unleavened bread seven days**. And there was no passover like to that kept in Israel from the days of Samuel the prophet; neither did all the kings of Israel keep such a passover as Josiah kept, and the priests, and the Levites, and all Judah and Israel that were present, and the inhabitants of Jerusalem. In the eighteenth year of the reign of Josiah was this passover kept" (II Chron. 35:1, 17-19).

After Josiah's reformation, he reigned only twelve more years and was killed in 607 BC in a battle against Necho, king of Egypt. Soon afterward, the nation of Judah fell once more into apostasy. A mere eighteen years after Josiah's death—through the course of three invasions by king Nebuchadnezzar's armies—the Jews were finally carried off to Babylon, to be held captive for 70 years, from 585 to 515 BC.

The Passover and Feast of Unleavened Bread After Babylon. A pitiful remnant of the Jews returned from captivity in Babylon to rebuild the small Jewish kingdom within the Persian Empire. They were allowed to rebuild their temple, have freedom of religion and be self-governing—but they no longer had a king. With only a governor (appointed by the king of Persia), they too were subject to the laws of the Persian Empire.

During the days of Ezra, the priest, and Nehemiah, the governor, the city and temple were rebuilt in troublesome times (see the books of Ezra and Nehemiah). Historically, a great religious renewal began when the temple was finished and dedicated. As in the reformations of Hezekiah and Josiah, the people again kept the Passover and the Feast of Unleavened Bread. "And the children of the captivity **kept the passover upon the fourteenth *day* of the first month**. For the priests and the Levites were purified together, all of them *were* pure, and killed the passover for all the children of the captivity, and for their brethren the priests, and for themselves. And the children of Israel, which were come again out of captivity, and all such as had separated themselves unto them from the filthiness of the heathen of the land, to seek the LORD God of Israel, did eat, **and kept the feast of unleavened bread seven days with joy: for the LORD had made them joyful**…" (Ezra 6:19-22).

In order to ensure that the new reforms would last, Ezra and Nehemiah led the Jews into a special covenant, known as the covenant of the Great Synagogue. Consisting first of 120 members, the Great Synagogue was later reduced to 70. Representing the nation, it was made up of five divisions: 1) the chief priests; 2) the chief Levites; 3) the chiefs of the people; 4) the representatives of the cities; and 5) the doctors of the law. The Great Synagogue lasted for 210 years, from 515 to 305 BC—down to the time of the high priest, Simon the Just.

As one can see, there are many passages in the Old Testament concerning the keeping of the Passover and the Feast of Unleavened Bread—all of which demonstrate how important these feasts are to God.

The Feast of Firstfruits—Pentecost. After Israel crossed the Red Sea, they journeyed six more weeks into the wilderness until they came to Mount Sinai—three days before God spoke the Ten Commandments. On the day of their arrival, God revealed to Moses His awesome purpose for the nation of Israel—they were to represent Him to all the nations of the world. "And Moses went up unto God, and the LORD called unto him out of the mountain, saying, 'Thus shalt thou say to the house of Jacob, and tell the children of Israel; "ye have seen what I did unto the Egyptians, and *how* I bare you on eagles' wings, and brought you unto myself. Now therefore, if ye will obey my voice indeed, and keep my covenant, then ye shall be a peculiar treasure unto me above all people: for all the earth *is* mine: and **ye shall be unto me a kingdom of priests, and an holy nation**." These *are* the words which thou shalt speak unto the children of Israel' " (Ex. 19:3-6).

God said, "Israel *was* holiness unto the LORD, and **the firstfruits** of his increase…" (Jer. 2:3). As the firstfruits of the nations of the world, it was fitting that they received the Ten Commandments, spoken by God Himself, on the Feast of Firstfruits—the Day of Pentecost. From the book of

Jasher—a non-canonical, secondary history of the children of Israel, which is mentioned in Joshua 10:13 and II Sam. 1:18—we read: "And in the third month from the children of Israel's departure, on the sixth day thereof, the Lord gave to Israel the ten commandments on Mount Sinai" (Jasher 82:6). The sixth day of the third month is a traditional Jewish date for Pentecost. Undoubtedly, this account is the basis for the Hebrew tradition that God gave the Ten Commandments to Israel, His firstfruit nation, on the Feast of Firstfruits, or Pentecost.

In Deuteronomy, Moses reiterated Israel's purpose as the firstfruit nation chosen by God to represent Him to the nations of the world: "Behold, I have taught you statutes and judgments, even as the LORD my God commanded me, that ye should do so in the land whither ye go to possess it. **Keep therefore and do** *them*; **for this** *is* **your wisdom and your understanding in the sight of the nations, which shall hear all these statutes, and say, 'Surely this great nation** *is* **a wise and understanding people.' For what nation** *is there so* **great**, **who** *hath* **God** *so* **nigh unto them**, as the LORD our God *is* in all *things that we* call upon him *for*? **And what nation** *is there so* **great**, that hath statutes and judgments *so* righteous as all this law, which I set before you this day?" (Deut. 4:5-8). As a nation, the twelve tribes of Israel were to share God's laws, commandments, statutes and judgments with the nations of the world.

Unfortunately, the only time Israel even partially fulfilled its purpose as God's representative firstfruit nation was during the first half of Solomon's reign. "And king Solomon passed all the kings of the earth in riches and wisdom. And all the kings of the earth sought the presence of Solomon, to hear his wisdom, that God had put in his heart" (II Chron. 9:22-23). When Solomon and the people apostatized and began to serve false gods, Israel ceased to represent God as a kingdom of priests to the rest of the world.

Pentecost Under Hezekiah. After Passover and the Feast of Unleavened Bread (kept in the second month), King Hezekiah continued in his zealous reforms, inspiring the people to observe the remainder of God's feasts—Pentecost, in the third month, and the fall festival season in the seventh month. "And Hezekiah appointed the courses of the priests and the Levites after their courses, every man according to his service, the priests and Levites for burnt offerings and for peace offerings, to minister, and to give thanks, and to praise in the gates of the tents of the LORD. *He appointed* also the king's portion of his substance for the burnt offerings, to *wit*, for the morning and evening burnt offerings, and the burnt offerings **for the sabbaths, and for the new moons, and for the set feasts, as** *it is* **written in the law of the LORD**.

"Moreover he commanded the people that dwelt in Jerusalem to give the portion of the priests and the Levites, that they might be encouraged in the law of the LORD. And as soon as the commandment came abroad, the children of Israel brought in abundance the firstfruits of corn, wine, and oil, and honey, and of all the increase of the field; and the tithe of all *things* brought they in abundantly. And *concerning* the children of Israel and Judah, that dwelt in the cities of Judah, they also brought in the tithe of oxen and sheep, and the tithe of holy things which were consecrated unto the LORD their God, and laid *them* by heaps. In the third month they began to lay the foundation of the heaps, and finished *them* in the seventh month" (II Chron. 31:2-7).

From the context of these verses, it is clear that under Hezekiah the Jews kept the Feast of Firstfruits as well as the feasts and holy days of the seventh month.

The Feast of Trumpets and War. The Feast of Trumpets was a memorial of the blowing of trumpets, because trumpets were blown throughout the day. We can learn much about the meaning of the Feast of Trumpets by looking at God's commands regarding the use of silver trumpets. As found in Numbers 10:1-10, the priests were to blow trumpets on the following occasions:

- The calling for assembly and for journeying
- To sound an alarm
- To go to war against an enemy
- In the day of gladness or on solemn days (i.e., holy days)
- To announce the beginning of months
- For holy day and new moon sacrifices

The predominant use of the trumpet was as an alarm for war. When God commanded Joshua to take the city of Jericho, He instructed him to have the priests (with the ark) march with the soldiers as they circled the city for seven days. The priest's were to blow trumpets the entire time (Joshua 6).

In I Samuel three and four, we see another example (albeit tragic) of the use of trumpets during war. Eli the priest's corrupt sons Hophni and Phineas led Israel in a fight against the Philistines while blowing trumpets. Defeat was inevitable, however, because this time God was not with Israel.

The Feast of Trumpets and the Dedication of Solomon's Temple. When Solomon's temple was completed, a feast of dedication was held for seven days beginning on the Feast of Trumpets. The priests brought the ark of the covenant from the city of David to the temple (I Kings 8:1-3, 65), where they placed it in the holy of holies. A special ceremony was held during which Solomon delivered a special prayer of dedication. After Solomon finished his prayer, the Lord established His presence in the holy of holies as demonstrated by a great white cloud that filled the temple. "And it came to pass, when the priests were come out of the holy *place*: (for all the priests *that were* present were sanctified, *and* did not *then* wait by course: also the **Levites** *which were* the singers, all of them of Asaph, of Heman, of Jeduthun, with their sons and their brethren, ***being* arrayed in white linen, having cymbals and psalteries and harps, stood at the east end of the altar, and with them an hundred and twenty priests sounding with trumpets**:) It came even to pass, as the trumpeters and singers *were* as one, to make one sound to be heard in praising and thanking the LORD; and when they lifted up *their* voice with the trumpets and cymbals and instruments of music, and praised the LORD, *saying*, 'For *he is* good; for his mercy *endureth* for ever:' that *then* **the house was filled with a cloud, *even* the house of the LORD**; so that the priests could not stand to minister by reason of the cloud: for the glory of the LORD had filled the house of God" (II Chron. 5:11-14).

This spectacular display of God's power and presence gave visual meaning to the Feast of Trumpets. As we will later see, this awesome event was a foreshadowing of the second coming of Jesus Christ and His literal return to the earth.

The Feast of Trumpets Under Ezra and Nehemiah. As we have observed, Ezra and Nehemiah initiated an immense reformation that truly brought the people back to God. After faithfully observing the Passover and Feast of Unleavened Bread, the Jews went on to keep the remainder of God's feasts, including the Feast of Trumpets: "And all the people gathered themselves together as one man into the street that *was* before the water gate; and they spake unto Ezra the scribe to bring the book of the law of Moses, which the LORD had commanded to Israel. And Ezra the priest brought the law before the congregation both of men and women, and all that could hear with understanding, upon **the first day of the seventh month**. And he read therein before the street that *was* before the water gate from the morning until midday, before the men and the women, and those that could understand; and the ears of all the people *were attentive* unto the book of the law" (Neh. 8:1-3).

Ezra established the standard of how services for the Sabbath and holy days would be conducted from that time forward. Ezra's method of reading the law, the prophets and the writings—combined with teaching from God's Word—became the format for services in all Jewish synagogues of the Diaspora.

The Day of Atonement. The Day of Atonement is the tenth day of the seventh month. It is a day of fasting (going without food or water). For Israel, Atonement was unique because on this day *only*, the high priest was allowed to enter the holy of holies to make atonement for himself, the priesthood and all the children of Israel (Lev. 16).

After the high priest had made an atonement for himself with the blood of animal sacrifices, he was to stand at the entrance of the temple with two identical goats. The priest drew lots over the goats to determine which would be "for the Lord," and which would be for Satan. The goat designated "for the Lord" was sacrificed as a sin offering (obviously picturing Christ's future sacrifice). The priest took its blood and sprinkled it before Lord on the mercy seat in the holy of holies to make atonement for all the sins, trespasses and uncleanness of the children of Israel. Afterwards its carcass was carried outside the camp to be wholly burned (where all sin offerings were burned).

The second goat represented Satan—"Azazel" (or, as the King James Version reads, "scapegoat"). However, the goat for Azazel was to remain alive and not be sacrificed. Before the entrance of the temple, the priest laid his hands upon the head of the live goat (for Azazel) and confessed upon it all the sins and transgressions of the children of Israel. This goat was then led by the hand of a "fit man" into the wilderness (where demons were known to dwell) and released.

This completed the annual atonement for all the sins, iniquities, transgressions and uncleanness of the children of Israel (Lev. 16:5-34).

The lessons of the Day of Atonement are twofold: 1) Only God can forgive sin, and 2) Satan will ultimately bear the responsibility for seducing the children of Israel into sin against God.

The Feast of Tabernacles and the Last Great Day. In God's instructions concerning the Feast of Tabernacles and the Last Great Day (the eighth day), He gives the children of Israel important insight into one aspect of the festival. "Also in the fifteenth day of the seventh month, when ye have gathered in the fruit of the land, ye shall keep a feast unto the LORD seven days: on **the first day** *shall be* **a sabbath, and on the eighth day** *shall be* **a sabbath**. And ye shall take you on the first day the boughs of goodly trees, branches of palm trees, and the boughs of thick trees, and willows of the brook; and ye shall rejoice before the LORD your God seven days. And ye shall keep it a feast unto the LORD seven days in the year. It *shall be* a statute for ever in your generations: ye shall celebrate it in the seventh month. Ye shall dwell in booths seven days; all that are Israelites born shall dwell in booths. **That your generations may know that I made the children of Israel to dwell in booths, when I brought them out of the land of Egypt**: I *am* the LORD your God" (Lev. 23:39-43).

God commanded the Israelites to dwell in booths or tents during the Feast of Tabernacles to commemorate their 40 years of wandering in the wilderness. After the Lord blessed them in the land (because of His promises to Abraham, Isaac and Jacob), the children of Israel were to never forget that God Himself had blessed them and given them their land and wealth (Deut. 8).

Meaning of Tabernacles for God. The Lord God made it clear that there was significant meaning as well for Himself in the Feast of Tabernacles—centering around the very purpose for the tabernacle/temple itself. "And let them make me a sanctuary; **that I may dwell among them**" (Ex. 25:8). The tabernacle and sanctuary of God was a special place of worship and sacrifice for the Israelites. God would dwell with them by establishing His presence in the holy of holies (Ex. 40:34-38). God was to dwell with His people, be their God and bless them—if they would, in turn, obey Him and keep His commandments.

When David desired to build a temple for God, Nathan the prophet gave him God's answer: "And it came to pass that night, that the word of the LORD came unto Nathan, saying, 'Go and tell my servant David, Thus saith the LORD, "Shalt thou build me an house for me to dwell in? Whereas **I have not dwelt in** *any* **house since the time that I brought up the children of Israel out of Egypt, even to this day, but have walked in a tent and in a tabernacle**" ' " (II Sam. 7:4-6).

God did not permit David to build the temple, because he was a bloody man of war. However, He did give all the plans for building the temple to David, who in turn gave them to Solomon, because God had chosen Solomon to build His temple (I Chron. 28-29). Witnessing the dedication of Solomon and the children of Israel, God blessed them with His presence in a majestic display of glory, as a brilliant cloud filled the temple. Affirming Solomon's prayer, the Lord again demonstrated his delight by consuming the burnt offerings with fire from heaven: "Now when Solomon had made an end of praying, the **fire came down from heaven, and consumed the burnt offering and the sacrifices; and the glory of the LORD filled the house**. And the priests could not enter into the house of the LORD, because the glory of the LORD had filled the LORD'S house. And when all the children of Israel saw how the fire came down, and the glory of the LORD upon the house, they bowed themselves with their faces to the ground upon the pavement, and worshipped, and praised the LORD, *saying*, 'For he *is good*; for his mercy *endureth* for ever' " (II Chron. 7:1-3),

After the dedication of the temple in Jerusalem, Solomon led all the people in keeping a great Feast of Tabernacles: "Also at the same time Solomon kept the feast [of Tabernacles] seven days [15th through the 21st of the 7th month], and all Israel with him, a very great congregation, from the entering in of Hamath unto the river of Egypt. And in the eighth day [the 22nd] they made a solemn assembly: for they kept the dedication of the altar seven days [1st through the 7th day of the 7th month], and the feast [of Tabernacles] seven days. And on the three and twentieth day of the seventh month [the day after the 8th day] he sent the people away into their tents, glad and merry in heart for the goodness that the LORD had showed unto David, and to Solomon, and to Israel his people" (verses 8-10).

God's presence was now with the children of Israel in the temple at Jerusalem, rather than in the tabernacle. With the temple completed, Solomon instructed the priests to begin bringing offerings to God in accordance with the laws God had given to Moses. "Then Solomon offered burnt offerings [through the priests] unto the LORD on the altar of the LORD, which he had built before the porch, even after a certain rate every day, offering according to the commandment of Moses, on **the sabbaths**, and on **the new moons**, and on **the solemn feasts, three times in the year, even in the feast of unleavened bread, and in the feast of weeks** [Pentecost], **and in the feast of tabernacles**" (II Chron. 8:12-13).

Feast of Tabernacles Under Ezra and Nehemiah. In the time of Ezra and Nehemiah, faithful Jews again returned to God and kept His commanded feasts, including the Feast of Tabernacles: "And they found written in the law which the LORD had commanded by Moses, that the children of Israel should dwell in booths in the feast of the seventh month: and that they should publish and proclaim in all their cities, and in Jerusalem, saying, 'Go forth unto the mount, and fetch olive branches, and pine branches, and myrtle branches, and palm branches, and branches of thick trees, to make booths, as *it is* written.' So the people went forth, and brought *them*, and made themselves booths, every one upon the roof of his house, and in their courts, and in the courts of the house of God, and in the street of the water gate, and in the street of the gate of Ephraim. And all the congregation of them that were come again out of the captivity made booths, and sat under the booths: for since the days of Jeshua the son of Nun unto that day had not the children of Israel done so. And there was very great gladness. Also day by day, from the first day unto the last day, he read in the book of the law of God. And they kept the feast seven days; and on the eighth day was a solemn assembly, according unto the manner" (Neh. 8:14-18; See Ezra 3:4).

As the biblical history of the children of Israel and Judah demonstrates, God blessed them when they faithfully kept His commandments, feasts and holy days. When they resumed their sinful ways, God sent prophets to warn them and call them to repentance. When Israel continued to transgress and, in rebellion, refused to repent—continuing to serve other gods, to worship the sun, moon and stars and to observe pagan occult holidays—God had no choice but to punish them and deliver them into the hands of their enemies. Thus, the repetitive cycle of apostasy and restoration continued even until the time of Jesus Christ.

This Old Testament overview of the feasts and holy days of God demonstrates that whenever the people of Israel and Judah **returned to God**—forsaking their idols and false gods—**they always kept God's Sabbath, His feasts and holy days** as He had commanded. In so doing, God blessed them for their repentance and obedience.

In chapter ten, we will see how the New Testament illustrates that the feasts and holy days of God continue to unveil and magnify the plan of God for the Church, Israel and all mankind—beginning with the sacrifice of Jesus Christ, "The Lamb of God Who takes away the sin of the world."

CHAPTER TEN

God's Spring Feasts and
Holy Days in the New Testament

A major key to understanding the New Testament is found in the knowledge of the feasts and holy days of God. Far from being abolished—as "Christianity" would have us believe—the New Testament reveals deeper and greater meanings for God's holy days. Without an understanding of these all-important feast days, a person's comprehension of the New Testament will, in fact, be deficient and incomplete.

In this chapter we will examine how God is using His festivals and holy days to fulfill His plan, purpose and prophecies.

From Matthew to Revelation, it can be clearly established that Christ's disciples **did not** observe occult holidays. Rather, Jesus Christ, the apostles, and the Jewish and Gentile converts all observed the commanded feast days of God. True Christians always love God and keep His commandments (Rev. 14:12). In fact, the term "Christian" means a **follower of Jesus Christ**—one who exhibits the qualities demonstrated and taught by Jesus. A Christian follows Christ regardless of circumstances (Rev. 14:4), and has the testimony and the faith of Christ (Rev. 12:17; 14:12).

The apostle John summed up the conduct and way of life of a true Christian: "*If* anyone is keeping His Word, truly in this one the love of God is being perfected. By this *means* we know that we are in Him. **Anyone who claims to dwell in Him is obligating himself also to walk even as He Himself walked**" (I John 2:5-6). And again, "For to this you were called because Christ also suffered for us, leaving us **an example**, that **you should follow in His footsteps**" (I Pet. 2:21).

Therefore, we are to believe in Jesus Christ and to follow His example—to walk as He walked, for He (as God manifested in the flesh) is the only basis for true Christianity. "**For no one is able to lay any other foundation besides that which has been laid, which is Jesus Christ**" (I Cor. 3:11). Not only is He the foundation of our faith, He is also called "the Chief Cornerstone" (Eph. 2:20 and I Pet. 2:6-7). The entire New Testament is built upon the foundation of Jesus Christ. It is through **His** perfect life, **His** death for our sins, and **His** resurrection that we receive salvation. Truly, from Genesis to Revelation, the focus of the entire Bible is Jesus Christ, the Savior of the world.

Jesus Christ—Our Passover—Died on Passover Day

To grasp the deeper meaning of Passover, we must look to the beginning—as the first prophecy concerning the Messiah is found in Genesis three. After Adam and Eve sinned, the Lord God Himself—the one Who later became Jesus Christ of the New Testament—prophesied of His future death as God manifested in the flesh. "And I will put enmity between thee [Satan] and the woman, and between thy seed [Satan and the demons] and her seed [Jesus Christ]; it [Christ, as Savior] shall bruise thy [Satan's] head [destroy his dominion], and thou [Satan] shalt bruise his [Christ's] heel [through the crucifixion]" (Gen. 3:15).

However, even before the creation of Adam and Eve, God had made provision for the redemption of mankind through Jesus Christ—as He is "the Lamb [of God, as good as] slain from *the* foundation of *the* world" (Rev. 13:8).

From the time of the first Passover in Egypt to the time of Jesus Christ, the Passover commemorated the sparing of Israel's firstborn. The male lamb without blemish sacrificed in the observance of the Old Testament Passover was a *type* that pointed to Jesus Christ, the "Lamb of God Who takes away the sin of the world" (John 1:29, 36).

Paul wrote that the Father had set an "appointed time [in which] Christ died for *the* ungodly" (Rom. 5:6)—for the sins of the world. What was that "appointed time"? Does this refer to one of the "appointed feasts" of God? The answer is, "Yes!" Paul made this crystal clear when he wrote to the Gentile church in Corinth: **"For Christ our Passover [Lamb] was sacrificed for us"** (I Cor. 5:7).

As the Gospels narrate, Paul fully understood that Jesus Christ died on the appointed day, the Passover day, at the precise time that God had determined "before the foundation of the world" (Rev. 13:8). The events recorded in the Scriptures concerning Jesus' last Passover—His betrayal, arrest, trials, beatings, the scourging, the crucifixion, His death and burial—all took place within one 24-hour day reckoned from sunset to sunset. That day was the Passover day in 30 AD, Nisan 14 on the Hebrew calendar, April 5 on the Julian Roman calendar. By virtue of these historical and spiritual facts, **the Passover day is the most important commanded feast of God—because Jesus Christ was crucified and died on that day!** Moreover, at least twenty-eight specific Old Testament prophecies were fulfilled on this appointed day (Fred R. Coulter, *The Day Jesus the Christ Died*, pp. 35-43).

As the supreme sacrifice of God the Father, Jesus Christ is indeed our Passover, Who died for us. He took upon Himself the full penalty of our sins to redeem and rescue us from the author of sin, Satan the devil.

Jesus Christ's Last Passover. The importance of Jesus Christ's last Passover is demonstrated in the fact that out of a total of eighty-nine chapters in the Gospels, thirty-two chapters (over one-third) are devoted to events just before and after Jesus' death. On the night of His last Passover, Jesus Christ instituted the **New Covenant Christian Passover**—a ceremony consisting of:

Footwashing (John 13:2-17);

Partaking of unleavened bread (Matt. 26:26; Luke 22:19; I Cor. 11:23-24);

Partaking of wine (Matt. 26:27-29; Luke 22:18-20; I Cor. 11:25-29).

Jesus began the New Covenant Christian Passover service by instituting the ordinance of footwashing. In so doing, Jesus "rose from supper and laid aside *His* garments; and after taking a towel, He secured it around Himself. Next, He poured water into a washing basin and began to wash the disciples' feet, and to wipe *them* with the towel which He had secured.... [And] when He had washed their feet, and had taken His garments, *and* had sat down again, He said to them, 'Do you know what I have done to you? You call Me the Teacher and the Lord, and you speak rightly, because I am. **Therefore, if I, the Lord and the Teacher, have washed your feet, you also are duty-bound to wash one another's feet; for I have given you an example, *to show* that you also should do exactly as I have done to you**. Truly, truly I tell you, a servant is not greater than his lord, nor a messenger greater than he who sent him. If you know these things, blessed are you if you do them' " (John 13:4-5, 12-17).

Thus, through example, Jesus taught His disciples to wash one another's feet as part of the Christian Passover service.

Jesus then broke unleavened bread—symbolizing His broken body—and instructed His disciples to eat of it. Afterwards, He instructed them to drink of wine, symbolizing His shed blood. The Gospel of Mark reads: "And as they were eating, Jesus took bread; *and* after blessing *it*, He broke *it* and gave *it* to them, and said, '**Take, eat; this is My body**.' And He took the cup; *and* after giving thanks, He gave *it* to them; and they all drank of it. And He said to them, '**This is My blood, the blood of the New Covenant**, which is poured out for many' " (Mark 14:22-24). Luke gives this account: "And He took bread; *and* after giving thanks, He broke *it* and gave *it* to them, saying, 'This is My body, which is given for you. **This do in the remembrance of Me**.' In like manner also, *He took* the cup after supper, saying, 'This cup *is* the New Covenant in My blood, which is poured out for you' " (Luke 22:19-20).

Though somewhat veiled, Jesus had earlier revealed to the Jews the meaning of the New Covenant Christian Passover: "Jesus said to them, 'I am the bread of life; the one who comes to Me shall never hunger; and the one who believes in Me shall never thirst at any time.... Truly, truly I say to you, the one who believes in Me has eternal life. **I am the bread of life**. Your fathers ate manna in the desert, but they died. This is the bread which comes down from heaven so that anyone may eat of it and not die. **I am the living bread, which came down from heaven; if anyone eats of this bread, he shall live forever; and the bread that I will give is even My flesh, which I will give for the life of the world**.' Because of this, the Jews were arguing with one another, saying, 'How is He able to give us *His* flesh to eat?'

"Therefore, Jesus said to them, 'Truly, truly I say to you, unless you eat the flesh of the Son of man, and drink His blood, you do not have life in yourselves. The one who eats My flesh and drinks My blood has eternal life, and I will raise him up in the last day; for My flesh is truly food, and My blood is truly drink. **The one who eats My flesh and drinks My blood is dwelling in Me, and I in him. As the living Father has sent Me, and I live by the Father; so also the one who eats Me shall live by Me.** This is the bread which came down from heaven; not as your fathers ate manna, and died. The one who eats this bread shall live forever' " (John 6:35, 47-58).

In Psalm 34, David foretold of this very concept when He wrote: "**O taste and see that the LORD *is* good: blessed *is* the man *that* trusteth in him**" (verse 8). What David wrote is very similar to what Jesus said—that is, "trusting in the Lord" is essentially the same as "living by" the Lord. Just as David did not mean that one was to *literally* taste and eat the Lord, Jesus likewise did not mean that a person was to eat His literal flesh and drink His literal blood—both somehow supposedly transubstantiated in bread and wine taken at the command of a priest. The bread and wine are **symbolic of His flesh and blood**. As David wrote, the literal action of "trusting" in the Lord was symbolized by the idea of "tasting" the Lord. In a similar manner, **actively living by Jesus Christ** is symbolized by our eating of the bread and drinking of the wine of the Christian Passover—the symbolic flesh and blood of Jesus Christ.

As an annual event, the New Covenant Christian Passover is to be observed on the night of Nisan 14. The practice of those who partake of "communion," "the Lord's Supper," or the "Eucharist" is to observe such occasions several times a month or year. They are not, however, partaking of the *true* New Covenant Christian Passover as Jesus commanded His disciples. Rather, they are partaking of a Christianized, apostate, pagan counterfeit. (See Appendix J, *The Eucharist or the Sacrifice of the Mass*, page 249.)

Paul Commanded Gentile Converts to Keep the Passover. The New Testament teaches that the Passover was not for the Jews only. After Jesus was resurrected, He commanded His apostles: " 'All authority in heaven and on earth has been given to Me. Therefore, go *and* **make disciples in all nations**, baptizing them into the name of the Father, and of the Son, and of the Holy Spirit; **teaching them to observe all things that I have commanded you**. And lo, I am with you always, *even* until the completion of the age' " (Matt. 28:18-20). Teaching disciples in all nations to observe the New Covenant Christian Passover is clearly part of "all things" commanded by Jesus. It is clearly evident that the observance of the Passover was not limited to Jews only.

In obedience to Jesus' command—some twenty-six years after His death and resurrection—the apostle Paul instructed Gentile converts to keep the Christian Passover as a yearly reminder of the sacrifice of Jesus Christ. He emphatically declared that he had received his instructions concerning Passover directly from the Lord. In the strongest terms possible He made it clear that when they kept the Passover, they were not to eat a supper with it, nor were they to call it the "Lord's Supper" (which they had done). "Therefore, when you assemble together in one place, it is not to eat *the* Lord's supper. For in eating, everyone takes his own supper first; now on the one hand, someone goes hungry; but on the other hand, another becomes drunken. WHAT! Don't you have houses for eating and drinking? Or do you despise the church of God, and put to shame those who have nothing? What shall I say to you? Shall I praise you in this? I do not praise *you*!... But if anyone is hungry, let him eat at home, so that *there will be* no *cause* for judgment *when* you assemble together" (I Cor. 11:20-22, 34).

Paul again gave them the Lord's instructions on when and how to properly partake of the bread and wine in renewing the New Covenant each year. "For I received from the Lord that which I also delivered to you, that **the Lord Jesus in the night in which He was betrayed** [the Passover night, Nisan 14] took bread; and after giving thanks, He broke *it* and said, 'Take, eat; this is My body, which *is* being broken for you. This do in **the remembrance of Me**.' In like manner, *He* also *took* the cup after He had supped, saying, 'This is *the* cup *of* the New Covenant in My blood. This do, as often as you drink *it*, in **the remembrance of Me**.' For as often as you eat this bread and drink this cup, you *solemnly* proclaim **the death of the Lord** until He comes. For this reason, *if* anyone shall eat this bread or shall drink the cup of the Lord unworthily, he shall be guilty of the body and *the* blood of the Lord" (I Cor. 11:23-27).

In these verses we find four factors that clearly *limit* the partaking of the Passover to **once each year**, on Nisan 14. They are: 1) "**in the night** in which He was betrayed," limits the observance to the Passover night only; 2) "**in the remembrance of Me**"—not "a remembrance" but, as the Greek reads, "**the** remembrance"—revealing that Passover is a specific, yearly memorial; 3) the phrase "as often as" cannot be taken to mean "as often as one desires" to partake of the bread and wine (the practice of Orthodox Christendom—daily, weekly, monthly, quarterly). Rather, this phrase means that as often as they partook of the Passover—year by year—they would remember and proclaim the Lord's death **until He would come**. (Remember, at this time the Church was expecting Christ's second coming to take place within a few years.) And finally, 4) the Greek syntax, not translatable into English, limits Passover to an annual observance (Fred R. Coulter, *The Christian Passover*, pp. 247-265).

Editor's note: A complete, detailed study of the Old Testament and New Testament Passover is contained in the 500-page book, *The Christian Passover* by Fred R. Coulter. It is the most comprehensive book ever written on this vital biblical subject. The book may be ordered from York Publishing Company (see address in front of book) or from *www.amazon.com*.

At midnight on the original Passover in Egypt, God passed over the blood-marked houses of the children of Israel and spared their firstborn. At midnight on Jesus' last Passover, God the Father did not pass over His Beloved Son—the firstborn of the virgin Mary. He did not spare His only begotten Son; rather, He delivered Jesus into the hands of His enemies—betrayed by the kiss of a friend. At the time of His arrest, no one knew (except God the Father and Jesus Christ) that His passion, beating, scourging, crucifixion and death as the *true* Passover Lamb of God marked the beginning of the plan of salvation for the world.

In the most solemn way possible, God used the Passover day itself for the crucifixion of Jesus Christ as the perfect sacrifice for the sins of the world. It was God the Father's **appointed day** that He had specifically set aside to fulfill His will and the promise of a Savior—one Who would redeem us from our sins. "For all have sinned, and come short of the glory of God; *but* are being justified freely by His grace through the redemption that *is* in Christ Jesus; Whom God has openly manifested *to be* a propitiation through faith in His blood, in order to demonstrate His righteousness, in respect to the remission of sins that are past, through the forbearance of God; *yes*, **to publicly declare His righteousness in the present time**, that He might be just, and the one Who justifies the one who *is* of *the* faith of Jesus" (Rom. 3:23-26). It is through Jesus Christ that we may receive eternal life, as the apostle John wrote: "For God so loved the world that He gave His only begotten Son, so that everyone who believes in Him may not perish, but may have everlasting life" (John 3:16).

Without the shedding of Jesus' blood, His death and His resurrection from the dead, there would be no forgiveness of sins or eternal salvation (I Cor. 15). Therefore, the Passover day—the remembrance of His death for our sins—is the most important feast of God for New Testament Christians. Those who have the Spirit of God and partake of the New Covenant Christian Passover on Nisan 14 each year are actually **renewing** their baptismal covenant of eternal life in Jesus Christ. This is accomplished through: 1) footwashing—walking in God's way of service through Jesus Christ; 2) partaking of the broken, unleavened bread—symbolizing Jesus' broken body for our healing; and 3) partaking of the wine—symbolizing His shed blood for the forgiveness of our sins. As Jesus said, "**Unless you eat the flesh of the Son of man, and drink His blood, you do not have life in yourselves**. The one who eats My flesh and drinks My blood has eternal life, and I will raise him up in the last day" (John 6:53-54).

The Gospels are the record of the life and teachings of Jesus Christ as God manifested in the flesh, the Savior of the world. Jesus' death by crucifixion on the Passover day is the awesome fulfillment of the meaning of Passover—and is central to the gospel message and the convergence and fulfillment of hundreds of prophecies in the Old and New Testaments.

This is why true Christians are duty-bound by the command of the Lord Jesus Christ to observe the New Covenant Christian Passover on the night of Nisan 14—once a year and once a year only. **Any other practice is disobedience against the Word of God and makes a self-righteous mockery of the greatest act of love by God the Father and Jesus Christ—the sacrifice of our Savior.** All other practices have been derived, to one degree or another, from the occult practices of Babylon and Egypt and are not of God.

Jesus was Placed in the Tomb as the Passover Day was Ending. Jesus died on the cross at the ninth hour of the day, approximately 3 PM, on Nisan 14, after one of the Roman soldiers thrust a spear into His side (Matt. 27:46-51; Mark 15:34-38). The apostle John, an eyewitness to all the events of that Passover day, wrote this account of Jesus' death: "And so, when Jesus had received the vinegar, He said, 'It is finished.' And bowing His head, He yielded up *His* spirit. The Jews therefore, so that the bodies might not remain on the cross on the Sabbath, because it was a preparation *day* (for that Sabbath was a high day [the first day of the Feast of Unleavened Bread, a holy day that began at sunset]), requested of Pilate that their legs might be broken and *the bodies* be taken away. Then the soldiers came and broke the legs of the first *one*, and *the legs* of the other who was crucified with Him. But when they came to Jesus *and* saw that He was already dead, they did not break His legs; but one of the soldiers had pierced His side with a spear, and immediately blood and water had come out. And he who saw *this* has testified, and his testimony is true; and he knows that *what* he says *is* true, so that you may believe. For these things took place so that the scripture might be fulfilled, 'Not a bone of Him shall be broken.' And again another scripture says, 'They shall look upon Him Whom they pierced' " (John 19:30-37).

Shortly afterward, Nicodemus and Joseph of Arimathea removed Jesus' body from the cross and wrapped it with wide strips of linen cloth (with spices) according to the Jewish burial custom of the time. They placed His body in the garden tomb just as the sun was setting, ending Nisan 14 and beginning Nisan 15 (verses 38-42).

Through the Passover, God fulfilled His promise to Abraham made when He pledged His own death in the covenant promise of Genesis 15:17. Christ also fulfilled His own words to His disciples concerning His death (Matt. 16:21; Mark 8:31; Luke 9:22; also see *The Day Jesus the Christ Died*, pp. 2-43). Thus, Jesus, as God manifested in the flesh, began His three days and nights in the tomb, which was the only sign that He gave to the Jews and to the world that He was the true Messiah (Matt. 12:39-40).

The New Testament Meaning of the Feast of Unleavened Bread

God commanded the children of Israel to remove all leaven from their houses prior to the Passover, which is also a separate day of eating unleavened bread (Ex. 12:8). They were to have put all leaven out of their houses before the seven-day Feast of Unleavened Bread began. The only bread they were to eat for the entire feast was unleavened bread (verses 15-20; 13:6-7; Lev. 23:6, etc.).

In the New Testament, we find that Paul taught the Gentiles to observe the Feast of Unleavened Bread in the same way that God had commanded the children of Israel. In writing to the Corinthians, Paul **defined leaven as a symbol of sin and sinful human nature**—a nature that is "puffed up" with vanity and pride. The brethren in Corinth had been tolerating a gross sin of immorality—in which a man was having sexual relations with his stepmother. Paul wrote: "Your glorying [in this] *is* not good. Don't you know that a little leaven leavens the whole lump?" (I Cor. 5:6.) Instead of abhorring such conduct, they were condoning it—even glorying over it. Paul had to correct them severely, because this individual's sin had begun to **leaven the whole congregation** with a sinful attitude, which would in turn lead to sinful conduct. He then commanded them to remove the individual from the congregation, just as they had removed leaven from their houses.

Paul had to remind them that just as they had unleavened their homes in preparation for keeping the feast, they were to also "unleaven" their spiritual lives from sin through Jesus Christ, our Passover. "Therefore, purge out the old leaven [of sin], so that you may become a new lump [sinless in Christ], *even* as you are unleavened [in your homes]. **For Christ our Passover was sacrificed for us**. For this reason, **let us keep the feast, not with old leaven, nor with *the* leaven of malice and wickedness, but with *the* unleavened *bread* of sincerity and truth**" (verses 7-8).

Paul's statement, "Let us keep the feast," is quite emphatic—and should quiet those who falsely teach that Paul was busy abolishing God's feasts. Clearly, this is a direct command to New Testament Gentile converts to keep the Feast of Unleavened Bread! Paul backs up his authority by stating: "If anyone thinks that he is a prophet or spiritual, let him acknowledge that **the things I write to you are *the* commandments of the Lord**" (I Cor. 14:37). This is what Paul taught in all the churches (I Cor. 7:17).

Paul again emphasized the spiritual meaning of Unleavened Bread when he admonished the Colossians to forsake their sinful ways and nature and replace them with the character of Christ and His attributes of love and righteousness (Col. 3:1-17).

As Abraham's spiritual seed, baptized Christians are to put on Jesus Christ—to become like Him (Gal. 3:26-29). "Christ in you, [is] the hope of glory" for Christians (Col. 1:27). By observing the Feast of Unleavened Bread, Christians learn that through the power of the Holy Spirit they are to overcome sin, live by every word of God, develop the character of Christ, walk in faith, believe in hope and live in the love of God.

The Night to be Much Observed. This night, the night of Nisan 15, begins the Feast of Unleavened Bread for seven days. The children of Israel were commanded to observe the Night to be Much Observed in commemoration of their Exodus from Egypt, and their deliverance from the bondage of slavery (Ex. 12:40-42). It was also on the same night—the "self same day" of Nisan 15—430 years before when the Lord God promised in His covenant with Abraham to deliver his descendants from their slavery (Gen. 15:12-18).

For true Christians, the Night to be Much Observed has intense spiritual meaning. That very night Jesus Christ's dead body was lying in the tomb—beginning His three days and nights "in the heart of the earth" (Matt.

12:40). This night was a fulfillment of God's covenant promise to Abraham—in which God pledged to die in order to fulfill His spiritual contract. Jesus' death was confirmed when his dead body was placed in the tomb as the Passover day was ending at sunset and the Night to be Much Observed was beginning. Just as the children of Israel were to rejoice in that God had delivered them and released them from their Egyptian bondage, true Christians, the spiritual seed of Abraham, are to rejoice on this night because it is the beginning of their deliverance from the bondage of sin and their exodus from spiritual Egypt (Coulter, *The Christian Passover*, pp. 266-277).

"Ex" means "out" and "odus" means "way." Hence, the word "Exodus" means, "the way out." The Exodus was Israel's "way out" of Egypt (symbolic of sin and bondage to sin). Likewise, for mankind the only "exodus" out of the bondage of sin is through Jesus Christ. At His Passover Jesus said, "I am the way"—Greek, οδος—the "way out," the exodus from sin. Our Christian walk with Jesus Christ begins after we have our sins forgiven through His shed blood as pictured by the Passover. We then begin our **journey out of sin** and a destructive way of life through love, faith devotion and obedience to Jesus Christ—walking in the love and grace of God, living by every Word of God and keeping His commandments, as pictured by the Feast of Unleavened Bread.

Jesus' Resurrection from the Dead. After being in the tomb exactly three days and three nights, Jesus was raised from the dead by the power of the Father as the regular weekly Sabbath, Nisan 17, was ending at sunset during the Feast of Unleavened Bread (Coulter, *The Day Jesus the Christ Died*, pp. 71-81). He was *not* resurrected on a Sunday morning—*not* on Orthodox Christendom's so-called Easter Sunday. He was resurrected at the close of the weekly Sabbath, just before the first day of the week began.

In the early morning on the first day of the week, when Mary Magdalene and others came to the tomb, an angel specifically told them that Jesus had already risen, that He was not there (Mark 16:2-7; Luke 24:1-6; John 20:1-10). A literal translation for "the first day of the week" is "the first of the weeks"—i.e., the first of the seven weeks to Pentecost. The Greek indicates that this "first day of the week" was the Wave Sheaf offering day.

The Wave Sheaf Offering Day. The offering of the first of the firstfruits is highly significant to God. Israel was instructed: "The **first of the firstfruits** of thy land thou shalt bring into the house of the LORD thy God" (Ex. 23:19). On this day, the first day of the week and the first day of the fifty-day count to Pentecost, the High Priest was to take a special, premier sheaf of the first of the firstfruits of the barley/wheat harvest and elevate or wave it before the Lord to be accepted by Him (Lev. 23:9-11). This incomparable ritual was **symbolic of Jesus Christ's ascension to the throne of God the Father** after He was resurrected from the dead—to be accepted as the first of the firstfruits of God.

The apostle John verified Jesus' ascension on this day: "But Mary stood outside the tomb weeping; and as she wept, she stooped down *and looked* into the tomb. And she saw two angels in white who were sitting, one at the head and the other at the feet, where the body of Jesus had been laid. And they said to her, 'Woman, why are you weeping?' She said to them, 'Because they have taken away my Lord, and I do not know where they have laid Him.'

"And after saying these things, she turned around and saw Jesus standing, but did not know that it was Jesus. Jesus said to her, 'Woman, why are you weeping? Whom are you seeking?' Thinking that He was the gardener, she said to Him, 'Sir, if you have carried Him off, tell me where you have laid Him, and I will take Him away.' Jesus said to her, 'Mary.' Turning around, she said to Him, 'Rabboni;' that is to say, 'Teacher.' Jesus said to her, '**Do not touch Me, because I have not yet ascended to My Father**. But go to My brethren and tell them that I am ascending to My Father and your Father, and My God and your God' " (John 20:11-17).

Later that same day at evening, Jesus appeared to the disciples and showed them His wounds from the crucifixion: "Afterwards, **as evening was drawing near that day, the first** *day* **of the weeks**, and the doors were shut where the disciples had assembled for fear of the Jews, Jesus came and stood in the midst, and said to them, 'Peace *be* to you.' And after saying this, He showed them His hands and His side. Then the disciples rejoiced *because* they had seen the Lord" (John 20:19-20).

Paul confirmed that Jesus Christ was the "first fruit" of the resurrection of the dead, the first of the spiritual harvest of God. At His return, at the time of the first resurrection, all those who are Christ's will be resurrected to eternal life: "But now Christ has been raised from *the* dead; He has become the first fruit of those who have fallen asleep. For since by man *came* death, by man also *came the* resurrection of *the* dead. For as in Adam all die, so also in Christ shall all be made alive. But each in his own order: **Christ** *the* **firstfruit; then, those who are Christ's at His coming**" (I Cor. 15:20-23). (For more detail about the Wave Sheaf offering day, see *The Day Jesus the Christ Died*, pp. 83-93.)

Additional References to the Feast of Unleavened Bread in the Gospels. The Passover and Feast of Unleavened Bread are two distinct feasts that fall on separate, yet consecutive, days—the 14th and the 15th. The two feasts have different, *but related*, meanings. Luke, however, records that it had become a common practice to refer to the entire eight-day festival season as "Passover." "Now the feast of unleavened *bread,* which *is* called Passover, was approaching" (Luke 22:1).

With this in mind we can better understand certain "difficult" references to the Passover and Feast of Unleavened Bread in the Gospel of John. "Now the **Passover of the Jews was near**.... Now when He was in Jerusalem **at the Passover, during the feast**, many believed on His name, as they observed the miracles that He was doing" (John 2:13, 23). "Now **the Passover, a feast of the Jews**, was near" (John 6:4). As the time of Jesus' last Passover approached, John wrote: "Now the **Passover of the Jews** was near" (John 11:55); "Six days before **the Passover**" (12:1); "Now before **the feast of the Passover**" (13:1).

In these and other passages John points to the importance of the Passover and Feast of Unleavened Bread. Few realize, however, that the Gospel of John is structured on the framework of the feasts and holy days of God. This makes John's gospel not only a record of Jesus' teachings, but a historical record as well.

- The harvest of Pentecost—John 4:35
- Feast of Trumpets—John 5:1
- Feast of Tabernacles and Last Great Day—John 7

Throughout the Gospels, the feasts and holy days of God provide the framework for the chronology of the ministry of Jesus Christ. Interestingly, however, there are "zero" written testimonies indicating that the true apostolic Church ever sanctioned the holidays now observed by Orthodox Christendom.

Other References to the Feast of Unleavened in the New Testament. The book of Acts is a microcosm of the Church of God and the ministry of the apostle Paul from about 30 AD to 67 AD. When examined carefully, it becomes apparent that Luke chronicled events relative to the feasts and holy days. This means that the apostles were using the sacred, calculated Hebrew calendar to record the times of these events, rather than the Roman calendar. Writing about Peter's imprisonment in 44 AD, Luke records: "Now about that time, Herod the king stretched forth *his* hands to persecute some of those of the church; and he killed James, the brother of John, with the sword. And when he saw that it pleased the Jews, he proceeded to take Peter also. (**Now those were *the* days of unleavened bread**.) And after arresting him, he put *him* in prison, delivering *him* to four sets of four soldiers to guard him with the intent of bringing him out to the people **after the Passover** *season*" (Acts 12:1-4).

In a deceitful attempt to give the appearance that the apostolic Church observed Easter, the translators of the King James Version incorrectly translated the Greek word for Passover (πασχα, *pascha*) in Acts 12:4 as "Easter." In all other places they correctly translated *pascha* as "Passover." However, as we have seen, "Passover" was also used in reference to the entire eight days of Passover and Unleavened Bread, which should be properly translated as "Passover *season*"—and never "Easter."

The Seventh Day of the Feast of Unleavened Bread. Undoubtedly, Jesus Christ, the apostles and the early New Testament Church observed all seven days of the Feast of Unleavened Bread. Although we do not find a specific reference to the seventh day of the feast, Luke's account of Paul's journeys in 58 AD demonstrates that he kept the full seven-day feast with Gentiles in northern Greece. "But we sailed away from Philippi **after the Days of Unleavened Bread**; and in five days we came to them at Troas, where we stayed *for* seven days" (Acts 20:6). This clearly indicates that Paul and his party observed the entire feast, including the seventh day.

In the account of the Exodus, God rescued the children of Israel from Pharaoh and his armies on the seventh day of the feast by bringing them safely through the Red Sea on dry ground. When the Egyptians followed them into the sea, God released the waters, destroying Pharaoh and his army.

As a nation steeped in the satanic occult worship of the sun and other false gods, Egypt is depicted in Scripture as a symbol of sin. Pharaoh was a type of Satan and his army symbolized evil demonic spirits. Just as Pharaoh and his armies pursued the children of Israel after God had rescued them from Egypt, so Satan and his demons can (and do) bring spiritual attacks upon converted Christians, God's spiritual children, attempting to enslave them again in the bondage of sin.

Thus we can see that, in the New Testament, the seventh day of the Feast of Unleavened Bread pictures how God, through Jesus Christ, has rescued us from the power of Satan. "Being strengthened with all power according to the might of His glory, unto all endurance and long-suffering with joy; giving thanks to the Father, Who has made us qualified for the share of the inheritance of the saints in the light; **Who has personally rescued us from the power of darkness and has transferred *us* unto the kingdom of the Son of His love**; in Whom we have redemption through His own blood, *even* the remission of sins" (Col. 1:11-14).

When Jesus called Saul to become Paul, the apostle to the Gentiles, He told him why He was chosen: "Now arise, and stand on your feet; for I have appeared to you for this purpose: to appoint you *as* a minister and a witness both of what you have seen and what I shall reveal to you. I am personally selecting you from among the people and the Gentiles, to whom I now send you, **to open their eyes, that *they* may turn from darkness to light, and *from* the authority of Satan to God**, so that they may receive remission of sins and an inheritance among those who have been sanctified through faith in Me' " (Acts 26:16-18).

As the "god of this world," Satan blinds the minds of those he has deceived (II Cor. 4:4). He is also called the "prince of the power of the air," who leads those of this world into living lives of sin and disobedience: "Now you were dead in trespasses and sins, in which you walked in times past according to the course of this world, according to **the prince of the power of the air**, **the spirit that is now working within the children of disobedience**; among whom also we all once had our conduct in the lusts of our flesh, doing the things willed by the flesh and by the mind, and were by nature *the* children of wrath, even as the rest *of the world*" (Eph. 2:1-3).

Paul went on to instruct them on how to fight their spiritual battles against Satan the devil and to overcome him through the power of God and the blood of Jesus Christ: "Finally, my brethren, be strong in *the* Lord, and in the might of His strength. Put on the whole armor of God so that you may be able to **stand against the wiles of the devil**, because we are not wrestling against flesh and blood, but against principalities *and* against powers, against the world rulers of the darkness of this age, against the spiritual *power* of wickedness in high *places*. Therefore, take up the whole armor of God so that you may be able to resist in the evil day, and having worked out all things, to stand.

"Stand therefore, having your loins girded about with truth, and wearing the breastplate of righteousness, and having your feet shod with *the* preparation of the gospel of peace. Besides all *these*, **take up the shield of the faith, with which you will have the power to quench all the fiery darts of the wicked one**; and put on the helmet of salvation, and the sword of the Spirit, which is the Word of God; praying at all times with all prayer and supplication in *the* Spirit" (Eph. 6:10-18).

Christians are to overcome Satan and resist his attacks through the blood of the Lamb, even if it costs them their physical lives: "And the great dragon was cast out, **the ancient serpent who is called the Devil and Satan**, who is deceiving the whole world; he was cast down to the earth, and his angels were cast down with him. And I heard a great voice in heaven say, 'Now has come the salvation and the power and the kingdom of our God, and the authority of His Christ because the accuser of our brethren has been cast down, who accuses them day and night before our God. **But they overcame him through the blood of the Lamb, and through the word of their testimony; and they loved not their lives unto death**' " (Rev. 12:9-11).

Jesus prayed to the Father that His people would be delivered from "the evil one"—Satan (John 17:15). He also told us we are to pray and entreat God daily that He would rescue us from the evil one (Matt. 6:13). There are many passages in the New Testament that show how God rescues us from sin and Satan. This ongoing spiritual battle—of overcoming sin, Satan and the world—reflects the special meaning of the seventh day of the Feast of Unleavened Bread in the New Testament.

Pentecost in the New Testament

Typically, God uses His feasts and holy days as benchmarks as He fulfills His will and purpose—often involving powerful historical events as well as spiritual events. For example, after God led the children of Israel to Mount Sinai, He personally spoke the Ten Commandments to them from the top of the mount in an awesome display of power and glory **on the day of Pentecost** (Ex. 20:1-17). As the New Testament shows, God again **used the day of Pentecost** in a wondrous demonstration of the power of His Holy Spirit—as He initially granted his Spirit to His Church.

In 30 AD, after Jesus was seen by His apostles and disciples for forty days, He instructed them to go to Jerusalem and wait until they had received the power of the Holy Spirit. "And while *they* were assembled with *Him*, He commanded them not to depart from Jerusalem but to 'await the promise of the Father, which,' *He said*, 'you have heard of Me. For John indeed baptized with water, but **you shall be baptized with *the* Holy Spirit after not many days**.... But you yourselves **shall receive power when the Holy Spirit has come upon you**, and you shall be My witnesses, both in Jerusalem and in all Judea and Samaria, and unto *the* ends of the earth' " (Acts 1:4-5, 8). Jesus then ascended into heaven and disappeared out of sight.

Ten days later, when the apostles and disciples were assembled together in a meeting room on the temple grounds to observe the day of Pentecost, God sent the Holy Spirit upon them in a unique display of His spiritual power. "And when the day *of Pentecost*, the fiftieth day, was being fulfilled, they were all with one accord in the same place. And suddenly *there* came from heaven a sound like *the* rushing of a powerful wind, and filled the whole house where they were sitting. And there appeared to them divided tongues as of fire, and sat upon each one of them. And they were all filled with *the* Holy Spirit; and they began to speak with other languages, as the Spirit gave them *the words* to proclaim.

"Now *there* were *many* Jews who were sojourning in Jerusalem, devout men from every nation under heaven. And when word of this went out, the multitude came together and were confounded, because each one heard them speaking in his own language. And they were all amazed, and marveled, saying to one another, 'Behold, are not all these who are speaking Galileans? Then how is it *that* we hear each one in our own language in which we were born? Parthians and Medes and Elamites, and those who inhabit Mesopotamia, and Judea and Cappadocia, Pontus and Asia, both Phrygia and Pamphylia, Egypt and the parts of Libya which *are* near Cyrene, and the Romans who are sojourning *here*, both Jews and proselytes, Cretes and Arabians; we hear them speaking in our own languages the great things of God.' And they were all amazed and greatly perplexed, saying to one another, 'What does this mean?' " (Acts 2:1-12).

By the power of His Holy Spirit, God miraculously caused the apostles to speak simultaneously in a multitude of languages. Thousands of Jews and proselytes from all over the world heard the apostles powerfully preach the message of God about the crucifixion and resurrection of Jesus Christ in their own languages.

Because God had placed His name and presence in the temple in Jerusalem, He likewise began the Church there. This was the reason He sent the Holy Spirit in the way that He did on this particular holy day. Had it been done in Nazareth or Bethlehem, no one would have believed that this was an act of God. However, the manner in which God poured out His Spirit—in the presence of multiple thousands of Jews assembled at the temple observing Pentecost—left no doubt that this was a powerful act of God. It was clearly His personal, divine intervention—not the work of men. This amazing display of God's power also provided the spiritual seal of authority confirming the apostles as His called and chosen witnesses (Luke 24:43-49).

Silencing the few detractors, Peter stood up to preach a dynamic message about the crucifixion and resurrection of Jesus Christ to the thousands gathered at the temple. After convicting them in conscience, he called on them to repent to God for their sins which killed Christ: " 'Therefore, let all *the* house of Israel know with full assurance that God has made this *same* Jesus, Whom you crucified, both Lord and Christ.' Now after hearing *this*, they were cut to the heart; and they said to Peter and the other apostles, 'Men *and* brethren, what shall we do?' Then Peter said to them, '**Repent**

and be baptized each one of you in the name of Jesus Christ for *the* **remission of sins, and you yourselves shall receive the gift of the Holy Spirit**' " (Acts 2:36-38). As a result, three thousand were baptized and added to the Church on that momentous day of Pentecost in 30 AD—the day the true Church of God began.

Few are Chosen Because few Repent. With the beginning of the Church on Pentecost, God revealed that He was selecting only those few who repent and accept the sacrifice of Jesus Christ for the forgiveness of their sins. Continuing in Acts two: " 'For the promise is to you and to your children, and to all those who are afar off, **as many as** *the* **Lord our God may call**.' And with many other words he earnestly testified and exhorted, saying, 'Be saved from this perverse generation.' **Then those who joyfully received his message were baptized**; and about three thousand souls were added that day. And they steadfastly continued in the teachings of the apostles and in fellowship, and *in* the breaking of bread and *in* prayers" (verses 39-42). While there were thousands of Jews at the temple on Pentecost, only 3,000 repented and were baptized because they were the **only ones who answered God's call**. God gave His Holy Spirit *only* to those individuals—*not* to the other thousands who did not repent. This confirms the truth that God only gives the Holy Spirit to the few who answer His call, repent of their sins and are baptized. From the time of Jesus' ministry until His second coming, God the Father and Jesus Christ are choosing only the ones who **answer** God's call. As Jesus said, "For many are called, but few *are* chosen"—because few repent (Matt. 22:14, Luke 13:1-5).

Because they refuse to repent, the vast majority have not been chosen by God at this time. Instead of believing God, people tend to believe in traditional religions—and many indeed claim that they are "Christian" because they "preach Christ's name." Typically, however, they reject God's commands concerning the weekly Sabbath and holy days.

But Jesus emphasized that professing His name is not enough: "Not everyone who says to Me, 'Lord, Lord,' shall enter into the kingdom of heaven; **but the one who is doing the will of My Father, Who** *is* **in heaven**. Many will say to Me in that day [the day of judgment], 'Lord, Lord, did we not prophesy through Your name? And *did we not* cast out demons through Your name? And *did we not* perform many works of power through Your name?' And then I will confess to them, 'I never knew you. Depart from Me, you who work lawlessness' " (Matt. 7:21-23).

Without **genuine belief** in the teachings of God the Father and Jesus Christ, such people become blinded and deceived: "And His disciples came to Him and asked, 'Why do You speak to them in parables?' And He answered *and* said to them, 'Because it has been given to you to know the mysteries of the kingdom of heaven, but to them it has not been given. For whoever has *understanding*, to him more shall be given, and he shall have an abundance; but whoever does not have *understanding*, even what he has shall be taken away from him. For this *reason* I speak to them in parables, because seeing, they see not; and hearing, they hear not; neither do they understand. And in them is fulfilled the prophecy of Isaiah, which says, "**In hearing you shall hear, and in no way understand; and *in* seeing you shall see, and in no way perceive; for the heart of this people has grown fat, and their ears are dull of hearing, and their eyes they have closed; lest they should see with their eyes, and should hear with their ears, and should understand with their hearts, and should be converted, and I should heal them.**" But blessed *are* your eyes, because they see; and your ears, because they hear' " (Matt. 13:10-16). (As we will see later, because God has blinded them at this time, their opportunity for salvation will come after the Millennium is over. We will thoroughly cover this vital truth when we come to the meaning of the Last Great Day.)

Indeed, at this present time very few are called and chosen, because very few actually believe God or Jesus Christ—or believe their Word, the Bible. Few are willing to repent, be baptized, obey God and strive to live by every word of God (Matt. 4:4; John 14:20-24; Acts 4:10-12, 19-20; 5:29-32).

It is God the Father and Jesus Christ Who do the choosing: "Blessed *be* the God and Father of our Lord Jesus Christ, Who has blessed us with every spiritual blessing in the heavenly *things* with Christ; according as **He has personally chosen us for Himself**" (Eph. 1:3-4). Jesus told His disciples: "You yourselves did not choose Me, but **I have personally chosen you**, and ordained you, that you should go *forth* and bear fruit, and that your fruit should remain; so that whatever you shall ask the Father in My name, He may give you" (John 15:16). This is why Jesus said, "I am the way, and the truth, and the life; **no one comes to the Father except through Me**" (John 14:6) and "**No one can come to Me unless the Father, Who sent Me, draws him**" (John 6:44). In these two verses Jesus clearly shows that this special calling is a *joint act* on the part of God the Father and Jesus Christ. It is simply not a matter of human determination or effort— but of God's choosing.

The Meaning of Pentecost. God's unique use of the day of Pentecost in the past has magnified and added to its meaning. Today, when we observe Pentecost, we may recall the lessons of this feast in both the Old and New Testaments:

1) God gave the Ten Commandments to the children of Israel (Ex. 20:1-17; Deut. 5:7-21).
2) Israel celebrated the completed wheat and barley harvest of the firstfruits (Ex. 23:16).
3) God sent the Holy Spirit to begin His Church.
4) After our repentance and conversion, with the Holy Spirit dwelling in us, God begins to write His laws and commandments in our hearts and minds (Heb. 10:16).
5) The apostles' miraculous preaching in many languages fulfilled, in part, Christ's command that the gospel be preached in all the world, to all nations (Matt. 28:18-20; Luke 24:44-47).

6) By sending the Holy Spirit, God signaled that He was going to reject and ultimately destroy the temple and its system of worship, as prophesied (Isa. 66:1-5; Matt. 22:1-7; Acts 7:44-50).

7) All who desire to worship God the Father could now do so in spirit and in truth—from any location, not just at the temple in Jerusalem (John 4:20-24; Heb. 10:16-22).

There is also a prophetic aspect to the Feast of Pentecost, in which God will again use this feast to fulfill His will and purpose. Christians are called spiritual "firstfruits" (James 1:18), and the harvest of the spiritual firstfruits is at the end of this age (Matt. 13:18-43; Rev. 14:14-16). This spiritual harvest, as pictured by Pentecost, will be a resurrection to eternal life for all who are called and chosen. This is the first resurrection at Jesus' coming (I Cor. 15:20-23; Rev. 20:6).

Visualize the blowing of a trumpet on the day of Pentecost. The children of Israel were assembled at the foot of Mount Sinai to receive the Ten Commandments spoken by God: "And it came to pass on the third day in the morning [Pentecost], that there were thunders and lightnings, and a thick cloud upon the mount, and **the voice of the trumpet exceeding loud**; so that all the people that *was* in the camp trembled. And Moses brought forth the people out of the camp to meet with God; and they stood at the nether part of the mount. And mount Sinai was altogether on a smoke, because the LORD descended upon it in fire: and the smoke thereof ascended as the smoke of a furnace, and the whole mount quaked greatly. **And when the voice of the trumpet sounded long, and waxed louder and louder**, Moses spake, and God answered him by a voice" (Ex. 19:16-19).

In Numbers 10:10 we read that the trumpet was to be blown on each holy day, including the Feast of Pentecost. This served to remind the children of Israel of the Pentecost at Sinai on which they received the Ten Commandments.

The apostle Paul draws a special comparison between the giving of the Ten Commandments at Mount Sinai and the assembling of the resurrected saints as they meet Jesus Christ. He emphasizes how much greater this event will be when compared to what the children of Israel had experienced: "For you [the Church] have not come to *the* mount [Sinai] that could be touched and that burned with fire, nor to gloominess, and fearful darkness, and *the* whirlwind; and to *the* **sound of *the* trumpet**, and to *the* voice of *the* words, which those who heard *begged* that *the* word not be spoken *directly* to them. (For they could not endure what was being commanded: 'And if even an animal touches the mountain, it shall be stoned, or shot through with an arrow'; and so terrifying was the sight *that* Moses said, 'I am greatly afraid and trembling.')

"But you [the Church] have come to [spiritual] Mount Sion, and to *the* city of *the* living God, heavenly Jerusalem; and to an innumerable company of angels; *to the* **joyous festival gathering** [Pentecost resurrection]; and to *the* church of *the* firstborn [the firstfruits of God], registered *in the* *book of life* in heaven; and to God, *the* Judge of all; and to *the* spirits of the just who have been perfected; and to Jesus, *the* Mediator of *the* New Covenant; and to sprinkling of *the* blood of *ratification*, proclaiming superior things than *that of* Abel" (Heb. 12:18-24).

The prophetic significance of the trumpet blown on Pentecost is that it pictures the "last trumpet"—blown at the time of the resurrection of the saints. Jesus Himself foretold this: "But immediately after the tribulation of those days, the sun shall be darkened, and the moon shall not give her light, and the stars shall fall from heaven, and the powers of the heavens shall be shaken. And then shall appear the sign of the Son of man in heaven; and then shall all the tribes of the earth mourn, and they shall see the Son of man coming upon the clouds of heaven with power and great glory. And **He shall send His angels with a great sound of a trumpet**; and **they shall gather together His elect** from the four winds, from one end of heaven to *the* other" (Matt. 24:29-31).

The apostle Paul also declared that the first resurrection to eternal life would occur at the **last trump**: "And as we have borne the image of the *one* made of dust, we shall also bear the image of the heavenly *one*. Now this I say, brethren, that flesh and blood cannot inherit *the* kingdom of God, nor does corruption inherit incorruption. Behold, I show you a mystery: we shall not all fall asleep, but **we shall all be changed, in an instant, in *the* twinkling of an eye, at the last trumpet; for *the* trumpet shall sound, and the dead shall be raised incorruptible, and we shall be changed**. For this corruptible must put on incorruptibility, and this mortal must put on immortality. Now when this corruptible shall have put on incorruptibility, and this mortal shall have put on immortality, then shall come to pass the saying that is written: 'Death is swallowed up in victory' " (I Cor. 15:49-54).

In Paul's first epistle to the Thessalonians, he wrote that the first resurrection takes place at the last trumpet: "But I do not wish you to be ignorant, brethren, concerning those who have fallen asleep, that you be not grieved, even as others, who have no hope. For if we believe that Jesus died and rose again, in exactly the same way also, those who have fallen asleep in Jesus will God bring with Him. For this we say to you by *the* Word of *the* Lord, that we who are alive and remain unto the coming of the Lord shall in no wise precede those who have fallen asleep because **the Lord Himself shall descend from heaven with *a* shout of command, with *the* voice of an archangel and with *the* trumpet of God; and the dead in Christ shall rise first**; then we who are alive and remain shall be caught up together with them in *the* clouds for *the* meeting with the Lord in *the* air; and so shall we always be with *the* Lord" (I Thes. 4:13-17).

The book of Revelation confirms that the last trump is the seventh trumpet—when the first resurrection takes place: "**Then the seventh angel sounded *his* trumpet**; and *there* were great voices in heaven, saying, 'The kingdoms of this world have become *the kingdoms* of our Lord and of His Christ, and He shall reign into the ages of eternity.' And the twenty-four elders, who sit before God on their thrones, fell on their faces and worshiped

God, saying, 'We give You thanks, O Lord God Almighty, Who is, and Who was, and Who *is* to come; for You have taken *to Yourself* Your great power, and have reigned. For the nations were angry, and Your wrath has come, and **the time for the dead to be judged, and to give reward to Your servants the prophets, and to the saints, and to *all* those who fear Your name, the small and the great**; and to destroy those who destroy the earth' " (Rev. 11:15-18).

When the first resurrection takes place, **angels will carry the saints** to a gigantic sea of glass in the clouds (conceivably over Jerusalem) to meet Christ. "And I saw a **sea of glass** mingled with fire, and those who had gotten the victory over the beast, and over his image, and over his mark, *and* over the number of his name, **standing on the sea of glass**, having *the* harps of God. And they were singing the song of Moses, *the* servant of God, and the song of the Lamb, saying, 'Great and awesome *are* Your works, Lord God Almighty; righteous and true *are* Your ways, King of the saints. Who shall not fear You, O Lord, and glorify Your name? For *You* only *are* holy; and all the nations shall come and worship before You, for Your judgments have been revealed' " (Rev. 15:2-4).

Several things will take place on this sea of glass before Christ and the saints return to the earth to establish the kingdom of God on earth:

1) The saints will receive their new names (Rev. 2:17).
2) The saints are given their rewards (I Cor. 3:8; Rev. 11:18; 22:12; II John 8).
3) The saints will receive their assignments as kings or priests (Rev. 20:6).
4) The marriage of the Lamb and His bride will take place (Rev. 19:6-8).
5) The marriage supper will take place (Rev. 19:9; Matt. 22:1-13).
6) The saints will witness the seven last plagues poured out—the vengeance of God (Rev. 15:5-8; 16:1-21; Psa. 149:4-9). The seventh plague will be the battle of Armageddon.
7) They will be gathered into God's army and will fight with Christ as they return to the earth with Jesus to establish the kingdom and government of God on the earth (Rev. 19:11-21; Zech. 14:1-9).

It will take time for all these things to transpire, undoubtedly extending from the day of Pentecost unto the Feast of Trumpets, about four months.

Thus, the Word of God reveals that just as God began the Church on Pentecost by sending the Holy Spirit, He will complete the harvest of His Church—the spiritual firstfruits—on Pentecost. On that day God will resurrect from the dead all the righteous saints—from Abel, the first martyr, to the two witnesses, the final martyrs. In the resurrection they will all be changed in a twinkling of an eye and given glorious, immortal bodies as the spiritual sons and daughters of God the Father. "[W]e are waiting for *the* Savior, *the* Lord Jesus Christ; **Who will transform our vile bodies, that they may be conformed to His glorious body**, according to the inner working of His own power, *whereby He is able* to subdue all things to Himself" (Phil. 3:20-21). As glorified spirit beings, they will shine as the stars of heaven (Dan. 12:1-3; Matt. 13:43).

They will share the same eternal existence and glory as Jesus Christ: "The Spirit itself bears witness conjointly with our own spirit, *testifying* that we are *the* children of God. Now if *we are* children, *we are* also heirs—truly, **heirs of God and joint heirs with Christ**—if indeed we suffer together with Him, so that **we may also be glorified together with Him**" (Rom. 8:16-17). This is why Paul calls the first resurrection a superior resurrection (Heb. 11:35-40). Finally, John writes: "Behold! What *glorious* love the Father has given to us, that we should be called the children of God.... [And] we know that when He is manifested, we shall be like Him, because we shall see Him exactly as He is" (I John 3:1-2).

The book of Revelation proclaims: "Blessed and holy is the one who has part in the first resurrection; over these the second death has no power" (Rev. 20:6). As pictured by the Feast of Pentecost, Christians look forward to receiving eternal life and glory in the first resurrection (Rom. 8:14-18; I John 3:1-3).

Other references to Pentecost. There are two other references showing that Paul kept the Feast of Pentecost. As we have clearly seen, Paul continually taught the Gentile converts to keep the feasts and holy days of God, which included the Feast of Pentecost.

• Paul wrote to the Corinthians from Ephesus of his intentions to visit and stay with them. However, he let them know that he would remain in Ephesus until Pentecost. This means that **he and all the brethren in Ephesus kept the Feast of Pentecost**. "But I will come to you after I pass through Macedonia, for I am going through Macedonia. It may be *that* I shall stay with you, or *that* I may even winter *there*, so that you may send me forth *on my journey* wherever I may go. For *at this time* I will not *stop* to see you, but I hope at some *future* time to stay with you, if the Lord permits. But **I will remain in Ephesus until Pentecost**. For a great and effective door has been opened to me, and there *are* many adversaries" (I Cor. 16:5-9).

• On another occasion, Paul was journeying to Jerusalem and intended to keep Pentecost there: "For Paul had decided to sail by Ephesus, because he did not want to spend time in Asia; for he hastened in order to be in Jerusalem **on the day of Pentecost**, if possible" (Acts 20:16).

• In the Gospel of John, Jesus points out the ripening harvest to His disciples, which apparently is a direct reference to Pentecost: "Do not say that there are yet **four months, and *then* the harvest comes.**

I say to you, look around. Lift up your eyes and see the fields, for they are already **white to harvest**" (John 4:35). From Pentecost until the Fall harvest season and the Fall festivals and holy days is four months—so Christ must have been referring to the time of Pentecost. As we have seen, 3,000 new converts were added to the Church on Pentecost in 30 AD.

In this chapter, we have taken a broad overview of the Spring feasts and holy days of God in the New Testament—where we find overwhelming evidence that the apostolic New Testament Church kept and revered these days. The "God-breathed" beautiful writings of the apostles truly expand the scope and spiritual significance of God's feasts and holy days. Far from being abolished by Jesus Christ and His true apostles, these days continue to foreshadow and crystallize God's purpose and plan for us all.

In the next chapter, we will learn how the Fall feasts and holy days continue to reveal God's prophetic master plan, outlining His loving purpose for all of humanity.

CHAPTER ELEVEN

A Survey of God's Fall Feasts and Holy Days in the New Testament

Occurring in the seventh month of the sacred calendar, the Fall feasts and holy days portray the future fulfillment of God's plan for all mankind. These vital days foretell *how* and approximately *when* endtime events prophesied in the Old and New Testaments will unfold.

We will begin our survey of the Fall holy days by focusing on the Feast of Trumpets—which falls on the first day of the seventh month (Lev. 23:23-25). Trumpets is the fourth (or "middle") of God's seven annual holy days, and thus functions much like a *fulcrum* or a "tipping point" in the history of the world. Why? Because Trumpets pictures God's direct, climatic intervention in the affairs of man—leading directly to the literal return of Jesus Christ and His establishment of the kingdom of God on earth.

Historically, God required the priests and Levites to blow silver trumpets as a memorial throughout the day of Trumpets (Psa. 81:3). They also blew a number of *shofars*, which were trumpets made from ram's horns, used primarily in time of war. During such times, God would lead Israel into battle as the priests carried the Ark of the Covenant—often blowing trumpets (Josh. 6:1-16; Judges 7:8, 16-18). If the people had been obedient to God and faithful to His covenant, He would fight for them and give them victory over their enemies (Deut. 28:7; Lev. 26:7-8).

In addition, guards who watched over the cities and villages of Israel were to blow the *shofar* if an enemy attack was eminent (Ezk. 33:1-6; Joel 2:1, 15).

The Feast of Trumpets in the New Testament

There is no a direct reference (by name) to the Feast of Trumpets in the New Testament. However, based on the chronological structure of John's Gospel, we can surmise that the feast mentioned in John 5:1 was probably the Feast of Trumpets. John's framework for his Gospel is: Passover, John 2; Pentecost, John 4; a feast of the Jews, John 5; Passover, John 6; Tabernacles and Last Great Day, John 7 and 8; and Passover, John 12-19. Based on the seasons, John has the following sequence: Spring, Fall, Spring, Fall, and Spring.

Since the feast in John 5:1 was *after* Jesus' reference to Pentecost in John 4, it must have been a Fall feast. (If it had been the Feast of Tabernacles, it is likely that John would have mentioned it, as he did in chapter 7. If it had been the Day of Atonement—a fast day characterized by absolutely no work whatsoever—the Jews would have been even more vehement against Jesus for healing a man and telling him to pick up his bedroll and walk.) We can conclude, therefore, that the feast mentioned in John 5:1 was probably the Feast of Trumpets.

   The Birth of Jesus Christ and the Feast of Trumpets. As the Word of God demonstrates, God has always used His feasts and holy days to fulfill His will as well as certain major prophesies. We have already seen that the "appointed time" for Jesus to die was the Passover day in 30 AD, which God had set "before the foundation of the world." But what about Jesus' birth—was it likewise predetermined "before the foundation of the world" to occur on a particular day? Was that day a holy day? And if so, which holy day? What do the Scriptures and history reveal about Jesus' birth?

   Paul confirms that Jesus was born at the precise time appointed by God: "But when the [appointed] time for the fulfillment came, God sent forth His own Son, born of a woman" (Gal. 4:4). This indicates that the time of Jesus' birth was predetermined. While the Gospels do not announce the specific day of Jesus' birth, He was clearly **born at a particular time preordained by God** to fulfill His will and prophetic plan.

   There is a preponderance of evidence found in the New Testament, the writings of Josephus, and other historical sources, as well as information relating to the calculated Hebrew calendar and specific astronomical events, from which we are able to determine approximately when Jesus was born— perhaps even the exact day. A chronicle of pertinent information documenting when Jesus was born is, unfortunately, too expansive to be included in this book. Such details, however, are carefully documented in two books: *A Harmony of the Gospels in Modern English—the Life of Jesus Christ* and *The New Testament In Its Original Order—a Faithful Version with Commentary,* both by Fred R. Coulter. It is sufficient to assert that the complex scriptural and historical evidence systematically compiled in these books supports the Feast of Trumpets in 5 BC as the most probable date of Jesus' birth. These books may be obtained from York Publishing (see address in the front of this book) or from *www.amazon.com*.

   The Prophetic Meaning of the Feast of Trumpets. The book of Revelation unveils the prophetic meaning of the Feast of Trumpets, as the book depicts the "day of the Lord" described in several Old Testament prophecies. These prophecies give us many details regarding the day of the Lord—the time of God's direct intervention in the affairs of man, when Jesus Christ returns in glory as King of kings and Lord of lords, to take control of this world (Rev. 11:15; 19:11-21). The Bible informs us that often a *day* in prophecy is a *year* in actual fulfillment (Num. 14:34, Ezek. 4:6). Isaiah 34:8 describes it as a "*day* of vengeance" and a "*year* of recompenses." Therefore, reckoned from Trumpets to Trumpets, the "day" of the Lord is the final *year* leading up to and including Jesus Christ's return to earth.

   This coming day of the Lord is a time of disaster, famine, pestilence and war with death and destruction unparalleled in all of human history.

The prophet Jeremiah indicates that ultimately **all nations will be involved** in the endtime day of the Lord (Jer. 25:15-17, 26-27). God will intervene powerfully from heaven against all the nations of the world—none shall escape (verses 30-33). In fact, when Jesus Christ intervenes mightily in this world, He is going to shake the earth so violently that it will be nearly thrust out of its orbit (Isa. 13:6-13; also see Hag. 2:6-7). The prophet Isaiah describes the awesome power of God when He "arises to shake terribly the earth" and begins to make Himself known to the world. There will be no doubt that such events are from the hand of God (see Isa. 2:10-12, 18-21).

God gave Daniel a vision of this time, saying, "there shall be a time of trouble, such as never was since there was a nation even to that same time" (Dan. 12:1). Jesus described for His disciples a time of tribulation coming at the end of the age—a time so devastating and destructive that if He did not intervene to limit those days, no flesh would be saved alive. "For then shall there be great tribulation, **such as has not been from *the* beginning of *the* world until this time, nor ever shall be *again*.** And if those days were not limited, there would no flesh be saved; but for the elect's sake those days shall be limited" (Matt. 24:21-22).

Throughout history mankind has suffered greatly from war, famine, pestilence and natural disasters. But nothing will compare to the day of the Lord: "**The great day of the LORD is near, it is near, and hasteth greatly**, even the voice of the day of the LORD: the mighty man shall cry there bitterly. **That day is a day of wrath, a day of trouble and distress, a day of wasteness and desolation, a day of darkness and gloominess, a day of clouds and thick darkness, a day of the trumpet and alarm** against the fenced cities, and against the high towers. And I will bring distress upon men, that they shall walk like blind men, because they have sinned against the LORD: **and their blood shall be poured out as dust, and their flesh as the dung**. Neither their silver nor their gold shall be able to deliver them in the day of the LORD'S wrath; but the whole land shall be devoured by the fire of his jealousy: for he shall make even a speedy riddance of all them that dwell in the land" (Zeph. 1:14-18).

The book of Revelation documents the fulfillment of such prophecies—describing an electrifying demonstration of power as Jesus Christ directly intervenes and personally manifests Himself. The opening of the sixth seal sets the stage for the day of the Lord to begin: "And when He [Jesus Christ] opened the sixth seal, I looked, and behold, there was a great earthquake; and the sun became black as *the* hair *of* sackcloth, and the moon became as blood; and the stars of heaven fell to the earth, as a fig tree casts its untimely figs when it is shaken by a mighty wind. **Then *the* heaven departed like a scroll that is being rolled up, and every mountain and island was moved out of its place**. And the kings of the earth, and the great men, and the rich men, and the chief captains, and the powerful men, and every bondman, and every free *man* **hid themselves in the caves and in the rocks of the mountains**; and they said to the mountains and to the rocks,

'Fall on us, and hide us from *the* face of Him Who sits on the throne, and from the wrath of the Lamb because **the great day of His wrath has come**, and who has the power to stand?' " (Rev. 6:12-17).

Trumpets and the Day of the Lord. The day of the Lord actually begins with the opening of the seventh seal—in which seven angels successively sound their trumpets, signaling various phases of God's direct intervention. Ultimately, this great "day" will climax in angelic war from heaven against the united armies of men and demons on the earth.

John describes what he saw in vision regarding the seven trumpet plagues sent from God by the hands of angels: "Then I saw the seven angels who stand before God, and seven trumpets were given to them. And another angel, who had a golden censer, came and stood at the altar; and much incense was given to him, so that he might offer *it* with the prayers of all the saints on the golden altar that *was* before the throne. And the smoke of the incense went up before God from *the* hand of the angel, ascending with the prayers of the saints. And the angel took the censer, and filled it with fire from the altar, and cast *it* into the earth; and there were voices, and thunders, and lightnings, and an earthquake.

"Then the seven angels who had the seven trumpets prepared themselves to sound *their* trumpets. And **the first angel sounded *his* trumpet**; and there was hail and fire mingled with blood, and it was cast upon the earth; and a third of the trees were burnt up, and all green grass was burnt up. Then **the second angel sounded *his* trumpet**; and *there* was cast into the sea as *it were* a great mountain burning with fire, and a third of the sea became blood; and a third of the living creatures that *were* in the sea died, and a third of the ships were destroyed. And **the third angel sounded *his* trumpet**; and *there* fell out of heaven a great star, burning like a lamp; and it fell on a third of the rivers, and on the fountains of waters. Now the name of the star is Wormwood; and a third of the waters became wormwood; and many men died from *drinking* the waters because they were made bitter. Then **the fourth angel sounded *his* trumpet**; and a third of the sun was smitten, and a third of the moon, and a third of the stars; so that a third of them were darkened; and a third part of the day did not shine, and likewise *a third part of* the night. And I looked; and I heard an angel flying in the midst of heaven, saying with a loud voice, '**Woe, woe, woe to those who are dwelling on the earth, because of the voices of the remaining trumpets of the three angels who *are* about to sound *their* trumpets**' " (Rev. 8:2-13).

When the fifth angel sounds his trumpet, hordes of demons will be released from an Abyss to join human armies using futuristic weapons: "And **the fifth angel sounded *his* trumpet**; and I saw a star *that* had fallen from heaven to the earth, and there was given to him the key to the bottomless abyss. And he opened the bottomless abyss [to release the imprisoned demons]; and there went up smoke from the pit, like *the* smoke of a great furnace; and the sun and the air were darkened by the smoke from the pit. Then locusts [demons] came onto the earth from the smoke; and power was given to them, as the scorpions of the earth have power. And it was said to them that they should not damage the grass of the earth, or any green thing, or any tree, but only the men who did not have the seal of God in their foreheads. And it was given to them that they should not kill them, but that they should be tormented five months; and their torment *was* like *the* torment of a scorpion when it stings a man. And in those days men will seek death but will not find it; and they will desire to die, but death will flee from them.

"And the appearance of the locusts *was* like horses prepared for war; and on their heads *were* crowns like *those* of gold; and their faces *were* like *the* faces of men; and they had hair like women's hair; and their teeth were like *those* of lions. And they had breastplates like iron breastplates; and the sound of their wings *was* like *the* sound of chariots *drawn* by many horses running to war; and they had tails like scorpions, and stingers; and they were *given* power to injure men with their tails *for* five months. And they have over them a king, the angel of the abyss; his name in Hebrew *is* Abaddon, but *the* name he has in Greek *is* Apollyon [Satan the devil]. **The first woe is past**. Behold, after these things two more woes are still to come" (Rev. 9:1-12). John is no doubt graphically describing futuristic weapons to be used by human·armies and demons. This fifth trumpet represents the aggressive attack by the prophetic "beast" of Revelation 13 against nations north and east of Jerusalem (Dan. 11:44).

After the five months, a coalition of kings from the east will retaliate against the "beast" with the largest army ever amassed in history. This massive, 200-million-man force will be armed with powerful, sophisticated weapons—and backed by the supernatural strength of hordes of demons. **"And the sixth angel sounded** *his* **trumpet**; and I heard a voice from the four horns of the golden altar that *is* before God; *and* it said to the sixth angel, who had the trumpet, 'Loose the four angels who are bound in the great river Euphrates.' Then the four angels, who had been prepared for the hour and day and month and year, were loosed, so that they might kill a third of men; and the number of *the* armies of the horsemen *was* two hundred thousand thousand; and I heard the number of them.

"And so I saw the horses in the vision, and those sitting on them, who had fiery breastplates, even like jacinth and brimstone. And the heads of the horses *were* like heads of lions, and fire and smoke and brimstone shoot out of their mouths. **By these three, a third of men were killed: by the fire and the smoke and the brimstone that shoot out of their mouths**. For their power is in their mouths; for their tails *are* like serpents, *and* have heads, and with them they inflict wounds. But the rest of the men who were not killed by these plagues still did not repent of the works of their hands, that they might not worship demons, and idols of gold and silver and brass and stone and wood, which do not have the power to see, nor to hear, nor to walk. **And they did not repent of their murders, nor of their sorceries, nor of their fornications, nor of their thievery**" (Rev. 9:13-21).

The prophet Joel describes this battle that takes place between the armies of the fifth and sixth trumpets: "**Blow ye the trumpet in Zion**, and sound an alarm in my holy mountain: let all the inhabitants of the land tremble: **for the day of the LORD cometh**, for it is nigh at hand; a day of darkness and of gloominess, a day of clouds and of thick darkness, as the morning spread upon the mountains: **a great people and a strong; there hath not been ever the like, neither shall be any more after it**, even to the years of many generations.

"A fire devoureth before them; and behind them a flame burneth: the land is as the garden of Eden before them, and behind them a desolate wilderness; yea, and nothing shall escape them. The appearance of them is as the appearance of horses; and as horsemen, so shall they run. Like the noise of chariots on the tops of mountains shall they leap, like the noise of a flame of fire that devoureth the stubble, as a strong people set in battle array. Before their face the people shall be much pained: all faces shall gather blackness. **They shall run like mighty men**; they shall climb the wall like men of war; and they shall march every one on his ways, and they shall not break their ranks: neither shall one thrust another; they shall walk every one in his path: and **when they fall upon the sword, they shall not be wounded**. They shall run to and fro in the city; they shall run upon the wall, they shall climb up upon the houses; they shall enter in at the windows like a thief. **The earth shall quake before them; the heavens shall tremble: the sun and the moon shall be dark, and the stars shall withdraw their shining**: and the LORD shall utter his voice before his army: for his camp is very great: for he is strong that executeth his word: **for the day of the LORD is great and very terrible; and who can abide it**?" (Joel 2:1-11.)

These wars of vast destruction will envelop the entirety of the Middle East—as well as extend from the western seat of the "beast" into the lands of the Far East, the origin of the kings of the east. Once these armies have fought to a standstill, **the seventh angel sounds his trumpet, and the first resurrection takes place on Pentecost** (Rev. 11:15-19).

The time from Pentecost to Trumpets is approximately four months. During this time, another seven angels will pour out the seven last plagues. The final, seventh plague will culminate in the battle of Armageddon. This colossal, epoch-ending war will pit God and His angels against the "beast," the "false prophet," and armies from all nations of the world—as well as against Satan himself, with his demons. "And after these things I looked, and behold, the temple of the tabernacle of the testimony in heaven was opened. And the seven angels who had the seven *last* plagues came out of the temple; they were clothed in linen, pure and bright, and girded about the chest with golden breastplates. And one of the four living creatures gave to the seven angels seven golden vials, full of the wrath of God, Who lives into the ages of eternity. And the temple was filled with smoke from the glory of God, and from His power; and no one was able to enter inside the temple until the seven plagues of the seven angels were fulfilled" (Rev. 15:5-8).

"Then I heard a loud voice from the temple say to the seven angels, '**Go and pour out the vials of the wrath of God onto the earth**.' And the **first** *angel* went and poured out his vial onto the earth; and an evil and grievous sore fell upon the men who had the mark of the beast, and upon those who were worshiping his image. And the **second angel** *went and* poured out his vial into the sea; and it became blood, like *that* of a dead *man*; and every living soul in the sea died. And the **third angel** poured out his vial upon the rivers, and into the fountains of waters; and they became blood.

"Then I heard the angel of the waters say, 'You are righteous, O Lord, Who are, and Who was, even the Holy One, in that You have executed this judgment. For they have poured out *the* blood of saints and of prophets, and You have given them blood to drink; for they are worthy.' And I heard another *voice* from the altar say, 'Yes, Lord God Almighty, true and righteous *are* Your judgments.'

"And the **fourth angel** poured out his vial upon the sun; and *power* was given to it to scorch men with fire. Then men were scorched with great heat; and they blasphemed the name of God, Who has authority over these plagues, and did not repent to give Him glory. And the **fifth angel** poured out his vial upon the throne of the beast; and his kingdom became full of darkness; and they gnawed their tongues because of the pain, and blasphemed the God of heaven because of their pains and their sores; yet they did not repent of their works. And the **sixth angel** poured out his vial into the great river Euphrates; and its waters were dried up, so that the way of the kings from the rising of *the* sun might be prepared. Then I saw three unclean spirits like frogs *come* out of the mouth of the dragon, and out of the mouth of the beast, and out of the mouth of the false prophet; for they are spirits of demons working miracles, going forth to the kings of the earth, even of the whole world, to gather them together to *the* battle of that great day of the Almighty God.

"Behold, I come as a thief. Blessed *is* the one who is watching and is keeping his garments, so that he may not walk naked and they *may not* see his shame. And he gathered them together to the place that in Hebrew is called Armageddon. Then the **seventh angel** poured out his vial into the air; and a loud voice came out of the temple of heaven, from the throne, saying, 'IT IS FINISHED.'

"And there were voices and thunders and lightnings; and there was a great earthquake, such as was not since men were on the earth, so mighty an earthquake, *and* so great. And the great city was divided into three parts; and the cities of the nations fell; and Babylon the Great was remembered before God to give her the cup of the wine of the fury of His wrath. And every island disappeared, and no mountains were found; and great hail, *each stone* the weight of a talent, fell down from heaven upon men; and men blasphemed God because of the plague of the hail, for the plague was exceedingly great" (Rev. 16:1-21).

After the last of the seven plagues has been poured out, Jesus and the resurrected saints will descend to the earth from the sea of glass in a final battle against the beast, false prophet and their armies. As they are descending to the earth with clarity and singleness of purpose on this Feast of Trumpets, the seven angels will **continue blowing the trumpets of God mightily for all the earth to hear**. "And I saw the beast and the kings of the earth and their armies, gathered together to make war with Him Who sits on the horse, and with His army. And **the beast was taken, and with him the false prophet** who worked miracles in his presence, by which he had deceived those who received the mark of the beast and those who worshiped his image. **Those two were cast alive into the lake of fire**, which burns with brimstone; and the rest were killed by the sword of Him Who sits on the horse, *even the sword* that goes out of His mouth; and all the birds were filled with their flesh" (Rev. 19:19-21).

The prophecy of this climactic battle—as pictured by the Feast of Trumpets—is found in Zechariah: "Then shall the LORD go forth, and fight against those nations, as when he fought in the day of battle. And his feet shall stand in that day upon the mount of Olives, which is before Jerusalem on the east, and the mount of Olives shall cleave in the midst thereof toward the east and toward the west, and there shall be a very great valley; and half of the mountain shall remove toward the north, and half of it toward the south.... **[And] the LORD my God shall come, and all the saints with thee**.... And the LORD shall be king over all the earth: in that day shall there be one LORD, and his name one.... And this shall be the plague wherewith the LORD will smite all the people that have fought against Jerusalem; Their flesh shall consume away while they stand upon their feet, and their eyes shall consume away in their holes, and their tongue shall consume away in their mouth" (Zech. 14:3-5, 9, 12). Thus, the battle of Armageddon ends.

This overview summarizes the prophetic meaning of the Feast of Trumpets, with a focus on its final fulfillment when Jesus Christ and all the saints return to the earth. There are numerous additional prophecies in the Bible that magnify the meaning of this pivotal "day of the Lord"—the *fulcrum* or "tipping point" in the history of humanity. The reader is encouraged to thoroughly study the Word of God—Old and New Testaments—for a more complete understanding of these events. The time is *at hand*. The prophesied events of the last days and the return of Jesus Christ *are near*.

The Day of Atonement

The tenth day of the seventh month is the Day of Atonement. It is a special fast day—with no food or water for the entire day—as reckoned from sunset to sunset (Lev. 23:26-32). As recorded in Leviticus 16, special sacrifices were offered on Atonement.

On this day, the high priest was first required to make special sacrifices for himself and his house. Atonement was the only day of the year the high priest was allowed entry into the "holy of holies"—to access the "mercy seat," a type of God's throne in heaven (Heb. 9:24). (The mercy seat is also known as the "Ark of the Covenant," as it contained the two tables of stone.) Thus, he entered the holy of holies and ceremoniously sprinkled the blood of a bullock on the mercy seat to make an "atonement" for himself and his family. Having done so, he was then allowed to perform "atonement" sacrifices for the people of Israel.

Next, he presented two, identical, live goats before the Lord and drew lots wherein God Himself selected one goat for a sin offering and the other for Azazel (KJV, "scapegoat").

The goat for the sin offering was then sacrificed and its blood sprinkled upon the mercy seat to make atonement for all the sins, transgressions and uncleanness of the children of Israel. The goat for Azazel was not sacrificed, but was presented alive before the Lord. The priest laid his hands upon the live goat's head, confessing over it all of Israel's iniquities and transgressions. Finally, the goat was led by the hand of a fit man into the wilderness and released.

The New Testament Meaning of the Goat Sacrificed for Sin. The symbolic meaning of this unique ritual involving the two goats could not be fully understood until the apostle John had written the book of Revelation and canonized the New Testament. With the books of Hebrews and Revelation, however, the meaning becomes clear. It is generally recognized that the sacrifice of the one goat and the sprinkling of its blood upon the mercy seat was symbolic of the sacrifice and shed blood of Jesus Christ for sin. The high priest represented Jesus Christ Himself, our High Priest. In the book of Hebrews, the apostle Paul gives the interpretation of the Atonement goat sacrificed for sin and the high priest of Leviticus 16. "But **Christ has become** *the* **High Priest** of the coming good things, through the greater and more perfect tabernacle, not made by *human* hands (that is, not of this *present physical* creation). Not by *the* blood of goats and calves, but **by the means of His own blood, He entered once for all into the holiest** [holy of holies], having *by* Himself secured everlasting redemption *for us....* But now, once and for all, in *the* consummation of the ages, **He has been manifested for** *the* **purpose of removing sin through His sacrifice** *of Himself*" (Heb. 9:11-12, 26).

Paul adds that, unlike the temporary purpose of the sacrificed goat, Christ's sacrifice is **once for all time**, and thus supersedes all temple rituals and sacrifices. "For the law, having *only* a shadow of the good things that are coming, *and* not the image of those things, with the same sacrifices which they offer continually year by year, is never able to make perfect those who come *to worship....* Because *it is* impossible *for the* blood of bulls and goats to take away sins.... Then He said, 'Lo, I come to do Your will, O God.' He takes away the first *covenant* in order that He may establish the second *covenant*; **by Whose will we are sanctified through the offering of the body of Jesus Christ once for all....** But He, after offering

one sacrifice for sins for ever, sat down at *the* right hand of God. Since that time, He is waiting until His enemies are placed *as* a footstool for His feet. For **by one offering He has obtained eternal perfection *for* those who are sanctified**" (Heb. 10:1, 4, 9-10, 12-14).

The Meaning of the Goat for Azazel. First, we need to realize that "Azazel" is another name for Satan the devil. Beginning with Adam and Eve unto this day, Satan and his demons have led all human beings into sin. He is a liar and the author of sin (John 8:44), as well as the "god of this world" (II Cor. 4:4). Although it is through the sacrifice of Jesus Christ that we have our sins forgiven, **Satan, as the originator of sin, must be removed** in order to fulfill God's plan for mankind. Through His sacrificial death and His resurrection, the living Jesus Christ has triumphed over Satan, his demons and their power: "After stripping the principalities and the powers, He made a public spectacle of them, *and* has triumphed over them **in it** [that is, through His death and resurrection]" (Col. 2:15).

Clearly, at the cross, Jesus triumphed over Satan and the demons—but they have not yet been removed. Until they are put away and prevented from influencing and deceiving human beings, there will never be an end to human sin (Rev. 12:9; Eph. 2:1-3; 6:10-17). Because **Satan is the author of all sin**, the high priest was to confess the sins of the children of Israel upon the head of the live goat, Azazel. The Azazel goat was not sacrificed because Satan and the demons are spirit beings and cannot die. Rather, they must bear their own sins, for there is no atonement for them.

The book of Revelation completes the picture—showing that the removal of the live goat into the wilderness by the hand of a fit man **symbolizes the removal of Satan the devil** just prior to the establishment of the kingdom of God on the earth. "Then I saw an angel [symbolized by the *fit man* of Lev. 16] descending from heaven, having the key of the abyss, and a great chain in his hand. And he took hold of the dragon, the ancient serpent, who is *the* Devil and Satan, and bound him *for* a thousand years. Then he cast him into the abyss [symbolized by the *wilderness* of Lev. 16], and locked him *up*, and sealed *the abyss* over him, so that he would not deceive the nations any longer until the thousand years were fulfilled; and after that it is ordained that he be loosed *for* a short time" (Rev. 20:1-3).

During the final generation of the Millennium, God will exile the incorrigibly wicked—those who refuse His salvation—to the geographical area of Gog and Magog. At the conclusion of the Millennium, Satan and his demons are released from the abyss for a short time—with one, final mission: to go out and deceive the wicked into gathering themselves to battle against Jerusalem. When they attack the holy city however, fire comes down out of heaven from God and consumes them—which is their first death (verses 7-9).

The final judgment and second death of all the incorrigibly wicked from the creation of Adam and Eve will take place at a later time (Rev. 20:14-15).

In the ultimate fulfillment of the Day of Atonement, Satan and the demon's final judgment will take place: "And the Devil, who deceived them, was cast into the lake of fire and brimstone, where the beast and the false prophet *had been cast*; and they, *Satan and the demons*, shall be tormented day and night into the ages of eternity" (Rev. 20:10).

While Satan and the demons will be tormented day and night forever, apparently the lake of fire will not continue into eternity. Rather, their torment will be to live in the blackness of darkness forever: "*They are* clouds without water [the incorrigibly wicked], being driven by the winds; trees of late autumn, without *any* fruit, uprooted, twice dead [the second death in the lake of fire]; raging waves of *the* sea, casting up like foam their own *ignominious* shame; **wandering stars** [Satan and the fallen angels], **for whom has been reserved the blackest darkness forever!**" (Jude 12-13).

Becoming "At One" with God. An understanding of the term "atonement" leads to a deeper spiritual meaning of the Day of Atonement for true Christians. The word is made up of three parts—"at-one-ment"— meaning, "to be **at one** with God." When we fast (with no food or water), we become acutely aware of how utterly dependent we are on God for life, breath, food and water. We realize that God created everything to sustain our temporary physical lives, which are subject to death. We understand that we have no capacity within ourselves to live forever. The gift of eternal life can come *only* from God the Father through Jesus Christ—by His love, grace and mercy.

During one of David's fasts, he wrote these moving words, describing how he desired to be at one with God: "My soul longeth, yea, even fainteth for the courts of the LORD: my heart and my flesh crieth out for the living God.... O God, thou art my God; **early will I seek thee: my soul thirsteth for thee, my flesh longeth for thee in a dry and thirsty land, where no water is; to see thy power and thy glory, so as I have seen thee in the sanctuary. Because thy lovingkindness is better than life, my lips shall praise thee**.

"Thus will I bless thee while I live: I will lift up my hands in thy name. My soul shall be satisfied as with marrow and fatness; and my mouth shall praise thee with joyful lips: when I remember thee upon my bed, and meditate on thee in the night watches. Because thou hast been my help, therefore in the shadow of thy wings will I rejoice. My soul followeth hard after thee: thy right hand upholdeth me" (Psa. 84:2; 63:1-8).

When Jesus faced the agony of His torture and crucifixion, He kept His mind **fixed** on the Father's **promise** that His flesh would not see corruption—that He would be resurrected back to eternal life and be with the Father once again. "I have set the LORD always before me: because he is at my right hand, I shall not be moved. Therefore my heart is glad, and my glory rejoiceth: my flesh also shall rest in hope. **For thou wilt not leave my soul in hell [the grave]; neither wilt thou suffer thine Holy One to see corruption**. Thou wilt show me the path of life: in thy presence is fullness of joy; at thy right hand there are pleasures for evermore…. **As for me, I will behold thy face in righteousness: I shall be satisfied, when I awake, with thy likeness**" (Psa. 16:8-11: 17:15).

In Jesus' passionate and agonizing prayer to the Father just before He was betrayed by Judas Iscariot, He epitomized the whole purpose of God for all who will receive **eternal life and be at one with God the Father and Himself** in the first resurrection: "Jesus spoke these words, and lifted up His eyes to heaven and said, 'Father, the hour has come; glorify Your own Son, so that Your Son may also glorify You; since You have given Him authority over all flesh, in order that He may give eternal life to all whom You have given Him. **For this is eternal life, that they may know You, the only true God, and Jesus Christ, Whom You did send**.

" 'I have glorified You on the earth. **I have finished the work that You gave Me to do. And now, Father, glorify Me with Your own self, with the glory that I had with You before the world existed**. I have manifested Your name to the men whom You have given Me out of the world. They were Yours, and You have given them to Me, and they have kept Your Word. Now they have known that all things that You have given Me are from You. For I have given them the words that You gave to Me; and they have received *them* and truly have known that I came from You; and they have believed that You did send Me. I am praying for them; **I am not praying for the world**, but for those whom You have given Me, for they are Yours. All Mine are Yours, and all Yours *are* Mine; and I have been glorified in them.

" 'And I am no longer in the world, but these are in the world, and I am coming to You. Holy Father, keep them in Your name, those whom You have given Me, so that they may be one, even as We *are one*. When I was with them in the world, I kept them in Your name. I protected those whom You have given Me, and not one of them has perished except the son of perdition, in order that the Scriptures might be fulfilled. But now I am coming to You; and these things I am speaking *while yet* in the world, that they may have My joy fulfilled in them.

" 'I have given them Your words, and the world has hated them because they are not of the world, just as I am not of the world. I do not pray that You would take them out of the world, but that You would keep them from the evil one. **They are not of the world, just as I am not of the world. Sanctify them in Your truth; Your Word is the truth**. Even as You did send Me into the world, I also have sent them into the world. And for their sakes I sanctify Myself, so that they also may be sanctified in *Your* truth.

" 'I do not pray for these only, but also for those who shall believe in Me through their word; **that they all may be one, even as You, Father, *are* in Me, and I in You; that they also may be one in Us**, in order that the world may believe that You did send Me. And I have given them the glory that You gave *to* Me, in order **that they be may one, in the same way *that***

We are one: I in them, and You in Me, that they may be perfected into one; and that the world may know that You did send Me, and have loved them as You have loved Me. Father, I desire that those whom You have given Me may also be with Me where I am, so that they may behold My glory, which You have given Me; because You did love Me before *the* foundation of *the* world. Righteous Father, the world has not known You; but I have known You, and these have known that You did send Me. And I have made known Your name to them, and will make *it* known; **so that the love with which You have loved Me may be in them, and I in them**' " (John 17:1-26).

In this beautiful and loving prayer, Jesus begins to reveal what it truly means to be "at one" with God and Jesus Christ for all eternity. In the last chapter of Revelation, the apostle John saw in vision how all those who receive eternal life will be "at one" with the Father and Christ for all eternity in the New Jerusalem. "And there shall be no more curse; and the throne of God and of the Lamb shall be in it [New Jerusalem]; and **His servants shall serve Him, and they shall see His face; and His name *is* in their foreheads**. And there shall be no night there; for they have no need of a lamp or *the* light of *the* sun, because *the* Lord God enlightens them; and they shall reign into the ages of eternity. And he said to me, 'These words *are* faithful and true; and *the* Lord God of the holy prophets sent His angel to show His servants the things that must shortly come to pass.' 'Behold, I am coming quickly. Blessed *is* the one who keeps the words of the prophecy of this book' " (Rev. 22:3-7).

This is the glorious meaning of the Day of Atonement for all true Christians who love and obey God the Father and Jesus Christ. Observing this special fast day in spirit and in truth brings us into the awesome reality of being "at one with God."

The Feast of Tabernacles

The Feast of Tabernacles is a seven-day festival beginning on the 15th day and continuing through the 21st day of the seventh month (Lev. 23:34). Also called the "Feast of Ingathering," this festival **celebrates the completed harvest** of all the abundant blessings of God (Ex. 23:16; 34:22). Additionally, God commanded the children of Israel to **dwell in booths for the seven days of the feast** to remind them that they dwelt in booths, or tents, when God brought them out of the land of Egypt (Lev. 23:39-43).

This feast also commemorates God Himself dwelling with Israel by placing His presence in the Tabernacle (Ex. 25:8) and later the Temple (II Chron. 5:11-14). For Israel, this feast also pictured the time when God had given them rest from their enemies after they settled in the Promised Land during Joshua's time (Josh. 21:43-44).

The primary Old Testament fulfillment of the Feast of Tabernacles occurred during Solomon's reign when all twelve tribes of the children of Israel were settled in the kingdom. At that time, they celebrated a seven-day feast to dedicate the temple, after which they celebrated the Feast of Tabernacles (II Chron. 7:8-11). For a brief time, Israel was the model nation God had intended them to be, representing Him to all the world. Thus, they were in the Promised Land; they had rest from their enemies, plus the abundant blessings of God; and He was dwelling among them with His presence in the Temple—all a type of the coming kingdom of God under Jesus Christ.

The New Testament is the Key to Understanding. When Jesus first appeared to the disciples after His resurrection, He gave them clear discernment of the Scriptures: "And He said to them, 'These *are* the words that I spoke to you when I was yet with you, that all *the* things which were written concerning Me in the Law of Moses and *in the* Prophets and *in the* Psalms must be fulfilled.' Then **He opened their minds to understand the Scriptures**" (Luke 24:44-45).

From Luke's account, we recognize that Jesus is the one Who unlocks the hidden meanings of Old Testament teachings and prophecies. After all, as God of the Old Testament, Christ was the one Who inspired the Old Testament writers; He was also the one Who inspired the apostles to write the words of the New Testament (II Tim. 3:15-17). Thus, the New Testament interprets the Old Testament.

Likewise, it is the New Testament that interprets the meaning of all of God's feasts and holy days—providing insight into the little-understood plan of God (Eph. 1:8-10; 3:1-5), and opening our understanding of the Word of God.

What follows is a short summary of the Feast of Tabernacles, viewed through the perspective of the New Testament.

The Meaning of the Feast of Tabernacles in the New Testament. The Scriptures teach that the Feast of Tabernacles held a special meaning for Jesus Christ during His fleshly life—because He was literally God in a human "tabernacle," dwelling with men. The apostle John concisely authenticates Who Jesus was, and why He came in the flesh: "In *the* beginning was the Word, and the Word was with God, and the Word was God. He was in *the* beginning with God. All things came into being through Him, and not even one *thing* that was created came into being without Him.... **And the Word became flesh, and tabernacled among us** (and we ourselves beheld His glory, *the* glory as of *the* only begotten with *the* Father), full of grace and truth.... Behold the Lamb of God, Who takes away the sin of the world" (John 1:1-3, 14, 29).

In John chapter seven, we find Jesus preparing to keep the Feast of Tabernacles in Jerusalem. At that time, because the Jews sought to kill Him, He instructed His mother and brothers to go on ahead of Him to Jerusalem. Thus, Jesus traveled in secret, and did not reveal His presence until the middle of the feast when He began to teach the people. On this occasion, He revealed the profound truth that **all of His teachings were from the Father**: "But then, about the middle of the feast, Jesus went up into the temple and was teaching. And the Jews were amazed, saying, 'How does this man know letters, having never been schooled?' [He was taught by the Father, not in rabbinical schools.] Jesus answered them and said, 'My doctrine is not Mine, but His Who sent Me. **If anyone desires to do His will, he shall know of the doctrine, whether it is from God, or** *whether* **I speak from My own self**. The one who speaks of himself is seeking his own glory; but He Who seeks the glory of Him Who sent Him is true, and there is no unrighteousness in Him' " (John 7:14-18).

Jesus emphasized that He had come from God the Father in heaven: "Then Jesus spoke out, teaching in the temple and saying, '**You know Me, and you also know where I come from; yet I have not come of Myself; but He Who sent Me is true, Whom you do not know. But I know Him because I am from Him, and He sent Me**.' Because of this *saying*, they were looking *for a way* to take Him; but no one laid a hand on Him because His time had not yet come. Then many of the people believed in Him, saying, 'When the Christ comes, will He do more miracles than those that this *man* has done?' The Pharisees heard the crowds debating these things about Him, and the Pharisees and the chief priests sent officers to arrest Him" (verses 28-32).

Following this encounter with the Jews and Pharisees, Jesus declared that He would be with them only a while longer, confirming that He was "tabernacling" among them. "Then Jesus said to them, 'I am with you yet a little while, and *then* I go to Him Who sent Me. You shall seek Me, but shall not find *Me*; and where I am *going*, you are not able to come' " (verses 33-34).

As Jesus told the Jews during the Feast of Tabernacles, He was God "manifested in the flesh" (I Tim. 3:16)—temporarily dwelling among men (or as John wrote, He "tabernacled among us"), teaching the Word of God, and ultimately destined to give his life to save mankind from sin and Satan. *Then* He would return to the Father.

As the Lord God of the Old Testament, Jesus created Adam and Eve, and they dwelt in the Garden of Eden with Him. After they had sinned, however, they were driven from His presence and no longer allowed to dwell with Him. Later, God dwelt among the children of Israel by placing His presence in the holy of holies in the tabernacle or temple. In the end, however, that too proved unworkable, as the temples were all destroyed because of sin.

But since Pentecost, 30 AD, God has begun to dwell—*to tabernacle*—through the Holy Spirit in each truly converted Christian.

True Christians are a Tabernacle or Dwelling Place for God. For converted members of the body of Christ—who have the indwelling of God's Spirit—the Feast of Tabernacles also has a special, personal meaning. There exists a unique, spiritual relationship between true believers, God the Father and Jesus Christ—by and through the power of the Holy Spirit. Upon conversion, when we receive the begettal of the Holy Spirit of God, we **become a special dwelling place for God**—a tabernacle or temple of

God! As Paul writes, "Don't you understand that you are God's temple, and *that* the Spirit of God is dwelling in you? If anyone defiles the temple of God, God shall destroy him because the temple of God is holy, which temple you are" (I Cor. 3:16-17).

Today, God no longer dwells in a physical tabernacle or temple made by human hands—He dwells in us by the power of the Holy Spirit. In fact, Jesus promised: **"If anyone loves Me, he will keep My word; and My Father will love him, and We will come to him and make Our abode with him**. The one who does not love Me does not keep My words; and the word that you hear is not Mine, but the Father's, Who sent Me" (John 14:23-24). And again, "Dwell in Me, and I in you" (John 15:4). Also see Galatians 2:20.

In his first general epistle, John wrote concerning this special indwelling of the Holy Spirit: "No one has seen God at any time. *Yet*, if we love one another, **God dwells in us**, and His own love is perfected in us. By this *standard* **we know that we are dwelling in Him, and He** *is dwelling* **in us: because of His own Spirit,** *which* **He has given to us**.... And we have known and have believed the love that God has toward us. **God is love, and the one who dwells in love is dwelling in God, and God in him**. **By this** *spiritual indwelling*, **the love** *of God* **is perfected within us**, so that we may have confidence in the day of judgment because even as He is, so also are we in this world" (I John 4:12-13, 16-17).

At the present time, our fleshly bodies are likened to a temporary tabernacle. However, in order to live with God forever, we need to be clothed with eternal life—changed from fleshly beings to spirit beings. "For we who are in *this* tabernacle [this fleshly body] truly do groan, being burdened; not that we wish to be unclothed, but to be clothed upon so that the mortal *flesh* may be swallowed up by life [in the resurrection (I Cor. 15:49-50)]. Now He Who is working out this very thing for us *is* God, Who has also given us the earnest of the Spirit" (II Cor. 5:4-5).

In addition, although we live *in* this world (society), Jesus said that we are **not** *of* **this world** (John 17:14-15). Likewise, as Paul admonished the Corinthians, we are to be separate from the world and its ways: "Do not be unequally yoked with unbelievers. For what do righteousness and lawlessness *have* in common? And what fellowship *does* light *have* with darkness? And what union *does* Christ *have* with Belial? Or what part *does* a believer *have* with an unbeliever? And what agreement *is there between* a temple of God and idols? **For you are a temple of** *the* **living God, exactly as God said: 'I will dwell in them and walk in** *them*; **and I will be their God, and they shall be My people**. Therefore, come out from the midst of them and be separate,' says *the* Lord, 'and touch not *the* unclean, and I will receive you; and I shall be a Father to you, and you shall be My sons and daughters,' says *the* Lord Almighty" (II Cor. 6:14-18).

It is through the indwelling of the Spirit of God that we receive the power to overcome sin and to develop the character of God for eternal life.

Paul emphasizes the central importance of the indwelling of the Holy Spirit in overcoming the pulls of the flesh and human nature and receiving eternal life: "However, you are not in *the* flesh, but in *the* Spirit, **if *the* Spirit of God is indeed dwelling within you**. But if anyone does not have *the* Spirit of Christ, he does not belong to Him. Now if Christ *be* within you, the body *is* indeed dead because of sin; however, **the Spirit *is* life because of righteousness**.

"Now if the Spirit of Him Who raised Jesus from *the* dead is dwelling within you, He Who raised Christ from *the* dead will also quicken your mortal bodies because of His Spirit that dwells within you. So then, brethren, we are not debtors to the flesh, to live according to *the* flesh; because if you are living according to *the* flesh, you shall die; but **if by *the* Spirit you are putting to death the deeds of the body, you shall live**. For as many as are led by *the* Spirit of God, these are *the* sons of God. Now you have not received a spirit of bondage again unto fear, but you have received *the* Spirit of sonship, whereby we call out, 'Abba, Father.' The Spirit itself bears witness conjointly with our own spirit, *testifying* that we are *the* children of God. Now if *we are* children, *we are* also heirs—truly, heirs of God and joint heirs with Christ—if indeed we suffer together with Him, so that we may also be glorified together with Him" (Rom. 8:9-17). In the resurrection, we will each be glorified with a new, *spiritual*, **permanent dwelling** as it were—with an immortal, incorruptible, eternal spirit body and mind (I Cor. 15:35-55). With this glory, we will shine like the stars of heaven (Dan. 12:2-3; Matt. 13:43; Gen. 15:5).

Through the indwelling of the Holy Spirit of God, we become special, *temporary* tabernacles or temples for God's abode—until the resurrection, when we receive the fullness of our inheritance. "In Whom you also trusted after hearing the Word of the truth, the gospel of your salvation; in Whom also, after believing, you were sealed with the Holy Spirit of promise, which is *the* earnest of our inheritance until *the* redemption of the purchased possession, to *the* praise of His glory" (Eph. 1:13-14).

While we now enjoy this special relationship with God the Father and Jesus Christ, we are looking forward to **dwelling with Them in the New Jerusalem**—and with all the spiritual family of God in the kingdom of God for all eternity. "Behold! What *glorious* love the Father has given to us, that we should be called the children of God! For this very reason, the world does not know us because it did not know Him. Beloved, now we are the children of God, and it has not yet been revealed what we shall be; but we know that when He is manifested, we shall be like Him, because we shall see Him exactly as He is" (I John 3:1-2).

This confirms another promise Jesus made to His disciples—that He would prepare a special dwelling place for them in the New Jerusalem. On the night of His last Passover Jesus told His disciples: "In My Father's house [the New Jerusalem] are many [permanent, eternal] dwelling places; if it were otherwise, I would have told you. I am going to prepare a place for you. And if I go and prepare a place for you, I will come again and receive you to Myself; so that where I am, you may be also" (John 14:2-3). This then is the *unique*, spiritual meaning of the Feast of Tabernacles for all true Christians—a dwelling place with God, *now* and **for all eternity**.

The Prophetic Fulfillment of Tabernacles for All Nations

As with the Feast of Trumpets and the Day of Atonement, the book of Revelation is the key that unlocks the prophetic meaning of the Feast of Tabernacles. After Jesus Christ and the resurrected saints return to the earth from the sea of glass, the beast and the false prophet are cast into the lake of fire and their armies are destroyed, as pictured by Trumpets (Rev. 19:11-21). Then, Satan and the demons are bound in the abyss, as portrayed by Atonement (Rev. 20:1-3).

What follows these two climactic events epitomizes the meaning of the Feast of Tabernacles: Jesus Christ and the saints **establish the kingdom of God** and rule the world for a thousand years. "And I saw thrones; and they that sat upon them, and judgment was given to them; and *I saw* the souls of those who had been beheaded for the testimony of Jesus, and for the Word of God, and those who did not worship the beast, or his image, and did not receive the mark in their foreheads or in their hands; **and they lived and reigned with Christ a thousand years**.... This *is* the first resurrection. **Blessed and holy is the one who has part in the first resurrection**; over these the second death has no power. But **they shall be priests of God and of Christ, and shall reign with Him a thousand years**" (Rev. 20:4-6).

Jesus Christ as King of the World. Before Christ's crucifixion, Pilate interrogated Him, asking if He was "the King of the Jews." Jesus answered, "My kingdom is not of this world. If My kingdom were of this world, then would My servants fight, so that I might not be delivered up to the Jews. However, My kingdom is not of this world." Pilate then asked, "Then You are a king?" Again, Jesus replied, "*As* you say, I am a king. **For this *purpose* I was born, and for this *reason* I came into the world**, that I may bear witness to the truth. Everyone who is of the truth hears My voice." (See John 18:33, 36-37.)

With His answer, Jesus laid bare the *truth* that He had indeed fulfilled the prophecy of Isaiah which says, "**For unto us a child is born, unto us a son is given: and the government** [of the kingdom of God] **shall be upon His shoulder**: and His name shall be called Wonderful, Counselor, The mighty God, The everlasting Father, The Prince of Peace. **Of the increase of *His* government and peace *there shall be* no end, upon the throne of David, and upon his kingdom, to order it, and to establish it with judgment and with justice from henceforth even for ever**. The zeal of the LORD of hosts will perform this" (Isa. 9:6-7). And, "**the LORD shall be king over all the earth**" (Zech. 14:9).

The Millennial reign of Jesus Christ as King will bring a righteous world government over all nations. The heavens and earth will rejoice:

"Say among the heathen *that* the LORD reigneth: the world also shall be established that it shall not be moved: He shall judge the people righteously. Let the heavens rejoice, and let the earth be glad; let the sea roar, and the fulness thereof. Let the field be joyful, and all that *is* therein: then shall all the trees of the wood rejoice before the LORD: **for He cometh, for He cometh to judge the earth: He shall judge the world with righteousness, and the people with His truth**" (Psa. 96:10-13).

When Jesus establishes the kingdom of God on earth, His capital will be Jerusalem. All wars will cease. There will be universal peace, and man will rebuild the desolate cities: "And it shall come to pass in the last days, *that* the mountain [kingdom] of the LORD'S house shall be established in the top of the mountains [kingdoms], and shall be exalted above the hills; and all nations shall flow unto it. And many people shall go and say, 'Come ye, and let us go up to the mountain of the LORD, to the house of the God of Jacob; and He will teach us of His ways, and we will walk in His paths:' for out of Zion shall go forth the law, and the word of the LORD from Jerusalem. And He shall judge among the nations, and shall rebuke many people: and they shall beat their swords into plowshares, and their spears into pruning hooks: nation shall not lift up sword against nation, neither shall they learn war any more…. And they shall build the old wastes, they shall raise up the former desolations, and they shall repair the waste cities, the desolations of many generations" (Isa. 2:2-4; 61:4).

God will even change mankind's nature—from its present carnal hostility toward Him and His righteous, perfect laws, to a nature of obedience and love. All people will be offered the opportunity for salvation and eternal life. "Then will I sprinkle clean water upon you, and ye shall be clean: from all your filthiness, and from all your idols, will I cleanse you. **A new heart also will I give you, and a new spirit will I put within you: and I will take away the stony heart out of your flesh, and I will give you an heart of flesh**. And I will put my spirit within you, and cause you to walk in my statutes, and ye shall keep my judgments, and do *them*. And ye shall dwell in the land that I gave to your fathers; and ye shall be my people, and I will be your God" (Ezek. 36:25-28).

The knowledge of the Lord will cover the earth as the seas do today. People will enjoy unbelievable wealth and the private ownership of land. "And there shall come forth a rod out of the stem of Jesse, and a Branch shall grow out of his roots: And the spirit of the LORD shall rest upon him, the spirit of wisdom and understanding, the spirit of counsel and might, the spirit of knowledge and of the fear of the LORD; and shall make him of quick understanding in the fear of the LORD: and he shall not judge after the sight of his eyes, neither reprove after the hearing of his ears: but with righteousness shall he judge the poor, and reprove with equity for the meek of the earth: and he shall smite the earth with the rod of his mouth, and with the breath of his lips shall he slay the wicked. And righteousness shall be the girdle of his loins, and faithfulness the girdle of his reins.

"The wolf also shall dwell with the lamb, and the leopard shall lie down with the kid; and the calf and the young lion and the fatling together; and a little child shall lead them. And the cow and the bear shall feed; their young ones shall lie down together: and the lion shall eat straw like the ox. And the sucking child shall play on the hole of the asp, and the weaned child shall put his hand on the cockatrice's den. **They shall not hurt nor destroy in all my holy mountain: for the earth shall be full of the knowledge of the LORD, as the waters cover the sea**.... For brass **I will bring gold, and for iron I will bring silver, and for wood brass, and for stones iron**.... **Violence shall no more be heard in thy land**, wasting nor destruction within thy borders; but thou shalt call thy walls 'Salvation,' and thy gates 'Praise' (Isa. 11:1-9; 60:17-18). Also, "they shall sit every man under his [own] vine and under his [own] fig tree; and none shall make *them* afraid: for the mouth of the LORD of hosts hath spoken *it*" (Micah 4:4).

All nations will keep the Sabbath and holy days of God: " 'And it shall come to pass, *that* from one new moon to another [month in and month out], and from one sabbath to another, shall all flesh come to worship before me,' saith the LORD" (Isa. 66:23). "And it shall come to pass, *that* every one that is left of all the nations which came against Jerusalem shall even go up from year to year to worship the King, the LORD of hosts, and to keep the feast of tabernacles" (Zech. 14:16).

As the Feast of Tabernacles pictured the great ingathering harvest for Israel, the coming Millennial reign of Jesus Christ and the saints (as kings and priests) will be a great spiritual harvest of God. During this one-thousand-year period, literally billions of people will be converted—and at the end of their lives, they will receive immortality as they enter the spiritual kingdom of God for all eternity. "I saw a new heaven and a new earth; for the first heaven and the first earth were passed away, and there was no more sea. And I, John, saw the holy city, *the* new Jerusalem, coming down from God out of heaven, prepared as a bride adorned for her husband. And I heard a great voice from heaven say, **'Behold, the tabernacle of God *is* with men; and He shall dwell with them, and they shall be His people; and God Himself shall be with them *and be* their God. And God shall wipe away every tear from their eyes; and *there* shall be no more death, or sorrow, or crying; neither shall *there* be any more pain, because the former things have passed away.'** And He Who sits on the throne said, 'Behold, I make all things new.' Then He said to me, 'Write, for these words are true and faithful' " (Rev. 21:1-5).

From the beginning of creation, the whole plan and purpose of God has been simply to dwell with His people—His spiritual family—for all eternity. It is the desire of God the Father and Jesus Christ to unselfishly share the endless wealth of the universe with their family. Thus, the Feast of Tabernacles pictures **a major stage in the fulfillment of God's master plan**.

However, the Feast of Tabernacles does not *complete* God's plan. There is one more holy day—the **"eighth day"** following the Feast of Tabernacles—which will consummate the awesome plan of God. In chapter twelve we will examine the scriptures that fully explain the meaning of this little-understood **eighth day**, called the "Last Great Day" (John 7:37).

CHAPTER TWELVE

God's Greatest Mystery of the Ages Revealed in the Eighth Day— the Last Great Day

When viewing the panorama of human history—from individuals to great civilizations, from the forgotten, unwanted and rejected, to the famous, idolized and celebrated—one is compelled to ask, "Why is there life and death, good and evil? Why does God allow and/or cause disasters, floods, tidal waves, earthquakes, volcanic eruptions, destruction, war, famine, pestilence, sickness, disease, pain and suffering, violence and death to befall all mankind throughout every generation and civilization?"

If God is a God of love, why does He not stop or prevent the wretchedness and misery of human suffering and accidental death—especially of innocent children and babies—and the abortion of the unborn? Why does God allow rape, murder, sadistic torture and cruelties of man against man— the strong against the weak, the wicked against the righteous? If God really hears the mournful cries of desperate humans suffering such horrific tragedies, disasters, sicknesses and death, why does He not intervene?

Throughout the ages, questions of life and death have haunted mankind—especially religionists and philosophers. Attempting to find answers to these mysterious realities of human life and death, men often find themselves separated from the true knowledge of God. As a result, men have cultivated countless theories and religious philosophies about the nature of God—as well as about the origin and purpose of life, the immortal soul, heaven, hell, purgatory and reincarnation. In the final analysis, however, they all admit that they simply do not have the answers to these seemingly inexplicable mysteries of life and death—and in particular, the ultimate mystery of all, why death?

Why Do Human Beings Die?

When a person dies, we are at once confronted with the ultimate weakness and the absolute helplessness of being human. Death brings us face-to-face with the stark reality that human life is temporary, and that no person has the power to escape death. Why does an immortal, eternal God of love consign the apex of His creation—man and woman made in His image and likeness—to death? Before we can appreciate the biblical answer, we need to understand why people die.

In the beginning when He created Adam and Eve, "God said, 'Let us make man in our image, after our likeness: and let them have dominion over the fish of the sea, and over the fowl of the air, and over the cattle, and over all the earth, and over every creeping thing that creepeth upon the earth.' So God created man in his *own* image, in the image of God created he him; **male** and **female** created he them. And God blessed them, and God said unto them, 'Be fruitful, and multiply, and replenish the earth, and subdue it: and have dominion over the fish of the sea, and over the fowl of the air, and over every living thing that moveth upon the earth...' And God saw every thing that he had made, and, behold, *it was* very good" (Gen. 1:26-28, 31). Everything that God created on the earth had been given to man to be used for his benefit. What a tremendous blessing God gave to mankind—dominion over the entire world!

Subsequent details regarding the creation of Adam and Eve are described in Genesis 2. As the account shows, Adam was created first: "And the LORD God formed man of the dust of the ground, and breathed into his nostrils the breath of life; and man became a living soul" (Gen. 2:7). God then created Eve, his wife, from one of Adam's ribs. He also gave them minds with full intelligence, freedom of choice and a fully functioning language (Gen. 2:16-17; 3:2-3).

God made man in His image and likeness, but of an inferior nature. Of all the creatures created to dwell on earth, only man has been given the attributes of God—including the mental ability to think and reason, to speak, write, plan, create, build, teach, learn, judge and rule. God gave human beings the capacity to love, hate, laugh, cry, forgive, repent and experience every type of emotion. All of these are godlike characteristics which humanity is privileged to possess, howbeit inferior to God.

Man is able to exercise these godlike attributes because he has been given a unique spiritual dimension that God did not give to the rest of His earthly creation. Every human being has this quality, which makes each one "a little lower than God" (Psa. 8:1-5, NASB). The Bible describes this spiritual aspect as the "spirit of man," **which is not an immortal soul**. It is this spiritual dimension of the mind that imparts human life and intelligence (Job 32:8, 18; 33:4; Zech. 12:1; I Cor. 2:11 and James 2:26). (See Appendix J, *What Happens to the Dead?,* page 255.)

Though they were made of the dust of the earth, both Adam and Eve were created in a state of innocence—sinless and blameless before God. They were not yet subject to the penalty of death, because they had not sinned (Gen. 2:25). In contrast, neither did they yet possess eternal life, because they had not eaten of the tree of life.

Adam and Eve—Free Moral Agents with the Power to Choose

God created Adam and Eve as free moral agents—with the power of intelligence, independent thought and personal choice. He has since given the same to every human being. The ultimate choice that each must decide is whether to love and obey God. As Creator and Lawgiver, God has decreed that the penalty for disobedience to His commands is death. However, through faith, love and obedience, God grants the gift of eternal life (Rom. 6:23). When God placed Adam in the Garden of Eden, He gave him clear instructions. He also gave Adam distinct choices as depicted by the two trees. "And the LORD God planted a garden eastward in Eden; and there he put the man whom he had formed. And out of the ground made the LORD God to grow every tree that is pleasant to the sight, and good for food; **the tree of life also in the midst of the garden, and the tree of knowledge of good and evil**... And the LORD God took the man, and put him into the garden of Eden to dress it and to keep it" (Gen. 2:8-9, 15). The tree of life represented the way of God that leads to eternal life. The tree of the knowledge of good and evil symbolized the way of sin, disobedience and death.

God warned Adam that the consequences of making the wrong choice would be death. "And the LORD God commanded the man, saying, 'Of every tree of the garden thou mayest freely eat: but of the tree of the knowledge of good and evil, thou shalt not eat of it: for in the day that thou eatest thereof thou shalt surely die [Hebrew, in dying you shall surely die]' " (Gen. 2:16-17).

Enter Satan, Sin and Death. God must have thoroughly instructed Adam and Eve about His laws and commandments and the path to eternal life before allowing Satan the devil, in the form of a serpent, to tempt them. They were acutely aware that if they ate of the tree of the knowledge of good and evil, they would be subject to death (Gen. 3:3).

When the serpent entered the Garden of Eden, Adam and Eve had to determine who they would believe and obey—God or Satan. They had to decide between the commandments of God or the blatant lies of Satan. It was their decision. Would they trust in God and choose His way—the way of life? Or would they believe Satan and choose the way that seemed right to them—the way of sin and death? (See Prov. 14:12; 16:25.)

The Bible records that Adam and Eve elected to believe Satan. Had they believed God, they could have rejected Satan's lying temptations. Believing Satan's lies, they choose to eat of the fruit of the tree of the knowledge of good and evil. "And the serpent said unto the woman, 'Ye shall not surely die: for God doth know that in the day ye eat thereof, then **your eyes shall be opened, and ye shall be as gods, knowing good and evil**.' And when the woman saw that the tree was good for food, and that it was pleasant to the eyes, and a tree to be desired to make one wise, she took of the fruit thereof, and did eat, and gave also unto her husband with her; and he did eat and the eyes of them both were opened" (Gen. 3:4-7).

The Consequences of Adam and Eve's Sin. First, their sin brought God's judgment upon the serpent—Satan (Gen. 3:14). The Lord God then promised a future Savior to die for the sins of Adam and Eve, as well as the sins of their offspring (verse 15). Finally, He pronounced His judgment against Adam and Eve: "Unto the woman he said, 'I will greatly multiply thy sorrow and thy conception; in sorrow thou shalt bring forth children; and thy desire *shall* be to thy husband, and he shall rule over thee.' And unto Adam he said, 'Because thou hast hearkened unto the voice of thy wife, and hast eaten of the tree, of which I commanded thee, saying, "Thou shalt not eat of it:" cursed *is* the ground for thy sake; in sorrow shalt thou eat *of* it all the days of thy life; thorns also and thistles shall it bring forth to thee; and thou shalt eat the herb of the field; in the sweat of thy face shalt thou eat bread, **till thou return unto the ground; for out of it wast thou taken: for dust thou *art*, and unto dust shalt thou return**' " (verses 16-19).

When their eyes were opened to "know" good and evil (that is, to decide for themselves what was good and evil), their eyes became closed to the way of God and His righteousness—not only for themselves, but also for all their progeny. Moreover, Adam and Eve were denied access to the tree of life. "And the LORD God said, 'Behold, the man is become as one of us, to know [decide what is] good and evil: and now, lest he put forth his hand, and take also of the tree of life, and eat, and live for ever:' therefore **the LORD God sent him forth from the garden of Eden**, to till the ground from whence he was taken. So he drove out the man; and he placed at the east of the garden of Eden Cherubims, and a flaming sword which turned every way, to keep the way of the tree of life" (verses 22-24).

With Adam and Eve's first acts of disobedience, sin entered the world. Importantly, they lost their innocence and their human nature was changed to a nature of sin and death. As Paul explains, this nature of sin and death became an inherent part of their very being, and through heredity has passed on to all mankind. "Therefore, as by one man [Adam] sin entered into the world, and by means of sin *came* death; and in this way, death passed into all mankind [as part of their heredity]; *and it is* for this reason that all have sinned" (Rom. 5:12).

Using himself as an example, Paul described man's sinful nature as the "sin *that is* dwelling within me ... **a law within my own members**, warring against the law of my mind, and leading me captive to **the law of sin that is within my own members**" (Rom. 7:17, 23). Though he could know and do good, sin was always present to defeat the good that he desired to do: "Consequently, I find this law *in my members*, that when I desire to do good, evil is present with me" (Rom. 7:21).

Paul further characterizes carnal human nature as irrevocably subject to "the law of sin and death" (Rom. 8:2). Consequently, all humans are naturally hostile to the laws of God: "Because the carnal mind *is* enmity against God, for it is not subject to the law of God; neither indeed can *it be*. But those who are in *the* flesh cannot please God" (verses 7-8).

This is the reason all human beings sin and die: "For all have sinned, and come short of the glory of God" (Rom. 3:23) —and, "in Adam all die" (I Cor. 15:22).

In the final analysis, our inherited human nature is a mixture of good and evil with the downward pull of the "law of sin and death." Because of the deceitfulness of the human heart and mind (Jer. 17:9), very few people would be willing to admit that humans are basically evil. Instead, the average person feels that he or she is essentially good and only tends to look at the apparent good of their behavior. As humans, we are inclined to excuse our sinfulness and inner evil thoughts, and to justify ourselves as good. "All the ways of a man *are* clean in his own eyes; but the LORD weigheth the spirits" (Prov. 16:2).

As a result, people view mankind as a whole as good, sincere, loving and mostly law-abiding. Indeed, those who practice good and help the needy and destitute with acts of kindness and mercy are genuine in their endeavors. These are the "good, sincere people" of the world who actually live by basic principles and have a sense of morality. Any good that they do can always be traced back to some form of the laws and commandments of God, as found in the Holy Bible. However, that does not mean they are called of God the Father and Jesus Christ unto salvation—though they may profess a form of Christianity and even attend church. From a human perspective, the observation and experience that humans are fundamentally good appears to be valid—especially when compared to the evil and wickedness of those who commit heinous crimes.

Paradoxically, the Bible portrays human nature much differently: "For we have already charged both Jews and Gentiles—ALL—*with* being under sin ... for there is not a righteous one—not even one! There is not one who understands; there is not one who seeks after God.... For all have sinned, and come short of the glory of God" (Rom. 3:9-11, 23).

God's perspective of mankind differs from the way we look at ourselves in that God looks primarily at the human spirit. God judges man's behavior by the **intents of the heart**—and thus weighs our "heart" against the spirit-of-the-law requirements of His holy, righteous laws and commandments. People, however, tend to look only at exterior behavior, which on the surface appears good or actually is good. Such manifest good behavior does not erase the nature of one's mind and heart. However, although a person may be righteous in their outward behavior—doing good as they see it, as did Job (Job 1:8)—they must come to repent deeply of their sins as he did (Job 42:1-6).

Because we all die in Adam, even those who are redeemed, converted and receive God's salvation in this life, must still die and await the resurrection at Jesus' second coming. (See Appendix J, *What Happens to the Dead?*, page 255.)

Salvation from Adam to Jesus' Second Coming

After Adam and Eve sinned, God promised a Redeemer would come to save mankind from their sins. He then drove them from the Garden of Eden and cut off access to the tree of life—showing that salvation for mankind in general was withheld until a future time when the Savior would come (Gen. 3:24). At that point God determined that He would call only a select few to receive salvation—only those who would truly love and obey Him—from that time forward until the prophesied death of the Messiah, Jesus Christ, in 30 AD.

The Bible lists a few righteous men who lived prior to the flood who will be resurrected to eternal life with the saints at Jesus' return. They are

Abel, Enoch and Noah (Heb. 11:4-7), and some of the other patriarchs listed in Genesis 5. God turned the rest of humanity over to their own devices to learn the lesson that the consequences of man's way without God, in rebellion against Him, results in misery, suffering and death (Prov. 14:12).

Irresponsibly, they choose to follow the way of Cain. The generation preceding the flood was exceedingly evil, wicked and sinful: "And GOD saw that the **wickedness of man** *was* **great in the earth, and** *that* **every imagination of the thoughts of his heart** *was* **only evil continually**. And it repented the LORD that he had made man on the earth, and it grieved him at his heart. And the LORD said, 'I will destroy man whom I have created from the face of the earth; both man, and beast, and the creeping thing, and the fowls of the air; for it repenteth me that I have made them....' **The earth also was corrupt before God, and the earth was filled with violence**. And God looked upon the earth, and, behold, it was corrupt; **for all flesh had corrupted his** [God's] **way upon the earth**. And God said unto Noah, 'The end of all flesh is come before me; for the earth is filled with violence through them; and, behold, I will destroy them with the earth' " (Gen. 6:5-7, 11-13).

Because Noah found grace in the sight of God, He spared Noah, his wife, and their three sons with their wives, from the flood—as well as various animals and living creatures that God sent to Noah to put into the ark. Approximately 1656 years after God created Adam and Eve, He destroyed all life with the universal deluge (Gen. 6:14-8:13). With the exception of a few righteous from Adam to Noah, God deliberately withheld salvation from mankind. They all lived and died without an opportunity for salvation. Are these lost forever or will God yet give them an opportunity for salvation? If so, how and when will He do it? As we will discover, the answers are found in the meaning of the Last Great Day.

After the Flood. In God's covenant with Noah and his descendents, He promised that although man's heart was evil from his youth onward, He would never again severely curse the ground nor destroy all life: "...the LORD said in his heart, 'I will not again curse the ground any more for man's sake; for **the imagination of man's heart** *is* **evil from his youth**; neither will I again smite any more every thing living, as I have done. While the earth remaineth, seedtime and harvest, and cold and heat, and summer and winter, and day and night shall not cease.' And God blessed Noah and his sons, and said unto them, 'Be fruitful, and multiply, and replenish the earth' " (Gen. 8:21-9:1).

While God did not offer spiritual salvation to the descendents of Noah's sons, He required that they obey Him and keep His laws and commandments in the letter of the law. However, because of human nature, it did not take long for mankind to once again rebel against God. In the third generation following the flood, Nimrod and his wife Semiramis led most of mankind into apostasy against God and promoted the worship of Satan as god. At the pinnacle of this rebellion, Nimrod's kingdom of Babel was established by ruthless conquest. Genesis gives this account: "And Cush begat Nimrod: he began to be a mighty one in the earth. He was a mighty hunter before [in place of] the LORD: wherefore it is said, 'Even as Nimrod the mighty hunter before [in place of] the LORD.' And the beginning of his kingdom was **Babel**, and Erech, and Accad, and Calneh, in the land of Shinar" (Gen. 10:8-10).

To usurp God's authority and dominion, they sought to build a tower to reach into the heavens. "And the whole earth *was* of one language, and of one speech. And it came to pass, as they journeyed from the east, that they found a plain in the land of Shinar; and they dwelt there. And they said one to another, 'Go to, let us make brick, and burn them thoroughly.' And they had brick for stone, and slime had they for mortar. And they said, 'Go to, let us build us a city and a tower, whose top *may reach unto* heaven; and let us make us a name, lest we be scattered abroad upon the face of the whole earth.'

"And the LORD came down to see the city and the tower, which the children of men builded. And the LORD said, 'Behold, **the people *is* one, and they have all one language; and this they begin to do: and now nothing will be restrained from them, which they have imagined to do**. Go to, let us go down, and there confound their language, that they may not understand one another's speech.' So the LORD scattered them abroad from thence upon the face of all the earth: and they left off to build the city. Therefore is the name of it called Babel; because the LORD did there confound the language of all the earth: and from thence did the LORD scatter them abroad upon the face of all the earth" (Gen. 11:1-9).

Ancient secular history records that when God scattered the people around the entire world, they took with them their false gods, their religion and the government of Nimrod and Semiramis. In Alexander Hislop's epochal book, *The Two Babylons*, he meticulously documents from a myriad of ancient records that the biblical account in Genesis 1 through 11 is accurate.

In spite of the evil and rebellion of mankind, God continued to manifest Himself to successive generations through His creation and His laws that govern the heavens and earth and the human physical environment. God further revealed Himself to men through His Word—His commandments and laws. But since men did not want to retain God in their knowledge, humanity became increasingly sinful. Ultimately, God gave them over to reprobate minds and abandoned them to their own lusts and idolatry, to learn the ultimate lesson that man's way leads to death and only God's way leads to life (Rom. 1:18-32). From the time of Adam and Eve to this day, God has left mankind to their own devices under the sway of Satan—to live and die, to develop their own societies, civilizations, religions and laws with Satan as their god (Rom. 1:18-32; Eph. 2:1-3; II Cor. 4:4; Rev. 12:9). The history of the Bible and the world verifies this to be true.

Abraham, Isaac, Jacob and Israel. In 1940 BC, approximately 300 years after the flood, God called Abraham and established His covenant with him and his descendents Isaac and Jacob, also named Israel, who had twelve sons from whom came the twelve tribes of Israel. Some 456 years later, in 1486 BC, God called Moses to lead the children of Israel out of their Egyptian slavery.

When God established His covenant with Israel at Mount Sinai, He did not make the Holy Spirit available to them nor did this covenant include the promise of eternal life. Rather, God required that the children of Israel obey Him in the letter of the law. Accordingly, they received physical blessings and national greatness for obedience and cursings for disobedience. Although worded differently, the choices God set before the twelve tribes of Israel were identical to the choices He set before Adam and Eve: "See, **I have set before thee this day life and good, and death and evil; in that I command thee this day to love the** LORD **thy God, to walk in his ways, and to keep his commandments and his statutes and his judgments, that thou mayest live and multiply: and the** LORD **thy God shall bless thee in the land whither thou goest to possess it.**

"But if thine heart turn away, so that thou wilt not hear, but shalt be drawn away, and worship other gods, and serve them; I denounce unto you this day, that ye shall surely perish, *and that* ye shall not prolong *your* days upon the land, whither thou passest over Jordan to go to possess it. **I call heaven and earth to record this day against you,** *that* **I have set before you life and death, blessing and cursing: therefore choose life, that both thou and thy seed may live**: that thou mayest love the LORD thy God, *and* that thou mayest obey his voice, and that thou mayest cleave unto him: for he is thy life, and the length of thy days: that thou mayest dwell in the land which the LORD sware unto thy fathers, to Abraham, to Isaac, and to Jacob, to give them" (Deut. 30:15-20).

This cycle of blessing and cursing continued with the children of Israel and the Jews until the promised Savior came. In Hebrews chapter 11, the apostle Paul lists those few who received salvation and the promise of eternal life from the time of Abel to Jesus Christ's first coming. In addition, Peter informs us that the prophets of God were included among those God called in a special way to receive salvation unto eternal life (I Pet. 1:10-12). All of these will be in the first resurrection, along with all the New Covenant apostles and saints (Rev. 11:18).

What Is God Going to Do?

From the creation of Adam and Eve until the first coming of Jesus Christ, the vast majority of all mankind has lived and died without the knowledge of the true God. Selectively, from Jesus' first coming, some have been called to redemption and salvation. Relatively few, however, have truly repented and become converted (Matt. 7:13-14; 22:14). Historically, the majority of humanity has consistently refused to believe and obey God. Deliberately, God has given mankind over to unbelief—to their own devises under the sway of Satan (Deut. 5:29; 29:1-4; Eph. 2:1-3; II Cor. 4:3-4; II Thess. 2:11; Rev. 12:9).

As Jesus explained to His disciples, those who refused to hear or believe Him and His teachings would be blinded, kept from spiritual understanding and given over to unbelief. In addition, they would loose what little discernment they already had. However, Jesus told His disciples that they would be given an abundance of understanding: "For whoever has *understanding*, to him more shall be given, and he shall have an abundance; but whoever does not have *understanding*, even what he has shall be taken away from him." He continued: "For this *reason* I speak to them in parables, because seeing, they see not; and hearing, they hear not; neither do they understand. And in them is fulfilled the prophecy of Isaiah, which says, 'In hearing you shall hear, and in no way understand; and *in* seeing you shall see, and in no way perceive; for the heart of this people has grown fat, and their ears are dull of hearing, and their eyes they have closed; lest they should see with their eyes, and should hear with their ears, and should understand with their hearts, and should be converted, and I should heal them' " (Matt. 13:12-15).

What Jesus declared was a mystery! He purposely blinded the unbelievers and closed their understanding so they could not be converted. Some might ask, "Doesn't it seem unfair that God would call some to salvation and exclude others?" From a raw human perspective, it does appear that God is unrighteous and partial if He only grants eternal life to the few He calls and rejects all others with no hope whatsoever of salvation. As Paul writes, "But Isaiah cried out concerning Israel, 'Although the number of the children of Israel shall be as the sand of the sea, **a remnant shall be saved**' " (Rom. 9:27).

What an incredible statement! What about the rest of Israel and the remaining nations of the world? Is God only going to save the remnant of Israel and those few that He has called to the exclusion of all others? By showing such partiality, is God unfair and unrighteous? Concerning these very questions, Paul declares, "What then shall we say? *Is there* unrighteousness with God? MAY IT NEVER BE!" (Rom. 9:14.)

Why then has God turned most of humankind over to spiritual blindness and unbelief? Paul gives an answer: "**For God has given them all over to unbelief in order that He might show mercy to all** (Rom. 11:32). Down through the ages the billions of people that God has deliberately blinded and given over to unbelief have died. How, then, is it possible for God to show them mercy and offer them salvation?

Does God Contradict Himself? Within the space of a few verses, Paul seems to contradict Jesus' statement that most have been blinded and given over to unbelief. He also seems to contradict his own account that only "a remnant will be saved." He declares, "**So all Israel shall be saved**" (Rom. 11:26). And again, "[God] Who **desires all men to be saved** and to come to *the* knowledge of *the* truth.... He is long-suffering toward us, **not desiring that anyone should perish**, but that **all should come to repentance**" (I Tim 2:4; II Pet. 3:9). How is God going to resolve these apparent discrepancies? In one place, He says that only a remnant will be saved. In another, He asserts that all Israel will be saved and that **He desires for all to come to repentance and have salvation**. Since God cannot lie, how is He going to accomplish this?

The answers are found in the meaning of the Last Great Day (John 7:37). The Last Great Day in the Old Testament is simply called "the eighth day … [a] holy convocation … a Sabbath"—following the seven-day Feast of Tabernacles (Lev. 23:36, 39; II Chron. 7:8-10). It is the least mentioned (and consequently the least understood) of all the feasts and holy days of God. Yet, with God, that "which is least of all shall become great" (Luke 9:48; Matt. 13:32). More than any other holy day, this seemingly obscure "eighth day" has perhaps the greatest meaning for all of mankind.

As with the other fall festivals and holy days, the meaning of the Last Great Day could not be fully understood without Revelation 20. We saw earlier that Revelation 20 brings out the fact that the Feast of Tabernacles portrays the establishment of the kingdom of God on earth. Tabernacles pictures the unique, 1000-year period (often called the Millennium) which will offer universal salvation for all peoples and nations—with Christ as King and those of the first resurrection serving as kings and priests (Rev. 20:6).

At the beginning of the 1000-year period, Satan and his demons are to be cast into the lake of fire. At the conclusion of the Millennium, God's final judgment is executed against Satan and his angels—sentencing them to the blackness of darkness forever, never again to be free (Rev. 20:10; Matt. 25:41; Jude 12-13).

However, the plan of God is not yet finished. Revelation 20 depicts another final age of universal salvation portrayed by the eighth day—the Last Great Day. In biblical numerology, the number eight signifies a "new beginning" or a "new order of things … and thus [eight] stands for the NEW in contrast to the old" (Vallowe, Biblical Mathematics, p. 85). The meaning of this "eighth day" reveals a fantastic, yet little realized or understood aspect of God's magnificent plan of salvation for mankind. Indeed, it is a "new beginning" for the rest of the dead.

The Rest of the Dead Will Live Again—The Second Resurrection

It is by Jesus Christ that all will be resurrected back to life: "For as in Adam all die, so also **in Christ shall ALL BE MADE ALIVE**" (I Cor. 15:22). But each in his own order (verse 23). In addition to the first resurrection, Revelation 20:5 reveals that all the rest of the dead (who were not in the first resurrection) are to live again also: "But **the rest of the dead** did not **live again** until the thousand years were completed…."

This verse answers what has been a mystery to mankind—the question of life after death. What John was inspired to write in Revelation 20 confirms Jesus' declaration concerning the dead: "Truly, truly I say to you, *the* hour is coming, and now is, when **the dead shall hear the voice of the Son of God; and those who hear shall live**. For even as the Father has life in Himself, so also has He given to the Son to have life in Himself; and has also given Him authority to execute judgment because He is *the* Son of man. Do not wonder at this, **for *the* hour is coming in which ALL WHO ARE IN THE GRAVES** [meaning all who have died regardless of circumstances] **shall hear His voice** and shall come forth: those who have practiced good unto a resurrection of life, and those who have practiced evil unto a resurrection of judgment" (John 5:25-29). In this passage, Jesus speaks of two separate resurrections, just as John describes in Revelation 20.

"The resurrection to life" is the first resurrection to eternal life as depicted by the firstfruit harvest of Pentecost. As immortal spirit beings, those of the first resurrection will not be subject to death: "Blessed and holy is the one who has part in the first resurrection; over these **the second death has no power**" (Rev. 20:6).

The Second Resurrection—to Judgment. Revelation 20 shows that the resurrection to judgment—which Jesus spoke of in John 5:29—occurs a thousand years after the first resurrection. Rightfully, it can be designated as **the second resurrection**. It is also referred to as "The Great White Throne Judgment" (Rev. 20:11-12).

Those in this resurrection will not be raised as spirit, with eternal life. Rather, they will be raised to a second life in the flesh—subject to death.

God separates those in this resurrection into two distinct classes:

1) From the creation of Adam and Eve to Christ's return—**all** who God did not call during their first lifetime. Because God deliberately bound them to a life of spiritual blindness and unbelief, they did not commit the unpardonable sin. In God's gracious generosity, He resurrects them to a second life in the flesh to have their **first** opportunity for salvation. This includes **all**, whether young or old, who died untimely deaths as a result of war, disease, natural disasters, accidents, murder, suicide—as well as those who died as newborns, those stillborn and even those who suffered death by abortion.

2) All those who, in their first lifetime, rejected the salvation of God and blasphemed against the Holy Spirit. Having committed the unpardonable sin, they will be raised back to physical life for their final judgment, to be cast into the lake of fire and die the second death. (See Appendix K, *What is the Unpardonable Sin?,* page 263.)

Forgivable and Unforgivable Sin. Jesus explained there are two categories of sin against God—forgivable and unforgivable. "I say to you, **every sin and blasphemy shall be forgiven to men** except the blasphemy against the *Holy* Spirit; *that* shall not be forgiven to men. And whoever speaks a word against the Son of man, it shall be forgiven him; but **whoever speaks against the Holy Spirit, it shall not be forgiven him, neither in this age nor in the coming *age***" (Matt. 12:31-32; Mark 3:28-29).

The coming age Jesus spoke of is the period of the resurrection to judgment that occurs after the thousand years are complete (John 5:29; Rev.

20:5). Those who have committed forgivable sins will include all who God did not call and were given over to unbelief (Matt. 13:10-15; Mark 4:11-12). Paul writes that they were given over to unbelief in order that God might have mercy upon them in a **coming age** (Rom. 11:32). These will be resurrected in the **first phase** of the second resurrection and have an opportunity for repentance and salvation. Finally, those who committed unforgivable sins will be resurrected in the **second phase** of the second resurrection.

Jesus added that this general resurrection of "the rest of the dead" will include people from all nations who lived out their first lives at different times throughout history. In fact, those from different nations and times will be raised back to life at the same time as the unbelieving Jews (and others) of Christ's generation. "*The* men of Nineveh [800 BC] shall stand up [be raised from the dead] **in the judgment with this generation** [the Jews of 28 AD] and shall condemn it, because they [those of Nineveh] repented at the proclamation of Jonah; and behold, a greater [one] than Jonah is here. *The* queen of *the* south [1000 BC] shall rise up [be raised from the dead] **in the judgment with this generation** [the Jews of 28 AD] and shall condemn it, because she came from the ends of the earth to hear the wisdom of Solomon; and behold, a greater [one] than Solomon *is* here" (Matt. 12:41-42). Clearly, Jesus is referring to the resurrection of judgment—"the coming age"—which is reserved for the rest of the dead as described in Revelation 20.

The Valley of Dry Bones—A Prophecy of the Second Resurrection. When Paul wrote to the believers in Rome, he maintained that during this present age only, "a remnant of Israel will be saved." He further elaborated that "all Israel shall be saved"—although he did not fully understand when that would occur.

Centuries prior to Paul, God gave the prophet Ezekiel a vision of the time when all the dead of Israel would be resurrected to a second physical life to have their first opportunity for salvation. "The hand of the LORD was upon me, and carried me out in the spirit of the LORD, and set me down in **the midst of the valley which** *was* **full of bones** [these human bones showed that they once lived and had died], and caused me to pass by them round about: and, behold, *there were* very many in the open valley; and, lo, *they were* very dry. And he said unto me, 'Son of man, **can these bones live**?' And I answered, 'O Lord GOD, thou knowest.'

"Again he said unto me, 'Prophesy upon these bones, and say unto them, O ye dry bones, hear the word of the LORD. Thus saith the Lord GOD unto these bones: "**Behold, I will cause breath to enter into you, and ye shall live: and I will lay sinews upon you, and will bring up flesh upon you, and cover you with skin, and put breath in you, and ye shall live; and ye shall know that I am the LORD.**" ' So I prophesied as I was commanded: and as I prophesied, there was a noise, and behold a shaking, and the bones came together, bone to his bone. And when I beheld, lo, **the sinews and the flesh came up upon them, and the skin covered them** above: but *there was* no breath in them.

"Then said he unto me, 'Prophesy unto the wind, prophesy, son of man, and say to the wind, 'Thus saith the Lord GOD; "Come from the four winds, O breath, and breathe upon these slain, that they may live." ' So I prophesied as he commanded me, and **the breath came into them, and they lived, and stood up upon their feet, an exceeding great army**. Then he said unto me, 'Son of man, **these bones are the whole house of Israel** [all the twelve tribes of Israel from all ages of time]: behold, they say, "Our bones are dried, and our hope is lost: we are cut off for our parts [for sins and transgressions]" ' " (Ezek. 37:1-11).

God instructed Ezekiel to continue prophesying: "Therefore prophesy and say unto them, 'Thus saith the Lord GOD; 'Behold, O my people, **I will open your graves**, and cause you to come up out of your graves [a resurrection to a second life in the flesh], and bring you into the land of Israel. **And ye shall know that I *am* the LORD, when I have opened your graves, O my people, and brought you up out of your graves**. And **shall put my spirit** [repentance, redemption and conversion] **in you**, and ye shall live, and I shall place you in your own land: then shall ye know that I the LORD have spoken *it*, and performed *it*, saith the LORD' " (verses 12-14).

There can be no doubt that Ezekiel is graphically describing a resurrection to a second physical life, because the passage describes bones, sinew, flesh and breath—as well as refers to "graves" four times. These scriptures emphasize the vital truth that the rest of house of Israel throughout history—which God had previously blinded because of unbelief—**will be resurrected to a second life in the flesh to be given their first opportunity for salvation**. It also confirms that in God's first covenant with Israel at Mount Sinai, He did not offer them the Holy Spirit, salvation or eternal life (Deut. 5:29). However, because God purposely blinded them, they did not commit the unpardonable sin in their first lifetime. Therefore, upon repentance, God will forgive their sins.

When they do repent, God will give them His Holy Spirit. They will have their hearts changed, become converted and have a chance to receive eternal life. Notice: "Then will I sprinkle clean water upon you, and ye shall be clean: from all your filthiness, and from all your idols, will I cleanse you. **A new heart also will I give you, and a new spirit will I put within you**: and I will take away the stony heart out of your flesh, and I will give you an heart of flesh. And **I will put my spirit within you, and cause you to walk in my statutes, and ye shall keep my judgments, and do *them***" (Ezek. 36:25-27).

In these two phrases of Ezekiel 37:13-14—"[Y]e shall know that I *am* the LORD" and "[I] shall put my spirit in you—" God is demonstrating that these raised to life will receive their opportunity for salvation and eternal life.

Jesus' statement about this resurrection to judgment—that "all who are in their graves" would hear His voice—is confirmed by Paul to also include Gentiles from all nations. "For as many as have sinned without law shall perish without law; and as many as have sinned within *the* law **shall be**

judged by *the* **law**" (Rom. 2:12). He adds that the Gentiles "which do not have *the* law, [yet] practice by nature the things contained in the law … are a law unto themselves" (verse 14). Thus, they too will be "judged by the law." When? Verse 16: "**In a day** [the second resurrection] **when God shall judge the secrets of men** by Jesus Christ, according to my gospel." As with Israel, God has blinded all uncalled Gentiles and has chosen to not give them His Holy Spirit. Therefore, because they committed forgivable sins, God will likewise raise them back to a second physical life for an opportunity for salvation.

Why Resurrected to a Second Physical Life?

The billions of people who are raised back to physical life in the second resurrection will not have to contend with Satan the devil or his demonic angels. They will have already lived their first lives under the authority of the "god of this world." Revelation 20:10 shows that before the second resurrection occurs, Satan and his demons will have been judged, sentenced, cast into the lake of fire and, finally, consigned to the blackness of darkness forever (Jude 13).

Since the second resurrection period is the final age of salvation, those of that time will not reproduce because the cycle of human birth and death must come to an end. As we will see, however, there will be an innumerable number of children of all ages who will be raised in this resurrection who will grow up to be adults and qualify for salvation.

Those in the second resurrection will have new bodies and minds, but they will still have memories of their first lives. As prophesied in Ezekiel 37:11, when the Israelites are raised to physical life again, they will exclaim, "Our bones are dried, and our hope is lost; we are cut off for our parts"—showing they understand that their first lives led them into spiritual blindness, lust and sin.

But why is God going to raise them back to life as physical human beings again? What is the purpose of living a second life in the flesh?

All Must Qualify for Salvation or Reject it While Living in the Flesh. Because God created mankind in His image and likeness from the dust of the earth, it is His purpose that all must qualify for salvation (or reject it) while living in the flesh. As we have seen, however, because of sin, God has blinded the majority of mankind and cut them off from salvation— so that, in the end, He might have mercy upon them all. Since God is love and desires to grant salvation to all through Jesus Christ, He has determined that all those who committed forgivable sins in their first lives will be raised back to a second physical life for their **first and only opportunity for eternal life**. Down through history, the vast majority of people who have lived and died are in this category. Undoubtedly, there will be billions and billions of people in the first phase of the second resurrection. John writes: "Then I saw a great white throne and the one Who was sitting on it, from Whose face the earth and the heaven fled away; and **no place was found for**

them. And **I saw the dead** [the "rest of the dead" described in verse 5], small and great, standing before God…" (Rev. 20:11-12).

During the final years of the Millennium the whole world will be prepared for the billions of people to be raised in the second resurrection. Those billions will immediately require housing, clothing, food, water, etc. In preparation, the whole earth will be transformed into a Garden of Eden—a fantastic utopia—ready and waiting to receive them.

When those of the judgment period are raised back to life, they **will repent** of their sins and God will forgive them. "And ye shall dwell in the land that I gave to your fathers; and ye shall be my people, and I will be your God. **I will also save you** from all your uncleannesses: and I will call for the corn, and will increase it, and lay no famine upon you. And I will multiply the fruit of the tree, and the increase of the field, that ye shall receive no more reproach of famine among the heathen. **Then shall ye remember your own evil ways, and your doings that *were* not good, and shall loathe yourselves in your own sight for your iniquities and for your abominations**" (Ezek. 36:28-31).

With their sins forgiven, they will be begotten by God's Holy Spirit—the earnest of their salvation. Although they will be converted, they will still have human nature and be subject to sin. However, upon "true, heartfelt" repentance they will be forgiven (as long as they commit forgivable sins), and—because they will be living under the grace of God—the sacrifice of Jesus Christ will be a continual propitiation for their sins (Rom. 3:23-26; I John 1:7-10; 2:1-2). Furthermore, they will be given ample time to live in faith, hope, love and obedience to God the Father and Jesus Christ in order to qualify for eternal life.

How Long Will They Live? It takes time to overcome human nature, grow in spiritual knowledge, and develop faithful, godly character in order to qualify for eternal life. But how long will this take? How long will those in the judgment live? As we previously learned, people will live to be one hundred years old during the Millennium in order to prove whether they will faithfully live in love, devotion and obedience to God (Isa. 65:20). Based on this precedent, we can conclude that God will likewise grant those in the first phase of the second resurrection one hundred years in which to live their second life in the flesh. This will allow ample time to learn to love God the Father and Jesus Christ—to keep the laws and commandments of God, overcome human nature, build godly character and develop the deep abiding faith required for salvation—thereby qualifying for God's gracious gift of eternal life.

The Resurrection of Children, Infants and the Spirit of Man. The second resurrection will also include countless children of all ages who had their lives cut short by war, murder, sacrifice to satanic gods, violence, torture, rape, famine, disaster, disease or accident. In His great love and tender mercy, God will raise them all to a second physical life in which they will be able to enjoy their lives to the full, receive the salvation of God and qualify for eternal life. These innocent babies and children—who in their first life were often unloved, rejected, considered inconvenient, or "legally" murdered—will become the loved, the accepted, the desired, and held and embraced in tender loving care.

What about babies that were aborted, miscarried, stillborn or died at birth—or newborn "throw-away" infants? The destruction of these innocent infants and the abortion of the unborn constitute one of the most heinous, fiendish works of Satan and his demons. What will God do for these most innocent ones? Are they lost forever? God the Father has promised that Jesus Christ will annul and completely undo all the works of Satan the devil (Heb. 2:14). Therefore, in His great love, tender mercy and forgiveness, God will raise them all back to a new physical life. Furthermore, **He will give them back** to their mothers and fathers in one of the most beautiful acts of redemption and reconciliation God could ever perform.

But, how will God raise the dead back to life?

God is able to transform the dead back to physical life because, at conception, He gives to **each person** the "spirit of man"—which is also the spirit of life. This human spirit functions much like "spiritual DNA" in that it "records" everything that is unique about a person. In addition, this "spirit of man" is **permanently locked in at conception, thus no man can destroy it**.

This guarantees that from the instant of conception—the uniting of the father's sperm with the egg of the mother—the newly begotten human life has within itself everything he or she will need to become a living person. The spirit of man gives life and enables the physical development of a new human being in the mother's womb—directing the genes and chromosomes to form each boy or girl in a continuous process. Without this spirit of man there would be no life—or, as the apostle James writes, "[T]he body without *the* spirit is dead…." (Jas. 2:26).

When talking to Job, Elihu declared that he fully understood he was made by the spiritual power of God. "The spirit of God hath made me, and the breath of the Almighty hath given me life" (Job 33:4). The prophet Zechariah tells us that God "…formeth the spirit of man within him" (Zech. 12:1).

While David was praying and meditating on how God created him in his mother's womb, he wrote, "For thou hast possessed my reins: **thou hast covered me in my mother's womb**. I will praise thee; for I am fearfully *and* wonderfully made: marvellous *are* thy works; and *that* my soul knoweth right well. **My substance was not hid from thee, when I was made in secret…. Thine eyes did see my substance, yet being unperfect; and in thy book all** *my members* **were written,** *which* **in continuance were fashioned, when** *as yet there was* **none of them**" (Psa. 139:13-16). The word "substance"—used by David to describe himself after he was conceived—is the identical word used today by so-called "modern science" to describe the initial mass of cells that begin developing immediately following conception.

More on the Spirit of Man. Since the spirit of man contains the complete master "genetic blueprint" of every individual from conception, the only difference between a newly conceived person and a full grown man or woman is development and growth. Consequently, when the aborted and stillborn are raised to life, they will probably be resurrected as full term babies and given to their mothers and fathers, who will then lovingly care for them. They will grow up, live their lives to the full, and have an opportunity to be converted and qualify for eternal life.

However, the spirit of man is **not** an immortal soul. Neither does it have consciousness outside of a human brain. In order for it to function, the spirit of man must be united with the human brain. When a person dies, the thought process stops (Psa. 146:4), the spirit of man returns to God, and the body returns to dust. "Then [at death] shall the dust [from which man is made] return to the earth as it was: and the spirit shall return unto God who gave it" (Eccl. 12:7). When Jesus died on the cross, His last words were, "Father into your hands I commit My spirit" (Luke 23:46; Matt. 27:50; John 19:30). (See Appendix J, *What Happens to the Dead?*, page 255.)

The apostle Paul writes that after death the "spirit of man" is stored with God in heaven until the time of the resurrection (Heb. 12:23). Through conversion, this human spirit is perfected by the indwelling of the Holy Spirit during the Christian's physical lifetime. For the dead who qualify for salvation in this age, God will use the "spirit of man" to impart to each resurrected saint a glorious, spiritual, immortal body and mind. (See Rom. 8:14-17; Phil. 3:20-21; I John 3:1-2.)

Likewise, Ezekiel 37 describes the second resurrection in which the entire house of Israel will be raised to a second physical life. Each will at that time be given a new physical body and a new mind reconstructed from the dust of the earth according to their unique "human spirit."

What Kind of Judgment Will They Receive? Before this question can be answered, we need to emphasize that today, during this age, true Christians are being judged by God according to their spiritual works only after they have repented of their sins, have been baptized and have received the Holy Spirit. Such are saved by the grace of God through faith: "For by grace you have been saved through faith, and this *especially* is not of your own selves; *it is* the gift of God, not of works, so that no one may boast. **For we are His workmanship, created in Christ Jesus unto *the* good works that God ordained beforehand in order that we might walk in them**" (Eph. 2:8-10).

Consequently, once a person has been converted, they are to conduct their lives by walking in the good works of God—His laws and commandments. Through daily prayer and study, they are to spend the rest of their lives growing in grace and knowledge, and overcoming human nature and sin by the power of God's Holy Spirit in them. This is how a Christian develops godly character (II Pet. 1:3-11), loves God with all his or her heart, mind and strength, and qualifies for eternal life through the grace of God.

Although true Christians live in the love of God and stand in His grace, God judges them according to their spiritual works of faith, hope and love. The apostle Peter writes that this judgment for eternal life is now on the people of God: "For the time *has come for* judgment [for eternal life] to begin with the household of God..." (I Pet. 4:17). Jesus also said, "The one who endures to *the* end, that one will be saved" (Matt. 24:13). In Jesus' messages to the seven churches, He repeatedly declares that everyone who is called to the first resurrection is being judged according to their works. Where their works are deficient or sinful, He calls them to repentance (Rev. 2-3).

Since God is not a respecter of persons (Rom. 2:11), those in the second resurrection will receive the same opportunity for salvation and eternal life. Christians in this age are continuously under God's judgment from the time of their conversion until they die in the faith. Likewise, God's judgment on those of the second resurrection will not begin until they too repent of their sins, are baptized and receive the Holy Spirit. They will then each have to grow in grace and knowledge, develop godly character and be faithful for one hundred years—the end of their second life in the flesh.

Although eternal life is the gracious gift of God, each will be judged according to the spiritual works of his or her second physical life, not the sinful works of their first life. As John writes, "[*T*]*he* books [the books of the Word of God] were opened [to their understanding]; and another book was opened, which is *the book* of life [an opportunity for salvation]. And the dead were judged [after their resurrection] out of the things written in the books [the Word of God], according to their works [in their second physical lives]. And the sea gave up the dead *that were* in it, and death and *the* grave gave up the dead *that were* in them; and they were judged individually, according to their works" (Rev. 20:12-13).

At the end of the one-hundred-year period, all that have qualified for eternal life will be instantaneously changed from flesh to spirit. They will enter the spiritual kingdom of God as part of God's extended family—which by then will have expanded greatly, becoming "the nations which are saved" (Rev. 21-22). Jesus proclaims, "Blessed *are* those who keep His commandments, that they may have the right to eat *of* the tree of life, and may enter by the gates into the city [New Jerusalem]" (Rev. 22:14).

The Second Phase of the Second Resurrection and the Lake of Fire. While the vast majority of those in the first phase of the second resurrection will attain eternal life, there will be **some who will refuse** God's gracious gift of immortality. In so doing, they will have committed the unforgivable sin—blasphemy against the Holy Spirit of God the Father. At the end of the one hundred years, these will remain alive in the flesh for a while longer—until the rest of the dead who had previously committed the unpardonable sin are resurrected. This second phase of the second resurrection will include all who had committed the unpardonable sin from Adam's time to the return of Jesus Christ and during the Millennium. They will be raised briefly to life in the flesh in order to receive their final judgment with all of the other incorrigibly wicked. (See Appendix K, *What is the Unpardonable Sin?*, page 263.)

Jesus sternly warned those who had received the Holy Spirit that if they did not have the godly, righteous works of love and obedience required for salvation, they would not receive eternal life. He warned that if anyone rejected God's salvation and blasphemed against the Holy Spirit of God, they would be rejected, accursed and cast into the lake of fire—the same fate that awaits Satan and his demons. "Then shall He also say to those on the left, 'Depart from Me, *you* cursed ones, into the eternal fire, which has been prepared for the devil and his angels' " (Matt. 25:41).

All those who have committed the unforgivable sin will not have their names written in the book of life—and will be cast into the lake of fire to die the second death. "And if anyone was not found written in the book of life, he was **cast into the lake of fire**" (Rev. 20:15). Verse 14: "And death and *the* grave were **cast into the lake of fire. This is the second death**." And again, "But *the* cowardly, and unbelieving, and abominable, and murderers, and fornicators, and sorcerers, and idolaters, and all liars, shall have their part in **the lake that burns with fire and brimstone**; which is *the* **second death**... And nothing that defiles shall ever enter into it [the New Jerusalem], nor shall *anyone* who practices *an* abomination or *devises* a lie; but *only* **those who are written in the Lamb's book of life**" (Rev. 21:8, 27).

After the incorrigibly wicked are cast into the lake of fire, the fire will then expand to encompass the whole earth and its atmosphere. Peter writes: "However, the day of *the* Lord [for those who face the second death] shall come as a thief in *the* night in which heaven itself shall disappear with a mighty roar, and *the* elements shall pass away, **burning with intense heat, and *the* earth and the works in it shall be burned up**" (II Pet. 3:10). At that time, Peter adds, "*the* **heavens, being on fire, shall be destroyed, and *the* elements, burning with intense heat, shall melt**" (verse 12). Thus, the wicked will be consumed in the lake of fire.

The New Heaven and New Earth—the Final Fulfillment of the Last Great Day

The apostle Peter writes that the earth and its atmosphere are to be burned up in preparation for a new heaven and a new earth: "But according to His promise, we look forward to a new heaven and a new earth, in which righteousness dwells" (II Pet. 3:13).

Jesus Christ gave the apostle John a vision of the new heaven and new earth: "Then I saw a new heaven and a new earth; for the first heaven and the first earth were passed away, and there was no more sea. And I, John, saw the holy city, *the* new Jerusalem, coming down from God out of heaven, prepared as a bride adorned for her husband. And I heard a great voice from heaven say, 'Behold, the tabernacle of God *is* with men; and He shall dwell with them, and they shall be His people; and God Himself shall be with them *and be* their God. And God shall wipe away every tear from their eyes; and *there* shall be no more death, or sorrow, or crying; neither shall *there* be any more pain, because the former things have passed away.' And He Who sits on the throne said, 'Behold, I make all things new.' Then He said to me, 'Write, for these words are true and faithful.' And He said to me, 'It is done. I am Alpha and Omega, the Beginning and the End. To the one who thirsts, I will give freely of the fountain of the water of life. **The one who overcomes shall inherit all things; and I will be his God, and he shall be My son**' '' (Rev. 21:1-7).

The climatic fulfillment of the Last Great Day is the ushering in of the new heaven and earth. Thus, the "eighth day" (as the number eight signifies) is a "new beginning" in the plan of God—an open door to eternity. God then brings the New Jerusalem to the earth—to be the home of the Father and Jesus Christ, His bride and all the saints in the first resurrection. This is the place Jesus told His disciples He would prepare for them (John 14:2).

Notice its glorious description: "And one of the seven angels that had the seven vials full of the seven last plagues came and spoke with me, saying, 'Come here, *and* I will show you the bride, the Lamb's wife.' And he carried me away in *the* Spirit to a great and high mountain, and showed me the great city, holy Jerusalem [which is not the bride, but where the bride will dwell], descending out of heaven from God, having the glory of God. And her radiance *was* like a most precious stone, as crystal-clear *as* jasper stone. And *the* city also had a great and high wall, with twelve gates, and at the gates twelve angels; and inscribed on *the gates* were *the* names of the twelve tribes of the children of Israel. On *the* east *were* three gates; on *the* north *were* three gates; on *the* south *were* three gates; on *the* west *were* three gates. And the wall of the city had twelve foundations, and written on them *were the* names of the twelve apostles of the Lamb.

"And the one who was speaking with me had a golden measuring rod, so that he might measure the city, and its gates and its wall. And the city lies foursquare, for its length is as long as its breadth. And he measured the city with the rod, twelve thousand furlongs; the length and the breadth and the height of it are equal. And he measured its wall, one hundred *and* forty-four cubits; *the* angel's measure *was according to* a man's. And the structure of its wall was jasper; and the city *was* pure gold, like pure glass. And the foundations of the wall of the city *were* adorned with every precious stone: the first foundation *was* jasper; the second, sapphire; the third, chalcedony; the fourth, emerald; the fifth, sardonyx; the sixth, sardius; the seventh, chrysolite; the eighth, beryl; the ninth, topaz; the tenth, chrysoprasus; the eleventh, jacinth; the twelfth, amethyst. And the twelve gates *were* twelve pearls; each of the gates respectively was a single pearl; and the street of the city *was* pure gold, as transparent *as* glass" (Rev. 21:9-21).

New Jerusalem will also be the ultimate fulfillment of the meaning of the Feast of Tabernacles. God the Father and Jesus Christ will personally dwell with their spiritual family and, from this time on, there will be no temple: "And I saw no temple in it; for the Lord God Almighty and the Lamb are the temple of it. And the city has no need of the sun, or of the moon, that they should shine in it; because the glory of God enlightens it, and the light of it *is* the Lamb. And the nations that are saved shall walk in its light; and the kings of the earth shall bring their glory and honor into it. And its gates shall never be shut by day; for there shall be no night there. And they shall bring the glory and the honor of the nations into it" (Rev. 21:22-26).

New Jerusalem will become the capital city and center of the universe. It will always be filled with righteousness and the Holy Spirit of God, as John's final vision reveals: "Then he showed me a pure river of *the* water of life, clear as crystal, flowing out from the throne of God and of the Lamb. *And* in the middle of *the* street, and on this side and that side of the river, *was the* tree of life, producing twelve *manner of* fruits, each month yielding its fruit; and the leaves of the tree *are* for *the* healing of the nations. And there shall be no more curse; **and the throne of God and of the Lamb shall be in it; and His servants shall serve Him, and they shall see His face; and His name is in their foreheads**.

"And there shall be no night there; for they have no need of a lamp or *the* light of *the* sun, because *the* Lord God enlightens them; and **they shall reign into the ages of eternity**. And he said to me, 'These words *are* faithful and true; and *the* Lord God of the holy prophets sent His angel to show His servants the things that must shortly come to pass. Behold, I am coming quickly. Blessed *is* the one who keeps the words of the prophecy of this book' " (Rev. 22:1-7).

God the Father and Jesus Christ plan to share the never-ending vastness of the universe with the immortal, spirit Family of God—in fulfillment of God's purpose for the majestic universe He created (Rom. 8:17-18; Heb. 1:2-3). Indeed, the Last Great Day pictures a new beginning—an open door to eternity! AMEN

Conclusion

In Part One of this book, we provided a well-documented, historical account of the major occult holidays observed around the world—as well as concerning the practice of Sunday-keeping by mainstream Orthodox Christendom. The evidence conclusively demonstrates that such days are entrenched in ancient **pagan sun worship**.

The majority of professing "Christianity"—*led astray in ignorance*—has simply accepted the observance of these days as part of the "Christian" liturgy. With slight-of-hand and sanctimonious falsehoods, religious and authority figures have assured their followers that because these formerly pagan festivals have been officially "Christianized" by the church, they are free to celebrate them as acceptable "Christian" holidays.

In Part Two, we analyzed the biblical perspective concerning occult holidays and Sunday-keeping, noting that **God absolutely condemns the observance of such days** and the false gods they actually represent. As the profound example of the children of ancient Israel and Judah illustrates—as well as in the case of professing "Christians" today—all must come to understand that it is *impossible* to worship the God of Truth with religious lies and myths rooted in occultism and the worship of Satan the devil.

In Part Three, we surveyed the biblical, seventh-day Sabbath, holy days and feasts of God. As emphasized in *both* the Old and New Testaments, God has consistently commanded His people to obediently observe His seventh-day Sabbath, holy days and festivals. As we learned, God reveals His plan and purpose for mankind through the meaning of these days. **God gives this understanding to those who love Him** and obey His commandments—and who keep His feasts and holy days. This—*obedience to God's way of life*—is how true Christians are to worship God the Father and Jesus Christ in "spirit and truth."

Today, we are living in the "last days"—and will soon come face-to-face with the impending "crisis at the close of the age." The inconspicuous rise of the *final* world empire is already well under way—which will envelop all mankind into an evil New World Order. Numerous biblical prophecies depict just such a world-ruling system—led by the "Antichrist," a *false* Messiah—coupled with an amalgamation of the world's religions, all under the sway of a great "False Prophet."

Warning!
Open Satan Worship will Sweep the World
and Usher in the Antichrist!

Historically, Satan has cleverly manipulated false religion, occult practices and witchcraft in order to deceive and corrupt all civilizations. He continues, today, to **deceive the whole world** (Rev. 12:9) into following him and his way of evil as the undisputed god of this present age (II Cor. 4:4).

However, **Satan's final and greatest deception** is rapidly developing. Once reaching its zenith of satanic power, it will sweep all peoples and nations into blatant Satan worship—replete with false signs, miracles and lying wonders—all designed to usher in the Antichrist. Empowered by Satan himself, the False Prophet will call down fire from heaven, proclaiming the Antichrist as the savior of the world. With the exception of *true* Christians who have the Holy Spirit of God, **all the world will be utterly deceived** into believing that the Antichrist is indeed the manifestation of God in the flesh—the long-awaited Messiah.

The prophecies of the New Testament clearly show that this Antichrist will arise out of the world's extant political and religious system referred to in Scripture as the "mystery of lawlessness." The coming of the Antichrist will be a *spectacular* event. The apostle Paul warned of his coming: "Now we beseech you, brethren, concerning the coming of our Lord Jesus Christ and our gathering together to Him, that you not be quickly shaken in mind, nor be troubled—neither by spirit, nor by word, nor by epistle, as if from us, *saying* that the day of Christ is present. **Do not let anyone deceive you by any means because** *that day will not* **come unless the apostasy shall come first, and the man of sin shall be revealed—the son of perdition**, the one who opposes and exalts himself above all that is called God, or that is an object of worship; so that he comes into the temple of God and sits down as God, proclaiming that he himself is God" (II Thess. 2:1-4).

Thus, the "man of sin" will be revealed "in his time," appearing just before Jesus Christ's second coming. "Do you not remember that when I was still with you, I told you these things? And now you understand what is holding *him* [the Antichrist] back **in order for him to be revealed in his own set time. For the mystery of lawlessness is already working**; only *there is* one Who is restraining at the present *time* until it arises out of *the* midst. And then the lawless one [the Antichrist] will be revealed (whom the Lord will consume with the breath of His mouth, and will destroy with the brightness of His coming)" (verses 5-8).

It will be Satan's grand finale at the close of the age: "*Even* **the one whose coming is according to** *the* **inner working of Satan, with all power and signs and lying wonders, and with all deceivableness of unrighteousness in those who are perishing because they did not receive the love of the truth, so that they might be saved. And for this cause, God will send upon them a powerful deception that will cause them to believe** *the* **lie**, so that all may be judged who did not believe the truth, but who took pleasure in unrighteousness" (verses 9-12).

Confirming what Paul wrote, Jesus Christ gave the apostle John a startling vision (recorded in the book of Revelation) of the coming New World Order and of the Antichrist who will arise out of that system. John depicted this **political system** as a "beast" with "seven heads and ten horns" (Rev. 13:1-9). A second "beast"—Satan's unified, worldwide **reli-**

gious system—is described as having two horns "like a lamb;" it speaks, however, "like a dragon" and performs "great wonders" (verses 11-13).

The Beast with Seven Heads and Ten Horns. One of the political beast's "seven heads," the coming Antichrist, is to receive a "deadly wound." Once revived, however, he becomes the "man of sin," the "son of perdition" of II Thessalonians 2: "[T]he dragon [Satan the devil, Rev. 12:3, 9] **gave him his power, and his throne and great authority**. And I saw one of his heads as *if it were* slain to death, but **his deadly wound was healed**; and THE WHOLE WORLD WAS AMAZED AND FOLLOWED THE BEAST. **And they worshiped the dragon**, who gave *his* authority **to the beast. And they worshiped the beast**, saying, 'Who *is* like the beast? Who has the power to make war against him?' **And a mouth speaking great things and blasphemies was given to him; and authority was given to him to continue *for* forty-two months. And he opened his mouth in blasphemy against God, to blaspheme His name, and His tabernacle, and those who dwell in heaven. And he was given *power* to make war against the saints, and to overcome them; and he was given authority over every tribe and language and nation. And all who dwell on the earth will worship him, whose names have not been written in the book of life of the Lamb slain from *the* foundation of *the* world**" (Rev. 13:2-8).

Not only will *Satan himself be worshiped*, but the Antichrist will be *revered as very God!* This **worldwide manifestation of Satan the devil** will be the total fulfillment of all occult agendas—the **ultimate in occult worship** since the beginning of human history!

The Beast with Two Horns that Speaks as a Dragon. As world governments align themselves with the New World Order, there will also be a unified world religion. This **religious system** is portrayed by the second beast of Revelation 13, which features "two horns like a lamb," but speaks "like a dragon."

Because of its lamb-like horns, this second beast appears to be "Christian"—but will actually be personified by the False Prophet, the world leader of Satan's occult religions. "And I saw another beast rising out of the earth; **and he had two horns like a lamb, but spoke like a dragon**; and he exercises all the authority of the first beast before him; and he causes the earth and those who dwell therein to worship the first beast, whose deadly wound was healed. And **he performs great wonders, so that he even causes fire to come down to the earth from heaven in the sight of men**. And he deceives those who dwell on the earth by means of the wonders that were given to him to perform in the sight of the beast, saying to those who dwell on the earth that they should make an image for the beast, which had the wound by the sword, yet was alive" (Rev. 13:11-14).

Satan is preparing for his grand, worldwide finale by saturating every aspect of society with the occult. Satan, demon and goddess worship—the focal point of the occult—will be brought out into the open. The Antichrist and the False Prophet will deceive all of mankind, uniting them in open rebellion against God! **Only the few true Christians will not be deceived!** Christians today are openly hated by this satanic, occult system. Once the Antichrist is in complete control of the world, however, the beast system will (again!) be given the power to martyr the saints (Rev. 13:7).

In Revelation 17, Christ gave John yet another vision of this evil **religious system**—this time symbolized by a *woman* "riding" the beast with the seven heads and ten horns (that is, the **political system** or New World Order). The "woman" is the great Babylonian harlot with her daughters—symbolizing all the occult religious systems of the world. "And one of the seven angels who had the seven vials came and spoke with me, saying to me, 'Come here; I will show you the judgment of the great whore who sits upon many waters; with whom the kings of the earth have committed fornication, and those who dwell on the earth were made drunk with the wine of her fornication.' Then he carried me away in *the* spirit to a wilderness; and I saw a woman sitting upon a scarlet beast that had seven heads and ten horns, full of names of blasphemy. And the woman *was* clothed in purple and scarlet, and *was* adorned with gold and pearls and precious stones; *and* she had a golden cup in her hand, filled with abominations and *the* filthiness of her fornication; and across her forehead a name *was* written: MYSTERY, BABYLON THE GREAT, THE MOTHER OF THE HARLOTS AND OF THE ABOMINATIONS OF THE EARTH. And I saw the woman drunk with the blood of the saints, and with the blood of the martyrs of Jesus. And after seeing her, I wondered with great amazement.... Then he said to me, 'The waters that you saw, where the whore sits, are peoples and multitudes and nations and languages.... And the woman whom you saw is the great city that has royal power over the kings of the earth' " (Rev. 17:1-6, 15 and 18).

The ten "horns" on the beast symbolize ten kings or nations that will receive power from the beast system—and will ultimately fight against Christ at His second coming. "And the beast that was, and is not, he is also the eighth, and is from the seven, and goes into perdition [lead by the Antichrist, whom Paul called the "son of perdition"]. And the ten horns that you saw are ten kings, who have not yet received a kingdom, but shall receive authority as kings *for* one hour with the beast [the coming New World Order]. These *all* have one mind, and shall give up their power and authority to the beast. These will make war with the Lamb, but the Lamb shall overcome them; for He is Lord of lords and King of kings, and those who *are* with Him *are* called, and chosen, and faithful.... For God has put into their hearts to do His will, and to act with one accord, and to give their kingdom to the beast until the words of God have been fulfilled" (Rev. 17: 11-14, 17). No human power will be able to stop this final, ultimate, satanic plot to be played out by the beasts of Revelation. Only the dramatic return of Jesus Christ will bring it to an end: "And I saw heaven open; and behold, a white horse; and He Who sat on it *is* called Faithful and True, and in righteousness He does judge and make war. And His eyes *were* like a flame of fire, and on His head *were* many crowns; *and* He had a name written that no one knows except Him. And *He was* clothed with a garment dipped in blood; and His name is The Word of God. And the armies in heaven were following Him on white horses; *and* they were clothed in fine linen, white and pure. And out of His mouth goes a sharp sword, that with it He might smite the nations; and He shall shepherd them with an iron rod; and He treads the winepress of the fury and the wrath of the Almighty God. And on *His* garment and on His thigh He has a name written: King of kings and Lord of lords.

"Then I saw an angel standing in the sun; and he cried out with a loud voice, saying to all the birds that fly in *the* midst of heaven, 'Come and gather yourselves together to the supper of the great God so that you may eat *the* flesh of kings, and *the* flesh of chief captains, and *the* flesh of mighty *men*, and *the* flesh of horses, and of those who sit on them, and *the* flesh of all, free and bond, and small and great.' **And I saw the beast and the kings of the earth and their armies, gathered together to make war with Him Who sits on the horse, and with His army. And the beast** [the Antichrist] **was taken, and with him the false prophet who worked miracles in his presence**, by which he had deceived those who received the mark of the beast and those who worshiped his image. **Those two were cast alive into the lake of fire, which burns with brimstone**; and the rest were killed by the sword of Him Who sits on the horse, *even the sword* that goes out of His mouth; and all the birds were filled with their flesh" (Rev. 19:11-21).

God's Call to Repentance

Each of us must "weigh in the balance" our own beliefs to see how they compare to the teachings of the Bible and those of the true Savior of mankind, Jesus Christ. We each must ask, and answer, **"Will I believe God, the Word of God, Jesus Christ and His teachings—will I love the truth? Or, will I believe the teachings and doctrines of men, and continue to follow the teachings of Satan the devil?"**

There can be *no* middle ground. God will never compromise with evil, and God does not accept lying, satanic myths. If we *reject* the truth of God when shown to us, He will send a powerful delusion—and we will end up believing fully in Satan's lies.

God calls upon *you* to **repent of your sins**—to turn from the way that seems right to men and to come out of this modern "Babylon the Great"—out of its corrupt governments and religions. "And after these things I saw an angel descending from heaven, having great authority; and the earth was illuminated with his glory. And he cried out mightily with a loud voice, saying, '**Babylon the Great is fallen, is fallen**, and has become a habitation of demons, and a prison of every unclean spirit, and a prison of every unclean and hated bird; because **all nations have drunk of the wine of the fury of her fornication, and the kings of the earth have committed fornication with her, and the merchants of the earth have become rich through the power of her luxury**.'

"And I heard another voice from heaven, saying, 'COME OUT OF HER, MY PEOPLE, **so that you do not take part in her sins, and that you do not receive of her plagues**, for her sins have reached as far as heaven, and God has remembered her iniquities. Render to her as she has rendered to you; and give to her double, even according to her works. In the cup that she mixed, give her back double. To the degree that she glorified herself and lived luxuriously, give to her as much torment and sorrow. For she says in her heart, "I sit a queen enthroned, and am not a widow; and in no way shall I experience sorrow." **For this very reason, her plagues shall come in one day—death and sorrow and famine; and she shall be burned with fire; for** *the* **Lord God, Who executes judgment upon her,** *is* **powerful**' " (Rev. 18:1-8).

When He returns, Jesus Christ will *destroy* this entire world system—a system based on witchcraft and the occult, and empowered by Satan and his demons! "Then one strong angel took up a stone like a great millstone and cast *it* into the sea, saying, 'In this same way shall the great city Babylon be thrown down with violence, and shall never again be found; and never again shall *the* sound of harpers and musicians and flute players and trumpeters be heard in you; and never again shall any craftsman of any craft be found in you; and never again shall *the* sound of a millstone be heard in you; and never again shall *the* light of a lamp shine in you; and never again shall *the* voices of bridegroom and bride be heard in you; **for your merchants were the great ones of the earth, and by your sorcery all nations were deceived**" (Rev. 18:21-24).

Personal Repentance

God the Father and Jesus Christ directly **hold each one of us responsible** to repent and forsake this great Babylonian system! All religious practices of this world and all "traditions of men" are inspired by Satan and his demons—they are not from God! Halloween, Christmas, New Year's, Easter, Good Friday and Lent have all been reconfigured and "Christianized" in order to **deceive the masses**—as part of a system designed to hold people in bondage and in ongoing sin against God!

We are to repent of our sins before God the Father, asking Him to forgive us through the blood of Jesus Christ. When He began His ministry in Galilee, Jesus commanded the people to repent! "The time has been fulfilled, and the kingdom of God has drawn near; **repent, and believe in the gospel**" (Mark 1:15).

After Jesus' resurrection, He commissioned the apostles to preach the gospel in all the world and commanded them to preach repentance and remission of sins to all nations: "According as it is written, it was necessary for the Christ to suffer, and to rise from *the* dead the third day. And in His name, **repentance and remission of sins** should be preached to all nations, beginning at Jerusalem" (Luke 24:46-47).

On the Day of Pentecost, the apostle Peter preached a powerful message proving that it was the sins of the leaders *and* the sins of the people that resulted in the crucifixion of Jesus Christ. Once convicted in both heart and mind, Peter instructed them to **repent of their sins** and to be baptized: " 'Therefore, let all *the* house of Israel know with full assurance that God has made this *same* Jesus, Whom you crucified, both Lord and Christ.' Now after hearing *this*, they were cut to the heart; and they said to Peter and the other apostles, 'Men *and* brethren, what shall we do?' Then Peter said to them, '**Repent and be baptized each one of you in the name of Jesus Christ for *the* remission of sins, and you yourselves shall receive the gift of the Holy Spirit**' " (Acts 2:36-38).

Several days later—when Peter and John had healed a man through Jesus' name—Peter again called on the people to repent: "The God of Abraham and Isaac and Jacob, the God of our fathers, has glorified His Son Jesus, Whom you delivered up, and denied Him in the presence of Pilate, after he had judged to release *Him*. But you denied the Holy and Righteous One, and requested that a man *who was* a murderer be granted to you; **and you killed the Author of life Whom God has raised from *the* dead**, whereof we are witnesses. And through faith in His name, this *man* whom you see and know was made strong in His name; and the faith that *is* through Him gave this complete soundness to him in the presence of you all. And now, brethren, I realize that you acted in ignorance, as *did* your rulers also; but what God had before announced by *the* mouth of all His prophets, *that* Christ should suffer, He has accordingly fulfilled. **Therefore, repent and be converted in order that your sins may be blotted out**, so that *the* times of refreshing may come from *the* presence of the Lord" (Acts 3:13-19).

Witnessing to the deceived, elite philosophers and pagan religionists in Athens, Greece, the apostle Paul declared to them that in times past they were, in *ignorance*, devoted to false deities. Now, however, God commands that all repent of such idolatry: "Therefore, since we are the offspring of God, we should not think that the Godhead *is* like that which *is made* of gold, or silver, or stone—a graven thing of art *devised by the* imagination of man; For *although* God has indeed **overlooked the times of this ignorance**, He now commands all men everywhere to repent" (Acts 17:29-30).

As was true of the ancient Greeks, nearly all of Orthodox Christianity has been blindly and ignorantly worshiping the "unknown God" (verse 23). Today's religious leaders have pushed aside the truth of God's Word—His Sabbath, feasts and holy days—and replaced them with their own traditions, religious practices and observances. Under the guise of grace, liberty and church authority, those who have accepted such teachings have been **ignorantly led into sin** against God the Father and Jesus Christ.

Paul wrote: "For all have sinned and have come short of the glory of God" (Rom. 3:23). Sin is the transgression of the laws and commandments of God (I John 3:4)—and all sin is lawlessness! The religious practices of this world have been shown clearly to be *sin*. Many are clever counterfeits, and they may *seem* right—but they are all *sin*.

Yes, it is true that **Jesus Christ died for your sins**—but *you* must **repent and stop living in sin**—and *then* be baptized. You must repent not only of your personal sins, but repent also of the sins of observing Sunday and the holidays of this world—the "sanitized" occult holidays of Satan the devil.

You need to repent of *all* sin, and have such sins "covered" by the blood of Jesus Christ. **You will be forgiven—as God has promised!** "If we proclaim that we have fellowship with Him, but we are walking in the darkness, we are lying to ourselves, and we are not practicing the Truth. However, if we walk in the light, as He is in the light, *then* we have fellowship with one another, and the blood of Jesus Christ, His own Son, cleanses us from every sin. If we say that we do not have sin, we are deceiving ourselves, and the truth is not in us. **If we confess our own sins, He is faithful and righteous, to forgive us our sins, and to cleanse us from all unrighteousness**" (I John 1:6-9).

God calls *you* to repentance. We must follow the example of King David, who, when he sinned against God, cried out for forgiveness: "Be merciful unto me, O Lord: for I cry unto thee daily.... **For thou, Lord, art good, and ready to forgive; and plenteous in mercy unto all them that call upon thee**" (Psa. 86:3, 5).

Now that **you know the truth** about Satan's occult holidays, and the truth about God's Sabbath and holy days, **what will you do?** Will you be convicted of your sins, repent and forsake your past, and turn to God the Father and Jesus Christ with all your heart? Will you, like David, pour out your heart to Him, confessing your sins? You have God's sure promise that He will forgive you all your sins. Then will you do as Jesus commanded— "go and sin no more"?

May God the Father and Jesus Christ lead you to understanding and repentance!

Please visit our websites, www.cbcg.org and www.biblicaltruthministries.org, where you will find numerous articles available on God's way of life. We also have downloadable sermons on repentance, water baptism, how to keep the Sabbath and holy days—and much more. Be sure to download the nine-part series entitled, *Why God Hates Religion!*

PART FOUR

Appendices

Appendix A

Halloween and the Flood of Noah—Is There a Link?

Following the dispersion of mankind at the tower of Babel (Gen. 11), virtually every ensuing culture has maintained a legend regarding a "Great Flood." Often, as we will see, such traditions are also associated with a great "Day of Death," as well as a "new beginning" (linked to the salvation of Noah and his family). Interestingly, these traditions are all tied to the Fall of the year—specifically the end of October and the beginning of November. Is it possible, as the evidence suggests, that there is a connection between the flood of Noah's time and the pagan holiday known today as Halloween?

Was the flood in the Fall of the year? Many scholars believe that—much like today's Jewish calendar—the calendar employed in Genesis began in the Fall, with the first month beginning somewhere from mid-September to mid-October. Genesis 7:11 states that the flood began "in the second month, the seventeenth day of the month." Therefore, this could easily place the beginning of the flood at the end of October or the beginning of November. A year later—on the 27th day of the second month—Noah and his family left the ark, their "salvation" complete. Thus, a "new year" began around the first of November.

One scholar writes: "What is often overlooked, however, is that there is [in addition to the great flood legend] the remembrance of the 'Day of the Dead,' followed by a New Year. This occurs on our [Roman] calendar at the end of October or the beginning of November" (Frank Humphrey, *The Great Flood and Halloween*).

The following examples serve to illustrate how widespread the tradition of the "Day of the Dead" and a "November New Year" had become. Note the many "themes" that correspond to Halloween.

• In Egypt it has "long been known that the ship of Isis and the chest or coffin of Osiris [note the **death** theme] which floated on the waters for a year are confused Egyptian recollections of the [great] Flood. Plutarch says [that] Osiris was shut up in his box and set afloat 'on the seventeenth day of the month Athyr, when nights were growing long and the days decreasing.'… In Plutarch's time, Athyr did in fact coincide with October-November."

• "In ancient Assyria the **ceremonies for the souls of the dead** were in the month Arahsamna, which is Marcheswan [the month of Heshvan on the Jewish calendar, which is mid-October to mid-November]. In Arahsamna the Sun God became Lord of the **Land of the Dead**."

• In India, "the Hindu Durga **festival of the dead** was originally connected with their **New Year which commenced in November**."

• In Iran, "the Persians **commenced their New Year in November**, in a month which was named Mordad-month, i.e., the **month of the angel of death**."

• In the Fall of the year the Aboriginal Australians "painted white stripes on their legs and arms to **resemble skeletons**."

• In French Polynesia, "the inhabitants … **pray for the spirits of departed ancestors** at the end of their New Year celebration in November."

• In Peru, "the [Inca] **New Year commenced in November** and the festival called Ayamarka—[meaning, the] **carrying of a corpse**—concluded with [the] placing [of] food and drink on **graves**."

• "The Mexican [Aztecs], too, kept the **Day of the Dead** at the same [Fall] time of the year."

• In many parts of Europe, "November 2 is **All Souls' Day, the Day of the Dead**."

• In France "it is Le Jour des Morts, Christianized now for centuries, but still at [the] heart [of] the old **Day of the Dead** when flowers are taken to the tombs."

• The "early Anglo-Saxons called November **Blood-Month**," while Celtic inhabitants of Britain "kept their New Year in November."

• In Wales and Scotland "early November is the time for **ghosts to be remembered**."

(Adapted from *The Great Flood and Halloween*, bold emphasis and bracketed comments added; for website information see Bibliography.)

Humphrey concludes, "The legends cited above are found all over the world in cultures radically distinct from one another…. And yet they all have in common this **remembrance of death and a new beginning at the end of October** and the beginning of November" (bold emphasis added).

Is this mere coincidence? Or does the evidence presented hint at the true origin of Halloween? Is Halloween, in fact, a sort of morbid memorial to the wicked that God destroyed by Noah's flood?

Humphrey suggests that—perhaps *like* the "Great Flood"—Halloween itself is a sober "reminder both of God's judgment on human rebellion and His offer of deliverance to those who put their trust in His mercy."

Appendix B

The Weekly Sabbath and Annual Feasts and Holy Days

The Weekly Sabbath

The weekly Sabbath, known as Saturday today, is the seventh day of the week. In the beginning, the Sabbath was created by God. He blessed and sanctified the seventh day at creation as a special day for rest and fellowship with Him. The Sabbath is a memorial of creation and was made for all mankind. It was the commanded day of weekly worship for 3,000 years before the Ten Commandments were given to Israel. The Fourth Commandment is a reminder to observe and to keep the Sabbath day holy.

As Lord God of the Old Testament, Jesus Christ created the Sabbath by resting on the very first seventh day and by blessing and sanctifying it. In the New Testament, Jesus Christ proclaimed that He is Lord of the Sabbath day. During His ministry on earth, He reaffirmed the sacredness of the Sabbath and taught its proper observance. Jesus Christ Himself showed by example that it is right to do good on the Sabbath day, in addition to resting from one's physical labor and secular business. The apostles of Jesus Christ and the early New Testament church observed the Sabbath and taught Gentile Christians to observe it.

The keeping of the seventh-day Sabbath is a special sign of the covenant between God and His people. God commands that it be observed from sunset Friday to sunset Saturday. During this holy time, Christians are commanded to rest from their labor and to assemble to worship God and to receive instruction from His Word. Observance of the seventh-day Sabbath is essential for salvation and for true fellowship with God the Father and Jesus Christ.

Scriptural References

Gen. 2:1-3	Mark 2:27-28	Ex. 20:8-10
Ex. 31:13-17	Isa. 58:13-14	Isa. 56:1-7
Isa. 66:23	Ezek. 20:12, 20	Lev. 23:1-3
Luke 4:4	Acts 13:42-44	Acts 17:2
Acts 18:4, 11	Acts 19:8-10	Heb. 4:4-10

The Annual Feasts and Holy Days

The Scriptures teach that there are seven annual feasts and holy days, which were ordained by God to be observed as special commanded convocations. These feasts and holy days portray God's plan of salvation for mankind. The observance of these holy convocations is a sign between God and His people. God's annual feasts and holy days were observed by His people during Old Testament times. In the New Testament, Jesus Christ's entire ministry was centered around the spiritual meaning of these holy days. The New Testament apostolic church faithfully observed these annual feasts and holy days. The Scriptures reveal that they will be observed by all mankind after the return of Jesus Christ.

As the holy days are annual Sabbath days, they may fall on any day of the week (except Pentecost, which always falls on a Sunday). When a holy day falls on a weekly Sabbath, the special observance of the annual holy day takes precedence. God's feasts and holy days are to be observed from sunset to sunset in accordance with the calculated Hebrew Calendar as preserved by the Levitical Jews. The seven annual feasts and holy days are as follows:

Feast or Holy Day	Commanded Scriptural Date of Observance
1) Passover	14th day of the first month*
2) Unleavened Bread (7 days)	15th through 21st days of the first month (the 15th & 21st are holy days)
3) Pentecost	Counted annually**
4) Trumpets	1st day of the seventh month
5) Atonement	10th day of the seventh month
6) Tabernacles (7 days)	15th through 21st days of the seventh month (the 15th is a holy day)
7) Last Great Day	22nd day of the seventh month (a holy day)

*Not a holy day
**Fifty days are counted, beginning with the first day of the week during the Days of Unleavened Bread. The feast is observed on the fiftieth day, which always falls on the first day of the week.

Scriptural References

Lev. 23	Ex. 23:14-17; 31:13	Ex. 12:1-20
John 7:37	Matt. 26:17-18	I Cor. 5:7-8
Acts 2:1	Acts 18:21	Acts 20:16
I Cor. 16:8	Zech. 14:16-19	Isa. 66:23

Appendix C

The Biblical Truth About Sunday Keeping

Sunday, the *first day of the week*, is purported to be the Christian day of worship. It is commonly taught and believed today that Jesus Christ and the original 12 apostles (and especially the apostle Paul) taught that Christians are no longer required to observe the Fourth Commandment—to keep the seventh day Sabbath holy. It is alleged that commandment keeping—and in particular the Sabbath commandment—was "nailed to the cross." Thus, it is claimed that Sunday is now the *"Christian Day of Worship."*

Is this claim true? Can such a teaching be *proven* from the inspired Word of God, the Holy Scriptures?

The answer is a resounding *no!* The truth is, Sunday keeping cannot be supported by the Scriptures. Are you willing to believe the Word of God—or will you simply accept the *teachings of men* as more important than the biblical teachings of God?

If you believe that Sunday worship is Christian—and if you believe that God's inspired Word, the Holy Scriptures, actually teaches Sunday keeping—then **search the Scriptures again**. You will *not* find:

1. One text that says that the Sabbath was *ever changed* from the seventh to the first day of the week.
2. One text where the first day of the week is ever called a holy day.
3. One text where we are told to keep the first day of the week.
4. One text that says that *Jesus ever kept* the first day.
5. One text where the first day is ever given any sacred title.
6. One text that tells us to keep the first day in honor of the resurrection of Jesus Christ.
7. One text that affirms that *any of the apostles* ever kept the first day as the Sabbath.
8. One text from any apostolic writing that authorizes *Sunday observance* as the Sabbath of God.
9. One text where it says it was *customary* for the Church to observe, or meet on, the first day of the week.
10. One text where we are *told not to work* on the first day of the week.
11. One text where any blessings are promised for observing Sunday.
12. One text where any punishment is threatened for working on Sunday.
13. One text that says the seventh day is not *now* God's Sabbath day.

14. One text where the apostles ever *taught* their converts to keep the first day of the week as a Sabbath.
15. One text that says the seventh day Sabbath is abolished.
16. One text where the first day is *ever called the Lord's Day.*
17. One text where *the first day was ever appointed to be kept as the Lord's Day.*
18. One text that says that the *Father or the Son ever rested on the first day of the week.*
19. One text that says that the first day of the week was ever sanctified and hallowed as a day of rest.
20. One text that says that Jesus, Paul or any other of the apostles taught anyone to observe the first day of the week as the Sabbath.
21. One text that calls the seventh day the "*Jewish Sabbath*" or one text that calls Sunday the "*Christian Sabbath.*"
22. One text authorizing *anyone* to abrogate, abolish or set aside God's Holy Sabbath and observe any other day.

(Adapted from the *Bible Sabbath Association*, Fairview, Oklahoma)

Appendix D

Rome's Challenge
to the Protestants

Rome's Challenge—Why Do Protestants Keep Sunday??

Most Christians assume that Sunday is the biblically approved day of worship. The Roman Catholic Church protests that, indeed, it is not. The Roman Catholic Church itself without any Scriptural authority from God transferred Christian worship from the Biblical Sabbath (Saturday) to Sunday, and to try to argue that the change was made in the Bible is both dishonest and a denial of Catholic authority. If Protestantism wants to base its teachings only on the Bible, *it should worship on Saturday.*

Over one hundred years ago the *Catholic Mirror* ran a series of articles discussing the right of the Protestant churches to worship on Sunday—exposing their claim that the New Testament taught Sunday keeping to be false. The articles stressed that unless one was willing to accept the authority of the Catholic Church to designate the day of worship, the Christian should observe Saturday, the true Christian Sabbath, as the both the Old and New Testaments teach. Those articles are presented here in their entirety.

For ready reference purposes, here are links to verses quoted in the article below.

New Testament verses relating to the apostles assembling the "first day of the week"	All New Testament references to "the Lord's day" or "day of the Lord"

1. Luke 24:33-40
    John 20:19
2. John 20:26-29
3. Acts 2:1
4. Acts 20:6-7
    Acts 2:46
5. I Cor. 16:1-2
    Acts 18:4
	1. Acts 2:20
	2. I Cor. 1:8
	3. I Cor. 5:5
	4. 2 Cor. 1:13-14
	5. Phil. 1:6
	6. Phil. 1:10
	7. 2 Pet. 3:10
	8. 2 Pet. 3:12
	9. Rev. 1:10

FEBRUARY 24, 1893, the General Conference of Seventh-day Adventists adopted certain resolutions appealing to the government and people of the United States from the decision of the Supreme Court declaring this to be a Christian nation, and from the action of Congress in legislating upon the subject of religion, and remonstrating against the principle and all the consequences of the same. In March 1893, the International Religious Liberty Association printed these resolutions in a tract entitled *Appeal and Remonstrance.* On receipt of one of these, the editor of the *Catholic Mirror* of Baltimore, Maryland, published a series of four editorials, which appeared in that paper September, 2, 9, 16, and 23, 1893. <u>The *Catholic Mirror* was the official organ of Cardinal Gibbons and the Papacy in the United States.</u>

These articles, therefore, although not written by the Cardinal's own hand, appeared under his official sanction, and as the expression of the Papacy to Protestantism, and the demand of the Papacy that Protestants shall render to the Papacy an account of *why* they keep Sunday and also of *how* they keep it.

The following article (excepting the notes in brackets/minor formatting and section headings for readability and the two [internal] Appendixes) is a reprint of these editorials, including the title on the next page. [From the *Catholic Mirror* of Sept. 2, 1893](Bold emphasis added throughout).

VOL. XLIV. NO. 34.   BALTIMORE, SATURDAY, SEPTEMBER 2, 1893.   PRICE FIVE CENTS.

THE CHRISTIAN SABBATH
[Catholic Sunday]
THE GENUINE OFFSPRING OF THE UNION OF THE HOLY SPIRIT
AND THE CATHOLIC CHURCH HIS SPOUSE. THE CLAIMS OF
PROTESTANTISM TO ANY PART THEREIN PROVED TO BE
GROUNDLESS, SELF-CONTRADICTORY, AND SUICIDAL

Our attention has been called to the above subject in the past week by the receipt of a brochure of twenty-one pages, published by the International Religious Liberty Association, entitled, "Appeal and Remonstrance," embodying resolutions adopted by the General Conference of the Seventh-day Adventists (Feb. 24, 1893). The resolutions criticize and censure, with much acerbity, the action of the United States Congress, and of the Supreme Court, for invading the rights of the people by closing the World's Fair on Sunday.

The Adventists are the only body of Christians with the Bible as their teacher, who can find no warrant in its pages for the change of the day from the seventh to the first. Hence their appellation, "Seventh-day Adventists." Their cardinal principle consists in setting apart Saturday for the exclusive worship of God, in conformity with the positive command of God Himself, repeatedly reiterated in the sacred books of the Old and New Testaments, literally obeyed by the children of Israel for thousands of years to this day, and endorsed by the teaching and practice of the Son of God whilst on earth.

Per contra, the Protestants of the world, the Adventists excepted, with the *same* Bible as their cherished and sole infallible teacher, by their practice, since their appearance in the sixteenth century, with the time-honored practice of the Jewish people before their eyes, have rejected the day named for His worship by God, and assumed, in apparent contradiction of His command, a day for His worship never once referred to for that purpose, in the pages of that Sacred Volume.

What Protestant pulpit does not ring almost every Sunday with loud and impassioned invectives against Sabbath [Catholic Sunday] violation? Who can forget the fanatical clamor of the Protestant ministers throughout the length and breadth of the land against opening the gates of the World's Fair on Sunday? The thousands of petitions, signed by millions, to save the Lord's Day from desecration? Surely, such general and widespread excitement and noisy remonstrance could not have existed without the strongest grounds for such animated protests.

And when quarters were assigned at the World's Fair to the various sects of Protestantism for the exhibition of articles, who can forget the emphatic expressions of virtuous and conscientious indignation exhibited by our Presbyterian brethren, as soon as they learned of the decision of the Supreme Court not to interfere in the Sunday opening? The newspapers informed us that they flatly refused to utilize the space accorded them, or open their boxes, demanding the right to withdraw the articles, in rigid adherence to their principles, and thus decline all contact with the sacrilegious and Sabbath-breaking Exhibition [meaning Sunday].

Doubtless, our Calvinistic brethren deserved and shared the sympathy of all the other sects, who, however, lost the opportunity of posing as martyrs in vindication of the Sabbath observance.

They thus became a "spectacle to the world, to angels, and to men," although their Protestant brethren, who failed to share the monopoly, were uncharitably and enviously disposed to attribute their steadfast adherence to religious principle, to Pharisaical pride and dogged obstinacy.

Purpose of Article

Our purpose in throwing off this article, is to shed such light on this all-important question (for were the Sabbath question to be removed from the Protestant pulpit, the sects would feel lost, and the preachers be deprived of their "Cheshire cheese") that our readers may be able to comprehend the question in *all its bearings*, and thus reach a clear conviction.

The Christian world is, morally speaking, united on the question and practice of worshiping God on *the first day* of the week.

The Israelites, scattered all over the earth, keep *the last day* of the week sacred to the worship of the Deity. In this particular, the Seventh-day

Adventists (a sect of Christians numerically few) have also selected the same day.

[*Note:* There have *always* been seventh day Sabbath-keepers in the world since the First Century AD (other than the Seventh Day Adventists (SDA's)). Today, not only do SDA's number in the millions, but there are thousands of churches, groups and home fellowships that keep a Saturday Sabbath.]

Israelites and Adventists both appeal to the Bible for the divine command, persistently obliging the strict observance of Saturday.

The Israelite respects the authority of the Old Testament only, but the Adventist, who is a Christian, accepts the New Testament on the same ground as the Old: viz., an inspired record also. He finds that the Bible, his teacher, is consistent in both parts, that the Redeemer, during His mortal life, never kept any other day than Saturday. The Gospels plainly evidence to him this fact; whilst, in the pages of the Acts of the Apostles, the Epistles, and the Apocalypse, not the vestige of an act canceling the Saturday arrangement can be found.

The Adventists, therefore, in common with Israelites, derive their belief from the Old Testament, which position is confirmed by the New Testament, indorsed fully by the life and practice of the Redeemer and His apostles' teaching of the Sacred Word for nearly a century of the Christian era.

Numerically considered, the Seventh-day Adventists form an insignificant portion of the Protestant population of the earth, but, as the question is not one of numbers, but of truth, and right, a strict sense of justice forbids the condemnation of this little sect without a calm and unbiased investigation; this is none of our funeral.

The Protestant world has been, from its infancy, in the sixteenth century, in thorough accord with the Catholic Church, in keeping "holy," not Saturday, but Sunday. The discussion of the grounds that led to this unanimity of sentiment and practice of over 300 years, must help toward placing Protestantism on a solid basis in this particular, should the arguments in favor of its position overcome those furnished by the Israelites and Adventists, the Bible, the sole recognized teacher of both litigants, being the umpire and witness. If however, on the other hand, the latter furnish arguments, incontrovertible by the great mass of Protestants, both cases of litigants, appealing to their common teacher, the Bible, the great body of Protestants, so far from clamoring, as they do with vigorous pertinacity for the strict keeping of Sunday, have no other [recourse] left than the admission that they have been teaching and practising *what is Scripturally false for over three centuries,* by adopting the teaching and practice of what they have always pretended to believe an apostate church, contrary to every warrant and teaching of sacred Scripture. To add to the intensity of this Scriptural and unpardonable blunder, it involves one of the most positive and emphatic commands of God to His servant, man: "Remember the Sabbath day, to keep it holy."

No Protestant living today has ever yet obeyed that command, preferring to follow the apostate church referred to than his teacher the Bible, which, from Genesis to Revelation, *teaches no other doctrine*, should the Israelites and Seventh-day Adventists be correct. Both sides appeal to the Bible as their "infallible" teacher. Let the Bible decide whether Saturday or Sunday be the day enjoined by God. One of the two bodies must be wrong, and, whereas a false position on this all-important question involves terrible penalties, threatened by God Himself, against the transgressor of this "perpetual covenant," we shall enter on the discussion of the merits of the arguments wielded by both sides. Neither is the discussion of this paramount subject above the capacity of ordinary minds, nor does it involve extraordinary study. It resolves itself into a few plain questions easy of solution:

1. Which day of the week does the Bible enjoin to be kept holy?

2. Has the New Testament modified by precept or practice the original command?

3. Have Protestants, since the sixteenth century, obeyed the command of God by keeping "holy" the day enjoined by their infallible guide and teacher, the Bible? And if not, why not?

To the above three questions we pledge ourselves to furnish as many intelligent answers, which cannot fail to vindicate the truth and uphold the deformity of error.

[From the *Catholic Mirror* of Sept. 9, 1893]

"But faith, fanatic faith, one wedded fast to some dear falsehood,
hugs it to the last." —*Moore.*

Conformably to our promise in our last issue, we proceed to unmask one of the most flagrant errors and most unpardonable inconsistencies of the Bible rule of faith. Lest, however, we be misunderstood, we deem it necessary to premise that Protestantism recognizes no rule of faith, no teacher, save the "infallible Bible." As the Catholic yields his judgment in spiritual matters implicitly, and with the unreserved confidence, to the voice of his church, so, too, the Protestant recognizes *no teacher but the Bible.* All his spirituality is derived from its teachings. It is to him the voice of God addressing him through his sole inspired teacher. It embodies his religion, his faith, and his practice. The language of Chillingworth, *"The Bible, the whole Bible, and nothing but the Bible, is the religion of Protestants,"* is only one form of the same idea multifariously convertible into other forms, such as "the Book of God," "the Charter of Our Salvation," "the Oracle of Our Christian Faith," "God's Text-Book to the race of Mankind," etc. It is, then, an incontrovertible fact that *the Bible alone* is the teacher of Protestant Christianity. Assuming this fact, we will now proceed to discuss the merits of the question involved in our last issue.

Recognizing what is undeniable, the fact of a direct contradiction between the teaching and practice of Protestant Christianity—the Seventh-day Adventists excepted—on the one hand, and that of the Jewish people on the other, both observing different days of the week for the worship of God, we will proceed to take the testimony of the teacher common to both claimants, the Bible. The first expression with which we come in contact in the Sacred Word, is found in Genesis 2:2 "**And on the seventh day He [God] rested from all His work which He had made.**" The next reference to this matter is to be found in Exodus 20, where God commanded the seventh day to be kept, *because* He had himself rested from the work of creation on that day; and the sacred text informs us that *for that reason* He desired it kept, in the following words; "*wherefore,* **the Lord blessed the seventh day and sanctified it.**" (1) Again we read in chapter 31, verse 15: "**Six days you shall do work; in the seventh day is the Sabbath, the rest holy to the Lord**"; sixteenth verse: "*it is an everlasting covenant,*" "**and a perpetual sign,**" "**for in six days the Lord made heaven and earth, and in the seventh He ceased from work.**" [*Note:* Scriptures quoted throughout these editorials are from the Douay, or Catholic, Version of the Bible.]

Saturday Always the Sabbath

In the Old Testament, reference is made one hundred and twenty-six times to the Sabbath, and all these texts conspire harmoniously in voicing the will of God commanding the seventh day to be kept, because God Himself *first kept it,* making it obligatory on all as "*a perpetual covenant.*" Nor can we imagine any one foolhardy enough to question the identity of Saturday with the Sabbath or seventh day, seeing that the people of Israel have been keeping the Saturday from the giving of the law, A.M. 2514 to A.D. 1893, a period of 3383 years. With the example of the Israelites before our eyes today, there is no historical fact better established than that referred to; viz., that the chosen people of God, the guardians of the Old Testament, the living representatives of the only divine religion hitherto, had for a period of 1490 years anterior to Christianity, preserved the weekly practice, the living tradition of the correct interpretation of the special day of the week, Saturday, to be kept "holy to the Lord," which tradition they have extended by their own practice to an additional period of 1893 years more, thus covering the full extent of the Christian dispensation. We deem it necessary to be perfectly clear on this point, for reasons that will appear more fully hereafter. The Bible—the Old Testament—confirmed by the living tradition of a weekly practice for 3383 years by the chosen people of God, teaches, then, with absolute certainty, that God had, Himself, named the day to be "kept holy to Him,"—that the day was Saturday, and that any violation of that command was punishable with death. "**Keep you My Sabbath, for it is holy unto you; he that shall profane it shall be put to**

death; he that shall do any work in it, his soul shall perish in the midst of his people." Ex 31:14.

[*Note*: In other words, the people of Israel (made up of 12 tribes— *one* of which is Judah, which the term "Jew" comes from) anciently maintained the correct day of the Sabbath—and the Jews (who did not lose their identity) to this day STILL keep the correct time of God's Sabbath given to them through Moses! **Time has not been "lost"—we know that Saturday IS God's Sabbath Day!**]

It is impossible to realize a more severe penalty than that so solemnly uttered by God Himself in the above text, on all who violate a command referred to no less than one hundred and twenty-six times in the old law. The ten commandments of the Old Testament are formally impressed on the memory of the child of the Biblical Christian as soon as possible, but there is not one of the ten made more emphatically familiar, both in Sunday School and pulpit, than that of keeping "holy" the Sabbath day.

Having secured the absolute certainty the will of God as regards the day to be kept holy, from His Sacred Word, *because* He rested on that day, which day is confirmed to us by the practice of His chosen people for thousands of years, we are naturally induced to inquire *when and where* God changed the day for His worship; for it is patent to the world that a change of day has taken place, and inasmuch as no indication of such change can be found within the pages of the Old Testament, nor in the practice of the Jewish people who continue for nearly nineteen centuries of Christianity obeying the written command, we must look to the exponent of the Christian dispensation; viz., the New Testament, for the command of God canceling the old Sabbath, Saturday.

Investigating the Sabbath in the New Testament

We now approach a period covering little short of nineteen centuries, and proceed to investigate whether the supplemental divine teacher—the New Testament—contains a decree canceling the mandate of the old law, and, at the same time, substituting a day for the divinely instituted Sabbath of the old law, viz., Saturday; for, inasmuch as Saturday was the day kept and ordered to be kept by God, *divine authority alone*, under the form of a canceling decree, could abolish the Saturday covenant, and another divine mandate, appointing by name another day to be kept "holy," other than Saturday, is equally necessary to satisfy the conscience of the Christian believer. The Bible being the only teacher recognized by the Biblical Christian, the Old Testament failing to point out a change of day, and yet another day than Saturday being kept "holy" by the Biblical world, it is surely incumbent on the reformed Christian to point out in the pages of the New Testament the new divine decree repealing that of Saturday and substituting that of Sunday, kept by the Biblicals since the dawn of the Reformation.

Examining the New Testament from cover to cover, critically, we find the Sabbath referred to sixty-one times. We find, too, that the Saviour invariably selected the Sabbath (Saturday) to teach in the synagogues and work miracles. The four Gospels refer to the Sabbath (Saturday) fifty-one times.

In one instance the Redeemer refers to Himself as "the Lord of the Sabbath," as mentioned by Matthew and Luke,[2] but during the whole record of His life, whilst invariably keeping and utilizing the day (Saturday), *He never once hinted at a desire to change it.* His apostles and personal friends afford to us a striking instance of their scrupulous observance of it *after His death*, and, whilst His body was yet in tomb, Luke (23:56) informs us: "**And they returned and prepared spices and ointments,** *and rested on the* **sabbath day according to the commandment ... but on the first day of the week, very early in the morning, they came, bringing the spices they had prepared.**" The "spices" and "ointments" had been prepared Good Friday evening, because "the Sabbath drew near." (Verse 54.) This action on the part of the personal friends of the Saviour, proves beyond contradiction that *after His death* they kept "holy" the Saturday, *and regarded the Sunday as any other day of the week.* Can anything, therefore, be more conclusive than the apostles and the holy women never knew any Sabbath but Saturday, up to the day of Christ's death?

[*Note* [2]: It is also referred to in Mark 2:28.]

We now approach the investigation of this interesting question for the next thirty years, as narrated by the evangelist, St. Luke, in his Acts of the Apostles. Surely some vestige of the canceling act can be discovered in the practice of the Apostles during that protracted period.

But, alas! We are once more doomed to disappointment. *Nine* [3] *times* do we find the Sabbath referred to in the Acts, but it is the *Saturday* (the old Sabbath). Should our readers desire the proof, we refer them to chapter and verse in each instance. Acts 13:14, 27, 42, 44. Once more, Acts 15:21; again, Acts 16:13; 17:2; 18:4. "**And he** [Paul] **reasoned in the synagogue** *every Sabbath,* **and persuaded the Jews and Greeks**"; *thus the Sabbath (Saturday) from Genesis to Revelation!!!* Thus, it is impossible to find in the New Testament the slightest interference by the Saviour or his Apostles with the original Sabbath, but on the contrary, an entire acquiescence in the original arrangement; nay a *plenary indorsement* by Him, whilst living; and an unvaried, active participation *in the keeping of that day and not* [*any*] *other by the apostles*, for thirty years after His death, as the Acts of the Apostles has abundantly testified to us.

[*Note* [3]: This should be eight.]

Hence the conclusion is inevitable; viz., that of those who follow the Bible as their guide, the Israelites and Seventh-day Adventists have exclusive weight of evidence on their side, whilst the Biblical Protestant has not a word in self-defense for his substitution of Sunday for Saturday.

[From the *Catholic Mirror* of Sept. 16, 1893.]

When his satanic majesty, who was "a murder from the beginning," "and the father of lies," undertook to open the eyes of our first mother, Eve, by stimulating her ambition, "You shall be as gods, knowing good and evil," his action was but the first of many plausible and successful efforts employed later, in the seduction of millions of her children. Like Eve, they learn too late, alas! the value of the inducements held out to allure her weak children from allegiance to God. Nor does the subject matter of this discussion form an exception to the usual tactics of his sable majesty.

Over three centuries since, he plausibly represented to a large number of discontented and ambitious Christians the bright prospect of the successful inauguration of a "new departure," by the abandonment of the Church instituted by the Son of God, as their teacher, and the assumption of a new teacher—*the Bible alone*—as their newly fledged oracle.

The sagacity of the evil one foresaw but the brilliant success of this maneuver. Nor did the result fall short of his most sanguine expectations.

A bold and adventurous spirit was alone needed to head the expedition. Him his satanic majesty soon found in the apostate monk, Luther, who himself repeatedly testifies to the close familiarity that existed between his master and himself, in his "Table talk," and other works published in 1558, at Wittenberg, under the inspection of Melancthon. His colloquies with Satan on various occasions are testified to by Luther himself—a witness worthy of all credibility. What the agency of the serpent tended so effectually to achieve in the garden, the agency of Luther achieved in the Christian world. **(4)**

"Give them a pilot to their wandering fleet,
Bold in his art, and tutored to deceit;
Whose hand adventurous shall their helm misguide
To hostile shores, or 'whelm them in the tide."

As the end proposed to himself by the evil one in his raid on the church of Christ was the destruction of Christianity, we are now engaged in sifting the means adopted by him to insure his success therein. So far, they have been found to be misleading, self-contradictory, and fallacious. We will now proceed with the further investigations of this imposture.

[***Note*** (4): Of course, one would expect a Catholic to demonize someone such as Luther, a person who fought for reforms in the church. If Luther had continued his reforms by accepting the Bible's Sabbath day, papists would not now be taunting "Protestants" with the inconsistency of professing to accept the Bible alone yet following the traditions of the Catholic Church in regards to God's day of worship.]

Did Jesus Change the Sabbath Day?

Having proved to a demonstration that the Redeemer, *in no instance,* had, during the period of His life, deviated from the faithful observance of the Sabbath (Saturday), referred to by the four evangelists fifty-one times, although He had designated Himself "Lord of the Sabbath," He never having *once,* by command or practice, hinted at a desire on His part to change the day by the substitution of another and having called special attention to the conduct of the apostles and the holy women, the very evening of His death, securing beforehand spices and ointments to be used in embalming His body the morning after the Sabbath (Saturday), as St. Luke so clearly informs us (Luke 24:1), thereby placing beyond peradventure, the divine action and will of the Son of God during life by keeping the Sabbath steadfastly; and having called attention to the action of His living representatives after his death, as proved by St. Luke; having also placed before our readers *the indisputable fact* that the apostles for the following thirty years (Acts) never deviated from the practice of their divine Master in this particular, as St. Luke (Acts 18:4) assures us: "**And he** [Paul] **reasoned in the synagogues** *every Sabbath* [Saturday], **and persuaded the Jews and the Greeks.**" The Gentile converts were, as we see from the text, equally instructed with the Jews, to keep the Saturday, having been converted to Christianity on that day, "the Jews and the Greeks" collectively.

Having also called attention to the texts of the Acts bearing on the exclusive use of the Sabbath by the Jews and Christians for thirty years after the death of the Saviour as the *only* day of the week observed by Christ and His apostles, which period *exhausts the inspired record,* we now proceed to supplement our proofs that the Sabbath (Saturday) enjoyed this exclusive privilege, by calling attention to *every instance* wherein the sacred record refers to the first day of the week.

References to Sunday after Resurrection of Christ

The first reference to Sunday after the resurrection of Christ is to be found in St. Luke's Gospel, chapter 24, verses 33-40, and St. John 20:19.

[*Note*: Luke 24:33-40 reads "**And they rose up the same hour, and returned to Jerusalem, and found the eleven gathered together, and them that were with them. Saying, 'The Lord is risen indeed, and hath appeared to Simon.' And they told what things were done in the way, and how he was known of them in breaking of bread. And as they thus spake, Jesus himself stood in the midst of them, and saith unto them, 'Peace be unto you.' But they were terrified and affrighted, and supposed that they had seen a spirit. And he said unto them 'Why are ye troubled? and why do thoughts arise in your hearts? Behold my hands and my feet, that it is I myself: handle me, and see; for a spirit hath not flesh and bones, as ye see me have.' And when he had thus**

spoken, he shewed them his hands and his feet." (King James Version)]

[*Note:* John 20:19 says "**Then the same day at evening, being the first day of the week, when the doors were shut where the disciples were assembled for fear of the Jews, came Jesus and stood in the midst, and saith unto them, 'Peace be unto you.'** " (KJV)]

The above texts themselves refer to the sole motive of this gathering of the part of the apostles. It took place on the day of the resurrection (Easter Sunday)[according to Catholic tradition], not for the purpose of inaugurating "the new departure" from the old Sabbath (Saturday) by keeping "holy" the new day, for there is not a hint given of prayer, exhortation, or the reading of the Scriptures, but it indicates the utter demoralization of the apostles by informing mankind that they were huddled together in that room in Jerusalem *"for fear of the Jews,"* as St. John, quoted above, plainly informs us.

The second reference to Sunday is to be found in St. John's Gospel, 20th chapter, 26th to 29th verses: "**And after eight days, the disciples were again within, and Thomas with them.**" The resurrected Redeemer availed Himself of this meeting of all the apostles to confound the incredulity of Thomas, who had been absent from the gathering on Easter Sunday evening. This would have furnished a golden opportunity to the Redeemer to change the day in the presence of all His apostles, but we state the simple fact that, on this occasion, as on Easter day, not a word is said of prayer, praise, or reading of the Scriptures.

The third instance on record, wherein the apostles were assembled on Sunday, is to be found in Acts 2:1: "**The apostles were all of one accord in one place.**" (Feast of Pentecost—Sunday.) Now, will this text afford to our Biblical Christian brethren a vestige of hope that Sunday substitutes, at length, Saturday? For when we inform them that the Jews had been keeping *this Sunday* for 1500 years, and have been keeping it for eighteen centuries after the establishment of Christianity, at the same time keeping the weekly Sabbath, there is not to be found either consolation or comfort in this text. Pentecost is the fiftieth day after the Passover, which was called the Sabbath of weeks, consisting of seven times seven days; and the day after the completion of the seventh weekly Sabbath day, was the chief day of the entire festival, necessarily Sunday. [The count for Pentecost does not begin with the Passover day, but it begins with the first day of the week during the Feast of Unleavened Bread, making Pentecost always fall on a Sunday.] What Israelite would not pity the cause that would seek to discover the origin of the keeping of the first day of the week in his festival of Pentecost, that has been kept by him yearly for over 3,000 years? Who but the Biblical Christian, driven to the wall for a pretext to excuse his sacrilegious desecration of the Sabbath, always kept by Christ and His apostles, would have resorted to the Jewish festival of Pentecost for his act of rebellion against his God and his teacher, the Bible?

Once more, the Biblical apologists for the change of day call our attention to the Acts, chapter 20, verses 6 and 7: *"and upon the first day of the week,* **when the disciples came together to break bread,"** etc. To all appearances, the above text should furnish some consolation to our disgruntled Biblical friends, but being Marplot, we cannot allow them even this crumb of comfort. We reply by the axiom: *"Quod probat nimis, probat nihil"*—"What proves too much, proves nothing." Let us call attention to the same Acts 2:46: **"And they, continuing** *daily* **in the temple, and breaking bread from house to house,"** etc. Who does not see at a glance that the text produced to prove the exclusive prerogative of Sunday, vanishes into thin air—an *ignis fatuus*—when placed in juxtaposition with the 46th verse of the same chapter? What Biblical Christian claims by this text for *Sunday alone* the same authority, St. Luke, informs us was *common to every day of the week:* **"And they, continuing** *daily* **in the temple, and breaking bread from house to house."**

One text more presents itself, apparently leaning toward a substitution of Sunday for Saturday. It is taken from St. Paul, 1 Cor. 16:1, 2: **"Now concerning the collection for the saints,"** **"On the first day of the week, let every one of you lay by him in store,"** etc. Presuming that the request of St. Paul had been strictly attended to, let us call attention to what had been done each Saturday during the Saviour's life and continued for thirty years after, as the book of Acts informs us.

The followers of the Master met *"every Sabbath"* to hear the word of God; the Scriptures were read *"every Sabbath day."* **"And Paul, as his manner was to reason in the synagogue** *every Sabbath*, **interposing the name of the Lord Jesus Christ,"** etc. Acts 18:4. What more absurd conclusion than to infer that reading of the Scriptures, prayer, exhortation, and preaching, which *formed the routine duties of every Saturday,* as had been abundantly proved, were overslaughed by a request to take up a collection on *another day of the week?*

In order to appreciate fully the value of this text now under consideration, it is only needful to recall the action of the apostles and holy women on Good Friday before sundown. They brought spices and ointments after He was taken down from the cross; they suspended all action until the Sabbath "holy to the Lord" had passed, and then took steps on Sunday morning to complete the process of embalming the sacred body of Jesus.

Why, may we ask, did they not proceed to complete the work of embalming on Saturday?—Because they knew well that the embalming of the sacred body of their Master would interfere with the strict observance of the Sabbath, the keeping of which was paramount; and until it can be shown that the Sabbath day *immediately preceding the Sunday of our text* had not been kept (which would be false, inasmuch *as every Sabbath had been kept*), the request of St. Paul to make the collection *on Sunday* remains to be classified with the work of the embalming of Christ's body, which could not be effected on the Sabbath, and was consequently deferred to the next convenient day;

viz., Sunday, or the first day of the week.

Having disposed of every text to be found in the New Testament referring to the Sabbath (Saturday), and to the first day of the week (Sunday); and having shown conclusively from these texts, that, so far, not a shadow of pretext can be found in the Sacred Volume for the Biblical substitution of Sunday for Saturday; it only remains for us to investigate the meaning of the expressions "Lord's Day," and "day of the Lord," to be found in the New Testament, which we propose to do in our next article, and conclude with apposite remarks on the incongruities of a system of religion which we shall have proved to be indefensible, self-contradictory, and suicidal.

[From the *Catholic Mirror* of Sept. 23, 1893]

"Halting on crutches of unequal size,
One leg by truth supported, *one by lies,*
Thus sidle to the goal with awkward pace,
Secure of nothing but to lose the race."

In the present article we propose to investigate carefully a new (and the last) class of proof assumed to convince the Biblical Christian that God had substituted Sunday for Saturday for His worship in the new law, and that the divine will is to be found recorded by the Holy Ghost in apostolic writings.

We are informed that this radical change has found expression, over and over again, in a series of texts in which the expression, "the day of the Lord," or "the Lord's day," is to be found.

The class of texts in the New Testament, under the title "Sabbath," numbering sixty-one in the Gospels, Acts, and Epistles; and the second class, in which "the first day of the week," or Sunday, having been critically examined (the latter class numbering nine); and having been found not to afford the slightest clue to a change of will on the part of God as to His day of worship by man, we now proceed to examine the third and last class of texts relied on to save the Biblical system from the arraignment of seeking to palm off on the world, in the name of God, a decree for which there is not the slightest warrant or authority from their teacher, the Bible.

References to "Day of the Lord" or "Lord's Day"

The first text of this class is to be found in the Acts of the Apostles 2:20: **"The sun shall be turned into darkness, and the moon into blood, before that great and notable day of the Lord shall come."** How many Sundays have rolled by since that prophecy was spoken? So much for that effort to pervert the meaning of the sacred text from the judgment day to Sunday!

The second text of this class is to be found in 1 Cor. 1:8: "**Who shall also confirm you unto the end, that you may be blameless** *in the day of our Lord Jesus Christ."* What simpleton does not see that the apostle here plainly indicates the day of judgment? The next text of this class that presents itself is to be found in the same Epistle, chapter 5:5: "**To deliver such a one to Satan for the destruction of the flesh, that the spirit may be saved** *in the day of the Lord Jesus."* The incestuous Corinthian was, of course, saved on *the Sunday next following!!* How pitiable such a makeshift as this! The fourth text, 2 Cor. 1:13,14: "**And I trust ye shall acknowledge even to the end, even as ye also are ours in the day of the Lord Jesus.**"

Sunday or the day of judgment, which? The fifth text is from St. Paul to the Philippians, chapter 1, verse 6: "**Being confident of this very thing, that He who hath begun a good work in you, will perfect it** *until the day of Jesus Christ."* The good people of Philippi, in attaining perfection *on the following Sunday,* could afford to laugh at our modern rapid transit!

We beg to submit our sixth of the class; viz., Philippians, first chapter, tenth verse: "**That he may be sincere without offense unto** *the day of Christ."* That day was *next Sunday,* forsooth! Not so long to wait after all. The seventh text, 2 Peter 3:10: "**But** *the day of the Lord* **will come as a thief in the night.**" The application of this text to Sunday passes the bounds of absurdity.

The eighth text, 2 Peter 3:12: "**Waiting for and hastening unto** *the coming of the day of the Lord,* **by which the heavens being on fire, shall be dissolved,**" etc. This day of the Lord is the same referred to in the previous text, the application of both of which *to Sunday next* would have left the Christian world sleepless the next Saturday night.

We have presented to our readers eight of the nine texts relied on to bolster up by text of Scripture the sacrilegious effort to palm off the "Lord's day" for Sunday, and with what result? Each furnishes *prima facie* evidence of the last day, referring to it directly, absolutely, and unequivocally.

The ninth text wherein we meet the expression "the Lord's day," is the last to be found in the apostolic writings. The Apocalypse, or Revelation, chapter 1:10, furnishes it in the following words of John: "**I was in the Spirit on the Lord's day**"; but it will afford no more comfort to our Biblical friends than its predecessors of the same series. Has St. John used the expression previously in his Gospel or Epistles?—Emphatically, NO. Has he had occasion to refer to Sunday hitherto?—Yes, twice. How did he designate Sunday on these occasions? Easter Sunday was called by him (John 20:1) *"the first day of the week."*

Again, chapter twenty, nineteenth verse: "**Now when it was late that same day,** *being the first day of the week."* Evidently, although inspired, both in his Gospel and Epistles, he called Sunday "the first day of the week." On what grounds, then, can it be assumed that he dropped that designation? Was he *more inspired* when he wrote the Apocalypse, or did he adopt a new title for Sunday, because it was now in vogue?

A reply to these questions would be supererogatory especially to the latter, seeing that the same expression had been used eight times already by St. Luke, St. Paul and St. Peter, *all under divine inspiration,* and surely the Holy Spirit would not inspire St. John to call Sunday the Lord's day, whilst He inspired Sts. Luke, Paul, and Peter, collectively, to entitle the day of judgment "the Lord's day." Dialecticians reckon amongst the infallible motives of certitude, the moral motive of analogy or induction, by which we are enabled to conclude with certainty from the known to the unknown; being absolutely certain of the meaning of an expression, it can have only the same meaning when uttered the ninth time, especially when we know that on the nine occasions the expressions were *inspired by the Holy Spirit.*

Nor are the strongest intrinsic grounds wanting to prove that this, like its sister texts, containing the same meaning. St. John (Rev. 1:10) says **"I was in the Spirit on the Lord's day"**; but he furnishes us the key to this expression, chapter four, first and second verses: **"After this I looked and behold a door opened in heaven."** A voice said to him: **"Come up hither, and I will show you** *the things which must be hereafter."* Let us ascend in spirit with John. Whither?—through that "door in heaven," to heaven. And what shall we see?—"The things that must be hereafter," chapter four, first verse. He ascended in spirit to heaven. He was ordered to write, in full, his vision of what is to take place antecedent to, and concomitantly with, "the Lord's day," or the day of judgment; the expression "Lord's day" being confined in Scripture to the day of judgment exclusively.

We have studiously and accurately collected from the New Testament every available proof that could be adduced in favor of a law canceling the Sabbath day of the old law, or one substituting another day for the Christian dispensation. We have been careful to make the above distinction, lest it might be advanced that the third [6] commandment was abrogated under the new law. Any such plea has been overruled by the action of the Methodist Episcopal bishops in their pastoral 1874, and quoted by the New York *Herald* of the same date, of the following tenor:

"The Sabbath instituted in the beginning and confirmed again and again by Moses and the prophets *has never been abrogated.* A part of the moral law, not a part or tittle of its sanctity has been taken away." The above official pronouncement has committed that large body of Biblical Christians to the permanence of the third commandment under the new law.

[*Note* [6]: In their catechisms, Catholic enumeration of Exodus 20, the Sabbath commandment is the third of the Ten Commandments.]

We again beg leave to call the special attention of our readers to the twentieth of "the thirty-nine articles of religion" of the Book of Common Prayer; "It is not lawful for the church to ordain anything that is contrary to *God's written word."*

CONCLUSION

We have in this series of articles, taken much pains for the instruction of our readers to prepare them by presenting a number of *undeniable facts* found in the word of God to arrive at a conclusion absolutely irrefragable. When the Biblical system put in an appearance in the sixteenth century, it not only seized on the temporal possessions of the Church, but in its vandalic crusade stripped Christianity, as far as it could, of all the sacraments instituted by its Founder; of the holy sacrifice, etc., retaining nothing but the Bible, which its exponents pronounced *their sole teacher* in Christian doctrine and morals.

Chief amongst their articles of belief was, and is today, the permanent necessity of keeping the Sabbath [Catholic Sunday] holy. In fact, it has been for the past 300 years the only article of the Christian belief in which there has been a plenary consensus of Biblical representatives. The keeping of the Sabbath constitutes the sum and substance of the Biblical theory. The pulpits resound weekly with incessant tirades against the lax manner of keeping the Sabbath [Catholic Sunday] in Catholic countries, as contrasted with the proper, Christian, self-satisfied mode of keeping the day in Biblical countries. Who can ever forget the virtuous indignation manifested by the Biblical preachers throughout the length and breadth of our country, from every Protestant pulpit, as long as yet undecided; and who does not know today, that one sect, to mark its holy indignation at the decision, has never yet opened the boxes that contained its articles at the World's Fair?

These superlatively good and unctuous Christians, by conning over their Bible carefully, can find their counterpart in a certain class of unco-good people [the scribes and Pharisees] in the days of the Redeemer, who haunted Him night and day, distressed beyond measure, and scandalized beyond forbearance, because He did not keep the [seventh day]Sabbath in as straight-laced manner as themselves.

Protestants Have *Never* Kept God's Sabbath

They hated Him for using common sense in reference to the day, and He found no epithets expressive enough of His supreme contempt for their Pharisaical pride. And it is very probably that the divine mind has not modified its views today anent the blatant outcry of their followers and sympathizers at the close of this nineteenth century. But when we add to all this the fact that whilst the Pharisees of old kept the *true Sabbath,* our modern Pharisees, counting on the credulity and simplicity of their dupes, *have never once in their lives kept the true Sabbath* which their divine Master kept to His dying day, and which His apostles kept, after His example, for thirty years steward, according to the Sacred Record. The most glaring contradiction, involving a deliberate sacrilegious rejection of a most positive precept, is presented to us today in the action of the Biblical Christian world. The Bible and the Sabbath [Catholic Sunday] constitute the watchword of Protestantism; but we have demonstrated that it is *the Bible against their Sabbath* [Protestant Sunday]. We have shown that no greater contradiction ever existed than their theory and practice. We have proved that neither their Biblical ancestors nor themselves have ever kept one Sabbath day in their lives.

The Israelites and Seventh-day Adventists [and Sabbath keeping churches of God] are witnesses of their weekly desecration of the day named by God so repeatedly, and whilst they have ignored and condemned their teacher, the Bible, they have adopted a day kept by the Catholic Church. What Protestant can, after perusing these articles, with a clear conscience, continue to disobey the command of God, *enjoining Saturday to be kept,* which command his teacher, the Bible, from Genesis to Revelation, records as the will of God?

The history of the world cannot present a more stupid, self-stultifying specimen of dereliction of principle than this. The teacher demands emphatically in every page that the law of the Sabbath be observed every week, by all recognizing it as "the only infallible teacher," whilst the disciples of that teacher have not once for over three [now four] hundred years observed the divine precept! That immense concourse of Biblical Christians, the Methodists, have declared that the Sabbath has never been abrogated, whilst the followers of the Church of England, together with her daughter, the Episcopal Church of the United States, are committed by the twentieth article of religion, already quoted, to the ordinance that the Church cannot lawfully ordain anything *"contrary to God's written word."* God's written word enjoins His worship to be observed on *Saturday* absolutely, repeatedly, and most emphatically, with a most positive threat of death to him who disobeys. All the Biblical sects occupy the same self-stultifying position which no explanation can modify, much less justify.

How truly do the words of the Holy Spirit apply to this deplorable situation! *"Iniquitas mentita est sibi"*—"Iniquity hath lied to itself." Proposing to follow *the Bible only* as teacher, yet before the world, *the sole teacher* is ignominiously thrust aside, and the teaching and practice of the Catholic Church—"the mother of abomination," when it suits their purpose so to designate her—[they have] adopted, despite the most terrible threats pronounced by God Himself against those who disobey the command, "Remember to keep holy the Sabbath."

Sunday As Day of Worship Is Catholic Creation

Before closing this series of articles, we beg to call the attention of our readers once more to our caption, introductory of each; viz., 1. The Christian Sabbath [Catholic Sunday], [is] the genuine offspring of the union of the Holy Spirit with the Catholic Church His spouse. 2. The claim of

Protestantism to any part therein proved to be groundless, self-contradictory, and suicidal.

The first proposition needs little proof. The Catholic Church for over one thousand years before the existence of a Protestant, by virtue of her divine mission, changed the day from Saturday to Sunday. We say by virtue of her divine mission, because He who called Himself the "Lord of the Sabbath," endowed her with His own power to teach, "he that heareth you, heareth Me"; commanded all who believe in Him to hear her, under penalty of being placed with "heathen and publican"; and promised to be with her to the end of the world. She holds her charter as teacher from Him—a charter as infallible as perpetual [which is a lie]. (See Appendix L, *Matthew 16:19 and 18:18 Binding and Loosing in the New Testament Church*, p. 267.) The Protestant world at its birth found the Christian Sabbath [Catholic Sunday] too strongly entrenched to run counter to its existence; it was therefore placed under the necessity of acquiescing in the arrangement, thus implying the [Catholic] Church's right to change the day, for over three [now four] hundred years. The Christian Sabbath [Catholic Sunday] is therefore *to this day,* the acknowledged offspring of the Catholic Church as spouse of the Holy Ghost, without a word of remonstrance from the Protestant world.

Let us now, however, take a glance at our second proposition, with *the Bible alone* as the teacher and guide in faith and morals. This teacher *most emphatically forbids any change in the day for paramount reasons.* The command calls for a *"perpetual covenant."* The day commanded to be kept by the teacher *has never once been kept,* thereby developing an apostasy from an assumedly fixed principle, as self-contradictory, self-stultifying, and consequently as suicidal as it is within the power of language to express.

Nor are the limits of demoralization yet reached. Far from it. *Their pretense* for leaving the bosom of the Catholic Church was for apostasy from the truth *as taught in the written word.* They adopted the written word as their sole teacher, which they had no sooner done than they abandoned it promptly, as these articles have abundantly proved; and by a perversity as willful as erroneous, they accept the teaching of the Catholic Church in direct opposition to the plain, unvaried, and constant teaching of their sole teacher in the most essential doctrine of their religion, thereby emphasizing the situation in what may be aptly designated "a mockery, a delusion, and a snare."

[EDITORS' NOTE (Written by Michael Scheifler) — It was upon this very point that the Reformation was condemned by the Council of Trent. The Reformers had constantly charged, as here stated, that the Catholic Church had "apostatized from the truth *as contained in the written word.*" "The written word," "The Bible and the Bible only," "Thus saith the Lord," were their constant watchwords; and "the Scripture, as in the written word, the sole standard of appeal," was the proclaimed platform of the Reformation and of Protestantism. "The Scripture *and tradition.*" "The

Bible as interpreted by the Church and according to the unanimous consent of the Fathers," was the position and claim of the Catholic Church. This was the main issue in the Council of Trent, which was called especially to consider the questions that had been raised and forced upon the attention of Europe by the Reformers.

The very first question concerning faith that was considered by the council was the question involved in this issue. There was a strong party even of the Catholics within the council who were in favor of abandoning tradition and adopting *the Scriptures only* as the standard of authority. This view was so decidedly held in the debates in the council that the pope's legates actually wrote to him that there was "a strong tendency to set aside tradition altogether and to make Scripture the sole standard of appeal." But to do this would manifestly be to go a long way toward justifying the claims of the Protestants. By this crisis there was developed upon the ultra-Catholic portion of the council the task of convincing the others that "Scripture *and tradition*" were the only sure ground to stand upon. If this could be done, the council could be carried to issue a decree condemning the Reformation, otherwise not. The question was debated day after day, until the council was fairly brought to a standstill. Finally, after a long and intensive mental strain, the Archbishop of Reggio came into the council with substantially the following argument to the party who held for Scripture alone:

"The Protestants claim to stand upon the written word only. They profess to hold the Scripture alone as the standard of faith. They justify their revolt by the plea that the Church has apostatized from the written word and follows tradition. Now the Protestant claim, that they stand upon the written word only, is not true. Their profession of holding the Scripture alone as the standard of faith is false. PROOF: The written word explicitly enjoins the observance of the seventh day as the Sabbath. They do not observe the seventh day but reject it. If they do truly hold the scripture alone as their standard, they would be observing the seventh day as is enjoined in the Scripture throughout. Yet they not only reject the observance of the Sabbath enjoined in the written word, but they have adopted and do practice the observance of Sunday, for which they have only the tradition of the Church. Consequently the claim of 'Scripture alone as the standard,' *fails;* and the doctrine of 'Scripture *and tradition*' as essential, is fully established, the Protestants themselves being judges."

[The Archbisop of Reggio (Gaspar [Ricciulli] de Fosso) made his speech at the last opening session of Trent, (17th Session) reconvened under a new pope (Pius IV), on the 18th of January, 1562 after having been suspended in 1552.—J. H. Holtzman, *Canon and Tradition*, published in Ludwigsburg, Germany, in 1859, page 263, and Archbishop of Reggio's address in the 17th session of the Council of Trent, Jan. 18, 1562, in Mansi SC, Vol. 33, cols. 529, 530. Latin.]

There was no getting around this, for the Protestants' own statement of faith—the Augsburg Confession, 1530—had clearly admitted that "the observation of the Lord's day" had been appointed by "the Church" only [meaning the Catholic Church].

The argument was hailed in the council as of Inspiration only; the party for "Scripture alone," surrendered; and the council at once unanimously condemned Protestantism and the whole Reformation as only an unwarranted revolt from the communion and authority of the Catholic Church; and proceeded, April 8, 1546, "to the promulgation of two decrees, the first of which, enacts under anathema, that Scripture *and tradition* are to be received and venerated equally, and that the deutero-canonical [the apocryphal] books are part of the canon of Scripture. The second decree declares the Vulgate to be the sole authentic and standard Latin version, and gives it such authority as to supersede the original texts; forbids the interpretation of Scripture contrary to the sense received by the Church, 'or even contrary to the unanimous consent of the Fathers,' " etc. [7]

[*Note:* [7]: See the proceedings of the Council; Augsburg Confession; and Encyclopaedia Britannica, article "Trent, Council of."]

This was the inconsistency of the Protestant practice with the Protestant profession that gave to the Catholic Church her long-sought and anxiously desired ground upon which to condemn Protestantism and the whole Reformation movement as only a selfishly ambitious rebellion against the Church authority. And in this vital controversy the key, the chiefest and culminative expression, of the Protestant inconsistency was in the rejection of the Sabbath of the Lord, the seventh day, enjoined in the Scriptures, and the adoption and observance of the Sunday as enjoined by the Catholic Church.

And this is today the position of the respective parties to this controversy. Today, as this document shows, this is the vital issue upon which the Catholic Church arraigns Protestantism and upon which she condemns the course of popular Protestantism as being "indefensible," "self-contradictory, and suicidal." (end of editor's note)]

Should any of the reverend parsons, who are habituated to howl so vociferously over every real or assumed desecration of that pious fraud, the *Bible Sabbath,* think well of entering a protest against our logical and Scriptural dissection of their mongrel pet [that Sunday keeping is taught in the Bible], we can promise them that any reasonable attempt on their part to gather up the *disjecta membra* of the hybrid, and to restore to it a galvanized existence, will be met with genuine cordiality and respectful consideration on our part.

But we can assure our readers that we know these reverend howlers too well to expect a solitary bark from them in this instance. And they know us too well to subject themselves to the mortification which a further dissection of this antiscriptural question would necessarily entail. Their policy now is to "lay low," and they are sure to adopt it.

APPENDIX I

These articles are reprinted, and this leaflet is sent forth by the publishers, because it gives from an undeniable source and in no uncertain tone, the latest phase of the Sunday-observance controversy, which is now, and which indeed for some time has been, not only a national question with the leading nations, but also an international question. Not that we are glad to have it so; we would that Protestants everywhere were so thoroughly consistent in profession and practice that there could be no possible room for the relations between them and Rome ever to take the shape which they have now taken.

But the situation in this matter is now as it is herein set forth. There is no escaping this fact. It therefore becomes the duty of the International Religious Liberty Association to make known as widely as possible the true phase of this great question as it now stands. Not because we are pleased to have it so, but because it is so, whatever we or anybody else would or would not be pleased to have.

It is true that we have been looking for years for this question to assume precisely the attitude which it has now assumed, and which is so plainly set forth in this leaflet. We have told the people repeatedly, and Protestants especially, and yet more especially have we told those who were advocating Sunday laws and the recognition and legal establishment of Sunday by the United States, that in the course that was being pursued they were playing directly into the hands of Rome, and that as certainly as they succeeded, they would inevitably be called upon by Rome, and Rome in possession of power too, to render to her an account as to why Sunday should be kept. This, we have told the people for years, would surely come. And now that it *has* come, it is only our duty to make it known as widely as it lies in our power to do.

It may be asked, Why did not Rome come out as boldly as this before? Why did she wait so long? It was not for her interest to do so before. When she should move, she desired to move with power, and power as yet she did not have. But in their strenuous efforts for the national, governmental recognition and establishment of Sunday, the Protestants of the United States were doing more for her than she could possibly do for herself in the way of getting governmental power into her hands. This she well knew and therefore only waited. And now that the Protestants, in alliance with her, have accomplished the awful thing, she at once rises up in all her native arrogance and old-time spirit, and calls upon the Protestants to answer to her for their observance of Sunday. This, too, she does because she is secure in the power which the Protestants have so blindly placed in her hands. In other words, the power which the Protestants have thus put into her hands she will now use to their destruction. Is any other evidence needed to show that the *Catholic Mirror* (which means the Cardinal and the Catholic Church in America) has been waiting for this, than that furnished on page 21 of this leaflet? Please turn back and look at that page, and see that quotation clipped from the New York *Herald* in 1874, and which is now brought forth thus. Does not this show plainly that that statement of the Methodist bishops, the *Mirror,* all these nineteen years, has been keeping for just such a time as this? And more than this, the Protestants will find more such things which have been so laid up, and which will yet be used in a way that will both surprise and confound them.

This at present is a controversy between the Catholic Church and Protestants. As such only do we reproduce these editorials of the CATHOLIC MIRROR. The points controverted are points which are claimed by Protestants as in their favor. The argument is made by the Catholic Church; the answer devolves upon those Protestants who observe Sunday, not upon us. We can truly say, "This is none of our funeral." If they do not answer, she will make their silence their confession that she is right, and will act toward them accordingly. If they do answer, she will use against them their own words, and as occasion may demand, the power which they have put into her hands. So that, so far as she is concerned, whether the Protestant answer or not, it is all the same. And how she looks upon them henceforth is clearly manifested in the challenge made in the last paragraph of the reprint articles.

There is just one refuge left for the Protestants. That is to take their stand squarely and fully upon the "written word only," "the Bible and the Bible alone," and thus upon the Sabbath of the Lord. Thus acknowledging no authority but God's, wearing no sign but His (Eze. 20:12, 20), obeying His command, and shielded by His power, they shall have the victory over Rome and all her alliances, and stand upon the sea of glass, bearing the harps of God, with which their triumph shall be forever celebrated. (Revelation 18, and 15:2-4.)

It is not yet too late for Protestants to redeem themselves. Will they do it? Will they stand consistently upon the Protestant profession? Or will they still continue to occupy the "indefensible, self-contradictory, and suicidal" position of professing to be Protestants, yet standing on Catholic ground, receiving Catholic insult, and bearing Catholic condemnation? Will they indeed take the written word only, the Scripture alone, as their sole authority and their sole standard? Or will they still hold the "indefensible, self-contradictory, and suicidal" doctrine and practice of following the authority of the Catholic Church and of wearing the sign of her authority? Will they keep the Sabbath of the Lord, the seventh day, according to Scripture? Or will they keep the Sunday according to the tradition of the Catholic Church?

Dear reader, which will YOU do?

APPENDIX II

Since the first edition of this publication was printed, the following appeared in an editorial in the *Catholic Mirror* of Dec. 23, 1893:

"The avidity with which these editorials have been sought, and the appearance of a reprint of them by the International Religious Liberty Association, published in Chicago, entitled, 'Rome's Challenge: Why Do Protestants Keep Sunday?' and offered for sale in Chicago, New York, California, Tennessee, London, Australia, Cape Town, Africa, and Ontario, Canada, together with the continuous demand, have prompted the *Mirror* to give permanent form to them, and thus comply with the demand.

"The pages of this brochure unfold to the reader one of the most glaringly conceivable contradictions existing between the practice and the theory of the Protestant world, and unsusceptible of any rational solution, the theory claiming the Bible alone as teacher, which unequivocally and most positively commands Saturday to be kept 'holy,' whilst their practice proves that they utterly ignore the unequivocal requirements of their teacher, the Bible, and occupying Catholic ground for three centuries and a half, by the abandonment of their theory, they stand before the world today the representatives of a system the most indefensible, self-contradictory, and suicidal that can be imagined.

"We feel that we cannot interest our readers more than to produce the 'Appendix'[8] which the International Religious Liberty Association, and ultra-Protestant organization, has added to the reprint of our articles. The perusal of the Appendix will confirm the fact that our argument is unanswerable, and that the only recourse left to the Protestants is either to retire from Catholic territory where they have been squatting for three centuries and a half, and accepting their own teacher, the Bible, in good faith, as so clearly suggested by the writer of 'Appendix,' commence forth-with to keep the Saturday, the day enjoined by the Bible from Genesis to Revelation; or, abandoning the Bible as their sole teacher, cease to be squatters, and a living contradiction of their own principles, and taking out letters of adoption as citizens of the kingdom of Christ on earth—His Church—be no longer victims of self-delusive and necessary self-contradiction.

[*Note*: [8] At the close of this editorial, Appendix I of this pamphlet was reprinted in full.]

"The arguments contained in this pamphlet are firmly grounded on the word of God, and having been closely studied with the Bible in hand, leave no escape for the conscientious Protestant except the abandonment of Sunday worship and the return to Saturday, commanded by their teacher, the Bible, or, unwilling to abandon the tradition of the Catholic Church, which enjoins the keeping of Sunday, and which they have accepted in direct opposition to their teacher, the Bible, consistently accept her in all her teachings. **Reason and common sense demand the acceptance of one or the other of these alternatives**; either Protestantism and the keeping of Saturday, or Catholicity and the keeping of Sunday. Compromise is impossible."

Appendix E

The Biblical Truth About Sabbath Keeping

Sunday, the *first* day of the week, is almost universally observed today by "professing Christians." Yet, the Bible teaches that **the only day that is holy to God is the seventh day of the week, called the Sabbath day in the Word of God.**

The Roman calendar used today in the United States shows the seventh day of the week as *Saturday*. Throughout Europe, however, calendars have been changed to show Sunday as the seventh day of the week. In spite of that change, Saturday remains the *true* biblical Sabbath day, holy to God. The Bible clearly commands: "**Remember the Sabbath day to keep it holy**. Six days shall you labor and do all your work: But the seventh day is the Sabbath of the Lord your God..." (Ex. 20:8-10).

Here are a number of profound reasons from Scripture why we should be observing the seventh day Sabbath today, as the weekly day of worship to God:

1. In the beginning God created the Sabbath day (Gen. 2:3).
2. God rested from His labors on the seventh day (Gen. 2:2).
3. The Sabbath was made *for* man, that is, for all mankind (Mark 2:27).
4. God blessed the seventh day because, on it, He rested from the work of His creation (Gen. 2:2; Ex. 20:11).
5. God blessed the seventh day and named it the Sabbath (Ex. 20:10-11).
6. God not only blessed the seventh day, He also sanctified it—that is, made it holy by His presence and declaration (Gen. 2:3).
7. There is no record in all the Scriptures that God ever removed His blessing from the Sabbath and placed it upon another day of the week.
8. God's people kept the Sabbath *before* the Ten Commandments were given at Mount Sinai (Ex. 16:22-26).
9. God ordained that man should keep the Sabbath (Ex. 20; Heb. 4:3-9).
10. God forbade work on the Sabbath day even in harvest time (Ex. 34:21).
11. God promised the Gentiles, those of all nations, a blessing if they kept the Sabbath (Isa. 56:2).
12. God promised to bless anyone who keeps the Sabbath (Isa. 56:2).

13. Nowhere in the Bible do we find a command to observe any other day of the week as holy, as a substitute or replacement for the seventh-day Sabbath.
14. God calls the Sabbath His *holy day* (Ex. 20:10; Lev. 23:2-3; Isa. 58:13; Mk. 2:28).
15. The keeping of the Sabbaths, weekly and annually, is a sign between God and His people (Ex. 31:12-17).
16. The Sabbath commandment, one of the longest of the ten, is given to God's people so that they might show their love and obedience towards God (Ex. 20:8-11; Deut. 5:12-15; Matt. 22:37-40).
17. Jesus kept and observed the Sabbath as a habit, which expressed His love and obedience toward God the Father (Lk. 4:16).
18. Jesus Christ is Lord of the Sabbath—and as such, the Sabbath is the TRUE LORD'S DAY (Mk. 2:28; Isa. 58:13; Matt. 12:8).
19. Jesus Christ recognized the Sabbath commandment as binding (Matt. 12:12; 5:17-18; Mk. 3:4).
20. Jesus Christ kept His Father's commandments, which included the seventh-day Sabbath (John 15:10; 8:29; 5:46-47).
21. The Sabbath was observed at the time of the crucifixion (Lk. 23:56).
22. The observance of the Sabbath was Paul's practice years after the crucifixion (Acts 17:2).
23. Paul recognized and observed the Sabbath during his ministry, about AD 45 (Acts 13:27).
24. Paul taught the Gentiles on the Sabbath day, at their own request (Acts 13:42).
25. Paul preached to an entire city on the Sabbath day (Acts 13:44).
26. Paul attended a prayer meeting on the Sabbath day, when no synagogue was available (Acts 16:13).
27. It was Paul's custom to preach Jesus Christ on the Sabbath day (Acts 17:2-3).
28. At Corinth, Paul preached every Sabbath for eighteen months (Acts 18:1-4, 11).
29. James recognized the seventh day Sabbath many years after the resurrection of Christ (Acts 15:21).
30. The seventh-day Sabbath will be observed during the millennium (Isa. 66:23).
31. The apostle Paul made it clear that the day of rest, the seventh day Sabbath, was to be observed as a holy day (Heb. 4:4-9).
32. The sanctity of the seventh day was never transferred by Jesus Christ, nor by the apostles, to the first day of the week. Neither was it changed by the Jesus' resurrection—for Christ rose "in the end of the Sabbath" and not on Sunday (Matt. 28:1-6).

33. Sabbath-keeping is a requirement for eternal life—as the Christian must be keeping *all* of God's Ten Commandments (Matt. 19:17; Rev. 22:14).
34. The seventh day Sabbath remains as the day of rest for God's people (Heb. 4:9).
35. Jesus warned that in the end time, as the great tribulation is beginning, we should pray that we would not have to flee on the Sabbath (Matt. 24:20).
36. The sign of God's people in the end time is that they would be keeping the commandments of God (Rev. 12:17; 14:12).

(Adapted from the *Bible Sabbath Association*, Fairview, Oklahoma)

Appendix F

Rome's War Against the Christian Passover, God's Sabbath and Holy Days

From the death of the apostle John in AD 100, apostate religious leaders and church scholars systematically began to reject God's Sabbath, holy days and feasts. These so-called early "church fathers" found favor instead with Sunday as the weekly day of rest and worship, as well as with various holidays and feasts of pagan origin—all of which they had conveniently "Christianized." The same "theologians" that denigrated the seventh-day weekly Sabbath likewise put forth countless false arguments that Christians were no longer required to observe God's feasts. Their hatred of God's holy days and feasts was, in many cases, more pronounced than their loathing of the Sabbath.

The attack against the biblical feasts and holy days began with the Passover. The church in the West particularly detested the observance of the Christian Passover, which they saw as "Jewish." True Christians kept the Passover on the night of the 14th day of the first month, as commanded by God. A conflict arose over the keeping of Passover—known in history as the "Quartodeciman controversy"—in which Rome called for the abolition of the Passover and the institution of "Easter-Sunday" (derived from Baalism and Mithraism). Central to their efforts was the condemnation of any observance of the Passover and biblical holy days as "Judaizing." In so doing, the western church rejected the true Christ Jesus as the Passover Lamb of God, slain on Nisan 14, as well as the Christian Passover that He instituted.

Baalism was the primary stumbling block that turned both Israel and Judah away from their covenant relationship with God, and ultimately brought them into national captivity. Their worship of Baal focused on a "transubstantiation" ritual celebrated on the day of the sun, Sunday—and was particularly important in sunrise celebrations on Easter Sunday (see Appendix J, *The Eucharist or the Sacrifice of the Mass*, p. 249).

Orthodox Christendom has always favored the insidious influences of Baalism over adherence to the commandments of God. Deliberate attempts to pervert the true worship of God through the counterfeit teachings of Baalism are recorded in the writings of the New Testament. One motive behind such attempts was the elimination of the Nisan 14 Christian Passover. The epistles of Paul are rife with this doctrinal combat (e.g., Galatians, Colossians, Hebrews), and the Gospel of John attests to this spiritual and doctrinal battle in which all true Christians were fully engaged by AD 70 (see Jude 3-4, 11 and Rev. 2:14).

238

By AD 95, the leadership of the Roman church was fast abandoning the seventh-day Sabbath for Sunday, and the Nisan 14 Passover for Easter. Once the observance of Easter Sunday superseded the Christian Passover, the abandonment of the remaining biblical feasts and holy days soon followed. These were quickly replaced with "Christianized" occult holidays—Christmas, Halloween, Lent, etc.

This movement soon coalesced into a weekly ritual meal of transubstantiation to Mithras (the Baal of Persia)—and ultimately led to the annual observance of Easter sunrise services in honor of Mithras' supposed resurrection. Mithras was anciently known as the pagan deity Tammuz (Ezk. 8:13-16). This "Christian" celebration—now renamed as a "communion service"—was adopted by growing numbers of churches throughout the empire until it eventually replaced the true Passover service of Nisan 14. This push to "Christianize" the pagan worship as "sanctified Christian worship" of God was championed by apostate church leaders of Rome, Asia Minor, and Alexandria, Egypt.

In AD 135, the majority of church congregations in the Mediterranean region had already abandoned the true Passover in favor of Sunday communion and the yearly Easter sunrise service. By AD 195, a mere sixty years later, the Orthodox Gentile bishops of Palestine had fully succumbed to this onslaught. **It cannot be overstated that the first step in this departure from the true worship of God was the introduction of weekly Sunday worship by the leadership of Rome**.

By AD 200, the only remaining champions of truth were found in scattered congregations in Asia Minor, some of whom continued faithfully in the observance of the Passover, feasts and holy days of God well into the sixth century. As the book of Revelation and early church history records, there remained a number of true Christians in Asia Minor who, led by the church at Ephesus, stood fast for the righteousness they had received from the Lord Jesus Christ and the apostles, particularly the apostle John. Faithfully, they repelled assault after assault against the weekly seventh-day Sabbath, the Nisan 14th Passover, and the remaining holy days of God.

The church historian Eusebius records the testimony of Polycrates, the leader of the Ephesian resistance, who held fast against this invasion of false doctrine: "[B]ut the bishops in Asia were led by Polycrates in persisting that it was necessary to keep the custom which had been handed down to them of old [given by Jesus Christ as recorded in the four Gospels]. Polycrates himself in a document which he addressed to Victor and to the church of Rome, expounds the tradition which had come to him as follows: 'Therefore we keep the day undeviatingly, neither adding [to] nor taking away, for in Asia great luminaries sleep, and they will rise on the day of the coming of the Lord, when he shall come with glory from heaven and seek out [literally, to raise up] all the saints. Such were Phillip of the twelve apostles, and two of his daughters who grew old as virgins, who sleep in Hierapolis, and another daughter of his, who lived in the Holy Spirit, rests at Ephesus. Moreover, there is also John, who lay on the Lord's breast, who was a priest wearing the breastplate, and the martyr, and teacher. He sleeps at Ephesus. And there is also Polycarp at Smyrna, both bishop and martyr, who sleeps at Laodicea, and Papirius, too, the blessed, and Melito the eunuch, who lived entirely in the Holy Spirit, who lies in Sardis, waiting for the visitation from heaven when he will rise from the dead. All these kept the fourteenth day of the Passover according to the gospel, never swerving, but following according to the rule of the faith [as taught by Jesus and the apostles]. And I also, Polycrates, the least of you all, live according to the tradition of my kinsmen, and some of them have I followed. For seven of my family were bishops and I am the eighth, and my kinsmen ever kept the day when the people put away the leaven. Therefore, brethren, I who have lived sixty-five years in the Lord and conversed with the brethren from every country, and have studied all the holy Scriptures, am not afraid of threats, for they have said who were greater than I, "It is better to obey God rather than men" ' " (Eusebius, *The Ecclesiastical History*, Vol. I, pp. 505-507, bracketed comments added).

After the death of Polycrates and his faithful fellow Christian leaders in Asia Minor, the only remaining resistance to the relentless pagan conspiracy was in the distant Mesopotamian Valley and in the mountainous regions of Europe. The true Christian brethren of these regions faithfully preserved the Old and New Testaments from the ravages of the Roman Orthodox, Jewish Orthodox and Gnostic communities. Opposing all corrupting influences, they preserved the only true testimony of our Messiah and His Passover.

Samuele Bacchiocchi writes of Rome's leading role in replacing the true Nisan 14 Passover with Easter Sunday: "There seems to be no question as to Rome being the place of its origin. Later historical data confirm, in fact, the Roman origin of Easter-Sunday. J.B. Pitra, for instance, has discovered and edited the conciliar decree of the Council of Nicaea [by Emperor Constantine in] (AD 325) concerning the celebration of Easter, where it specifically enjoined: 'All the brethren in the East who formerly celebrated Easter [i.e., the Nisan 14 Passover] with the Jews, will henceforth keep it at the same time as the Romans, with us and with all those who from ancient times have celebrated the feast at the same time with us.'... Scholars usually recognize in the Roman custom of celebrating Easter on Sunday instead of the 14th of Nisan, to use Jeremias' words, 'the inclination to break away from Judaism.' Lightfoot holds, for instance, that Rome and Alexandria adopted Easter-Sunday to avoid 'even the semblance of Judaism.' M. Righetti, in his monumental history of liturgy, also points out that Rome and Alexandria, after 'having eliminated the Judaizing quartodeciman tradition,' repudiated even the Jewish computations, making their own calculations, since 'such dependence on the Jews must have appeared humiliating.' The Nicene conciliar letter of Constantine, referred to above, explicitly reveals a marked anti-Judaic motivation for the repudiation of the quartodeciman Passover. The Emperor in fact, desiring to establish a [new religion] completely free from any Jewish influences writes: 'It appeared an unworthy thing that in the celebration of this most holy feast we should follow the practice of the Jews, who have impiously defiled their hands with enormous sin, and are, therefore, deservedly afflicted with blindness of soul.... *Let us then have nothing in common with the detestable Jewish crowd*; for we have received from our Saviour a different way.... Strive and pray continually that the purity of your souls may not seem in anything to be sullied by fellowship with the customs of these most wicked men.... All should unite in desiring that which sound reason appears to demand, and in *avoiding all participation in the perjured conduct of the Jews.*'

"The anti-Judaic motivations for [the] repudiation of the Jewish reckoning of Passover could not have been expressed more explicitly and forcefully in the letter of Constantine. Nicaea represents the culmination of a controversy initiated two centuries earlier and motivated by strong anti-Judaic feelings and one which had Rome as its epicenter.

"In all this controversy Rome exercised a role of leadership. We have noticed that it was in Rome that the Easter-Sunday custom arose, possibly under bishop Sixtus; it was to Rome that Polycrates addressed himself to defend his different tradition; it was to Rome that the Council of Nicaea pointed as the example to follow on the Easter observance" (Bacchiocchi, *Anti-Judaism and the Origin of Sunday*, pp. 86-87, bracketed comments added).

Appendix G

The Fourteen Rules for Bible Study Spiritual Keys to Understanding the Word of God

There are spiritual keys to understanding the Scriptures. The primary key is that of being in a steadfast loving, faithful and obedient attitude and relationship toward God. Jesus said, "If you love Me, keep the commandments—namely, My commandments" (John 14:15). Likewise, in the Psalms we find that those who keep the commandments of God will be given understanding: "All His commandments *are* sure. They stand fast for ever and ever, *and are* done in truth and uprightness....The fear of the LORD *is* the beginning of wisdom: a good understanding have all they that do *Hs commandments*: His praise endures for ever:" (Psa. 111:7, 8, 10, KJV). This is the foundation of understanding the Word of God.

Another vital key is clearly taught in Isaiah 28: "Whom shall He teach knowledge? And whom shall He make to understand doctrine? *Them that are* weaned from the milk, *and* drawn from the breasts [that is, fully grounded in the Word of God]. For **precept** *must be* **upon precept**, precept upon precept; **line upon line**, line upon line; **here a little**, *and* there a little" (verses 9-10, *KJV*).

The Bible tells us that in order to understand doctrine, we must study it line upon line and precept upon precept. That is exactly how we need to study any Scriptural question. The New Testament confirms this approach to understanding the Word of God and establishing sound doctrine. Paul instructed Timothy in how to study and teach doctrine: "Diligently *study* to show yourself approved unto God, a workman [in the Word of God] who does not *need to be* ashamed, rightly dividing [precept upon precept, and line upon line] the Word of the truth" (II Tim. 2:15).

The Word of God is called the Word of truth. It is the Spirit of truth that teaches us all things. Jesus said, "But *when* the Comforter *comes, even* the Holy Spirit, which the Father will send in My name, that one **shall teach you all things**, and shall bring to your remembrance everything that I have told you" (John 14:26). This is the promise Jesus gave!

The Bible makes it clear that the Word of truth works together with the Spirit of truth to give understanding to those who love God and seek His will. It is self-evident that it is not possible for the carnal mind, which is deceitful above all things (Jer. 17:9), to come to the knowledge of the truth of God. In fact, the carnal, unconverted mind is enmity (that is, hostile) toward God and is not willing to be subject to God's laws (Rom. 8:7). Regardless of how brilliant or how great one's intellect may be, God's Word is not under-

242

stood by human wisdom or reasoning. It is only through the Spirit of God that the Word of God is understood.

The Apostle Paul taught that spiritual truths can only be discerned and understood through the Spirit of God: "But according as it is written, '*The* eye has not seen, nor *the* ear heard, neither have entered into *the* heart of man, *the* things which God has prepared for those who love Him.'

"But God has revealed *them* to us by His Spirit, for the Spirit searches all things—even the deep things of God. For who among men understands the things of man except *by* the spirit of man which *is* in him? In the same way also, the things of God no one understands except *by* the Spirit of God. Now we have not received the spirit of the world, but the Spirit that *is* of God, so that we might know the things graciously given to us by God; which things we also speak, not in words taught by human wisdom, but in *words* taught by *the* Holy Spirit *in order to* communicate spiritual things by spiritual *means*. But *the* natural man does not receive the things of the Spirit of God; for they are foolishness to him, and he cannot understand *them* because **they are spiritually discerned**' " (I Cor. 2:9-14).

Spiritual truth is revealed by the Spirit. Unfortunately, many people are caught up in the politics of religion, the organizational power structure of an ecclesiastical hierarchy, or the time-honored doctrines of various churches. These things prevent an unbiased study and obscure the spiritual truths in God's Word.

A biblically outlined method of study—"rightly dividing" the Word of God—is the proper way to study the Word of God. When one studies the Bible following the Fourteen Rules For Bible Study, he or she will find the truth of the Bible as revealed by the Holy Spirit of truth. These rules are not designed to bolster a previous doctrinal position, or justify a particular church doctrine. These things do not really matter; and even if they did, would God overlook such misuse of His Word?

Paul's words to Timothy show the danger in misusing the Scriptures: "See that *they* remain mindful of these things, earnestly charging *them* in the sight of the Lord not to argue over words that are not profitable in any way, *but which lead* to *the* subverting of those who hear" (II Tim. 2:14). Many Bible teachers have misused the Scriptures in this way. In order to justify doctrinal beliefs that are not taught in the Bible, they have twisted and distorted the Scriptures to fit their own private interpretations. Whole churches have been subverted by arguments and disputes over words that have undermined the faith of millions!

The apostle Peter warned the believers to be on guard against false teachers: "As *he has* also in all *his* [Paul's] epistles, speaking in them concerning these things; in which are some things *that are* difficult to understand, **which the ignorant and unstable are twisting *and distorting*, as *they* also *twist and distort* the rest of the Scriptures, to their own destruction**. Therefore, beloved, since you know this in advance, be on guard against *such practices,* lest you be led astray with the error of the lawless ones, *and* you fall from your own steadfastness" (II Pet. 3:16-17).

Peter understood that those who promote their own private interpretations are rejecting the Holy Spirit of God which inspired every word that is written in the Scriptures: "Knowing this first, that no prophecy of Scripture originated as anyone's own *private* interpretation; because prophecy was not brought at any time by human will, but the holy men of God spoke as they were moved by *the* Holy Spirit" (II Pet. 1:20-21). Paul also made it clear that the words of the scriptures were not humanly devised but were "God-breathed." Notice: "And that from a child you have known the holy writings, which are able to make you wise unto salvation through faith, which *is* in Christ Jesus. **All Scripture *is* God-breathed** and *is* profitable for doctrine, for conviction, for correction, for instruction in righteousness; so that the man of God may be complete, fully equipped for every good work." (II Tim. 3:15-17).

False doctrines and misinterpretations are continually being propagated because ministers and teachers use the Word of God deceitfully. How diabolical it is to take the Word of God, which is the truth, and misapply it to create a lie! Such deceptive use of God's Word has existed from the time of the apostles. In writing to the believers at Corinth, the apostle Paul contrasted his ministry with the deceitful approach of false teachers in his day: "Therefore, having this ministry, according as we have received mercy, we are not fainthearted. For **we have personally renounced the hidden things of dishonest gain, not walking in *cunning* craftiness, nor handling the Word of God deceitfully; but by manifestation of the truth we are commending ourselves to every man's conscience before God**" (II Cor. 4:1-2).

When studying the Bible, one should apply the Fourteen Rules for Bible Study that follow. These rules show the systematic method and the mechanics of proper Bible study.

One should never establish doctrine based on the traditions of men, regardless of how knowledgeable or authoritative they are reputed to be. Nor should one base doctrine solely on the commentaries or other writings of men. Any student of the Bible should strictly follow the Word of God by examining the subject's history and referring to the original languages, Hebrew and Greek, in order to determine precise definitions and meanings of key, critically important words. Such an approach will lead to a clear and complete understanding of what the Word of God truly teaches.

Fourteen Rules for Bible Study

1) Begin with Scriptures that are easy to understand.

2) Let the Bible interpret and prove the Bible. Don't look for what you want to prove; look for what the Bible actually proves.

3) Understand the context—the verses before and after, the chapters before and after. Does your understanding of a particular verse harmonize with the rest of the Bible?

4) As much as possible, understand the original language, Hebrew or Greek. Never try to establish dogmatic doctrine or teachings by using *Strong's Exhaustive Concordance of the Bible*. It can be helpful at times, but it is extremely limited.

5) Ask: what does the Scripture clearly say?

6) Ask: what does the Scripture not say?

7) Ask: who was the book written to?

8) Ask: who wrote it?

9) Ask: who said it?

10) Understand the time frame in history when the book was written.

11) Base your study on Scriptural knowledge that you already under stand. What do you know up to this point in time?

12) Do not allow your own personal assumptions or preconceived notions to influence your understanding and conclusions.

13) Do not form conclusions based on partial facts, insufficient information, or the opinions and speculations of others.

14) Opinions, regardless of how strongly you feel about them, don't necessarily count. Scripture must be your standard and guide.

Appendix H

The True Meaning of *Sabbatismos* in Hebrews 4:9

"There remaineth therefore a **rest** to the people of God" (King James Version).

Simple, to the point—but almost universally misunderstood. In fact, the true meaning of Hebrews 4:9 is the *very opposite* of the false interpretation assumed by many churches, ministers and theologians.

Mainstream "Christianity" teaches today that Christians are no longer required to observe the seventh-day Sabbath because, as this verse is taken to mean, Christ has given them "rest" (or, as some say, a "release") from commandment-keeping. The false claim put forth is that Jesus has "fulfilled the law" *for* them. As a result, they are told, the Christian has entered into a spiritual "rest" from sin, and that Jesus Himself *is* their "spiritual Sabbath."

Such reasoning, of course, is completely contrary to the Word of God. Jesus Himself said that He did not come to abolish or "do away with" the laws and commandments of God, but to fulfill them (Matt. 5:17-18). Nor did Christ fulfill any commandment in order to release Christians from their obligation to keep God's laws. Rather, He set the example for us—not to force us into obedience, but to *free us* from committing sin (I Pet. 2:21-22, I John 3:4). Years into his ministry, the apostle Paul said that he was still zealous for the laws of God (Acts 22:3)—which would certainly include the Sabbath commandment.

When we understand the full meaning of the Greek text of Hebrew 4:9, there is no question that the New Testament upholds the authority of the Fourth Commandment. The Greek word used here for "rest" is *sabbatismos* (σαββατισμος), which means "Sabbath rest, Sabbath observance" (Arndt and Gingrich, *A Greek-English Lexicon of the New Testament*).

This definition is confirmed by other historical works: "The words 'sabbath rest' is translated from the [Greek] noun *sabbatismos*, [and is] a unique word in the NT. This term appears also in Plutarch (*Superset. 3 [Moralia 166a]*) for sabbath observance, and in four post-canonical Christian writings which are not dependent on Heb. 4:9" (*The Anchor Bible Dictionary*, Vol. 5, p. 856).

While *sabbatismos* is a noun, the verb form of the word is *sabbatizo* (σαββατιζω), which means, "to keep the Sabbath" (*A Greek-English Lexicon of the New Testament*).

This definition of *sabbatizo* is confirmed by its use in the Septuagint, a Greek translation of the Old Testament dating from third century BC. (It is called the Septuagint, meaning "Seventy," because the first five books were translated by seventy Greek-speaking Jewish scholars in Alexandria, Egypt. Jews used the Septuagint in synagogues throughout the Roman Empire; Greek-speaking Jewish and Gentile coverts to Christianity used the translation throughout the early New Testament period. The apostle Paul quotes extensively from the Septuagint in his epistle to the Hebrews.)

When Paul used *sabbatismos* in Hebrews 4:9, he did so knowing that its meaning was **well known** to the Greek-speaking believers of that day. After all, its verb form (*sabbatizo*) was widely employed in the Septuagint—which, as a translation, was as familiar to the Greek-speaking Jews and Gentiles of the early Church as the King James Bible is to Christians today.

For example, the use of the verb *sabbatizo* in Leviticus 23:32 in the Septuagint leaves no doubt as to its meaning. *The Greek English Lexicon of the Septuagint* defines *sabbatizo* as "to keep [a] sabbath, to rest" (Lust, Eynikel, Hauspie). The English translation of this verse in the Septuagint reads: "It [the Day of Atonement] shall be a holy sabbath [literally, 'a Sabbath of Sabbaths'] to you; and ye shall humble your souls, from the ninth day of the month: from evening to evening **shall ye keep your sabbaths**" (*The Septuagint With the Apocrypha*, Brenton).

The phrase "shall ye keep your sabbaths" is translated from the Greek phrase, *sabbatieite ta sabbata* (σαββατιειτε τα σαββατα)—which literally means, "you shall **sabbathize** the Sabbaths." The form of the Greek verb *sabbatizo* is the second person plural *sabbatieite*, which means, "ye shall keep." In the entire Septuagint, the verb *sabbatizo* is never used except in relation to "Sabbath-keeping." In keeping with this definition, the KJV translates *sabbatieite* as, "shall ye celebrate your sabbath."

There is no question that the Greek verb *sabbatizo* in Leviticus 23:32 is specifically referring to Sabbath observance. This meaning applies equally to the noun form *sabbatismos,* used by Paul. Thus, the continuity of the Septuagint's use of *sabbatizo* and the use of *sabbatismos* in Hebrews 4:9 confirms that Paul was upholding the observance of the seventh-day Sabbath.

The use of *sabbatismos* in Hebrews 4:9 directly contradicts any false teaching that the Fourth Commandment has been abolished. As the context of Hebrews four shows, the observance of the seventh-day Sabbath as a day of rest and worship is as binding for the people of God today as it was for Israel of old.

It becomes clear then that Hebrews 4:9 does not mean that Christians enter into some sort of "spiritual rest" which exempts them from the obligation to keep the Sabbath, or any other commandments. Rather, this verse must be taken as *instructive*—that Christians are indeed commanded to keep the Sabbath day. Consequently, this verse should be translated as the original Greek meant, "**There remains, therefore, Sabbath-keeping for the people of God**."

Appendix I

The Eucharist—Sacrifice of the Mass

Is the bread and wine of the Eucharist transfigured at the command of a priest into Jesus' literal flesh and blood?

The Catholic Church claims that Jesus instituted the "Eucharist"—the so-called "Sacrifice of the Mass"—on the night of His last supper. According to Scripture, however, Jesus kept the Passover that night (Luke 22:15, etc.), adding bread and wine as symbols of the New Covenant. Thus, He instituted the Christian Passover service.

Just what is the "Eucharist," and what is its *true* origin? And what of the claim that, at the command of a priest, bread and wine actually *become* the literal flesh and blood of Christ in the "Sacrifice of the Mass"?

During the second to fourth centuries AD, the apostate "Christian" church in Rome grafted numerous pagan rituals into its "Christianized" practices. Among them was the "Sacrifice of the Mass"—called the "Eucharist"—in which it is claimed that bread and wine are transfigured into the literal flesh and blood of Jesus Christ. "In the celebration of the Holy Mass, **the bread and wine are changed into the body and blood of Christ**. It is called **transubstantiation**, for in the Sacrament of the Eucharist the substance of bread and wine do not remain, but the entire substance of bread is changed into the body of Christ, and the entire substance of wine is changed into his blood, the … outward semblance of bread and wine alone remaining" (*The Catholic Encyclopedia*, article "Consecration," bold emphasis added).

But is this belief founded on the Word of God?

Such a teaching ignores the plain teaching of the New Testament concerning the Passover. As symbols of the New Covenant, the bread and wine of Christ's last supper were clearly **representative** of His body and blood. To take Jesus' words literally—"this is my body" and "this is my blood"— is to grossly disregard a common literary tool of Scripture: **figurative language**.

Such language is widely used throughout the Bible. For example, when David's men risked their lives to bring him much-needed water, he said: "*Is not this* the blood of the men that went in jeopardy of their lives?" (II Sam. 23:17). To David, the water was symbolic of the blood of those who risked their lives for him. In a similar manner, Christ is called a "door" in John 10:9, a "vine" in John 15:5, and a "rock" in I Corinthians 10:4—none of which are to be taken literally.

Forcing a literal meaning on Christ's words concerning the bread and wine of Passover creates several problems. First, it ignores the fact that

Jesus Christ, Who is seated at the right hand of God the Father in heaven, is no longer composed of flesh and blood—but of spirit (see a description of His glorified form in Revelation chapter one). Secondly, the drinking of blood is expressly forbidden in Scripture (Deut. 12:16; Acts 15:20).

More importantly, however, the idea of transubstantiation seriously contradicts a pivotal New Testament teaching, that Jesus' sacrifice was efficacious **once for all time, for all human sin**—for Christ was "**offered once** to bear *the* sins of many" (Heb. 9:28). The Catholic Church teaches that in the Eucharist the wafer of bread (as Christ's literal body) is offered up by the priest **in sacrifice**. (The wafer is referred to as a "host," from a Latin word originally meaning "victim" or "sacrifice.") In a quote from the Council of Trent, the church says, "If any one saith that in the Mass **a true and proper sacrifice** is not offered to God ... let him be anathema" (*The Catholic Encyclopedia*, article "Sacrifice of the Mass," bold emphasis added. Note: "Sacrifice of the Mass" is another name for the Eucharist).

The Catholic idea of Christ being offered up repeatedly as a sacrifice stands in sharp disagreement with Jesus' own words when He said on the cross, "It is finished" (John 19:30). Again, Christ's sacrifice was accomplished **once, for all time, for all human sin**. Hebrews 10:10-14 says "we are sanctified through the offering of the body of Jesus Christ **once for all**. Now every high priest stands ministering day by day, offering the same sacrifices repeatedly, which are never able to remove sins; but He, after **offering one sacrifice for sins for ever**, sat down at *the* right hand of God.... For **by one offering** He has obtained eternal perfection *for* those who are sanctified."

Those who believe otherwise—and practice the Eucharist—should consider whether they are "crucifying [again] the Son of God for themselves, and are publicly holding *Him* in contempt" (Heb. 6:6).

Clearly, the "Sacrifice of the Mass" is unbiblical. But what, then, is its true origin?

Ancient Transubstantiation Rites

There is considerable evidence that transubstantiation rituals were carried out as part of the religious observances of numerous primitive cultures. Sir James George Frazer writes: "The custom of eating bread sacramentally as the body of a god was practised by the Aztecs before the discovery and conquest of Mexico by the Spaniards [in the sixteenth century]. Twice a year, in May and December, an image of the great Mexican god Huitzilopochtli or Vitzilipuztli was made of dough, then broken in pieces, and solemnly eaten by his worshippers.... They called these morsels [of bread] the flesh and bones of Vitzilipuztli" (*The Golden Bough—A Study in Magic and Religion*, pp. 566-567).

Frazer adds that "the ancient Mexicans, even before the arrival of Christian missionaries, were **fully acquainted with the doctrine of transubstantiation** and acted upon it in the solemn rites of their religion. They believed that by consecrating bread **their priests could turn it into the**

very body of their god, so that all who thereupon partook of the consecrated bread entered into a mystic communion with the deity by receiving a portion of his divine substance into themselves.... The ceremony was called *teoqualo*, that is, 'god is eaten' " (Ibid., pp. 568-569, bold emphasis added). Even the Catholics admit: "[Pagan] Mithraism had a Eucharist, but **the idea of a sacred banquet is as old as the human race** and existed at all ages and amongst all peoples" (*The Catholic Encyclopedia*, article "Mithraism," bold emphasis added).

"The doctrine of transubstantiation, or the magical conversion of bread into flesh, was also familiar to the Aryans of ancient India **long before the spread and even the rise of Christianity**. The Brahmans [of India] taught that the rice-cakes offered in sacrifice were substitutes for human beings, and that they were actually converted into the real bodies of men by the manipulation of the priest" (*The Golden Bough*, p. 568, bold emphasis added).

Amazingly, the concept of literally "eating a god" actually stems from cannibalism. Of the various cultures that practiced cannibalism, Frazer writes that "the flesh and blood of dead men [were] commonly eaten and drunk [in order] to inspire bravery, wisdom, or other qualities for which the [dead] men themselves were remarkable.... By this means the strength, valor, intelligence, and other virtues of the slain are believed to be imparted to the eaters" (Ibid., p. 576).

If the victim was considered to be a god, so much the better: "[B]y eating the flesh of an animal or man he [the savage] acquires not only the physical, but even the moral and intellectual qualities which were characteristic of that animal or man; so when the creature [or man] is deemed divine [a god], our simple savage naturally expects to **absorb a portion of its divinity** along with its material substance.... By eating the body of the god he **shares in the god's attributes and powers**" (Ibid., pp. 573 and 578, bold emphasis added).

Thus, the practice of cannibalism led to the idea of, literally, "eating a god." Over time, this custom evolved into various transubstantiation rituals in which consecrated bread was eaten—but only after it had been "magically" changed into the "literal" flesh of a god. Depending on the culture, wine was also often consumed as the "literal" blood of a god.

But how did this pagan transubstantiation concept find its way into "Christianity"?

The Babylonian Influence

Central to the ancient Babylonian religion was the supreme goddess "mother" Ishtar. Subsequently, every pagan civilization has worshipped its own version of a caring goddess-mother figure, such as Inanna, Fortuna, Hathor, etc. Of this "original goddess" figure, Alexander Hislop writes that "the goddess-mother has evidently radiated in all directions from Chaldea [Babylon]" (*The Two Babylons*, p. 158). As we will see, Babylonian goddess-mother worship was the forerunner of the Catholic reverence of

250

"Mother Mary"—and pivotal to the development of the Eucharist ritual.

Hislop continues: "Now, thus we see how it comes that Rome represents Christ … as a stern and inexorable judge, before whom the sinner 'might grovel in the dust, and still never be sure that his prayers would be heard,' while Mary is set off in the most winning and engaging light, as the hope of the guilty, as the grand refuge of sinners…. The most standard devotional works of Rome are pervaded by this very principle, exalting the compassion and gentleness of the mother at the expense of the loving character of the Son….

"All this is done only to exalt the Mother, as *more* gracious and *more* compassionate than her glorious Son. Now, this was the very case in Babylon: and to this character of the goddess queen her favourite offerings exactly corresponded. Therefore, we find the women of Judah represented as simply '**burning incense, pouring out drink** [wine] **offerings, and offering** *cakes* **to the queen of heaven**' (Jer. 44:19)" (Ibid., pp. 158-159, bold emphasis his).

In what were known as "bloodless" sacrifices, such "cakes" were offered to the "queen of heaven" (Ishtar) as a form of communion. Hislop adds that, after such sacrifices, Ishtar's worshippers also "**partook of [the cakes and wine]**, swearing anew fidelity to her" (Ibid., p. 159, bold emphasis added).

Riding on the skirts of Mary, as it were, this early form of the Eucharist found its way into the apostate Roman church. "In the fourth century, when the queen of heaven, under the name of Mary, was beginning to be worshipped in the Christian Church [at Rome], **this 'unbloody [bread and wine] sacrifice' also was brought in**…. [At] that time it was well known to have been **adopted from the Pagans**" (Ibid., p. 159, bold emphasis added). In the Catholic Eucharist, the "host" is a **round wafer**. Contrast this with the reality that when bread is broken, it never breaks into *round* shapes. The *broken* bread at Passover represents the body of Christ, *beaten* and *torn*. This awesome symbolism is completely lost in the "round" wafer.

History, however, links the "roundness" of the wafer with **sun worship**. "The importance … which Rome attaches to the *roundness* of the wafer, must have a reason; and that reason will be found, if we look at the altars of Egypt. 'The thin, *round* cake,' says Wilkinson, 'occurs on all [Egyptian] altars.' Almost every jot or tittle in the Egyptian worship had a symbolical meaning. The *round disk*, so frequent in the sacred emblems of Egypt, symbolised the *sun*.'… [The] 'round' wafer, whose 'roundness' is so important an element in the Romish Mystery … **is only another symbol of Baal, or the sun**" (Ibid., pp. 160, 163, bold emphasis added).

Of this Egyptian practice, Hislop writes: "Now, when Osiris, the sun-divinity, became incarnate, and was born, it was not merely that he should give his life as a *sacrifice* for men, but that he might also be **the life and** *nourishment* **of the souls of men**…. Now, this Son, who was symbolised as 'Corn,' was the SUN-divinity incarnate, according to the sacred oracle of the great goddess of Egypt…. What [could be] more natural then, if this incarnate divinity is symbolised as the '*bread* of God,' than that he should be represented as a '*round* wafer,' to **identify him with the Sun**?" Hislop adds that this god who was identified "under the symbol of the wafer or thin round cake, as 'the bread of life,' was in reality the fierce, scorching Sun, or terrible Moloch" (Ibid., pp. 160-161, 163, bold emphasis added).

In the end, says Hislop, "the practice of offering and eating this 'unbloody sacrifice' [of bread and wine] was patronised by the Papacy; and now, throughout the whole bounds of the Romish communion, it has super-seded the simple but most precious sacrament of the Supper instituted by our Lord Himself" (Ibid., p. 164).

Mary Worship—and Mary as "Mediatrix of Communion"

When it comes to understanding the "mystery" of the Eucharist, the role of Mary cannot be overstated. Mary is so intimately connected to the Eucharistic mystery that the late John Paul II—in his encyclical letter *Ecclesia de Eucharistia*—called her the "Woman of the Eucharist." "If we wish to rediscover in all its richness the profound relationship between the Church and the Eucharist, **we cannot neglect Mary**, Mother and model of the Church.... Mary can guide us towards this most holy sacrament, because **she herself has a profound relationship with it**" (Pope John Paul II, *Ecclesia de Eucharistia*, ch. 6: "At the School of Mary, Woman of the Eucharist," para. 53, bold emphasis added). The complete *Ecclesia de Eucharistia* is available at www.ewtn.com/library/encyc/jp2eucha.htm.

Mary's connection to the Eucharist stems in no small part from the fact that she is actually *worshipped* by the Catholic Church. Catholics, of course, deny this. However, while there is nothing in Catholic literature that *explicitly* states that Mary should be the object of worship, the sentiment is strongly *implied*. The Catholic reverence of Mary amounts, in practice, to worship because Catholics kneel before her image, pray to her, trust in her for salvation, and attribute to her titles and honors which alone belong to God. For example, a popular prayer in Mary's honor says, "Hail, holy Queen, Mother of Mercy! Our life, our sweetness and our hope! To thee do we cry, poor banished children of Eve. To thee do we send up our sighs, mourning and weeping, in this valley of tears. Turn, then, most gracious Advocate, thine eyes of mercy toward us." (Taken from *Mary Worship—A Study of Catholic Practice and Doctrine*, Mary Ann Collins, Jan. 2006, www.CatholicConcerns.com.)

Note the use of "Advocate," a title belonging to Christ (I John 2:1). In the official "Catechism of the Catholic Church"—as proclaimed by the Second Vatican Council (1962-1965) and approved in 1992 by Pope John Paul II—it is stated that **God has exalted Mary in glory** as "Queen of Heaven" (Catechism, no. 966), and that she is to be **praised with special devotion** (Catechism, no. 971; *Catechism of the Catholic Church*, Double-day, pp. 274-275).

One only has to read between the lines to see the high degree of reverence given to Mary. Connected to the worship of Mary is her presumed role as co-mediator with Christ of man's salvation—wherein she is often referred to as "Mediatrix." According to Catholic Creed, the "Blessed Virgin is invoked in the Church under the titles Advocate, Helper, Benefactress, and Mediatrix" (Catechism, no. 969; Ibid., p. 275).

History had already predicted as much. Hislop writes that "the goddess-queen [Ishtar] of Chaldea [the "Queen of Heaven"] differed from her son, who was worshipped in her arms. *He* was ... represented as delighting in blood. But *she* [like Mary in the Catholic Church], as the mother of grace and mercy ... was averse to blood, and was represented in a benign and gentle character. Accordingly, in Babylon [as in Rome today] she bore the name of Mylitta—that is, 'The Mediatrix' " (*The Two Babylons*, pp. 56-57). Scripture, of course, confirms that there is but "one Mediator between God and men—*the* man Christ Jesus" (I Tim. 2:5). Referring to Christ, Luke wrote: "And there is no salvation in any other, for neither is there another name under heaven which has been given among men, by which we must be saved" (Acts 4:12).

One of Catholicism's principal proponents of the Marianist Movement, which glorifies Mary, was priest-missionary Louis Marie de Montfort (1673-1716) of France—best know for his works *True Devotion to the Blessed Virgin* and *The Secret of Mary* (see montfort.org). In his commentary entitled *St. Louis Marie de Montfort on the Eucharist and Mary*, Catholic writer Corrado Maggioni describes Montfort's insight into the role of Mary in the Eucharist. "With great sensitivity and in great depth, Montfort draws attention to the **presence and action of Mary in the Eucharist** without detriment to the excellence of the redeeming work of Christ.... **Mary is mediatrix of Communion**." Maggioni quotes Montfort as saying that people "should go to confession and Holy Communion with the intention of **consecrating themselves to Jesus through Mary**" (from www.marys-touch.com/Saints/montfort3.htm, pp.1-2, bold emphasis added).

Not only has the Catholic Church exalted Mary to an idealized, larger-than-life position as goddess-Mother and Mediatrix, it has also made her a virtual **coequal with Christ in His sufferings**.

In his message to the 19th International Marian Congress (1996), Pope John Paul II said: "Mary is present, with the Church and as the Mother of the Church, **at each of our celebrations of the Eucharist**. If the Church and the Eucharist are inseparably united, the same ought to be said of Mary and the Eucharist. This is one reason why, since ancient times, **the commemoration of Mary** has always been part of the Eucharistic celebration....

"Every Holy Mass makes present in an unbloody manner that unique and perfect sacrifice, offered by Christ on the Cross, **in which Mary participated**, joined in spirit with her suffering Son ... **offering her own sorrow to the Father**. Therefore when we celebrate the Eucharist ... the memory of his Mother's suffering is **also made alive and present**.... Through spiritual communion with the sorrowful Mother of God, believers share in a special way in the paschal mystery" (*Mary Leads us to Eucharist*, bold emphasis added;

available at www.ewtn.com/library/PAPALDOC/JP96-815.htm).

In addition, John Paul says that "Mary, throughout her life at Christ's side and not only on Calvary, **made her own** *the sacrificial dimension* of the Eucharist.... Mary experienced a kind of 'anticipated Eucharist'—one might say a 'spiritual communion'—of desire and of oblation, which would culminate in her union with her Son in his passion... (*Ecclesia de Eucharistia*, para. 56, bold emphasis added).

It should be obvious that the Sacrifice of the Mass is as much about Mary as it is about Christ. Indeed, in the Catholic mind, Mary is inexorably bound to the Eucharist. What, then, if anything, does all of this suggest?

Namely, that Mary's so-called "presence" in the Eucharist is a huge understatement. Mary is worshipped, looked upon as co-mediator and co-sufferer with Christ, and she is inseparably "present" and "active" in every Eucharist ritual. The emphasis on her role as "mediatrix of Communion"—coupled with the stress placed on her "sacrificial" role—leads one to ask, *Is Mary also present in the host?*

While the Catholic Church clearly does *not teach* that Mary is co-present in the host in the way Jesus is said to be, the subtle *suggestion* nevertheless remains.

Montfort taught that "since Mary gave the Redeemer **his flesh and blood**, it follows that **she cannot but be involved in the mysteries that are a unique memorial of the same flesh and blood**, that is, the Eucharist" (Maggioni, p. 2, bold emphasis added). As Jesus' mother, *her* flesh and blood are now *His* flesh and blood—giving her at least, perhaps, **an indirect presence in the host**. After all, since the Eucharist is a memorial of the sacrifice of Christ—in which, as we have seen, Mary is said to have "participated"—does not the ritual equally become a memorial of Mary?

Certainly, it is possible to **unknowingly worship** some*one* or some*thing*. Of pagan forms of worship, Christ said, "You do not know [who or] what you worship" (John 4:22). Is the Eucharist just another form of *veiled* Mary-worship? Is this not the Babylonian mystery religion brought full circle?

To borrow from Jeremiah 44:17-19, "We Catholics burn incense to Mary, the Queen of Heaven, and pour out drink offerings of wine to her, and make Eucharistic bread with which to worship her"—and to paraphrase Hislop, "All this is done **only to exalt the Mother** above her glorious Son."

Whatever its intention, the Catholic doctrine of the Eucharist and transubstantiation stands exposed as nothing more than a fraudulent, *idolatrous*, **pagan tradition**—the product of a combination of Babylonian religious mysteries and primitive ideas of "eating a god." Regardless of the claims of the Roman church, and the prayers of her priests, Jesus Christ's flesh has never been present in any "communion wafer," nor has His blood ever been present in any "communion wine."

For a complete historical and theological dissertation on the subject, see Alexander Hislop's *The Two Babylons*, pp. 156-165. (Available at *www.biblicaltruthministries.org* or *www.cbcg.org*.)

Appendix J

What Happens to the Dead?

The Bible is quite clear and straightforward concerning death and the state of the dead. Orthodox Christendom, however, would have us believe that death is little more than the death of the body, while the still-conscious "immortal soul" goes on to **one place or another**. But what does the Bible teach about death and the state of the dead?

Billions of people today—and more billions throughout history—have never had even the slightest chance for salvation. In fact, most have never even **heard the name** of Jesus Christ—the **only name under heaven** by which man may be saved (Acts 4:12). Many have, however, known of the teachings of Christianity and the Bible, but never truly had their minds opened that they might understand.

What happens to such people when they die? Are they, as many believe, "lost"?

Orthodox Christendom, again, teaches that such people are sent immediately at death to be tormented in an ever-burning hell. But does the Bible teach such an outrageous idea? What really happens to the dead?

Is the Soul Immortal?

Interestingly, Orthodox Christendom as a whole does not even pretend to get its beliefs from the Bible alone. Many, in fact, are of pagan origin. The "immortal soul" concept, for example, **does not come from the Bible.** If you believe the Bible is the Word of God and the only reliable source of knowledge about God, then the question is, "What does the **Bible** teach about life after death?"

Most religious leaders today continue to teach the immortality of the soul, despite the fact that the Bible teaches the exact opposite—that the human soul is **mortal**. It can and does DIE (Ezek. 18:20). **God alone** has immortality (I Tim. 6:15, 16).

The immortal soul idea can be traced back to ancient Babylonian mythology, which in various forms spread through the then-civilized world, eventually centering in Egypt in the third and second millennia BC. Greek mythology came mostly from Egypt, and its gods were simply the old Egyptian gods under different names. In the so-called "Golden Age" of Greek civilization, belief in various deities was overlaid gradually with a body of philosophy promoted by Socrates, Plato and Aristotle. A major part of Platonic philosophy was based on the supposed **dualistic nature** of man—the idea of an immortal soul trapped inside a material body.

In the fourth century BC, Plato's disciple, Aristotle, served as teacher to the young Grecian prince Alexander—who later as Alexander the Great conquered the Persian Empire and the rest of the "known world." This conquest led to the spread of Hellenistic Greek philosophy throughout the empire.

Dualism teaches that the body and soul are two irreconcilably different aspects of man and are perpetually at odds with one another. Thus, the "inner person" is actually an "immortal soul" that originated in the heavens and came down to be trapped inside a material, physical body. For Plato, the only true and pure reality was the heavenly—the material was deemed temporary and essentially evil, and was at best only a faulty reflection of the heavenly. Accordingly, the hope of the "spiritual man" was that his conscious immortal soul could return to heaven at the death of the material body.

A few of the earliest "church fathers" were able to discern the fallacy of this doctrine, which had already begun to creep into the Church. Well studied in both the Old and New Testament scriptures, Justin Martyr (AD 100-167) is one such example. In an extended dialogue with a learned Jewish Rabbi, he states, "If you have fallen in with some who are called Christians ... and who say there is no resurrection of the dead, but that their souls, when they die, are taken to heaven; do not imagine that they are Christians..." (Justin, *Dialogue with Trypho,* LXXX, www.earlychristianwritings.com). Most post-apostolic "church fathers," however, were brought up believing ideas such as the immortality of the soul prior to becoming "Christian." Through their highly influential writings, they eventually infused such ideas into the doctrines of the Roman Church. The Protestant Reformation—while it did help to correct some doctrinal errors—continued to promote the immortal soul heresy, which today underlies Protestant as well as Catholic doctrine.

How Such False Teachings Hurt People

The heretical idea of an immortal soul living beyond the death of the body has proven most harmful. How? Many of today's false religions play upon the fears of those deceived about the state of the dead. Churches have used false ideas about death to get people to worship dead "saints" instead of God—as well as to deceive them into thinking they can actually buy a deceased loved one's way into heaven (thus filling church coffers).

The immortal soul idea also plays a part in many abominable occult practices such as necromancy—the attempt to contact the spirits of departed loved ones. Thousands of people have been given false hopes and bilked out of their hard-earned money by charlatans who claimed to be contacting the dead through séances. (If anything supernatural actually happens at such events, the "spirits" contacted are not those of any dead human beings—but demons pretending to be the spirits of the dead persons!)

Today, fanatical activists in the Middle East are promised that if they blow themselves up in a crowd and kill as many innocent civilians as possible, their immortal souls will go to heaven and be attended by many virgins.

(One wonders whether they would be as willing to do this if they knew their soul was not immortal—that they would simply be dead afterwards, eventually to face the judgment of God!)

The "Soul"—According to the Bible

What the Bible says about the soul requires some study. The Hebrew word translated "soul" is *nephesh,* defined as "a *breathing* creature, i.e., animal or (abstract) *vitality;* used very widely in a literal, accommodated or figurative sense (bodily or mentally)..." (*Strong's Exhaustive Concordance of the Bible,* Hebrew Lexicon, item 5315; abbreviations spelled out). The various uses of the Hebrew *nephesh* simply refer to the **physical life** of air breathing creatures—including human beings. Rather than being separate from the physical body, the soul is inextricably fused with the body.

When God created Adam in Genesis chapter one, He made him (not just his body) "of the dust of the ground"—and Adam "became a living soul" (*nephesh*). Notice—it does not say that Adam "received a soul," but that he **became a living soul**. The soul is what a person IS—not something he "has." It's the **complete package** of everything one is, both physical and nonphysical.

But can a soul die? In Ezekiel 18:4 we read, "The soul [*nephesh*] that sins, it [not just the body] shall die." For emphasis, the statement is repeated in verse 20. Some point to what Jesus said in Matthew 10:28—"Fear not them which kill the body, but are not able to kill the soul"—but they fail to read the rest of the passage. "But rather fear him [God] which is able to destroy both soul and body in hell [Greek, *gehenna*]" (KJV) Notice, Christ did NOT say this *gehenna* fire burns the soul for eternity, but that it DESTROYS the soul—burns it up, causing it to cease to exist. Christ made it clear that the soul is NOT immortal and has no life or consciousness apart from the body.

Confusing Soul with Spirit

Some misunderstanding of the biblical teaching on the soul may result from the fact that the Bible also teaches that man has a human spirit. The Hebrew word translated "spirit" is *ruach,* which in some places is also translated "breath."

Job 32:8 says there is a "spirit in man." Several passages in Proverbs refer to this human spirit (Prov. 15:13; 16:32; 20:27; 25:28). This inner spirit, which we all have, is **not a separate or additional "being"**—nor an "immortal soul" trapped inside of us. It is a non-physical dimension that God gives to each of us at conception and is what, in reality, makes us human (Isa. 42:5; Zech. 12:1).

It is the human spirit added to our brain which gives us a **conscious mind** with self-identity—through which we are able to learn complex subjects such as language, mathematics and design (I Cor. 2:11). The human spirit is the sum total of everything about us that is non-physical—our thoughts, imaginations, plans, hopes, dreams, feelings, emotions, attitudes—and makes us each who and what we are. The human spirit also provides God with what is comparable to a "recording" of all that we are—which at death returns to God (Eccl. 12:7). God can then use this "recording" to resurrect us back to physical (or spiritual) life with everything that was unique about us intact.

It is important to understand that even with the addition of the human spirit, it is the whole physical and spiritual package that makes up the person—the soul. The whole person **is a soul**—not "has" a soul. Neither the soul nor the human spirit retain any consciousness after death (Psalm 146:4).

Paul writes that through conversion our human spirit is conjoined by God's Holy Spirit (Rom. 8:16). It is through the workings of God's Spirit with our human spirit in our minds that enables us to be able to understand the things of God (I Cor. 2:11). Those who have God's Holy Spirit added to their human spirit in this life become, at death, the "dead in Christ."

Death—According to the Bible

Again, the Bible is clear in its teaching on death and the state of the dead. The difference between being alive and being dead, according to scripture, is not a matter of place or location—but a matter of being conscious or not conscious. Death, as we will see, is the **total cessation of life**, including consciousness. The only hope for the dead is through a resurrection back to conscious life.

The Bible describes the death of humans as being identical to the death of animals (Eccl. 3:19, 20). Death is the same for all—whether righteous or unrighteous, faithful or unfaithful (Eccl. 9:2). In death, a person's thoughts perish—he or she **knows nothing**, has no consciousness, no awareness (Eccl. 9:5; Psa. 146:4). They are neither looking down from "heaven" nor roasting in a "hell" somewhere in the bowels of the earth. They are simply "dead."

What about Heaven—or Purgatory?

Many are surprised to learn that the Bible does not teach that anyone goes to heaven. On the contrary, Jesus Christ—the very author of our Christian faith, whose words ought to carry far more weight than those of any would-be religious leader—stated emphatically, "No man has ascended up to heaven" (John 3:13). The apostle Peter adds, "David is not ascended into the heavens" (Acts 2:34)—he is simply dead.

Hebrews 9:27 tells us that it is appointed to **all to die once**. This **first death** (and lying dead for decades or centuries afterward) is neither a reward nor a punishment. It is simply what happens to everyone. In David's case—because he died "in the faith"—he will (in a future resurrection) receive the reward of the faithful. Like all the true saints who have died, he is simply waiting in his grave for the resurrection.

Another false teaching (also based on the "immortal soul" idea) insists that people go at death to a place called "Purgatory" where they suffer over long periods of time in order have their sins purged—after which they can go on to heaven.

Obviously, there are no references to such a myth in scripture. In fact, the idea denies the very sacrifice of Christ for the forgiveness of sin. When a person is truly converted—has repented of sin and accepted Christ as savior—his or her sins are totally and completely forgiven **at that time**. One does not have to undergo any punishment for such sins—now or after death. To teach otherwise borders on blasphemy!

The Resurrection—A Christian's True Hope

Job asked the question in chapter 14, verse 14, "If a man die, shall he live again?" He gives the answer: "All the days of my appointed time [in the grave] will I **wait till my change comes**. You shall call, and I will answer you: You will have a desire to the works of your hands." This change does **not** occur right at death. Job knew he would have to **wait in the grave** for an unknown period of time before God would raise him up to a CHANGED state—from being dead to being alive.

Again, we must look to the words of Jesus Christ, not to those of human church leaders. The most quoted verse of the Bible—John 3:16—may also be one of its least understood. "For God so loved the world that He gave His only begotten son, that whosoever believes in Him should not..."—what? Not go to hell, but go to heaven?

Is that what Christ said?

This passage is not about living forever in a horrible place or living forever in a good place. Location isn't the issue. Christ said those who believe in Him "should not **perish**"—which means to cease to exist—"but have everlasting life."

In the book of Acts and throughout the epistles, Paul and the other apostles describe the Christian hope as being the **resurrection from the dead**. In reassuring Christians of this hope, Paul makes it clear in I Corinthians 15 that Jesus' resurrection is absolute proof of a future resurrection of the saints. He encourages the Thessalonians with similar words in I Thess. 4:13-18. Referring to the resurrection of the true Christian, Christ repeatedly said, "I will raise him up **at the last day**" (John 6:39, 40, 44, 54; 11:24).

When does God make His final decision whether a person lives forever or perishes? Does God make that decision at the time of a person's death? For those few who have been called to conversion and God's grace, now is their time of judgment. But for the majority, the time for their judgment has not yet come. Remember, the first death is neither reward nor punishment—for in Adam, we all die (I Cor. 15:22). The vast majority of the dead are simply waiting for the resurrection, when they will have their opportunity for "judgment."

Is Today the Only Day of Salvation?

There is an assumption implicit in the teachings of mainstream Christianity that if a person doesn't "get saved" now, in this life, that he or she is lost forever. As sincere and well meaning as these teachers may be, they are simply in error. The Bible DOES NOT teach the idea that this life is the only time in which people may have salvation!

It is important that we understand something largely unknown to world leaders. Satan, the "god of this world" (II Cor. 4:4), currently holds most religious and civil leaders under his sway—having deceived such leaders at every turn (Rev. 12:9). The result is a world of culture and tradition in which whole populations are entrenched in false ways of life. Most people are so steeped in the ways of this world that they cannot possibly understand the truth of God—nor would they be willing to follow God's way of life even if they did understand. This is why, as Paul says in Rom. 11:32, God has "concluded them all in unbelief"—but only for a time—"that He might have mercy on them all" in a future time of judgment.

Add to that the fact that the natural human mind simply lacks the capacity or even the desire to understand spiritual truth (I Cor. 2:11, 14). Only if God by His spirit "calls" a person—that is, **opens the mind** of an individual and imparts understanding of His truth—does that person come to repentance and conversion in this life (II Cor. 7:9-11; John 6:44; Rom. 2:4; Phil. 2:13).

Christ indicated to His disciples that such a calling has NOT been extended to most people in this life. They asked Him why He spoke to the masses in parables. He answered, "Because it has been **given to you** to know the mysteries of the kingdom of heaven, but to them it has not been given.... For this reason **I speak to them in parables**, because seeing, they see not; and hearing, they hear not; neither do they understand. And in them is fulfilled the prophecy of Isaiah, which says, 'In hearing you shall hear, and in no way understand; and in seeing you shall see and in no way perceive; For the heart of this people has grown fat, and their ears are dull of hearing, and their eyes they have closed; lest they should see with their eyes, and should hear with their ears, and should understand with their hearts, and should be converted, and I should heal them' " (Matt. 13:11-15).

Up to now, only a tiny minority of all humankind has had the calling of God—and far fewer have actually come to conversion and received God's Holy Spirit. These few—this "little flock," as Christ refers to His true Church—constitute the "house of God." Peter tells us that **now**, in this life, **is the time that judgment must begin at the house of God** (I Pet. 4:17). Thus, when a converted person dies "in the faith" (or "in Christ") their judgment by God has already taken place. God has made the final decision that he or she is going to be in His Kingdom—and has written that person's name in the "Book of Life."

There will be some few who may have committed the "unpardonable sin"—that is, with full knowledge and understanding of the truth and the way to salvation—they have rejected God's grace and forgiveness, and have chosen not to repent and turn from the way of sin to God's way. For such— and only God knows who they are—their final judgment is complete. They await the resurrection of the wicked and their fate is the second death in the lake of fire. This lake of fire (Greek, *gehenna*) is a consuming fire that to- tally destroys the incorrigible wicked. Jesus warned us to fear Him who can "**destroy** both soul and body" in this fire (Matt. 10:28). Malachi 4:1-3 shows that the wicked will become ashes under the feet of the faithful.

A Second Resurrection

As we've seen, the dead in Christ remain **in their graves** UNTIL He raises them up "at the last day," as depicted by the Feast of Pentecost (Job 14:14; John 5:25; 6:39, 40, 44, 54; I Thess. 4:13-16; I Cor. 15:50-54; Matt. 24:30, 31; Rev. 20:4-6). At that time Christ will raise them to eternal life in a supernatural, spirit state—to be just like Christ Himself (I John 3:1, 2; Phil. 3:21; II Pet. 1:4; Daniel 12:3).

But what about the rest of the dead? Judgment for them has not yet occurred. When do they **get their chance** for salvation?

In Revelation 20, verse five, John writes that the resurrection of the "dead in Christ" (which occurs at Christ's second coming) is only the "first resurrection." He adds that, "the **rest of the dead** lived not again until the thousand years were finished."

But they DO LIVE AGAIN! There is a **second resurrection.** In that same chapter, verse 12, we read, "And I saw the dead, small and great, stand before God." Here we see pictured the "second resurrection"—the resurrection of all who have ever lived and **died NOT in the faith**—those not having been called and brought to conversion in their first life, now coming before Christ's "white throne" of judgment.

As with most biblical subjects, the whole story is not told all in one place. In Ezekiel 37 we have another view of the second resurrection— dealing specifically with the dead of Israel as they are brought back to **physical** life in the future. They are among the "rest of the dead"—the dead **not** in Christ—who appear before God's throne in Revelation 20:12. Re- member, "the rest of the dead" means **all of those** not in the first resurrec- tion—which would include the overwhelming majority of Israelites who had died throughout the ages.

Notice in Ezekiel 37 that after Israel is brought back to life, God gives them His Holy Spirit! In order to receive God's spirit, however, they must first repent as Peter brings out in Acts 2:38. These newly resurrected Israelites will, apparently, be called before the "white throne" of Christ like the rest of humanity—to account for the deeds of their past. Most if not all will come to see what sinners they were—and in repentance accept Jesus

Christ as their savior with forgiveness of their sins. They will be granted God's Spirit and happily live out their new physical life. (Isa. 65:20 seems to indicate that they may have up to 100 years to grow in grace and knowledge and to build spiritual character before ultimately going on into the Kingdom of God.)

Salvation for Gentiles too?

Clearly then, we see "unconverted" Israel resurrected in the future. But what about "unconverted" Gentiles? Chapters 9-11 of Romans shows us that **God will deal with Gentiles as He deals with Israel.** Revelation 20:12 pictures ALL of the "rest of the dead" before the white throne, not just Israel. ALL bow before God and confess their sins. ALL are judged based on their works, and ALL are found guilty of sin (Rom. 3:23).

But will the guilty stand condemned? II Peter 3:9 tells us that God is not willing that **any should perish** (be destroyed and miss out on eternal life). After being shown their sins before the throne of God, ALL will have their **first and only chance** for salvation through repentance, conversion and the indwelling of the Holy Spirit. Remember, those of the second resurrection NEVER had (in their first life) their minds opened to the truth of God by the Holy Spirit of God—and never had the opportunity (with a full understanding) to repent of their sins and receive God's grace.

Christ died once for ALL (I Tim. 2:6; Heb. 10:10; I Cor. 15: 22-24). Our Lord and Savior did not go through the torture, humiliation, scourging and beating He suffered, followed by His agonizing death on the cross—only to have His grace offered to just part of the human family!

By the time this "White Throne Judgment" takes place, Satan will have been put into the lake of fire and will no longer be able to pervert the truth and deceive humanity. Without Satan's distorting influence—and with their minds now opened by the Holy Spirit—people will for the **first time** be able to think spiritually. Only those very few who refuse, at that time, to repent and accept Christ as their Savior will go on to the ultimate punishment—the lake of fire pictured in Revelation 20:14-15.

Thank God for His incredible, merciful plan! Be encouraged by the truth of the Bible concerning death and the state of the dead—rejoice in the sure knowledge that all who have ever lived will one day have their full chance for eternal life!